booksonline

Read SAP PRESS online also

With booksonline we offer you online access to leading SAP experts' knowledge. Whether you use it as a beneficial supplement or as an alternative to the printed book – with booksonline you can:

- Access any book at any time
- Quickly look up and find what you need
- Compile your own SAP library

Your advantage as the reader of this book

Register your book on our website and obtain an exclusive and free test access to its online version. You're convinced you like the online book? Then you can purchase it at a preferential price!

And here's how to make use of your advantage

1. Visit www.sap-press.com
2. Click on the link for SAP PRESS booksonline
3. Enter your free trial license key
4. Test-drive your online book with full access for a limited time!

Your personal **license key** for your test access including the preferential offer

ez5u-rsmh-g8w9-q6fk

STEVE SMITH

Optimizing Value Flows with SAP® ERP

Andrea Hölzlwimmer

Optimizing Value Flows with SAP® ERP

Bonn • Boston

Galileo Press is named after the Italian physicist, mathematician and philosopher Galileo Galilei (1564–1642). He is known as one of the founders of modern science and an advocate of our contemporary, heliocentric worldview. His words *Eppur se muove* (And yet it moves) have become legendary. The Galileo Press logo depicts Jupiter orbited by the four Galilean moons, which were discovered by Galileo in 1610.

Editors Patricia Kremer, Eva Tripp
English Edition Editor Stephen Solomon
Translation Lemoine International, Inc., Salt Lake City, UT
Copyeditor Jutta VanStean
Cover Design Jill Winitzer
Photo Credit Getty Images RF/Studio Paggy
Layout Design Vera Brauner
Production Editor Kelly O'Callaghan
Assistant Production Editor Graham Geary
Typesetting Publishers' Design and Production Services, Inc.
Printed and bound in Canada

ISBN 978-1-59229-298-1

1st Edition 2010

Library of Congress Cataloging-in-Publication Data
Hölzlwimmer, Andrea.
Optimizing value flows with SAP ERP / Andrea Hölzlwimmer.
1st ed.
p. cm.
Includes bibliographical references and index.
ISBN-13: 978-1-59229-298-1 (alk. paper)
ISBN-10: 1-59229-298-4 (alk. paper)
1. Inventory control — Data processing. 2. Value — Data processing.
3. Cash flow — Data processing. 4. SAP ERP. I. Title.
TS160.H57 2010
658.500285'53 — dc22 2009045225

Contents at a Glance

Contents

Acknowledgments

Writing a book is no easy task, with plenty of highs and lows. However, all the effort and input are quickly forgotten when the finished work lies completed. It often occurred to me during the writing process that writing a book is like giving birth to a child: the start of the "pregnancy" is characterized by feelings of euphoria, the last few weeks are difficult, and the "mother" longs for the end. And once the baby is born, the feeling of joy is overwhelming. That joy is all the greater if the mother's commitment and dedication are enthusiastically supported by her helpers and assistants.

It is in this spirit that I would like to thank everyone who supported this book project with both moral and practical support. Special thanks are due to my co-authors and the many other co-workers at J&M who provided every kind of support and advice.

- Thank you to everyone who answered specific questions and provided proofreading and ghostwriting services.
- Thanks to the team at Galileo Press for always being available to listen and for offering lots of useful advice.
- And thanks to everyone who may have been neglected due to this book in the last few months.

But the biggest thanks of all are due to you, the reader. I hope that this book gave you the information that you needed. Do not hesitate to get in touch with me if you have any questions, or if this book gave you new, additional ideas. Although 443 pages is a lot, it is still not enough to deal with every possible aspect and detail, so please do let me know what you liked and did not like about the book.

In spite of the help and support I received from all sides, there may still be some errors in this book, for which I alone bear full responsibility.

I look forward to hearing from you at *ValueFlow@jnm.com*, and I can also be contacted at XING.

Andrea Hölzlwimmer

Foreword

When my colleague Andrea Hölzlwimmer first came up with the idea of writing a book about integrated workflows and how to map them using SAP ERP, her initial proposal quickly turned into a lively debate on the central questions. Why write a book like this? Havenít books already been written on this topic? What material would it have to cover? What could Andrea Hölzlwimmer and J&M Management Consulting contribute from their many years of professional consulting experience to make this book a useful addition to the existing body of literature on the mapping and implementation philosophies used in SAP ERP systems?

It did not take too long to find the answers. The book title, *Optimizing Value Flows with SAP ERP*, specifies the three main subject areas of the book, which are as follows: supply chain management and logistics; a comprehensive view of these from the accounting viewpoint; and all topics relating to mapping in an *enterprise resource planning* (ERP) system. Although having a solid ERP platform has become the industry standard in Central European companies (as best-evidenced by the huge success of SAP) since the early 1990s, the actual implementation philosophy rarely does justice to all requirements in practice.

Most of the existing literature on this broad topic restricts itself to one or, at most, two of the three aspects mentioned; focusing either on a theoretical analysis of the *logistics* and *accounting* areas and their dependencies, or on a practical model of one of the disciplines using SAP ERP. In this literature, the interaction between logistics and accounting is usually regarded more as a necessary evil than as an opportunity.

Because neither of these two areas can function without the other, the opportunity is to enhance the companyís external competitive advantage by integrating internal processes from both areas, while at the same time leveraging all of the potential within the company to increase efficiency and cut costs and creating the transparency required by top management. This will ultimately allow the company to stay the course in bad times as well as in good times.

The author of this book, Andrea Hölzlwimmer, has expertise in three additional areas that greatly enhance the bookís usefulness: a comprehensive business education, professional experience in companies, and extensive project experience in a consulting capacity. After her vocational training in business, which included work placements, she completed a degree in business studies with majors in information management and project management. She is also familiar with the SAP project environment from the perspective of both companies and consultants. Her many years of consulting work in several SAP implementation projects, covering almost all aspects of Financials and Controlling, enabled her to extend her knowledge both in mid-sized German companies and in large international enterprises. With the launch of the new General Ledger Accounting — including segment reporting — in todayís SAP ERP landscape, her consulting focus in recent years has been on an integrated analysis of value flows in enterprises.

Andrea Hölzlwimmer and the team that supported her in the creation of this book have deliberately taken an approach to presenting the content that begins with a theoretical discussion of the term "integrated value flow." However, thanks to the teamís many years of consulting experience at J&M in SAP ERP implementation projects that focused almost exclusively on creating an integrated view of the Logistics and Financials environments, the material always has a strong and obvious practical relevance. It is this combined theoretical and practical focus that makes this book unique. Although the modeling methods and perspectives it contains have a solid theoretical basis, they are nonetheless easy to implement in real-world scenarios in companies and projects. This is the only way to ensure that an ERP implementation project or a re-engineering project fully exploits all of the available optimization potential to sustain the companyís competitive advantage in the long term.

I have no doubt that this book will provide readers from all areas of the enterprise with important modeling methods and philosophies they can use in ERP implementation and re-engineering projects. In addition to the authorís professional experience and that of her team members, the content also reflects the integrated approach to consulting taken at J&M Management Consulting. I hope that you enjoy reading this book and I look forward to hearing your feedback!

Lars Eickmann
Partner J&M Management Consulting AG

This chapter explains how this book is structured, what topics are covered in each chapter, and who "Lederwaren-Manufaktur Mannheim" is. Enjoy!

1 Introduction

A personal touch adds a certain something to the results of any work, be it a poem, a piece of music or, indeed, the implementation of an IT system. In the case of the first two, this personal touch is often precisely what makes the work special and unmistakable. But how special and unmistakable can an IT system really be without sacrificing functionality?

In my work as a consultant, I see countless systems that were created by specialists—specialists in sales, purchasing, or accounting. Without doubt, these people contributed valuable ideas and implemented impressive solutions. However, in many cases, these specialists concentrated on just one area or one module. Thus, over the years, SAP systems have come into existence that more resemble a series of islands than an integrated whole. This is a shame, as integration is one of the great strengths of SAP.

In the area of material flow, the problem of poor integration was tackled a number of years ago and today, *supply chain management* is a common concept. Many enterprises run programs to optimize their supply chains and expert forums such as *Supply Chain Days* in Heidelberg have come into existence.

But what is being done in the area of value flow? It is a concept that is taken for granted and is rarely recognized as the cause of problems in companies. Value flow re-design projects often start out with problems such as "We need to fix our CO-PA reporting," "Financial Accounting and Controlling are not integrated enough," or "Our CFO doesn't understand the figures." In many cases, the search for errors in CO-PA turns into a project to reorganize value flows. For example, a company may realize that not all its business transactions are transferred to CO-PA, or that this transfer is being undertaken with an incorrect valuation basis.

To find a solution in such situations, we have to look at how the company runs its operations and ask ourselves what we want to report on at the end of a period. This requires a holistic, cross-module understanding of the subject matter, and a process-based and value flow-based perspective.

1.1 Content and Structure

Chapter overview

The goal of this book is to give you the kind of holistic understanding of the subject matter mentioned previously and to sensitize you to the associated potential for optimization and conflict. The book is structured as follows:

Chapter 2, The Concept of Integrated Value Flows, explains the term *integrated value flows*. Because the SCOR model is referred to frequently from this point on, this chapter also introduces you to this model.

In **Chapter 3, Basic Principles of Integration in SAP ERP**, we will turn our attention to the SAP system. Some objects—both in the organizational structure and in the master data—influence all processes. This chapter describes this influence and the effects on the value flow. Because a powerful reporting concept is a major goal and a component of value flows, we will also analyze the important CO-PA component in this chapter.

After this general introduction, we start the discussion of the main processes in enterprises. In **Chapter 4, Procurement Process, Chapter 5, Sales and Distribution Process,** and **Chapter 6, Production Process**, you will learn in detail about the factors that affect the structure of processes and the system. You will become familiar with the most important objects such as orders in procurement and sales orders in sales and distribution, and you will analyze the main process steps, both from the technical side and in terms of how they are mapped in the system.

The goal of accounting is to ensure that the reporting concept is efficient and fit for purpose. The closing activities in Financial Accounting and Controlling are important steps toward achieving this goal. An example of a closing procedure document is used to illustrate the individual steps and dependencies. **Chapter 7, Closing and Reporting in SAP ERP**, takes a concise look at reporting in SAP ERP.

SAP NetWeaver BW offers a whole range of other reporting options, which are the subject of **Chapter 8, Reporting with SAP NetWeaver BW**.

To ensure that you understand the explanations fully and that you can apply them to your work in your own company more easily, the examples in this book are based on a fictional enterprise called *Lederwaren-Manufaktur Mannheim* (a leather goods manufacturing company in Mannheim, Germany). A description of this company's product range and organizational structure is provided at the end of this introduction.

The practical application of this book is emphasized by a project report that is provided in **Chapter 9, Optimizing Value Flows by Implementing the SAP General Ledger — A Real-Life Example.** The initial goal of the project described here was to roll out the new G/L. However, during the year it took to complete the project, the value flows were revised and the reporting concept was also re-designed.

When searching for individual topics, the topic overview for each chapter will point you in the right direction (see Figure 1.1).

Using this book

Throughout the book, you will also find icons that will alert you to special tips, warnings, and examples.

[!] This icon warns you about common errors or problems you may encounter in your work. Therefore, when you come across this icon, we recommend that you pay particular attention to the text.

[+] This icon identifies tips that will make your work easier. It is also used to alert you to additional information on the topic in question.

[Ex] This icon flags text that uses practical examples to explain and expand on the topic in question.

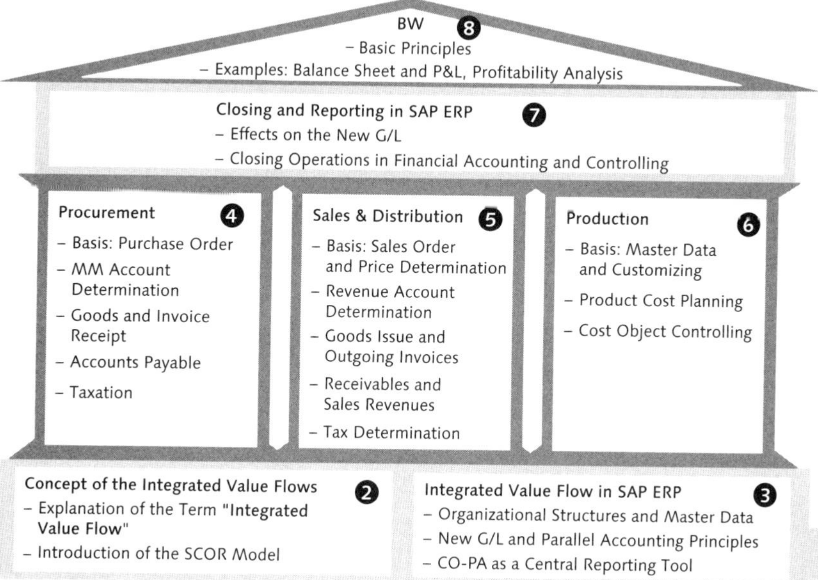

Figure 1.1 Overview of Topics and Chapters

As an enhancement to the topics covered in this book—Figure 1.1 shows an overview of these—the Appendices contain supplementary information. For example, Appendix A provides a sample closing procedure document, and Appendix B contains useful menu paths and transactions.

1.2 Lederwaren-Manufaktur Mannheim

Our sample company

To make it easier for you to understand the sample figures that are used throughout this book, we have created a fictional sample enterprise called Lederwaren-Manufaktur Mannheim. This is a limited liability company with headquarters in Mannheim, Germany.

Product range

The company's product range comprises three product lines:

- **Tailor-made leather shoes**
  Lederwaren-Manufaktur Mannheim manufactures hand-made leather shoes. Foot measurements can be taken in each of the company's retail outlets in Mannheim, Brussels, Paris, and Milan. The manufacturing of the lasts and, ultimately, the shoes is performed on a make-to-order basis by trained shoemakers in Brussels and Mannheim.
- **Luxury leather handbags**
  The company's handbags are made in small batches in Milan and Mannheim. They are sold under the company's own brand name, Lederwaren-Manufaktur Mannheim, and under customers' brand names. The main sales location for handbags is Paris.
- **Leather belts**
  The company's leather belts are mass-produced. Customers are fashion labels of all sizes. Most of the leather belts are sold under the company's own brand name, Lederwaren-Manufaktur Mannheim; however, occasionally, some are sold under a customer's brand name.

The company's product range is rounded off by its high-end leather handbags. However, because the production facilities are not designed to manufacture these items, the company buys its handbags as trading goods.

Organization

Lederwaren-Manufaktur Mannheim concentrates on the European market, especially Germany, Italy, and France. The corporate structure illustrated in Figure 2.2 was set up to facilitate this model.

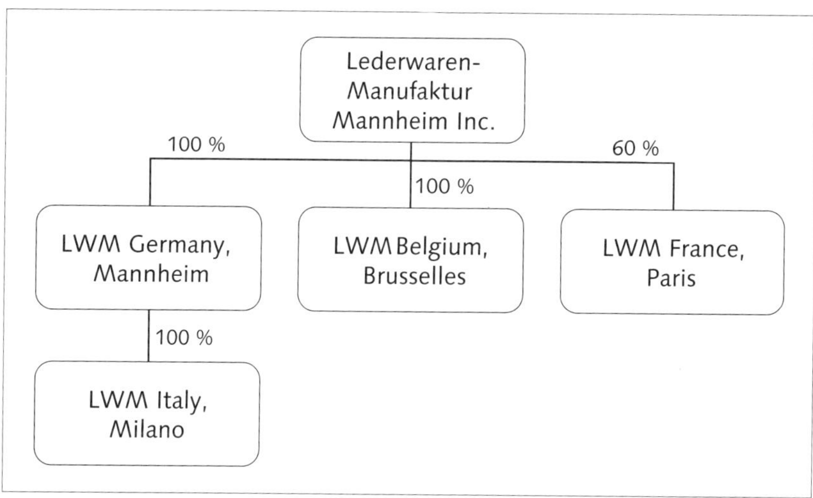

Figure 1.2 Organizational Structure of Lederwaren-Manufaktur Mannheim

All of the central functions and a large portion of the production process are located at the company's *original base* in Mannheim. During the course of the company's development, two additional *production locations* were set up in Brussels and Milan. Sales and distribution is organized on the basis of region, and is the responsibility of each international subsidiary. The international fashion labels and fashion houses are an exception; these are *key accounts* and are handled centrally in Mannheim.

Cost center structure

The company established a cost center structure (see Table 1.1) for a fair distribution of overhead among cost objects. This structure also makes it easier to control costs that arise from the company's business activities.

	Cost Center		Profit Center		Segment	
Services	D1000	IT services	M5000	Administration	M_OH	Overhead
	D2000	HR services	M5200	Human Resources	M_OH	Overhead
	D3000	Building and maintenance service	M5000	Administration	M_OH	Overhead

Table 1.1 Accounting Organization

	Cost Center		Profit Center		Segment	
Material and warehousing	M1000	Materials purchasing	M9999	Production, other	MANF	Production
	M2000	Materials warehousing	M9999	Production, other	MANF	Production
Production	P1000	Shoe workshop	M2100	Shoes, Mannheim	M_SHOES	Shoes
	P1100	Shoe workshop support staff	M2100	Shoes, Mannheim	M_SHOES	Shoes
	P2000	Bag production	M1200	Bags	M_BAGS	Bags
	P3000	Luggage production	M1300	Luggage	M_BAGS	Bags
	P4000	Belt production	M1400	Belts	M_BELT	Belts
	P9000	Production overhead	M9999	Production, other	MANF	Production
	P9500	Final inspection	M9000	Production, general	MANF	Production
Sales and distribution	S1000	Marketing	S1000	Sales	SALES	Sales
	S1000	Sales and distribution	S1000	Sales	SALES	Sales
Admin	A0000	Administration	M5000	Admin	M_OH	Overhead
	A1000	Management	M5000	Admin	M_OH	Overhead
	A2000	Finance	M5100	Accounting	M_OH	Overhead
	A3000	Controlling	M5100	Accounting	M_OH	Overhead

Table 1.1 Accounting Organization (Cont.)

As Table 1.1 shows, the company is structured on the basis of product lines as much as possible. A non-product-specific cost center is used only when there is no clear assignment, as is the case with Accounting. The representation of the company in the form of a limited number of cost centers, as shown in Table 1.1, assumes that the shoes, bags, and belts are each manufactured at one production location and with one production type. This is a greatly simplified representation that does not reflect reality, but will serve the purposes of our example.

Profit center structure

The profit center structure reflects the classic product division-based corporate model. In our structure, administrative areas are also used, to which costs and revenues can be added in line with the profit center concept. This model allows the company to better manage the activities of each area and keep track of each area's profitability.

Each profit center also has *segments* (see Figure 1.3). Lederwaren-Manufaktur Mannheim has two basic types of segments: those for manufacturing the individual product groups, and those that reflect the functional entities within the leather goods manufacturing process, such as sales and retail. As a general rule, segments provide a cross-section of the various profit centers and thus describe the areas of activity of the company.

Standard Hierarchy	Name	Activation status	Person Responsible
M1	M1		
DUMMY	DUMMY		
DUMMY	DUMMY	☐	E. Müller
ADMIN	ADMIN		
M5000	Admin	☐	C. Verwalter
M5100	Accounting	☐	E. Müller
M5200	HR	☐	A. Huber
S1000	Sales	☐	A. Kaufmann
M1000	Production		
K1000	Key-Accounts	☐	V. Schreiber
M1100	Handbag	☐	K. Franzl
M1150	Wallets	☐	K. Franzl
M1200	Bags - Office	☐	C. DeNiro
M1300	Luggage	☐	Z. Butt
M1400	Belts	☐	W. Pitter
M2100	Shoes - Mannheim	☐	M. Blanick
M9000	Production - cross	☐	M. Gucci
M9999	Raw material - other	☐	M. Gucci

Figure 1.3 Hierarchical Structure of Lederwaren-Manufaktur Mannheim

It is often a worthwhile exercise to take a critical look at the things we deal with on a daily basis. For example: what does "integrated value flow" really mean? Are there any models that make it easier for us to understand enterprise processes? After reading this chapter, you will be able to answer these questions.

2 The Concept of Integrated Value Flows

As you can already tell from the chapter structure of this book, enterprises have three main value flows, which run in parallel. These are in the areas of procurement, sales, and production. In this chapter, you will acquire a general understanding of *integrated value flows* and the factors that influence them from a business viewpoint.

To accomplish this, we will first look at the term *integrated value flow*. In doing so, we will examine the existing models for representing value flows and consider which of these models is best suited for representation purposes in this book.

At first glance, a correct value flow is important for accounting and controlling purposes, at the least. From the accounting viewpoint, the goal is clear: there has to be a certification-ready year-end closing by the end of the business year.

What is the goal in controlling? There is a concise, pragmatic answer to this question as well: the goal of controlling is a traceable, user-friendly reporting concept. But what is user-friendly and therefore suitable for the individual enterprise? The final section of this chapter considers these questions—and answers them, of course.

2.1 Explanation of the Term "Integrated Value Flow"

No fixed definition

The term *integrated value flow* is used widely in our everyday work, but it has no fixed, consistent definition. Even in discussions on the subject of value flow, the integration aspect is often neglected. Therefore, we would like to attempt to come up with a consistent definition. To this end, we will divide up the term into its two component parts: integration and value flow.

2.1.1 Value Flow

Related terms

We will take a circuitous route in approaching the term "value flow." What related terms are you familiar with from your daily work? Aside from *value flow*, we also frequently come across the terms *material flow* and *information flow*, in theory and in practice. As Figure 2.1 shows, these three flows do not run independently, in parallel; rather, they are interconnected.

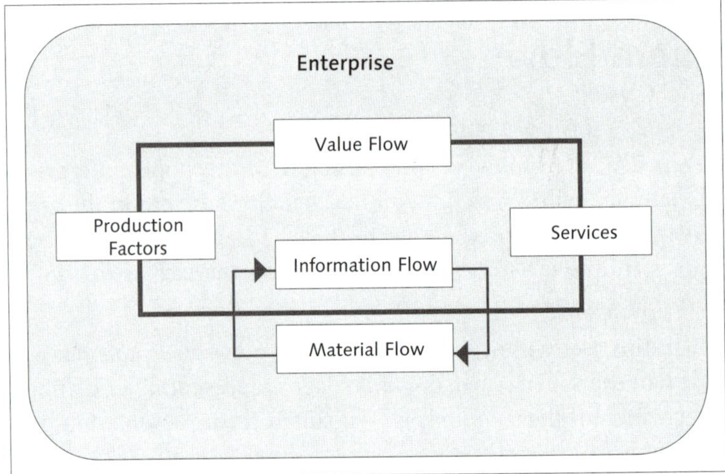

Figure 2.1 Relationships Between Material Flow, Information Flow, and Value Flow

Material flow

Material flow deals with different kinds of physical movement of goods. The material flow starts when materials are procured or yielded. It also comprises the stockholding, handling, and delivery of products. The boundaries of the material flow are individual and are set by each company. If we step beyond this boundary and extend our analysis to suppliers and customers, we are looking at what is known as the *supply chain*. The terms material flow and supply chain refer to the same principle, but with different scopes.

You can analyze the material flow in any producing company by looking at that company's production: materials are handled, products are transported by forklift to the warehouse, and trucks are loaded with goods in the delivery area. Using the classic factors of *labor*, *land*, and *capital*, services are performed or products are manufactured, and thus, ultimately, goods are made.

Information flow

The term *information flow* refers to the route taken by data to reach one or more recipients in the form of information. Ideally, this information triggers a reaction on the part of the recipient. The information flow thereby interacts with the material flow.

Interaction Example Between Information Flow and Material Flow

The information that the safety stock in the warehouse has been exceeded triggers the procurement process in the purchasing department and leads to the creation of an order. The result of the quality assurance checks causes the material stocks in the warehouse to be either released or locked.

Today, most companies manage the task of retrieving, distributing, and processing all of this data by using more or less modern enterprise resource planning (ERP) systems.

Document flow

The term *document flow* is frequently used in companies that use SAP solutions. This term refers to the chain of all of the documents associated with a business transaction that are created in the system. An example of this is the document flow in the sales process. In this process, a sales order, a delivery note, and a billing document may be created in the system. A document flow can map both the material flow and the value flow. A delivery, therefore, is a goods movement that is mapped in the system. A billing document represents only the issuing of an invoice to the customer, and is thus part of the value flow rather than the material flow. In summary, we can say that the document flow represents the information flow in the system.

Value flow

Now, after this brief digression, we will look at the concept of value flow, which is closely linked to that of material flow. In one sense, value flow means the representation of value creation along the logistical chain; that is, along the material flow.

The value flow, however, also contains purely monetary streams. These monetary streams have nothing to do with the movement or processing of goods. Examples are financial assets and financial transactions in general. As the company Porsche shows, enterprises can also create considerable monetary value outside of the scope of their operational business activities. However, because Porsche's situation is probably an exception, we will not consider financial transactions and treasury at this point. A financial issue we do look at in this book is the payment procedures that happen at the end of the logistics-like processes of procurement and sales.

We can divide up the material, information, and value flows not only by content, but also by perspective on enterprise processes:

- **Business perspective**
  The business perspective focuses on the management of production processes in the delivery of business activities and services. *Supply Chain Management* (SCM) is the concept of analyzing and optimizing material flows on a comprehensive level.
- **Value-based perspective**
  The value-based perspective focuses on the coordination of information flows. The goal is to represent material flows in the form of analyzable information or values. These values can then be used as a basis for strategic enterprise decisions.

Today, an integrated view of material and information flows is taken for granted and it should also be possible to view value flows in a similarly integrated fashion. But what do we mean when we say "integration?"

2.1.2 Integration

Meaning

The word *integration* is derived from the Latin *integer*, meaning "whole," and integration thus means "creating a whole." To put it another way, "integration" refers to the process of bringing together individual parts to form a single entity. Therefore, if we consider an issue such as a value flow in an integrated way, we analyze all of the components of the value flow together. Alternatively—that is, if we take a non-integrated view—we would divide up the value flow into its component parts and analyze each part separately.

Significance in the IT environment

In the IT environment, integration means interconnecting different areas, such as production, sales and distribution, and accounting, with as high a degree of automation as possible. The goal is to link data and information from different sources and pass it on to all of the parties involved. This interlinking of different sources in particular is central to the issue of value flow. IT is an area where a lot of effort is put into achieving a high degree of integration.

Interest groups

Integration, an essential part of the value flow, is often regarded as a given in this context and is therefore neglected at times. In value flows, we have to do more than just interlink different sources; however, it is not always entirely clear what the goal is because there are different interest groups that want their requirements fulfilled. Figure 2.2 shows the various interest groups within enterprises and the system-based support that is available.

Logistics

Let us take a closer look now at these interest groups. The *Logistics* requirements are focused on the material flow. What is required is all of the information that helps the production and delivery processes to run smoothly. The sources of this information can include Controlling and its sub-area, Product Cost Controlling. A product can be posted to or from the warehouse only after it has an actual price.

Controlling

Controlling, for its part, depends on logistical information because it uses this information as a basis for creating product costings. Examples of the information required by Controlling are receipts, bills of material, and routings from production planning. Controlling also depends on internal and external reporting requirements. The goal is to comprehensively map the enterprise situation so that corrective action can be taken in a timely manner if errors occur, or are likely to occur.

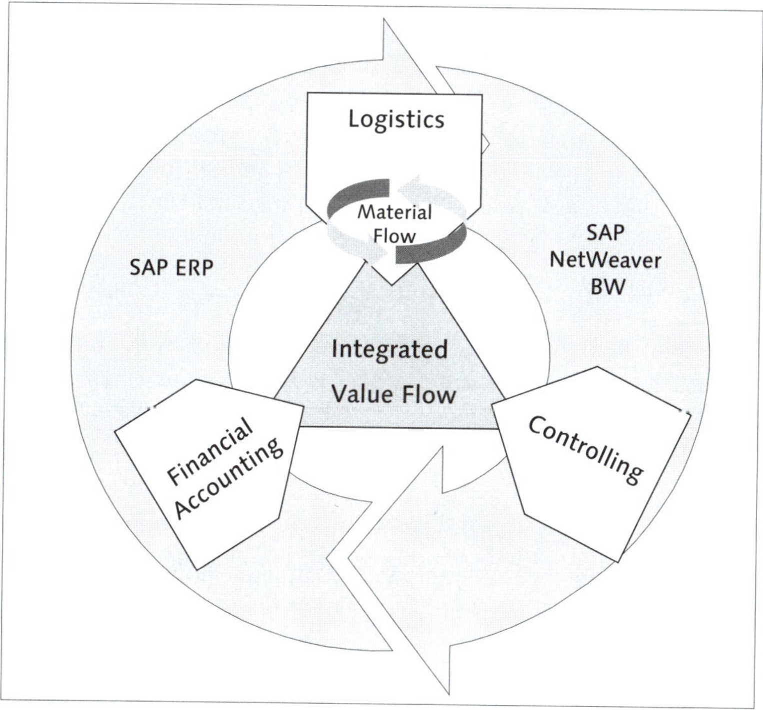

Figure 2.2 System-Based Support by Internal Interest Groups

The structure of value flows depends largely on the types and perspective of the relevant Controlling measures. Controlling types are influenced by the following factors:

- Functional requirements (for example, sales and distribution, or production requirements)
- Regional requirements (for example, local, national, or global requirements)
- Control-related requirements (for example, requirements on the operational, tactical, or strategic levels)
- System specifications (for example, Controlling specifications)

Financial Accounting

The requirements of Financial Accounting, on the other hand, are motivated mainly by statutory framework conditions (such as tax-related and commercial regulations) and other external requirements such as those of capital markets and banks. Other aspects such as liquidity management—implemented using cash flow optimization, for example—also play a role.

Representing enterprise processes

As you can see, Controlling has to fulfill a wide range of requirements. However, it is also affected by the way in which the enterprise processes are represented. The academic field of business studies provides a range of models for this purpose. The suitability of each model depends on the individual methodology and approach favored by both the enterprise as a whole and by the persons responsible in each case.

2.2 Models for Representing Enterprise Processes

The number of models for mapping enterprise processes is practically unlimited. One well-known classic model is *Porter's value chain model*. Another frequently used model is the *SCOR model*. We will look at both of these models in more detail.

2.2.1 Porter's Value Chain Model

No general discussion about value flows is complete without a mention of Porter's value chain model. Therefore, we will explain both the differences and the commonalities between Porter's value chain and our definition of an integrated value flow.

Primary and secondary activities

Michael E. Porter's *value chain model* enables you to systematically document all of the strategic activities in an enterprise. The model classifies the data into primary and secondary (supporting) activities (see Figure 2.3).

In Porter's model, competitive advantage can be gained from every activity, be it primary or secondary. He sees the value chain as a tool for value engineering, business analysis, and strategic development.

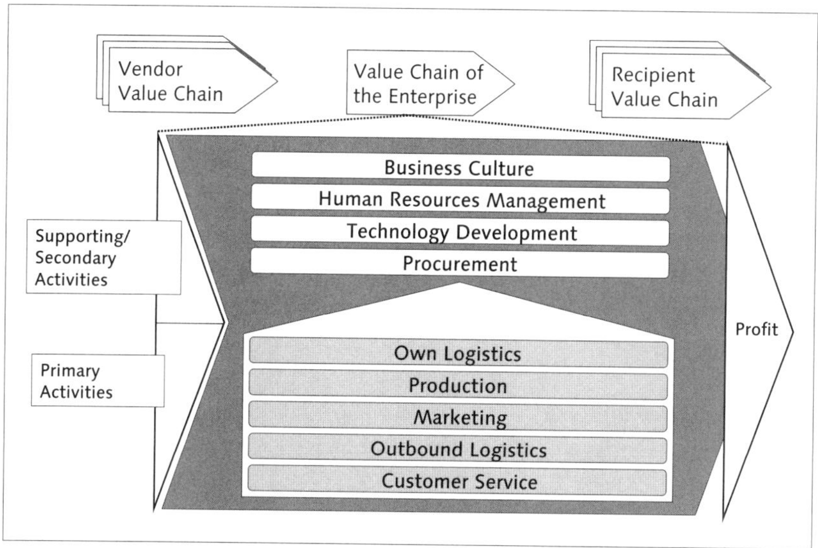

Figure 2.3 Porter's Value Chain Model

Increase value creation

Porter's main concern is to increase value creation in producing companies; however, there is also a close link between his model and the concept of integrated value flows. In his model, Porter represents the value creation chain in such a way that it can be regarded as the basis of an integrated value flow. Thus, the value flow is a systematic representation of the activities identified by Porter.

We will now look at another approach that is characterized by Logistics and the material flow. This will be useful because, as you have seen, an integrated value flow can exist only if there is an integrated material flow in the production process.

2.2.2 SCOR Model

We can use the *supply chain operation reference (SCOR) model* for material-based processes, which are the functional level of an enterprise. This model features a clear, level-based structure that represents the business activities of an enterprise. The levels in the model enable us to represent the values.

Analyze and describe business processes

The SCOR model was designed by the *Supply Chain Council* (SCC), an independent non-profit organization. The model is part of a standard method for analyzing and describing all internal and cross-company business processes in the supply chain, with the consistent goal of optimizing processes. The method can be used for both simple and complex enterprise activities.

The SCOR model links to and integrates the following aspects:

- **Business process reengineering**
  As-is analysis and development of a target situation as in Porter's value chain model.
- **Benchmarking**
  Quantifying operational performance and juxtaposing this with other, similar enterprises, and formulating internal goals on the basis of best-in-class results.
- **Best practice analyses**
  Analysis of management practices and IT solutions that enable best-in-class performance.

The scope of the SCOR model extends beyond internal company boundaries. Suppliers are included up to the first production level, and both customers and their customers are also considered. The goal of this broad approach is to recognize and implement all optimization potential.

Therefore, the SCOR model is located on the border between business and economics and incorporates value flows in both areas. In this book, we focus on internal flows within enterprises only.

As Figure 2.4 shows, the SCOR model is based on five central business process categories.

Business process categories at the first level

Let us take a closer look at the five business process categories in the SCOR model:

1. **Planning**
   The planning process (plan) synchronizes supply and demand and is a general process.
2. **Procurement**
   The *procurement* process (source) provides materials and services.
3. **Production**
   The *production* process (make) manufactures semi-finished and finished products.

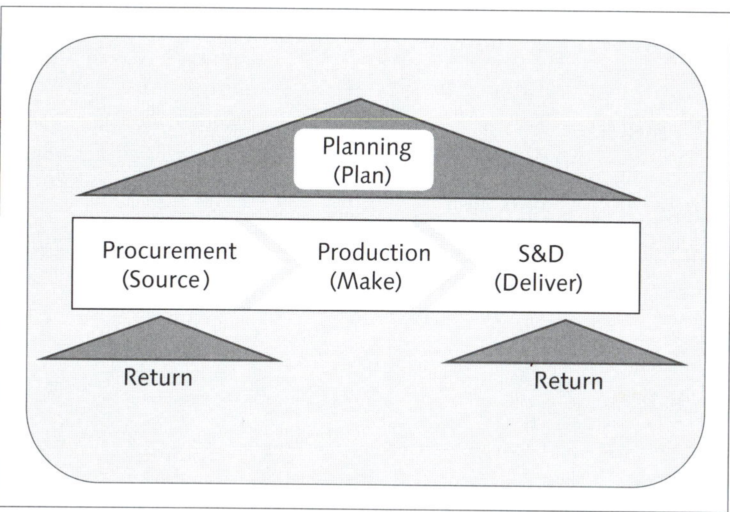

Figure 2.4 SCOR Model—First Level

4. **Sales and distribution**
   The sales and distribution process (deliver) comprises warehouse management, order management, and transport management in a company's customer relationships.
5. **Returns**
   The *returns* process comprises the returning of materials to the supplier and the receiving and processing of customer returns. Defects in materials or products are the most common reason for returns.

These business process categories are useful, but too wide in scope for our purposes. They are included here simply to give you an initial introduction to the internal workings of an enterprise. This is why these five processes are referred to as the *first level of the SCOR model*. It is at this level that a company defines the scope of its own supply chain.

Process types at the configuration level

The five process categories are assigned at the second level, which is the configuration level. The process types on the configuration level are explained below.

- **Planning processes**
  The *planning processes* (plan) should comply with the aggregated demand within a specific time period.

- **Execution processes**
  The *execution processes* (execute), which are triggered by the planning processes, change the status of a product.
- **Support processes**
  The *support processes* (enable) prepare information and make it available. This information is based on the planning and execution processes.

Linking the first and second levels

Figure 2.5 shows how the process categories at the first level and the process types at the second level can be represented in a matrix.

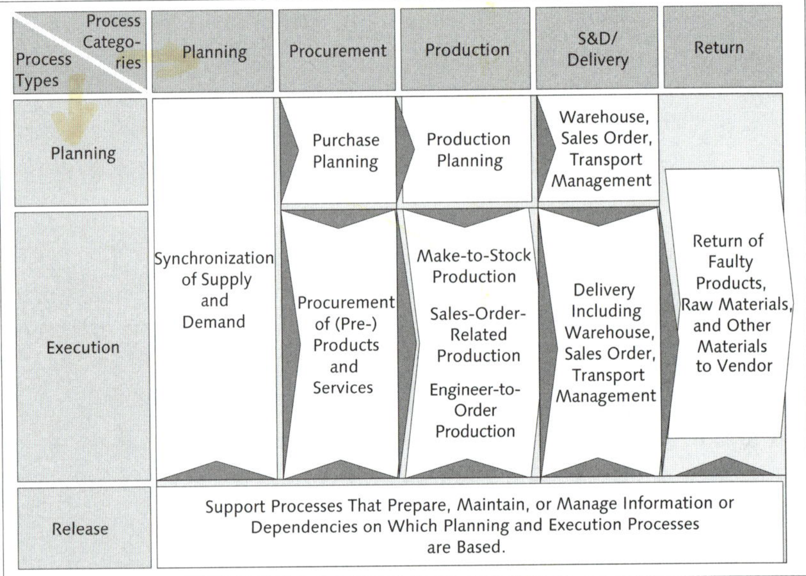

Figure 2.5 SCOR Model—Linking the First and Second Levels

In the figure, you can see the process types in each of the five process categories. As an example, we will combine the process category *production* with the process type *execution*. In this case, the SCOR model offers three possible types:

- Make-to-stock production
- Sales-order-related production
- Engineer-to-order production

Even without detailed knowledge of these process types, you can probably imagine that an engineer-to-order production process (e.g., a power station) is managed differently from a make-to-stock production process (e.g., bag manufacturing at Lederwaren-Manufaktur Mannheim).

Design level

The SCOR model contains a third level for mapping these additional details. This level is known as the *design level*. It contains sub-processes of the main processes at the second level. The individual process steps, their order, and input and output information are represented separately for each process category (such as production).

The design level can be illustrated in a flow chart, to which further detail can be added if required. For our purposes, no further detail is needed. Let us consider, then, what further subdivision we have selected for the example mentioned (execution in production, see Figure 2.6). The major production process is initially subdivided into the three types we mentioned: make-to-stock production, sales-order-related production, and engineer-to-order production. Make-to-stock production is further subdivided into the following steps:

- Production planning
- Withdrawal of raw materials, supplies, and consumables
- Actual production (manufacturing)
- Placement in storage
- Product release
- Waste disposal

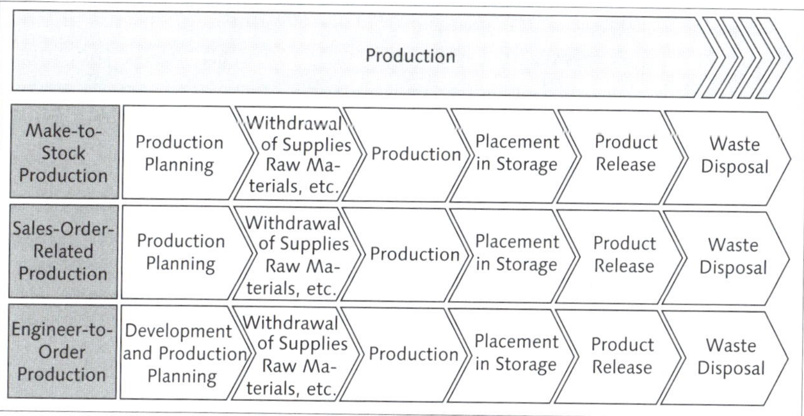

Figure 2.6 Production Process in the SCOR Model

This subdivision makes it possible for us to examine the individual activities in the overall process in an integrated but nonetheless discrete manner. These sub-steps usually also reflect the department structure within the company.

Implementation level

There is also an additional level called the implementation level. This level is not contained in the SCOR model because it relates to the individual software implementation process in each company. The goal at this level is to use software that fulfills the company's individual requirements. We assume that the readers of this book have by now decided to use SAP.

The SCOR model was developed to optimize the supply chain; that is, the material flow. For this reason, parts of the model fall short of our requirements. Therefore, we will extend the model so that it represents the entire value flow in companies.

2.3 Extending the SCOR Model

In extending the SCOR model, our goal is to be able to analyze in a unified and comprehensive way all of the business processes in a company and the resulting values.

Turning action into data

A term that is often used in projects that are set up to implement or restructure a business intelligence application such as SAP NetWeaver BW is "turning data into action." This means that the company must react in some way to the retrieved and analyzed data.

After all, it is only by actually implementing the findings that result from the retrieval and analysis processes that companies can change their business processes for the better and, ultimately, increase productivity and profitability.

In this book, we approach the matter from a different angle: the goal is to represent the route that value takes along the material and information flows in the enterprise. Therefore, when mapping integrated value flows, we like to use the term "turning action into data."

Forward and analyze data

By "action," we mean the business approach taken by a company; in other words, the material flow. When this flow is quantitatively mapped within an enterprise, action is turned into data. In addition to the process of data retrieval, data also has to be forwarded and analyzed so that an integrated value flow can be mapped. As in the standard SCOR model, we want to restrict ourselves to the operational processes.

Therefore, performance management—that is, strategic enterprise management—is not covered in this book. However, even though we restrict ourselves to operational controlling, there are still several different philosophies and schools of thought that influence our controlling systems.

2.4 Interaction Between Process Design and Controlling Approach

In Figure 2.6, we saw in the example production process that the design of the production process affects the sub-steps in the process. With make-to-stock and sales-order-related production, we manufacture a known product and can therefore start procuring the materials right away. In engineer-to-order production, we first have to develop the product and plan the production process.

When we compare make-to-stock production with engineer-to-order production in particular, it becomes clear that two completely different controlling approaches are required.

[Ex]

Different Controlling Approaches for Make-to-Stock and Engineer-to-Order

When goods are being produced for stock, we will primarily be concerned with any deviations that may occur in the production process. We cannot link the production order and the sales order.

In the case of engineer-to-order production, although we are still interested in any potential production deviations, our main focus is on the sales order. In sales-order-related production, we want to ensure that the individual order yields a profit. If the production costs turn out to be higher than expected, we can seek to re-negotiate with the customer. This is not possible in mass production with delivery to stock.

We can conclude that each enterprise handles its controlling in very different ways. Aside from the previously-mentioned production design consideration, enterprises also take into account a whole range of other factors such as size and industry when deciding to use one controlling approach or another. We will examine the following types of controlling in more detail below:

- Sales order controlling
- Production controlling
- Vendor management and controlling

Sales order controlling

A plant manufacturer typically carries out a *sales order controlling* process. This process determines and updates the costs associated with the sales order. It also has to be possible to periodically accrue the costs in case there are sales orders that require a processing time of several months or even years. This is the only way to identify and, if required, update the current costs and revenues before completing the order.

Production controlling

A company that mass-produces goods for stock has a different controlling focus. The kind of controlling done by companies like this is *production controlling*. The focus in production controlling is on costing quantities, overhead, and storage costs.

Vendor management and vendor controlling

Another, more extreme example of an approach to controlling taken by a company that mass-produces goods for stock can be found throughout the retail industry. Production controlling is not required in this case; the focus is on purchasing and selling retail goods. This model requires both intensive *vendor management* and *vendor controlling* and thorough *customer and market analysis*. The most important parameters for revenue maximization in a retail business are purchasing costs and sales targets.

However, that does not mean that a company follows one controlling strategy only. Let us take the example of our company, LeatherWorks Manufacturing:

- The company manufactures shoes on a make-to-order basis; that is, on the basis of sales orders only.
- It manufactures handbags in small batches.
- It mass-produces leather belts.
- To complete its product portfolio, it buys handbags as trading goods.

Clearly, the profitability of the belt production process will be calculated differently than that of the sales order-based shoe production process. For more information on this topic, see Chapter 6, Production Process.

In the following chapters, we will make recommendations and suggest alternatives for systematically mapping the various processes. We are concerned primarily with two things: representing a value flow that is as integrated as possible and closely analyzing the options that exist in an SAP system for designing a value flow.

2.5 Summary

In summary, we can say that there are several different models for representing enterprise processes. For our purposes, the SCOR model has proven to be the most suitable. This model is well equipped to represent the material flow in companies. It also takes sufficient account of various process types such as make-to-stock production and sales-order-related production. However, to use the SCOR model to represent the complete value flows throughout all enterprise processes, we have to add certain payment processes to the model.

It is important to create a shared understanding of the term *integrated value flow*. We define it as the representation of value creation along the logistical chain, plus the associated payment processes. From every process, we expect as high a degree as possible of integration and automation.

Using an SAP system can be compared to an expedition into a distant region of the world: fascinating, exciting, complex, and at first, obscure. This chapter is intended to help you understand the basic principles of integration in SAP ERP.

3 Basic Principles of Integration in SAP ERP

The structure of a model that is supposed to map enterprises and their value flows must not be separated from the everyday business. "Turning action into data" stands for the mapping and processing of transactions that take place within the enterprise in an IT solution (see Chapter 2, Section 2.3, Extending the SCOR Model).

To do this, large and medium-sized companies often use SAP systems. Due to the technical solutions and restrictions of its systems, SAP has created its own value flow model and because of the solutions provided in the standard system, companies that use an SAP system for basic processes such as posting an incoming payment proceed in a similar way.

This chapter first describes the current status of many SAP systems before it takes a detailed look at the entity model. An entity model represents a structured description of an enterprise and the corresponding structure of organizational units in an SAP system. The descriptions focus on the structures in accounting. In addition, the chapter discusses international requirements as well as master data, which play an essential role regarding establishing an integrated value flow.

Next, the chapter describes the CO-PA subcomponent for market and segment reporting, which represents an important reporting tool in SAP ERP. In this context, it makes sense to describe the component from a central and cross-process point of view because the analyses carried out in CO-PA and the resulting technical design have a major effect on the value flows.

3.1 Structure of SAP Systems

SAP ERP is an integrated business software that enables you to process business processes in real time. Parallel to the material flow, the software creates information and value flows that are both based on an entirely integrated document flow.

Value flow model in SAP ERP

The SAP system maps the value flow primarily in the application components *Financial Accounting* and *Controlling*. Although both components can be the origin of a value flow, the starting point can more often be found in one of the logistics components. For example, *Materials Management* (MM) for goods movements, *Production* (Production Planning and Control, PP) in the context of production processes, or *Sales and Distribution* (SD) when it comes to invoicing customers could represent the starting point of a value flow, to name but the core components of the SAP system.

Integrating Financial Accounting and Controlling

Cost-relevant data from all components automatically flows into the Financial Accounting and Controlling components, which in turn exchange data with one another. In this context, costs and revenues are assigned to different account assignments such as accounts and cost elements, cost centers, projects, or orders.

Lack of integration in historically evolved SAP systems

Frequently, enterprises prefer the sequential implementation of individual components to what is called a *big bang* with the simultaneous implementation of all SAP components required. In addition, the range of components has been considerably enhanced over time, which means that the production systems of customers must regularly be enhanced as well. As a result, SAP systems often grow and are enhanced by diverse modules or components.

Due to this growth, the integration aspect frequently disappears. Consequently, there are many SAP systems in operation today that have grown historically and do not contain any consistent customizing procedures or custom developments. After these SAP systems had been implemented, only the process areas that were either newly implemented or caused problems were discussed. However, the great strength of SAP ERP is its high level of integration for all components (see Figure 3.1). This level of integration is the prerequisite for mapping integrated value flows and it can only exist if the topic of integration is the primary focus throughout the entire lifecycle of the system.

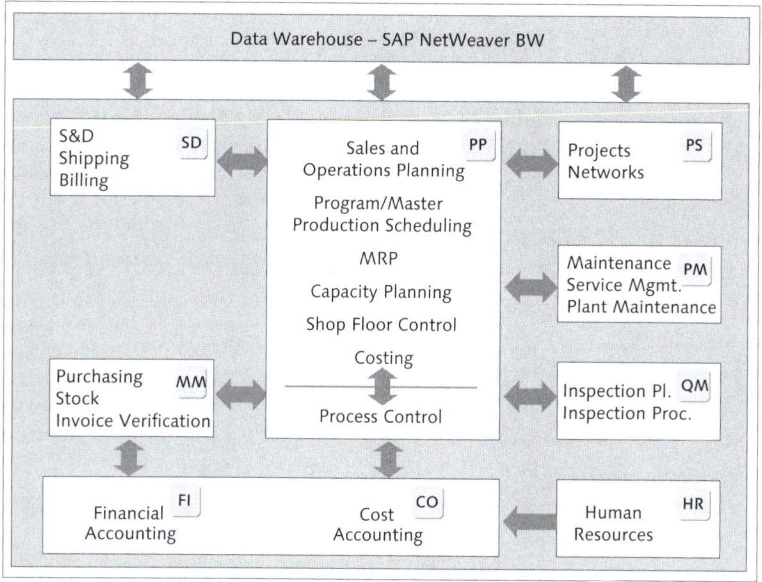

Figure 3.1 Overview of SAP Components (Excerpt)

Integrating processes

When it comes to the topic of *integration*, we tend to think only of processes that are mapped across multiple components in the system. However, we should not forget that the organizational structure and the master data already involve basic definitions that are relevant to the subsequent structuring of systems and processes. Also, the question as to where existing reporting requirements can be met is of similar importance. In this context, a subcomponent of Controlling assumes a particularly important role in the SAP ERP system: the CO-PA market and segment reporting tool (PA = Profitability Analysis).

3.2 Entity Model

From the point of view of financial accounting in particular, the definition of the organizational structure seems to be an easy task. Similarly, in cost accounting, this issue is often neglected. Here, the only issue usually seems to be whether reporting, and thus the controlling area, should cover more than one company code. However, an entity model, that is, the depiction of an enterprise's structure and organization, must always map the entire context. Accordingly, the structures of internal and external accounting must be harmonized and provide for the requirements of logistics as well as for potential structural changes in the future.

Organizational structures

Surprisingly, existing organizational structures often not only meet specific requirements but also have been created due to technical necessities or restrictions. For example, SAP systems often contain what are called *technical company codes* that have come into existence during the import of legacy data or that are used to map internal reporting units.

Therefore, even long-time SAP customers should take the discussion about how to map their enterprise structure seriously. There are many situations in which you should reconsider and, if necessary, reorganize the company structure.

[Ex]

Enterprise Reorganization during the Migration to the SAP General Ledger

The migration to the SAP General Ledger provides a good opportunity to reorganize the structures that are mapped in the SAP system.

- The SAP General Ledger contains new organizational elements and gives reason to rearrange internal structures.
- If, in addition, you want to replace classic profit center accounting with the SAP General Ledger, you must rebuild the entire customer-specific profit center reporting process from scratch (see Chapter 9, Optimizing Value Flows by Implementing the SAP General Ledger—A Real-Life Example).

When rebuilding the reporting structure, you can challenge the relevance of existing reports. In this context, you should also check whether the structure that is mapped in SAP is future-proof.

To find an appropriate way to map the enterprise structures in SAP, you must check whether you can actually use the organizational elements provided by SAP in your company.

3.2.1 Organizational Elements in the SAP System

The standard version of the SAP system contains the following organizational elements:

- Company code
- Company
- Business area
- Functional area
- Credit control area
- Controlling area
- Profit center

- Operating concern
- Segment

The following sections describe these organizational elements in greater detail.

Company Code

The *company code* represents the most important entity in financial accounting. It is well-suited to map a *legal entity* in the SAP system. In this context, a legal entity represents any organizational unit that has its own legal status and the statutory obligation to create an annual statement of accounts. At the company code level, the financial statement and profit and loss statement can be created at any time and the data to be posted can be assigned to the correct accounts without problem.

Company

Companies are used to map the enterprise structure from the consolidation viewpoint. They are stored in the master data of company codes and business partners and can be used as entities for legal consolidation. In contrast to this, management consolidation frequently uses profit center accounting.

Business Area

Another element of classical general ledger accounting is the *business area*. You can use the business area to present figures of the financial and profit and loss statements at a level that is lower than the company code. With the introduction of profit center accounting (EC-PCA), business areas have lost in importance because the derivation from profit centers is easier and more flexible. However, it was usually not possible to exactly map all values from the financial and profit and loss statements at the business area level; depending on the amount of work involved in this, it was only possible to get more or less good approximations. Thus, in some enterprises, the directive exists that a billing document can contain only one business area. Otherwise, it would be almost impossible to display accounts receivable and revenues in an exact manner at the business area level. From the point of view of logistics, however, it makes sense to submit only one invoice that covers multiple business areas to a customer. However, to be able to do so, a clear and unique reporting process must be in place, which in turn requires you to establish processes around system restrictions.

A major drawback of using the business area as compared to using classical profit center accounting in the EC-PCA (Enterprise Controlling – Profit Center Accounting) component was the higher level of integration between EC-PCA and Controlling. Therefore, any new SAP system implementation usually involves profit centers. However, there is no need to switch from using business areas to using profit centers in existing systems if all existing reporting requirements can be met with business areas. This is why business areas continue to exist in many enterprises although the problems and compromises described can occur.

Functional Area

Derivation can be performed much more easily in the *functional area*. Functional areas are used to present the profit and loss statement based on *cost-of-sales accounting*. The first cost-of-sales accounting implementations carried out many years ago did not allow for storing the functional area in the master data of Controlling account assignments, particularly cost centers and internal orders. This is why the derivation of characteristics had to be mapped via complex substitutions. The presentation of values then often took place in CO-PA. After SAP made it possible to store the functional area in Controlling master data, the cost-of-sales accounting ledger had established itself as a standard solution.

Cost-of-sales accounting ledger

The *cost-of-sales accounting ledger* is the only special ledger provided by SAP (FI-SL component). In addition to the G/L account, the ledger also maps the functional area. After the implementation of the SAP General Ledger, the functional area can also be depicted directly in the general ledger so that a separate cost-of-sales accounting ledger is no longer necessary.

The functional area can be stored in Controlling objects, G/L accounts, and cost elements. When defining the derivation of characteristics, you must take into account the following ranking of objects:

- Weakest object: Controlling account assignment
- Next level: G/L account and cost elements
- Strongest derivation: custom substitutions

[Ex]

OBBZ, KEDR

Example of a Functional Area Derivation Hierarchy

An accounting document contains an item with profit and loss account and cost center account assignment. If a functional area is maintained both in the cost center master and the G/L account, the functional area of the G/L account will be used. If, in addition to this, a substitution is active, the functional area from the G/L account can be overwritten as well.

Avoiding the Overwriting of Functional Areas in Substitutions [+]

You can prevent functional areas in substitutions from being overwritten by querying whether the functional area is empty and defining that this is the only case in which it is substituted.

Credit Control Area

The most important questions to be answered when defining the *credit control area* are as follows: At which level do you want to maintain credit limits for customers? Does it make sense if each company code provides a separate limit to a customer? The latter could result in a situation in which one company code continues to supply goods or services to a customer, while another company code has already terminated the supply because a credit limit has been exceeded. Although SAP assigned the credit control area to the Financial Accounting component, its characteristics are often decided upon in the sales and distribution (SD) team.

Controlling Area

The *controlling area* represents the organizational unit that serves as a basis for overhead cost controlling, product cost controlling, and profit center accounting. For example, the controlling area level influences the decision as to whether the posting to a G/L account in Financial Accounting also involves a posting activity in the Controlling component. In the standard SAP system, you can carry out clearings across different company codes only within one controlling area.

General controlling area

As mentioned at the start of this chapter, the question regarding how to assign company codes and controlling areas plays a key role in SAP implementation projects. Company codes that belong to a general controlling area can be analyzed together in cost accounting. However, at the same time, the controlling area also represents the entity in which the activities of financial accounting must be carried out in a synchronized manner. To be able to create monthly reports from the controlling area, all closing entries must have been made previously. In other words: In the best case, all company codes contained in a regional controlling area would be based on one common closing plan. You cannot generate reports from the controlling area until all closing operations have been completed. Because we are living in an age of fast closes, we must ask the question as to whether it is realistic to have all countries and companies follow only one common schedule. Very often this is not the case.

Regional organization

Rather, it is much more realistic that a controlling area comprises the company codes of one country or region. Usually, the controlling, and in particular, the closing processes can be standardized and synchronized without a problem within a specific country or region. Direct assignments are also frequently made; that is, one company code corresponds to one controlling area; the advantage of this is that you do not need to synchronize the closing processes of the individual company codes. However, the disadvantage of this approach is that it limits the option of a comprehensive reporting process in an SAP ERP system. In this case, the easiest way to carry out global reporting is to use a data warehouse.

Cross-company code transactions

The controlling area always provides the framework within which you can carry out cross-company code clearing transactions in Controlling. This restriction is also important when you define the organizational structure. If you decide on using multiple controlling areas, the standard system can map global business transactions only via invoices.

Profit Center

Prior to the introduction of the SAP General Ledger, *profit centers* used to be mapped in Enterprise Controlling (EC-PA). They are used to depict the enterprise structure from the management point of view. From the corporate point of view, profit centers are frequently used for management consolidation; that is, to provide an internal view of the corporate group, whereas companies are used for legal consolidations (based on statutory requirements). The cross-component position of profit center accounting—between Financial Accounting and Controlling—makes this type of accounting interesting and leads to a high level of integration.

Financial statement

However, what causes problems in this context is the mapping of financial statements at the profit center level because the derivation of characteristics of the profit center requires you to make compromises. Take, for example, postings that involve only balance sheet accounts. Because the profit center usually derives from Controlling account assignments, you must assign the profit center manually with these kinds of postings. Alternatively, you can also use dummy account assignments.

[!]

Interpreting Differences as Problematic Discrepancies

But watch out: At first glance, you may easily misinterpret the resulting differences between overhead cost controlling and profit center accounting as problematic discrepancies!

Deriving Profit Centers for Pure Balance Sheet Account Postings [+]

Via a substitution in Financial Accounting, you can use the profit center derivation of the standard SAP system for pure balance sheet account postings as well. To do so, you must define the Controlling account assignments as optional or mandatory entries in the field status of the balance sheet account. You then have to activate the transfer to EC-PCA for the respective balance sheet accounts in Transaction 3KEH.

Note that this does not entail the creation of Controlling documents, but of profit center documents. The profit center is derived from the Controlling object you assigned in the balance sheet item.

The controlling area represents the framework within which profit center accounting occurs. However, it is possible to use profit centers across different company codes.

Operating Concern

The *operating concern* is the comprehensive unit in Profitability Analysis (CO-PA) and you calculate the contribution margin at the level of the *operating concern*. From a technical point of view, each *operating concern* is stored in a separate table. Therefore, you cannot carry out any reporting across multiple *operating concerns* using standard tools. Consequently, you should thoroughly check whether you need one or several *operating concerns*.

To be able to make a decision regarding the design of the operating concern, you must take into account the structure of the CO-PA component. Section 3.5, CO-PA as a Central Reporting Tool, provides detailed information about this.

Aside from the objects discussed so far, no other organizational objects have been available for a long time. However, with the introduction of the SAP General Ledger in SAP ERP, SAP provided the new *segment* object.

Segment

The *segment* is an account assignment object in the SAP General Ledger. You can create complete financial statements and profit and loss statements at the level of segments. However, one major drawback of segment reporting is that segments are closely linked with profit centers. In the standard SAP system, segments are stored in the profit center master record. This raises the question as to whether you really want to use segments or rather choose to present the data via nodes in the profit center structure. The advantage of using segments is that you can create a zero balance at the segment level, which is not possible when you use a profit center hierarchy.

Removing links between profit centers and segments

You can remove links between profit centers and segments by using BAdIs. In turn, this also allows you to derive segments independently of the standard SAP system. However, in practice, this means that at any given time, you *must* be able to find a segment using a BAdI. Otherwise, the system will enter no segment or a dummy segment into the posting document, which impairs the overall reporting quality. This is a pretty challenging task in the context of implementing the SAP General Ledger.

If you prefer to use the standard SAP system, you can use a range of account assignment objects and organizational units. Figure 3.2 provides an overview of these elements.

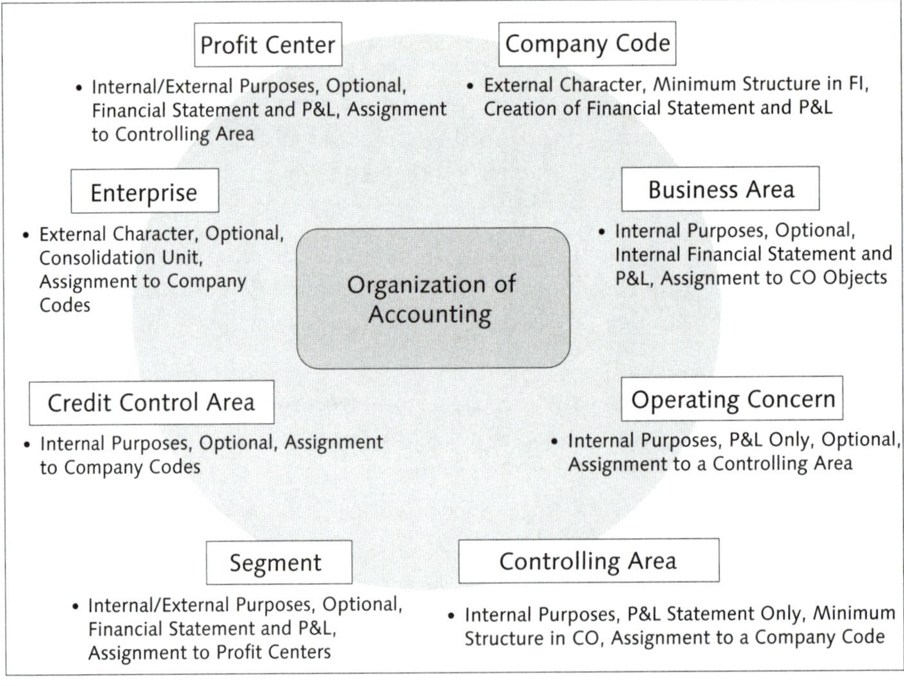

Figure 3.2 The Most Important Organizational Units in Financial Accounting and Controlling

3.2.2 Organizational Elements and Enhancements of the Standard SAP System

Custom account assignment objects

The SAP General Ledger allows you to implement *custom account assignment objects*. This way, you can create your own management structures and map them in Financial Accounting.

[!]

Effects of Using Custom Account Assignment Objects

When creating custom account assignment objects, you should always keep in mind the relatively low level of integration and the significant effects these objects have on table structures in the SAP system.

To benefit from using an account assignment object, you must enhance the Financial Accounting Document Segments (BSEG) table, among other things. Therefore, before implementing a custom field, you should always check whether alternative solutions exist with fewer technical implications.

In addition, you must define the derivation of custom account assignment objects via custom program coding.

However, aside from these aspects (which you must, without doubt, keep in mind), the use of custom account assignment objects represents a viable alternative if, for example, you want to report additional features in the context of management consolidation.

Changing the organizational structure

Many enterprises change their internal structures on a regular basis. This can have strategic reasons such as the acquisition or sale of parts of the enterprise, the restructuring of cost centers, or a new orientation of profit centers. Aside from this, *structural changes* can also become necessary at the operational level, for example, if you want to change a profit center in the cost center master because the cost center itself had been incorrectly created, or if you want to merge multiple cost centers for reasons of data protection.

With regard to structural changes, the question always arises as to when exactly the change should take effect: should it be valid as of a specific key date (e.g., from the current period on), or should the structure be changed retroactively?

Transaction KEND

SAP currently supports organizational changes only to a limited extent and only the CO-PA component provides technical support via Transaction KEND. This transaction enables you, for example, to retroactively implement changes to profit center assignments. In this context, Transaction KEND implements changes only at the object level, whereas individual items in CO-PA are not modified at all. These items remain unchanged so that, for example, they keep their account assignments to the old profit centers. In addition, the transaction does not allow you to specify a key date. Technically speaking, this means that the old structure never existed in reporting. It also means that by changing the structure, you also change reporting figures that have already been transferred to a data warehouse such as *SAP NetWeaver Business Warehouse* (SAP NetWeaver BW) and reported internally or externally.

For example, neither overhead cost controlling nor profit center accounting are aware that Transaction KEND exists in CO-PA. Therefore, after you have carried out a KEND run in CO-PA, you can no longer synchronize data within the Controlling component. Thus, to proceed in a consistent way, you should restrict changes to the organizational structure to a minimum and allow for those changes only at predefined points in time within the current or future periods.

3.2.3 Excursus: The SAP General Ledger and Changes to the Organizational Structure

This issue does not much affect financial accounting because changes to company codes do not occur very often and if they do occur, they usually involve a large-scale project such as the implementation of the SAP General Ledger (see Chapter 9, Optimizing Value Flows by Implementing the SAP General Ledger—A Real-Life Example).

A useful feature of the SAP General Ledger is the integration of profit center accounting in general ledger accounting. However, despite the benefits of this integration, you should also take into account that internal restructurings can cause problems that not only affect controlling aspects but also have an impact on financial accounting. As a result of this, problems caused by internal restructurings will be transferred from the profit and loss statement into the financial statement.

From a technical point of view, the SAP system issues an error message when you try to change the assigned segment in profit center master data. You can convert this error message into a warning; however, this does not really solve the problem caused by the restructuring. Let us look at the example of material stock to clarify this issue.

Changing Profit Center Assignments [Ex]

Suppose you have to post a receipt for a material to which profit center A is assigned in the master record. Next, you change the profit center assignment in such a way that you now assign profit center B to the material; then you post the goods issue.

This simple example illustrates that the total of material stock is displayed accurately. However, if you look at the inventory values of individual profit centers, you will immediately see that there is a mistake. The inventory shown for profit center A is too high, while profit center B is assigned a negative inventory value.

This shows that the implementation of the SAP General Ledger involves some content-related issues that can only be solved individually in the context of the implementation project.

This brief description already demonstrates that implementing the SAP General Ledger can trigger discussions about the entity model because not everything that is required and possible can be implemented without a problem and without adverse effects on the organization and processes.

3.3 International Requirements

A topic that is gaining in importance along with the implementation of the SAP General Ledger involves the mapping of international requirements in financial accounting.

You should first be clear about the fact that originally, the SAP system was a financial accounting and controlling software package designed for the German market. This concept, designed to meet national standards, became problematic when *parallel rendering of accounts* was called for in financial accounting. At that time, the software's ability to meet international requirements was limited.

Increasing level of internationalization

The problem first occurred in large, international corporations that had to procure both shareholders' capital and external capital at an early stage. With an increasing level of internationalization, small and medium-sized companies also became more and more obliged to create their financial statements according to IAS/IFRS or US-GAAP standards.

[+]

Mandatory Accounting Principles

The *International Accounting Standards* (IAS) represent a part of the international accounting principles referred to as *International Financial Reporting Standards* (IFRS). The accounting principles generally accepted in the US are referred to as *United States Generally Accepted Accounting Principles* (US-GAAP).

3.3.1 Parallel Accounting using the Classic General Ledger

The classic general ledger provided three options to map parallel accounting principles:

1. Mapping via parallel company codes
2. Mapping via an additional special ledger
3. Mapping via parallel accounts

The following sections describe these scenarios in more detail.

Mapping via parallel company codes

The concept of using *parallel company codes* is based on the assumption that the greater part of postings is identical in both accounting principles. Daily business is mapped in the operational company code, which is integrated with the logistical components. This company code is based on the accounting principles that are also used in controlling, that is, according to which the enterprise is run. To apply other accounting principles that are only mapped in financial accounting statements, you must create an additional company code that is not integrated with logistics and is primarily used for manual closing entries. To analyze the additional accounting results, both company codes must be evaluated together: the operational company code as well as the additional code that contains manual standardizing entries. Technically, this concept is supported only by asset accounting, although it has never played a major role in practice.

Mapping via an additional special ledger

The basic idea of using a *special ledger* for a second rendering of accounts is similar to the concept of mapping via parallel company codes. Because the general ledger maps only one set of accounting principles, the second set of principles is mapped in a special ledger. The advantage of this method is that all postings that occur in the general ledger can also be transferred to the special ledger where they can be adapted using local postings. Thus, the special ledger shows a complete dataset. However, this variant also has been rarely implemented.

Mapping via parallel accounts

The most widespread method to map different accounting principles is to use *parallel accounts*. This involves the mapping of all accounting principles in the general ledger and in the operational company code. For this purpose, all operational accounts—which can show different values depending on the accounting principles applied—must be identified and multiplied. The accounting principles to be applied are selected in reporting in such a way that the accounts of the respective other accounting principles are excluded. For example, for a financial statement to comply with the German trade law, all IFRS accounts contained in the chart of accounts must be placed among those accounts that have not been assigned. All accounts whose posted data is not affected by the accounting principles applied, such as cash accounts, are referred to as shared accounts and must be shown in reporting on the basis of all accounting principles.

Mickey Mouse model

The account logic can best be described using what is called the *Mickey Mouse model* shown in Figure 3.3. In this model, a financial statement comes into existence every time you look at one "ear" and the "face" together such as the right ear, which contains the pure IFRS accounts plus the shared accounts. The accounts contained in the other ear are not involved. In this context it is important that each "ear" by itself, as well as the "face," show a zero balance.

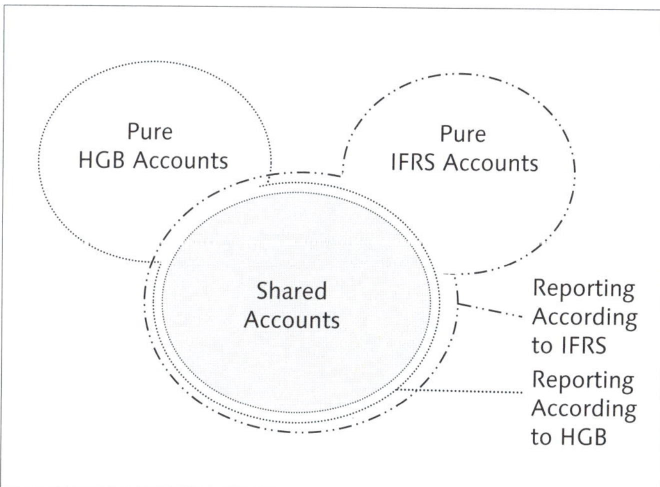

Figure 3.3 Mickey Mouse Model

3.3.2 Options of the SAP General Ledger for the Parallel Rendering of Accounts

Parallel ledgers

The list of parallel rendering of accounts is supplement by the SAP General Ledger, which is another option to map parallel ledgers within General Ledger Accounting. The technology corresponds to the technology that is provided by the long-established FI-SL component: You can create multiple ledgers in parallel, which all use a shared totals table. In the SAP General Ledger, you must use at least one ledger, called the *leading ledger 0L*. All other ledgers are optional and their names can be selected freely.

Posting to ledgers

Business transactions that are entered in another SAP component and result in a document in General Ledger Accounting always try to post in all ledgers. Only within the Financial Accounting component is it possible to generate a posting without addressing the leading ledger.

Parallel ledgers instead of parallel accounts

This almost revolutionary innovation enables you to replace the traditional method of parallel accounts with the use of *parallel ledgers*. This facilitates reporting and reduces the risk of incorrect postings because a non-leading ledger must be posted explicitly (see Figure 3.4).

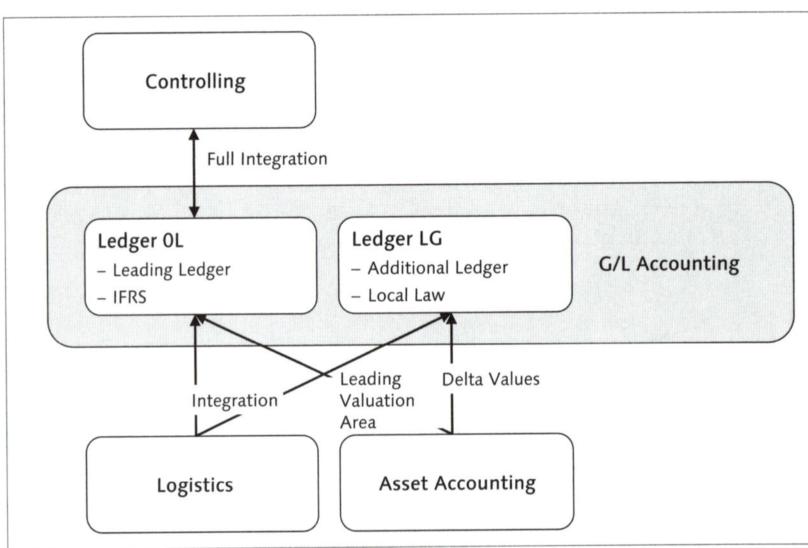

Figure 3.4 Parallel Rendering of Accounts with SAP General Ledger

Postings in General Ledger Accounting that result from logistics processes are not posted ledger-specifically and can therefore be evaluated in both ledgers, 0L and LG. Asset Accounting, however, supports parallel ledgers to the effect that the individual ledgers 0L and LG are addressed explicitly. Here, only the leading ledger 0L is posted with the complete value (e.g., the depreciation); the ledger LG only receives the delta value that together with the value of the ledger 0L results in the depreciation according to local law. This means that the value of the depreciation in ledger LG is based on two documents: the depreciation in ledger 0L plus the delta value that was directly posted in the ledger LG. If you use parallel ledgers, you must also consider that an integration with cost accounting is only possible for the leading ledger 0L, for instance, via real-time integration.

Migration to parallel ledgers

Within the framework of a migration to the SAP General Ledger and prior to implementing parallel ledgers, you must take into account that the design is elaborate for the following reasons:

- **Integration**
  Only the leading ledger is integrated with Controlling.
- **Delta method**
  Asset accounting supports a non-leading ledger only in the delta method; that is, you need a delta depreciation area in asset accounting. The overall value in the non-leading ledger results from the value of the leading depreciation area plus/minus the delta depreciation area.
- **Change management**
  The posting logic with parallel accounts is known within the enterprise and possibly well established. The changeover to parallel ledgers using a careful change management process must be forwarded to the internal organization.

Segment financial statements

The creation of *segment financial statements* is another step toward the internationalization of the SAP ERP system. As already described, the segment is an account assignment object that is available in the SAP General Ledger. Segment reporting enables you to create financial statements across individual business areas without considering the company code limits. In this context, segments are units that can be uniquely defined.

Fast close

Another important keyword that is often used in the international environment is *fast close*. Initially, you could assume that this refers to a shorter period of time from the start to the end of the closing process. In real life, however, the concept of fast close usually refers to an early closing. An early closing is implemented by decoupling the posting periods from the calendar months.

[Ex]

Early Closing

If, for example, the posting period ends on August 27 instead of August 31, you can report figures on the last day of the month already; that is, on August 31. The closing process itself, however, has not been accelerated.

Real-time integration

Regardless of this, however, the SAP General Ledger also provides options to abbreviate the closing process, for example, via *real-time integration*. Real-time integration is more or less the successor of the reconciliation ledger (Transaction KALC). The procedures of real-time integration and Transaction KALC are similar: As soon as a Controlling document results in an assignment change that is relevant for financial accounting, this change is transferred to the Financial Accounting component. Whereas the reconciliation ledger enables this transfer only if the functional and business area is changed and in case of cross-company code postings, real-time integration covers a wider range. In the standard version, real-time integration considers the change of the functional area, profit center, segment, and business area as well as cross-company code processes. However, it is also possible to transfer all transactions of Overhead Cost Controlling to Financial Accounting or to design the transfer completely independently using a BAdI.

Transfer of single documents

Whereas the reconciliation ledger is started periodically, that is, at the end of the month, and generates summarized postings in Financial Accounting, the real-time integration checks every transaction in Controlling as soon as it is posted and transfers the relevant documents individually to the Financial Accounting component. Upon closing, this spares you the run of the reconciliation ledger as well as the reconciliation efforts between Financial Accounting and Controlling. This enables you to reconcile Financial Accounting and Controlling not only directly after the run of the reconciliation ledger, but also permanently and within a period.

Regarding the reconciliation ledger and real-time integration, the topic is now within the area of period-end closing and we have reached the processes. At the beginning of this chapter you already learned that the integrative depiction of value flows not only requires a corresponding orientation of the organizational structure and processes; another important component is the master data, which we will discuss next.

3.4 Value Flow-Oriented Master Data Concept

Defining the master data lays an essential foundation for the integration of an SAP system. In this context, master data refers to the master data that is used in logistics and the pure Financial Accounting and/or Controlling master data.

3.4.1 General Ledger Account and Cost Element

General ledger account—mapping of general ledger accounting

The *G/L account* is primarily used to map G/L accounting in external accounting. The *cost element* is the corresponding equivalent of controlling. The technical structure for both objects is similar: There is what is called an *A segment* that contains the data that depends on the chart of accounts. This segment is enhanced with the *B segment* that contains the data that depends on the company code or the controlling area.

A segment—no influence on the value flow

We will first take a look at the G/L account. Essential settings are made at chart of accounts level, which have limited effect on the value flow. The most important setting in this context is the definition of whether the account is a balance sheet account or a profit and loss account. In addition, you define the account number and name here.

Open item control and document splitting

At the company code level, you are provided with several setting options. Only a few of these contribute to the control of the value flow. For example, the option to display line items or manage open items (*open item control*) on accounts is just one possibility to simplify the accountant's daily work. These options, however, have no effect on the value flow.

With the implementation of the document splitting in the SAP General Ledger, open item control is of great significance because it is a major influencing factor for document splitting.

[+]

Document Splitting in the SAP General Ledger

The *document splitting* is one of the most interesting developments SAP has implemented in accounting. Only with this function can you generate financial statements on an object other than the company code without having to work with approximated values on a large scale. To understand the function, you must take a closer look at the two forms of document splitting based on an example of profit center derivation:

- **Active document splitting**
  The active document splitting enables you to split a payables item and distribute it to multiple profit centers if the offsetting account also contains different profit centers. The splitting is based on distribution rules that are stored as fixed values in the system. These rules define which line item is used as the basis of document splitting and which items should be distributed by percentage; that is, according to the ratio in the base lines.

- **Passive document splitting**
  The passive document splitting takes effect in accounts that are managed on an open item basis. Here, it is possible, for example, to assume the profit center account assignment of an incoming invoice from the open invoice item and to pass it up to the bank or clearing account.

Primary and secondary cost elements

Cost elements are the cost-relevant items of the chart of accounts. Generally, all P&L accounts are also defined as cost elements. These are then referred to as *primary cost elements*, that is, cost elements whose costs originate outside of Controlling. *Secondary cost elements* are in contrast with these and are only available within Controlling and cannot be posted to in Financial Accounting.

General ledger accounts and cost elements

Figure 3.5 illustrates the relation of G/L accounts and cost elements.

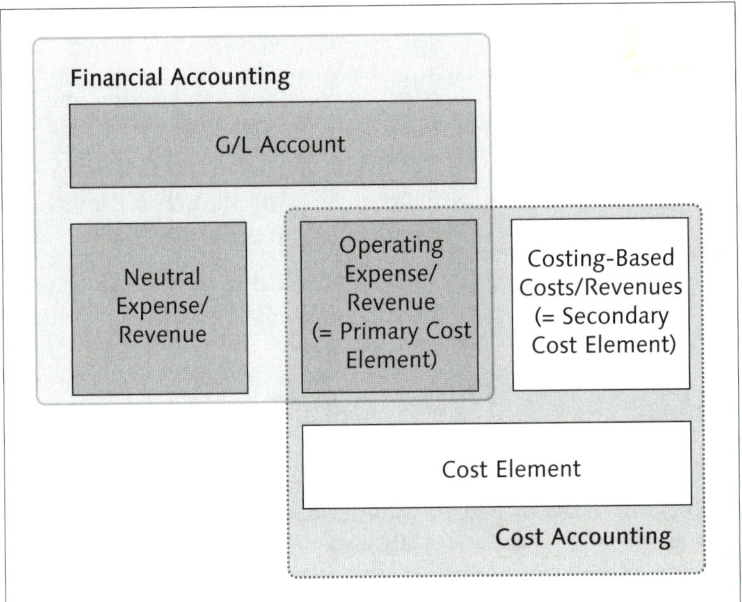

Figure 3.5 Relation of G/L Accounts and Cost Elements

You can see that not all profit and loss accounts must be created as cost elements in Controlling. If you do not create a cost element for a profit and loss account, this is referred to as nonoperating expenses or revenues. Due to the missing cost element, values that are posted to the G/L account are not transferred to the overhead cost controlling. Usually, the profit or loss is determined in parallel in Financial Accounting and Controlling. Whereas in Financial Accounting you also calculate the financial result, in Controlling, EBIT (*Earnings Before Interests and Taxes*) is frequently the last line of the calculation of profits. If you want to calculate a consistent EBIT in Financial Accounting and Controlling (which you should), neutral accounts in Financial Accounting may be incorporated in the P&L statement only below the EBIT.

In SAP ERP, two factors indicate whether a cost element is primary or secondary:

- **The number of the cost element**
  If a number is entered when a cost element is created and this number is already assigned to a G/L account in Financial Accounting, the cost element can only be created as a primary cost element.
- **The cost element category**
  Detailed control is implemented via the cost element category, a field in the master data of the cost element. Here, it is decided whether the cost element is primary or secondary. Additionally, you also determine the usability of the cost element within Controlling and in the integration with other components. The most important cost element categories are the following:

  01 (Primary costs/cost reducing revenues)
  Most primary cost elements are created with category 01. Cost elements that are created with this category can be posted to from other SAP components, such as Financial Accounting or MM.

  11 (Revenues) and 12 (Sales deduction)
  Cost element categories 11 and 12 are usually used for the primary cost elements of revenue account determination. Only with these categories can you transfer sales to CO-PA. Cost elements of these categories can be posted to internal orders or WBS elements (WBS = work breakdown structure) but not to cost centers. On cost centers, only the statistical maintenance of these items is possible.

  21 (Internal settlement)
  Cost element category 21 is used for the settlement of Controlling account assignments to other Controlling objects.

  41 (Overhead rates)
  Cost element category 41 is used to create cost elements if you are working with overhead rates.

42 (Assessments)
Cost element category 42 is used for assessments in Controlling.

43 (Internal activity allocation)
Cost element category 43 is a separate cost element category for internal activity allocation in Controlling.

90 (Statistical cost element balance sheet accounts)
Cost element category 90 is used to create cost elements for balance sheet accounts.

[+]

Special Cost Element Category 90

So far, we have assumed that the G/L accounts that are created as cost elements in Controlling are profit and loss accounts. However, it is also possible to create cost elements for balance sheet accounts using cost element category 90. This category is defined in the SAP standard.

If you want to evaluate asset or stock values in Controlling reporting, you can provide the corresponding accounts with a cost element of category 90. However, only statistical postings are possible to these cost elements.

As you can see, the cost element category not only differentiates between primary and secondary cost elements but also affects the value flow. Cost elements that are created with an incorrect category can interrupt the value flow.

[Ex]

Interrupting the Value Flow

For example, you must not create the account for updating a vendor account with category 12 and then assign the account to a cost center because this would only generate a statistical posting in overhead cost controlling. You would not be able to process such a statistical posting meaningfully; that is, you would not be able to forward it to CO-PA, for example.

Financial Accounting and Cost Element Accounting

Due to the close link between G/L accounts and cost elements, the chart of accounts must inevitably be a shared product of financial accounting and cost accounting. A general decision you have to make is whether and for which purpose you want to use the neutral accounts.

Avoiding neutral accounts

If you avoid neutral accounts, you get complete reconciliation between financial accounting and cost element accounting. This is, without doubt, an advantage. However, you must provide each posting to a profit and loss account with a Controlling account assignment, which is not always supported by the SAP system. An important example for the lack of support is the logistics integration via the MM account determination (see Chapter 4, Procurement Process). For instance, if you create all stock change accounts as a cost element, you must define a dummy account assignment for the goods issue to the customer. The question thus arises whether you should omit the reconcilability of Financial Accounting and Controlling because the postings in Controlling cannot be evaluated meaningfully.

3.4.2 Chart of Accounts

Importance of the chart of accounts

With the growing level of internationalization, the definition of the *chart of accounts* becomes a topic to which you must pay increased attention. Its positioning indicates the importance SAP attaches to the chart of accounts: directly at the client level, above the company code and the organizational elements of logistics. Each company code must be assigned to one operating chart of accounts.

The *controlling area* is assigned to a chart of accounts either directly via the assigned company code (for a 1:1 assignment) or directly via Customizing. The chart of accounts is therefore also a classification criterion in cost accounting. It contains not only the P&L accounts of external accounting that correspond to the primary cost elements, but also the secondary cost elements that are only available in cost accounting.

Additional charts of accounts

However, the central positioning of the chart of accounts is also problematic, as you will see. Customers frequently request additional charts of accounts; however, this request cannot be easily met because a company code can only be assigned to one chart of accounts in operational business. SAP solves this problem by connecting several charts of accounts. As a result, the additional fields GROUP ACCOUNT and ALTERNATIVE ACCOUNT NUMBER are provided, which you can use to map additional requirements (see Figure 3.6).

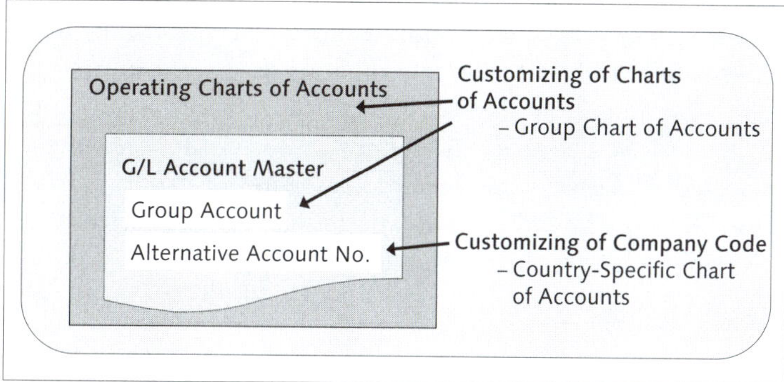

Figure 3.6 Hierarchy of Charts of Accounts

Operating Chart of Accounts

The *operating chart of accounts* is the chart of accounts whose G/L accounts you address in your daily work. Exactly one operating chart of accounts is assigned to every company code. The use of an operating chart of accounts is the minimum requirement in Customizing.

Group Chart of Accounts

A *group chart of accounts* can be assigned to the operating chart of accounts. This group chart of accounts has an n:1 relationship, which means that a group chart of accounts can be assigned to many different operating charts of accounts. This procedure makes sense if different operating charts of accounts are used within the group. Because you can never assign a group chart of accounts directly to a company code, the accounts only contain the data of the A segment.

An evaluation according to the group account number is possible in various reports and in consolidation, for example, for deductions in SAP SEM-BCS, a BI/BW-based consolidation tool of SAP. You can also use it to call financial statements. This enables you to call comparable financial statements for company codes without a major time effort, even if the company codes work with different operating charts of accounts.

Implementing a group chart of accounts

When you implement a group chart of accounts, you should not underestimate the effort required for mapping the operating accounts. You must also consider that the group chart of accounts must be able to map different international conditions.

Alternative: shared operating chart of accounts

However, there is an alternative approach to mapping an operating chart of accounts in a group chart of accounts. In this case, all company codes are forced to post to the group accounts in operational business. The chart of accounts that is specified by the group thus fulfills the role of the operating chart of accounts. The benefit of this approach is that the entire company uses the same account numbers. Unfortunately, this does not ensure that all accountants use the accounts identically. In real life, accounts are frequently posted to with diverse business cases in the various parts of the company. Consequently, the informative value and comparability of figures that are provided by these accounts must be questioned.

Counter-argument: legal regulations

In addition to the fact that the figures should be considered only conditionally, there are other reasons against a shared operating chart of accounts and a frequently mentioned point are the legal regulations regarding the chart of accounts. This can be addressed with a country-specific chart of accounts.

Country Chart of Accounts

Country-specific chart of accounts

In fact, some countries have regulations for the numbering of G/L accounts, for example, France. Like France, many countries have eased this regulation so that it is no longer an explicit requirement to post to account numbers that are predetermined by the respective national law for operational business. Only notifications must still be implemented using the defined account numbers. For this purpose, SAP provides the *country-specific chart of accounts*.

The country-specific chart of accounts is not defined in the operating chart of accounts but in the company code. This means that the ALTERNATIVE ACCOUNT NUMBER field is provided in the G/L account master record. This way, you can create financial statements using the country-specific chart of accounts so that reporting is possible according to national law.

Individual decision

As you can see, there are up to three charts of accounts that can be used for a company code: the operating chart of accounts, the group chart of accounts, and the country-specific chart of accounts. The decision which charts of accounts are used in a company depends on the respective given conditions. The use of an international operating chart of accounts calls for a determined head office that can enforce "its" chart of accounts in the subsidiaries. National varieties in the mapping of balance sheet values often result in prolonged discussions. In individual cases such as the *purchase account management*, which exists in many southern European countries, there are legally binding regulations that must be taken into account.

While the discussion of G/L accounts, cost elements, and charts of accounts revolved exclusively around Financial Accounting and Controlling, there is also other master data that is interesting for the integration with Logistics components. The material master is the most important integrated object in this context.

3.4.3 Material Master

Manifold links

The *material master* must satisfy the requirements of many technical areas and SAP components. There are links to bills of material, recipes, production, material requirements planning, warehouse management, quality management, and financial and cost accounting.

The material master can satisfy the different requirements thanks to its different *views*. The minimum requirement for a material is the general view, which primarily includes the material number and description. The respective use of the material number decides which other views are required. This way, you avoid that redundancies occur in the SAP data retention and you also enable scalability if individual applications (e.g., production) are used retroactively or not at all.

[Ex]

Necessary Views

Which views are necessary depends on each individual case. For example, the sales and distribution views are irrelevant for a raw material because the raw material is not sold but is used for production. On the other hand, a finished product that was produced in-house does not have a purchasing view but does have a sales and distribution view.

Because a comprehensive discussion of the material master would be beyond the scope of this book, our description is limited to the areas that are relevant for the integrated value flow.

The fields concerning the material valuation are of great interest from the point of view of financial and cost accounting.

You can find the specification for this in the material master on the tabs FINANCIAL ACCOUNTING and COSTING.

The following sections discuss the following:

- Valuation class
- Price control
- Costing

Valuation Class

Valuation class—classification criterion of Financial Accounting/ Controlling

The definition of the *valuation class* is fundamental because it is used to classify the account determination for goods movements. The requirements for the valuation classes should always be provided by financial and cost accounting. The desired aggregation level for the depiction of the values in the financial statements and profit and loss statement is decisive here. Do you want to manage all raw materials in one material stock account? Are there materials you want to analyze separately in cost accounting due to a high value or high price fluctuations? These and other questions must be discussed in this context.

Chapter 4, Section 4.5, Integration of MM and Financial Accounting/Controlling, provides a detailed description of the role of the valuation class.

The valuation class defines at which point in the financial statement and profit and loss statement you can find material movements and material stocks. It is also important for which value in the financial statement you apply the logistics processes. You specify this using price control, among other things.

Price Control

Price control defines how the price of a material is formed. In the standard SAP version, you can choose between *standard price* and *moving average price*.

Moving average price

The moving average price per material unit is calculated based on the stock's total value divided by the material stock. In this context, the price can be influenced by goods receipt and invoice receipt. Internal material movements such as a material withdrawal for production cannot influence the price. These have the price that is valid at the respective time of material valuation. The calculation is automatic. Table 3.1 shows an example for calculating a moving average price for suitcase locks:

Transaction	Stock (piece)	Value per piece	Total value	Moving average price
Opening stock	100	EUR 8.00	EUR 800.00	EUR 8.00
Goods issue to production	–40		EUR -320.00	EUR 8.00
Warehouse stock	60		EUR 480.00	EUR 8.00
Goods receipt for order	100	EUR 10.00	EUR 1,000.00	
Warehouse stock	160	EUR 9.25	EUR 1,480.00	EUR 9.25
Goods issue to production	–90		EUR -833.00	EUR 9.25
Closing stock	70		EUR 648.00	EUR 9.25

Table 3.1 Example of a Moving Average Price Calculation

As shown in this example, the price of the locks does not change on consumption but only when a material is received. The new goods value results from the mixed costing of new and existing goods. The third row of the example shows that a warehouse stock of 60 locks is in stock with a total value of EUR 480.00. Another 100 locks with a value of EUR 10.00 each are received; that is, EUR 1,000.00 in total. As a result, 160 locks with a value of EUR 1,480.00 are now in stock. Consequently the new price per piece is:

EUR 1,480.00 ÷ 160 pieces = EUR 9.25/piece

Raw materials are typically kept with a moving average price. However, if a raw material such as some types of metals is subject to high price fluctuations, you must consider whether you should define a fixed standard price so that the raw materials are incorporated in production costs with a fixed value.

Standard price

Stability is the advantage of standard price control. A standard price results from a price change in logistics (Transaction ME21) or from a recalculation in product controlling. In both cases, a change of the material master and a simultaneous revaluation of the current warehouse stock that affects the financial statement take place. The stability of the standard price can be considered a disadvantage for externally procured materials in particular because the material does not reflect the current market price.

Periodic unit price

If you use the material ledger, you can deploy the moving average price control to create a period unit price. This period unit price is a combination of the previously discussed moving average and standard prices.

Keeping parallel prices is possible

If you use standard prices, a price usually results from costing runs that are defined within the framework of planning at the end of the year for the following year or the following period. The SAP system presents the prices, which are the result of cost estimates, in parallel as future, current, and previous cost estimate value. This parallel presentation of prices enables you to retrace a material's price development at a glance (see Figure 3.7).

Balance sheet valuation for physical inventory prices

There is no such thing as *the* price of a material in the SAP system. Rather, you can define different prices in the material master depending on use. For this purpose, the SAP system provides additional fields in which you can update planned prices as well as valuation prices that are based on tax law and commercial law. These prices are referred to as *physical inventory prices* in the SAP system.

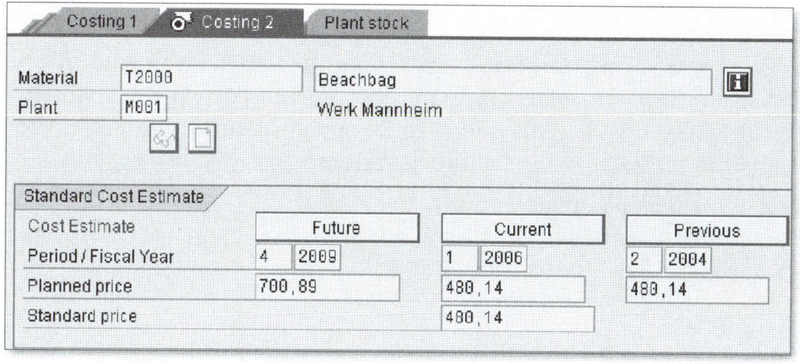

Figure 3.7 Price History in the Material Master

Physical inventory prices are not generated continuously but are only updated by the balance sheet valuation function. In the valuation, you can differentiate between *determination of lowest value*, *replacement cost valuation*, and valuation according to the *LIFO* or *FIFO method* (LIFO = Last In – First Out, FIFO = First In – First Out). However, none of these price determinations result in the posting of documents and a related change of the stock values in Financial Accounting. To change the value that is listed in the balance sheet, you have two options in the standard version:

- Posting of a price change and update as a standard price
- Manual posting in Financial Accounting

Valuation Procedure [+]

The valuation procedure decides which price is used for the inventory valuation. Alternatively, the *delivered price* and the *current price* are at least available for selection. The permissibility of the respective valuation procedure depends on the rendering of account.

- **Lowest Value Principle (LVP)**
  Here, another distinction is made between the strict and the moderate LVP. According to the strict LVP, you must select the lowest price from two possible prices; according to the moderate LVP, you can select between the current and the lower price.
- **LIFO valuation**
  The abbreviation LIFO (*Last In – First Out*) means that the last stock of a material to be received is the first to be consumed. For example, imagine the stack of paper in the copy room: New cartons of paper are always stacked on top, and the paper is taken from the top of the stack if required. This is only possible if the material's quality does not deteriorate with long storage times. Here, you apply the material prices of the oldest receipts for the material stock.

- **FIFO valuation**
  FIFO (*First In – First Out*) is the exact opposite of LIFO: Now, the goods that are in stock first are the first to be withdrawn. An example is silo stockholding where the silo is filled from above and the goods are withdrawn at the bottom. Here, the prices of the last receipts are used for valuation.
- **Replacement value valuation**
  This valuation method uses the current market price for valuation. Consequently, this value is not linked with the original receipt price.

You can see that physical inventory prices cannot be used for operational business in the standard version and have only informative value.

When talking about "values," the fields in the field group TAX DATA on the tab SALES: sales org. 1, are important in the material master. They are used to control the tax relevance of the material in the billing document. Chapter 5, Sales and Distribution Process, provides a detailed description of the fields and their effect. There, you will also find a description of the *account assignment group material.*

On the tab SALES:GENERAL/PLANT, you will find the PROFIT CENTER field. You can use this field to find a profit center for all material movements.

[+]

Maintaining the Price Unit

When you maintain the material masters, always ensure that the same price unit is used in all material views. This way, you can avoid incorrect entries.

An example:

[Ex]

Different Price Units

In the purchasing view, "1 piece" is maintained as the purchase order unit, whereas "1,000 pieces" is used in accounting. There is a risk that price and quantity variances occur in invoice verification that are caused by the price unit's control in the material master.

Costing

Costing data

Two tabs— COSTING 1 and COSTING 2—are provided for the costing data in the material stock. They are used to control how the material must be costed. Here, you can find specifications about the handling of overhead costs (overhead group) as well as for the determination and handling of variances in production (variance key). You can find further information on this topic in Chapter 6, Production Process.

3.4.4 Requirements Class

Effects of the requirements class

The *requirements class* is an important field for multiple topics of logistics and cost accounting; however, this is not apparent at first glance. The requirements class determines several definitions for the development of requirements in sales and the production environment.

You can find the Customizing of the REQUIREMENTS CLASS via Transaction OVZG or in the Implementation Guide under SALES AND DISTRIBUTION • BASIC FUNCTIONS • AVAILABILITY CHECK AND TRANSFER OF REQUIREMENTS • TRANSFER OF REQUIREMENTS • DEFINE REQUIREMENTS CLASSES (see Figure 3.8).

Reqmts class 040 Mke-to-ord.w/o cons.

Requirements	
Availability	☑
Req. transfer	☑
Allocation ind.	
Prod.allocation	☐
Ind.req.reductn	☐
No MRP	

Configuration	
Configuration	
Cons.of config.	

Costing	
Costing	
Costing ID	
Costing Method	2
Costing Variant	PC04
Costing Sheet	COGM
Copy cstg sheet	☐
CndTypLineItems	
CondTypLinItFix	

Assembly	
Assembly type	
Order costing	☐
Automatic plnng	☐
Special Stock	E
Order Type	
Avail.components	☐
Type comp.check	
Online assembly	
Capacity check	
No update	☐
OCM	☐

Account assignment	
Acct Assgt Cat.	E
Valuation	
W/o Val. Strat.	☐
Settlmt Profile	SD1
Strategy Seq.	
Changeable	0
RA Key	UNIT
Consumption	E
Functional Area	0100

Figure 3.8 Settings in the Requirements Class

We will first take a look at the most essential settings from the sales and distribution perspective. The requirements class controls whether an availability check is carried out for the material in the sales order (this is the case in our example; see the AVAILABILITY checkbox). Furthermore, it is defined whether a requirements transfer takes place (is carried out according to the Requirements transfer checkbox; see in Figure 3.8). This definition enables you to make schedule lines for the sales order later on.

Account assignment category

The *account assignment category* (ACCT ASSGT CAT. checkbox) is a critical definition for the Controlling component. The account assignment category decides whether the item should be settled to a Controlling account assignment. In our example, the entry E means that the sales order is a cost object.

Settlement profile/ settlement rule

Here, you also determine which *settlement profile* (SETTLMT PROFILE checkbox) is used for the sales order. The strategy sequence is then used to determine the *settlement rule*; that is, the target account assignment for settlement. By entering 0 in the CHANGEABLE field, you additionally determine that the settlement profile and the found settlement rule can no longer be changed in the sales order. Alternatively, you can also specify that a change is permissible prior to the first settlement or even at all times.

Results analysis key

The *results analysis key* (RA key CHECKBOX) is also critical. This key can have different meanings depending on the order type. Using this checkbox, you can determine the *Work In Process* (WIP) or carry out the results analysis.

The determination of the permitted account assignment categories is particularly essential for the value flow within the company. For example, cost accounting can use the sales order as the controlling characteristic only if the sales order item is also part of the value flow.

Derivation of the requirements class

The *requirements class* is not defined permanently in the master data but is derived in the background by the system. How the derivation works depends on the SAP components that are used.

Derivation without PP

If you only use the SD component but not the PP component, the requirements class is derived from the *requirements type*. The item category of the sales order item and the MRP group in the material master form the source of the requirements type.

Derivation if PP is used

If you use the PP component, the derivation of the requirements type is primarily based on the material. For this purpose, use the fields STRATEGY GROUP (MRP 3 VIEW), MRP GROUP (MRP 2 VIEW), and MATERIAL TYPE (general view) in the material master. If no requirements type can be derived in this process, the SAP system attempts to achieve the derivation using the combination of ITEM CATEGORY (the sales order item) and MRP GROUP or only via the ITEM CATEGORY. If this is still unsuccessful, the sys-

The billing documents, settlements from overhead cost controlling, as well as order and project settlements, however, can be displayed in both CO-PA variants.

In the sample enterprise, Lederwaren-Manufaktur Mannheim, only costing-based CO-PA is enabled. Although this reduces the reconciliability of CO-PA and Financial Accounting, this option utilizes the Financial Accounting-independent valuation in CO-PA. Deciding against an account-based CO-PA reduces the data volume and follows a common procedure.

3.5.2 Structure of Costing-Based CO-PA

Figure 3.9 illustrates the structure and functioning of costing-based CO-PA. If you have already worked with business intelligence systems, you will recognize the method.

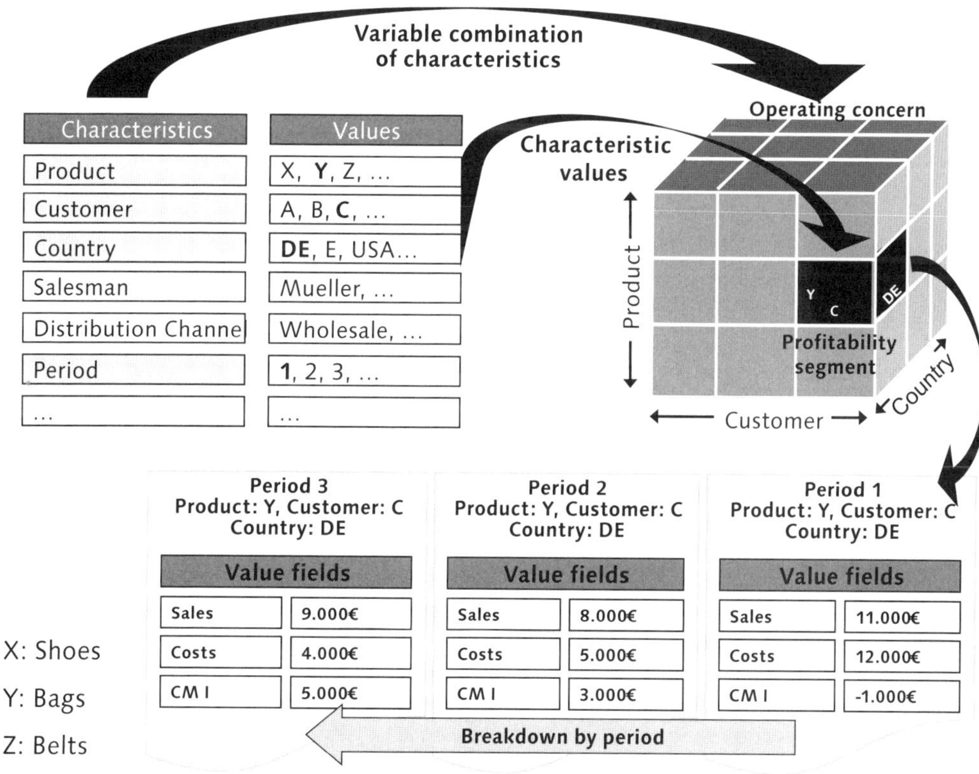

Figure 3.9 Structure and Evaluation of Costing-Based CO-PA

Imagine CO-PA as a multi-dimensional cube. In reporting, you can limit the dimensions to be considered using the selection criteria of a report. This narrows the view of the cube so that only those data records are left that fulfill your selection criteria. This approach is called the *slice-and-dice* procedure.

In this example, you can see that customer C from Germany has regularly procured product Y. To obtain this information from CO-PA, the system provides each data record in CO-PA, which results from a billing document in SD, with the listed characteristics.

In this example, you now want to display the sales generated with product Y at customer C, sorted by periods. By opposing the revenues to the costs of the sales, you can calculate the contribution margin 1 (CM I). Unfortunately, this reveals that in period 1, the products were sold at too low a price, which resulted in a negative contribution margin . Consequently, counter-measures were taken. Despite lower sales in the subsequent periods, the contribution margin has developed positively.

This is a basic example of how values can be updated in CO-PA and evaluated later on. In real life, this evaluation is usually considerably more complex. It is therefore indispensable to define the reporting requirements prior to configuring CO-PA. Only then can you collect data in a targeted manner.

Section 3.2, Entity Model, already described that the *operating concern* is the organizational unit of CO-PA. Establishing this area is the first step in Customizing. You can find the entire Customizing in the Implementation Guide under CONTROLLING • PROFITABILITY ANALYSIS.

Operating concern

In the operating concern, you initially decide whether you want to map costing-based and/or account-based CO-PA. In addition to the operating concern currency, you can also decide whether the company code currency should be recorded as well. Additionally, an operating concern has its own fiscal year variant, just like the company code and the controlling area. Here, you must ensure that you can store different variants in the individual entities and that the number of periods is identical respectively.

After you have made these few general specifications, you can start to define the data structure; that is, the list of characteristics and value fields.

If the characteristics and value fields that are available in the standard version are not sufficient, you can create own objects. We will first discuss the creation of *characteristics* using Transaction KEA5.

Naming Characteristics [+]

Do not use meaningful abbreviations for characteristics and value fields. This way, you can use outdated objects elsewhere in future.

Creating characteristics

After you have defined a characteristic ID, the system takes you to the input screen CREATE CHARACTERISTIC: ASSIGNMENT (see Figure 3.10).

At Lederwaren-Manufaktur Mannheim, diverse high-quality leathers are used. To be able to respond to new market trends, it is essential to monitor sales, sorted by leather. For this purpose, create a new characteristic WW200 (leather).

Because this characteristic is not available directly as a field in the sales order, create a new characteristic with its own value maintenance (see Figures 3.10, 3.11, and 3.12). Alternatively, it would also be possible to refer to existing field contents from the material or customer master or from the sales order. You can also create a characteristic completely without a check of the values entered. With this option, however, you presumably cannot ensure that a characteristic is filled meaningfully and thus is evaluable.

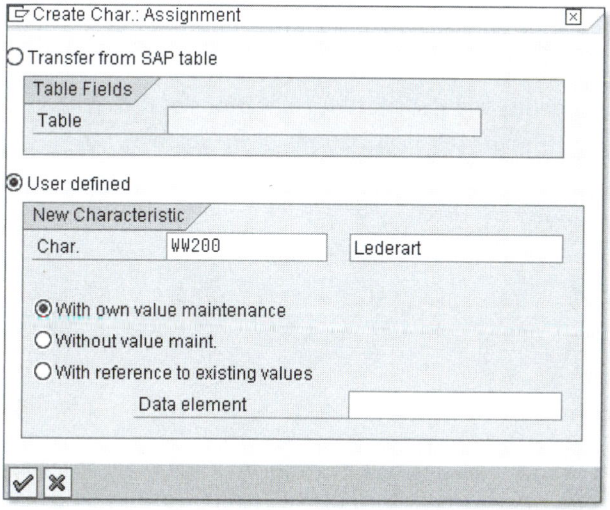

Figure 3.10 Creating Characteristic WW200

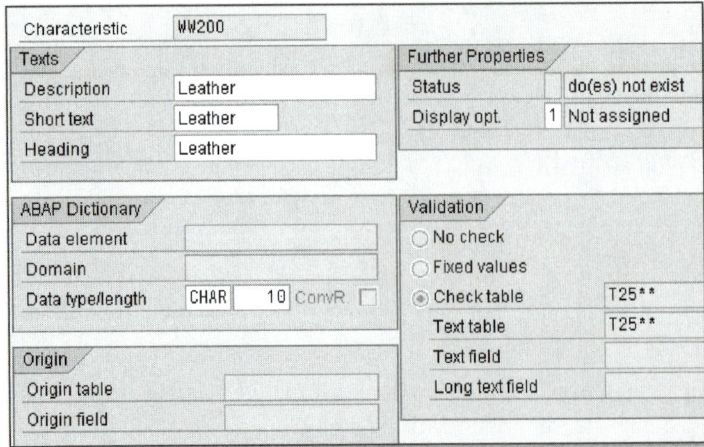

Figure 3.11 Details of Characteristic WW200

Value type and length of the characteristic

In the detail screen, you define the value type (alphanumeric or numeric) and the length with which the characteristic should be created. On the right side of Figure 3.11, you can see that the SAP system already displays a Check table, T25**, for the table (already masked, that is, not conclusively defined). The exact definition of the table is carried out in the next input screen. *T2550* was entered in this case.

In this table, you must define the necessary specifications of the characteristic values. Figure 3.12 shows the specifications of the leather.

Lederart	Descriptn
BOXCALF	Boxcalf
CALF	Calf
CHEVREAU	Goat
KROKO	Crocodile
STRAUSS	Ostrich

Figure 3.12 Values for Characteristic WW200

Assignment of characteristics

After you have created the characteristic, you must use Transaction KEA0 to assign it to operating concern LWAG. The SAP system "wants" to regenerate the operating concern at this point. As long as you are not in a live system that already contains the CO-PA documents, this does not constitute a problem. For operating concerns that already contain data, however, this can result in long runtimes. Because no postings can and may occur during the generation, long runtimes are very unfavorable in a live system.

Error Message for the Initial Generation

[+]

Frequently, an error message occurs during the initial generation. In this case, you should restart the generation manually before you begin to search for the error. Often, the operating concern can be generated without any problem with the second attempt.

Derivation of characteristic values

After you have created a new characteristic and assigned it to the operating concern, you must define the location where the system should derive the field content. There are several options to derive characteristic values:

- Derivation rule
- Table lookup
- Move
- Clear
- Customer hierarchy access
- Customer enhancement

Derivation rule

You can use derivation rules to create "if-then relationships." For the few sales materials available at Lederwaren-Manufaktur Mannheim, it is useful to populate characteristic WW200 using a derivation rule. Customizing would then be displayed as shown in Figure 3.13.

Product number	As	Leather	Leather Name
B1000	=	CALF	Calf
S1000	=	BOXCALF	Boxcalf
S1100	=	KROKO	Crocodile
S2000	=	BOXCALF	Boxcalf
S2100	=	CHEVREAU	Goat
S3000	=	BOXCALF	Boxcalf
S4000	=	BOXCALF	Boxcalf
S5000	=	BOXCALF	Boxcalf
S6000	=	BOXCALF	Boxcalf
S6100	=	CHEVREAU	Goat
S6200	=	KROKO	Crocodile
S7000	=	BOXCALF	Boxcalf
T100	=	BOXCALF	Boxcalf
T1000	=	STRAUSS	Ostrich
T110	=	KROKO	Crocodile

Figure 3.13 Derivation Rule for the Characteristic Derivation

Table access

Using table accesses, you can use field contents from all tables that are currently available for the interface to CO-PA. Typical examples are fields from the material or customer master or fields from the sales order. The derivation of the company code from the sales organization via Table TVKO (ORGANIZATIONAL UNIT: SALES ORGANIZATIONS) is a table access that is already contained in the standard version.

Assignment

Assignments enable you to write content of any source field to the target characteristic. An example of this is the filling of the ship-to party characteristic. A possible assignment could look like this: Search for "ship-to party" partner role in sales order and write customer number to "ship-to party" characteristic.

Initialization

An initialization is required if you want to set the content of the characteristic to the respective initial value. For character fields, the initial value is [BLANK], for numeric fields it is 0. An initialization is often required for deliveries free of charge or for returns, for example.

Customer hierarchy access

SAP also supports the access to data of customer hierarchies. For this purpose, you are provided with a special derivation type for characteristic values.

Customer enhancement

If these standard means for filling characteristics are not sufficient, you can use a user exit. For this purpose, the SAP system provides enhancement COPA0001. Using a user exit should always be the last resort because it is often possible to reach your objective in the standard if you use the derivation steps skillfully. In real life, however, users often revert to user exits to derive most of the characteristics. After a few years, however, users cannot recall how these user exits actually work.

With the definition and derivation of characteristics, you have now determined the criteria according to which CO-PA should evaluate the values and quantities. In the next step, you must map the values and quantities and transfer them to the CO-PA component.

Creating value fields

In CO-PA, values and quantities are updated in the *value* or *quantity fields* respectively. Like characteristics, value fields should also be created with a neutral abbreviation. To decide on the value fields you require, you must consider how your result calculations should be defined, that is, which lines you want to display. You create value fields using Transaction KEA6. You then need to fill the fields, which is described next.

Filling of value fields

The filling of value fields depends on the source of values (see Figure 3.14).

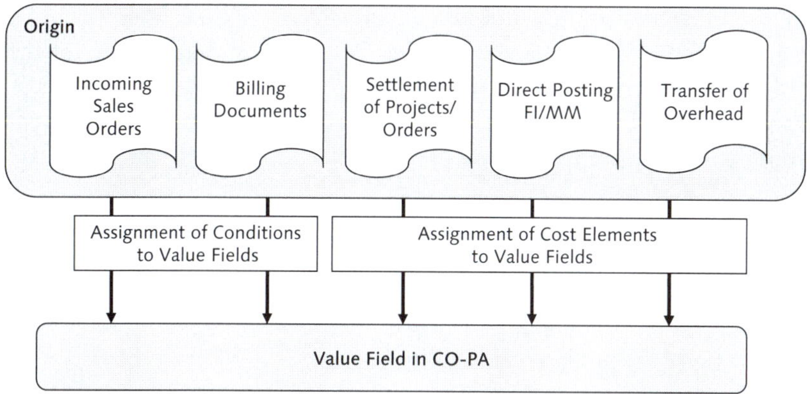

Figure 3.14 Filling Value Fields in CO-PA

Assigning conditions to value fields

As you can see, two basic options exist to fill value fields. On the one hand, you can assign the conditions of the SD price determination to the value fields of CO-PA. This option is available, for example, during the transfer of sales orders and billing documents.

PA transfer structure

On the other hand, you can assign cost elements or cost element groups to the value fields. You can use this option for the settlement of cost objects, that is, projects or orders. The assignment of cost elements to value fields is carried out using *PA transfer structures*.

In a PA transfer structure, you can define where the costs or revenues come from and where they are sent to; that is, to which value field. Because you want to fill value fields for the settlement of production orders to CO-PA that are different from the value fields for the recording of revenues from Financial Accounting using the account assignment to a profitability segment, you can use multiple PA transfer structures in parallel. These are always created specifically for the operating concern.

Figure 3.15 shows an example of a PA transfer structure that can be used for the settlement of internal orders to CO-PA.

PA transfer str: 10 — PA settlement, marketing actys
CO Area: M001 — Kokrs LVWM Mannheim

Assgnmnt	Text	Qty billed/deliver	Source assigned	Value field assigned
10	Total Costs	☐	☑	☑
20	Revenues	☐	☐	☐

Figure 3.15 Definition With PA Transfer Structure 10

Defining the source

You can find lines of the *contribution margin accounting* as lines of the PA transfer structure. Because you use the PA transfer structure only for the settlement of marketing costs, a subdivision by costs and revenues is sufficient. For each line, you now define which cost elements or cost element groups you want to transfer. The cost elements or cost element groups are the *source*.

Figure 3.16 shows the values for line 10 of PA transfer structure 10.

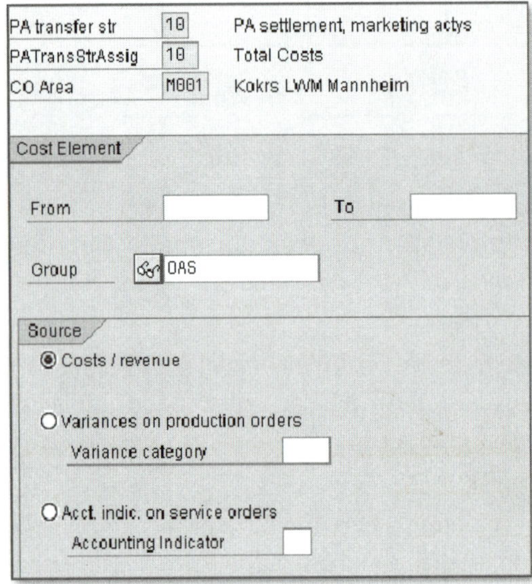

Figure 3.16 Example of the Source for the Transfer to CO-PA

Cost elements/ cost element groups

In the example shown, an entry in the GROUP field was selected. Entry 0AS is a cost element group in Controlling that was created via Transaction KAH1. A source must be maintained for each line of the PA transfer structure. It is important to note that not all cost elements of overhead cost controlling must be considered here. Nevertheless, only a single line may be assigned to the cost element within a PA transfer structure. The reason is obvious: If you assigned two lines of the PA transfer structure to one cost element, the costs would be double in the profitability analysis. Consequently, the result could be incorrect.

Figure 3.16 indicates that you can also select other sources in addition to costs and revenues:

- Variances on production orders
- Accounting indicators on service orders

Variance categories

You can also use variance categories for the settlement of production costs. This requires using Product Cost Accounting. When it is activated, you can pass the cost variances in production (e.g., due to price variances for the procurement of raw materials) to CO-PA. *Variance categories* are used to identify variances. You can use variance categories as the source for filling the value fields.

Accounting indicator

If you use customer service service orders, you can also enter the *accounting indicator* as the source. Accounting indicators enable you to differentiate between costs and revenues, between grace and warranty services, and, of course, sales.

You therefore have three options to select the values you want to enter in a value field. Furthermore, you also need to assign the value field. An example is shown in Figure 3.17.

PA transfer str.	10	PA settlement, marketing actys
PA TransStructAssig.	10	Total Costs
Operating concern	LWAG	Lederwaren-Manufaktur EUROPE

Quantity/value	F	Value fld	Name
Value field	3	VV380	General Market.costs

Figure 3.17 Assignment of the Value Field in CO-PA

Assignment of value fields

You can assign more than one value field to each line of the PA transfer structure. This is because of the second column shown in Figure 3.17: the indicator, fixed/variable (column F). You can use it to control whether you want to view only the fixed or variable costs from the amounts incurred or the total costs. Therefore, you could assign two value fields here: The first field would show the fixed costs from production and the second the variable costs.

In principle, the filling of CO-PA fields is not very complex. However, because you define completely independently which values are incorporated in CO-PA, you must ensure that you do not transfer too many or too few values. If you make a mistake, this results in incorrect reporting.

3.6 Summary

From a cost accounting perspective, CO-PA is the most important reporting tool. All values are gathered here, and there are many options for evaluations. Because the data is collected from different areas such as the sales order or billing data from SD, production costs and variances from PP, and values of overhead cost controlling from Controlling, it is important that you define what should be shown in reporting before you set up value flows.

This reporting-oriented approach is also important when you define organizational structures. The structures are determined by logistics requirements in the MM, PP, and SD components. In financial accounting, the structures are mainly defined by legal requirements. In cost accounting, however, the organization can be based on internal aspects. Here, you must consider, for example, to what extent you want to map the activity allocations between the companies. However, you should always consider integration an important but not the only influencing factor. From the reporting perspective, a controlling area that is as comprehensive as possible is desirable but it also requires coordinated activities in the closing process, which is not always possible or desirable.

Increasing international requirements also play an essential role. The result is not changed but extended reporting tasks, which an SAP system could perform only provisionally until the SAP General Ledger was implemented. The SAP General Ledger is now a very powerful tool of the SAP system but it is still "just" a G/L. Even if the SAP system could map a rudimentary cost center accounting in the SAP General Ledger, it would still be common for enterprises to use financial accounting and controlling—that is, the Financial Accounting and Controlling component—in parallel. Thus, we are back to the fundamental decision of which accounts should be transferred to Controlling—that is, which profit and loss accounts are created as cost elements. There is no universal answer, except for the dissatisfying answer that this is purely a matter of taste.

The discussion of master data has not yet concluded because the material master in particular assumes a central role in the entire SAP system. Here—as in many other areas—close cooperation of experts for Logistics components as well as for Financial Accounting and Controlling is necessary. Because the integration of a system can only be achieved if the project team already works on a cross-component basis—that is, on an integrated basis.

Three critical processes run in an enterprise. This chapter analyzes the first important process, the purchasing process. You should not underestimate its significance, because the products you generate can only be as good as the materials you purchase.

4 Procurement Process

The focus of business value added is usually on production, which requires various input factors such as material and labor. From the logistics perspective, the procurement process should provide the correct input factors in the correct quality and quantity at the correct location at the correct time. Although the tasks of procurement can be summarized in a plain and simple sentence, it comprises numerous aspects. This chapter discusses the different aspects of the procurement process as well as the related effects on the enterprise's value flows.

First, it describes how the procurement process is integrated with the operational performance. In this context, the extended SCOR model plays a significant role. Afterward, you learn how to statistically update and trace commitments in cost accounting during the procurement process to allow for early budget controlling. Additionally, this chapter focuses on account determination from Materials Management (MM account determination) because this considerably affects the interface between logistics and accounting. The descriptions on the goods receipt and invoice receipt then lay the foundation for discussing "genuine" value flows.

The explanations on mapping and further processing the resulting payables in accounting conclude the integration with logistics. Usually, the payables are what are called *payables for goods and services* (PGS). An outlook on the closing process rounds off this chapter.

We will now take a look at the steps and different design options in the procurement process. For this purpose, the adapted SCOR model from Chapter 2, Section 2.2.2 is used again as an example.

4.1 Procurement Process in the SCOR Model

SCOR model

Within the SCOR model the "purchasing" part (source) that comprises the ordering process and warehouse management is also the part that includes the procurement process. Depending on the production approach, the SCOR model differentiates between three basic procurement process types (see Figure 4.1).

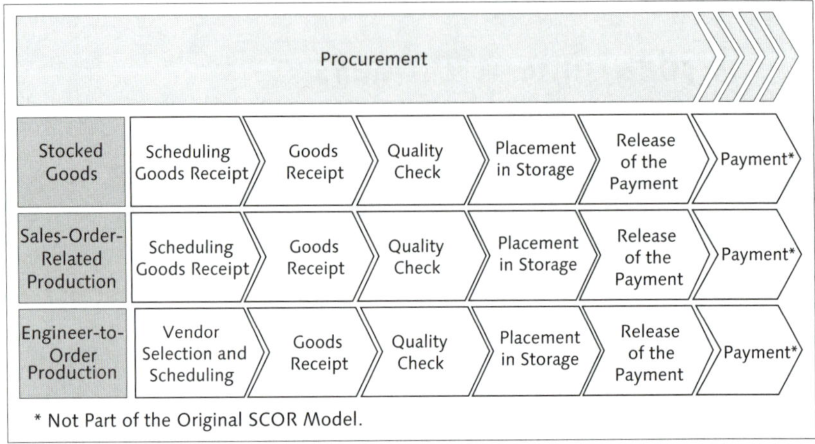

Figure 4.1 Procurement Process in the Adapted SCOR Model

As you can see, we added the payment process to the standard model (see Figure 2.5 in Chapter 2, Section 2.2.2, SCOR Model). Regarding logistics, it would be sufficient to consider the process complete after the payment for the invoice has been released. However, because this book focuses on the value flow, it is supposed to guide you through the complete flow, that is, up to paying the vendor invoice.

Process types in the SCOR model

In addition to this aspect, Figure 4.1 shows that the SCOR model differentiates between three procurement process types, which depend on the organization of the production:

- Procurement for make-to-stock production
- Procurement for sales-order-related production
- Procurement for projected sales-order-related production

Vendor selection

It is apparent that the three process types only differ in the first module. For make-to-stock production and sales-order-related production, the purchasing department is responsible for scheduling the goods receipt in the continuous process. For project production, this also includes the task of selecting the vendor, which also needs to be done for the first two process types. The difference is that selecting the vendor is only necessary for make-to-stock and sales-order-related production if new or modified products are used. For continuous replenishment orders, the purchasing department usually collaborates with known vendors with whom outline agreements may have been worked out.

For us, it is not relevant if and to which extent the purchasing department has to select the corresponding vendors for individual ordering processes because this does not generate value flows. It is also not important what kind of event has triggered the purchase requisition: reaching a minimum amount of raw materials in stock, a sales order, or the completion of project planning. From the perspective of accounting and cost accounting, this is not a transaction you can express in values.

However, the process type affects the procedure in cost accounting. This involves the question of which objects are used to assign the accounts for purchase orders, goods receipt, and invoice receipt. For more information, refer to Section 4.3.2, Purchase Order.

Reducing budgets for purchase orders

You already know that vendor selection is not relevant for the value flow. You can take adequate measures in cost accounting only if a purchase requisition or a purchase order is being created. You can now account the open purchase requisitions to possible existing budgets to be able to identify overruns at an early stage.

Goods receipt

In most cases, the *goods receipt* is the first event you have to include in the financial statement. Here, you must post a receipt in stock or, for goods that are not subject to inventory management, an expense. From the logistics view, the goods receipt consists of several substeps. After you have received the goods, you have to check the quality of the procured goods or repack them until they can be stored. From the accounting and cost accounting view, only the process of entering the stock in the system is relevant because it results in Financial Accounting and Controlling postings.

Invoice receipt

In an SAP system, you usually do not post the goods receipt to payables but to the goods receipt/invoice receipt account (GR/IR account). Received invoices are also posted to this account. This means that it serves as a buffer between the two processes (goods receipt and invoice receipt) and consequently enables you to separate the flow of goods from the value flow. This also provides additional benefits, which are discussed in detail in Section 4.8, GR/IR Account. It is not until the vendor invoice is received and posted that the open item is created in accounts payable accounting. Depending on the specific case, you must additionally post currency differences or other deviations.

Outgoing payments The open item is usually cleared within a payment run. From the accounting perspective, this is the last operation of the value flow in the procurement process.

Creation of values The different stages of the procurement process may lead to values in Financial Accounting and Controlling. Figure 4.2 provides an overview of the possible documents.

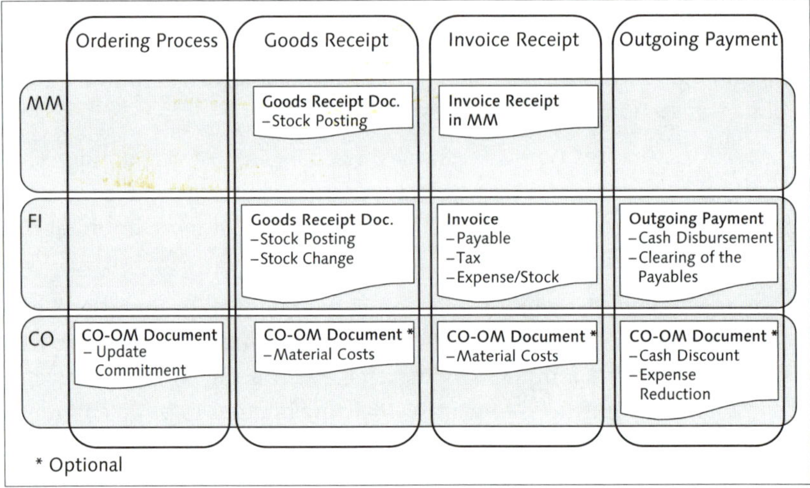

Figure 4.2 Value Flow of the Procurement Process

The updates of commitments within the ordering process takes on a special role in Figure 4.2. Here, in contrast to all other processes, only statistic values and no actual values are updated.

Before discussing the details of the procurement process, we will take a look at the involved master data. First, there is the material master. Because it is not only critical in procurement but also in production and sales and distribution, it was already described in Chapter 3, Section 3.4.3, Material Master. The use of the vendor master, which is detailed in the following section, is usually restricted to the procurement process. It is indispensable for both logistics and accounting.

4.2 Vendor Master as an Integrative Element

To meet the different requirements of the purchasing department and accounts payable accounting, the SAP system splits up the vendor master into three parts:

- General part
- Accounting view
- Purchasing data

General part

For every vendor for which the system should map business relationships, at least the general part must be created. This part stores all information that is relevant and clear for both the purchasing department and accounting. Here, you can find the vendor number, the name and address of the vendor, the corresponding tax information as well as all bank details. The benefit is that you have to maintain the bank details only once, even if the vendor exists in several company codes.

Accounting view

In the accounting view, you maintain all data based on the company code. The example of the reconciliation account clearly illustrates the benefit of this procedure.

"Reconciliation account" example

The reconciliation account is the link between accounts payable accounting and general ledger accounting. In general ledger accounting, it maps the payables. As soon as a posting is made for a vendor, the posting is also implemented on the reconciliation account in general ledger accounting (see Figure 4.3).

In the example, an invoice of EUR 1,190.00 shipment costs (gross) from vendor 90100 is received. To generate a posting to the vendor account, a reconciliation account must to be defined in the vendor master to ensure integration with the general ledger. In this case, account 160000 is specified in the vendor master. If you now specify the vendor number when entering the incoming invoice, the system generates a posting item of EUR 1,190.00 on the vendor account and on reconciliation account 160000. For an offsetting account assignment to the input tax account and freight account, the document in the general ledger balances to zero. In accounts payable accounting, only the open item for vendor 90100 in the amount of EUR 1,190.00 is shown.

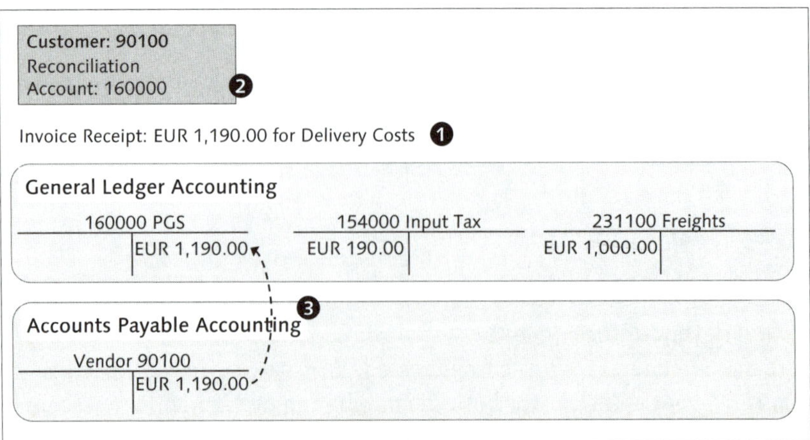

Figure 4.3 Posting Techniques for Reconciliation Accounts

Mapping of payables

A typical structuring for the mapping of payables in general ledger accounting is the following:

- Payables for goods and services, third-parties, domestic
- Payables for goods and services, third-parties, foreign
- Payables for goods and services, affiliated enterprises, domestic
- Payables for goods and services, affiliated enterprises, foreign

[Ex]

Mapping Payables in the Reconciliation Account of Lederwaren-Manufaktur Mannheim

Let us take our sample enterprise Lederwaren-Manufaktur Mannheim as an example and assume that all required ostrich leather is procured exclusively from one wholesaler in Frankfurt, Germany. The purchasing department has a decentralized organization; that is, each of the producing plants (Mannheim, Milan, and Brussels) has created the German wholesaler as a vendor.

For the German plants, the vendor is a domestic vendor; for all other plants, it is a foreign vendor. Whereas the German plant defines account 160000 (domestic vendor payables) in the vendor master, account 161000 (foreign vendor payables) must be specified for Belgium, France, and Italy.

Because you maintain the reconciliation account separately for each company code, this differentiation can be made without any problem. Additional accounting view data includes the terms of payment and the payment method. The accounting *terms of payment* are only relevant if the vendor invoice is directly entered in accounting and not via the MM component.

Payment methods

In the SAP world, *payment methods* are the different methods you can use to pay—for example, check or bank transfer—and you can assign more than one payment method to a vendor. This is useful, for example, if you want to pay large invoices via check and all invoices up to EUR 10,000.00 via bank transfer.

[+]

Check Function for Duplicated Invoices or Credit Memos

The accounting view of the vendor master also contains an indicator you can use to have the system check for invoices or credit memos that have been entered twice. If the indicator is set, the SAP system checks whether the document already exists when you enter an invoice or credit memo. It assumes that the document has been entered twice if fields such as the external document number, vendor, and amount correspond to the fields of an already existing document.

If this is the case, the system outputs a message to inform the user of the risk of a duplicate entry. You can customize this message using Transaction OBA5, for example. However, it should be an informational message and not an error message and should only inform the user of the risk of a duplicate entry and not prohibit entering the invoice.

If you want to use this system support, you have to define the CHECK FOR DUPLICATE INVOICE indicator as a mandatory field in the Customizing of the vendor master.

Purchasing data

The *purchasing data* of the vendor stores all information that you require for a smooth purchasing process but that does not affect the accounting processes. Here, you maintain the purchase order currency and the term of payment, for example, that are should be used for purchase orders for this vendor by default.

Required views

For vendors that are only required in accounting but for which no purchase order is entered in the system, you only have to create the *general* and the *accounting view*. Examples include employees to which travel expenses were paid via bank transfer. You also do not have to provide an accounting view for vendors that are required for the purchasing process but not for accounting. This includes, for example, potential vendors from which you request a quotation but for which no purchase order is generated. Of course, the purchasing department does not obtain a quotation for its own sake. Usually, a requirement is determined within the enterprise, for example, in production, in materials planning, or in stock. When the purchasing department receives the requirement, the ordering process starts.

4.3 Purchase Order as the Basis of the Procurement Process

In the context of the ordering process, this section focuses on two documents: purchase requisition and purchase order.

4.3.1 Purchase Requisition

You can transfer the requirements either manually without system support or, particularly if the SAP system works with MRP procedures, automatically. In the SAP world, the document that triggers the purchase order later on is called *purchase requisition*. Depending on the method of how the purchasing department is informed about a requirement, a purchase requisition can be entered directly; that is, manually, or indirectly; that is, via another SAP component.

A purchase requisition already contains all of the necessary information for the purchasing department. First, it defines a requisitioner. For every item, it also specifies the purchase order quantity and, preferably, the material number. Alternatively, a material group can be maintained.

[+]

Material Group

A *material group* is a grouping of materials for which no material may exist. You can derive the account assignment from the material group; that is, it supports automated processing.

A purchase requisition is an internal document. It is a request to the purchasing department to procure a material or service. After its release, you can fulfill a purchase requisition with a purchase order or an outline agreement.

Determining the source of supply

You may have to determine a *source of supply* before creating a purchase order. Here, the SAP system also supports the purchaser: You can create requests and enter the quotation afterward as well as access existing purchase orders and conditions in the system. By comparing the different quotations in the SAP system, you can determine the best vendor and then create the purchase order.

4.3.2 Purchase Order

Header data of the purchase order

Like many other documents in the SAP system, a purchase order consists of a header that is supplemented with individual items. Except for the stock transfer order, all purchase orders are sent to a vendor. The respective vendor number is entered in the purchase order header. As a result, the system proposes various values from the vendor master, as follows:

- Ordering address, invoice address, and delivery address
- Terms of payment
- Incoterms (terms of freight)

Purchase order item—item category

More interesting than the header information are the purchase order items. Their behavior—as well as the required information for each item—is controlled by what is called an *item category*. The type and attributes of the item category determine critical definitions (see Figure 4.4).

SPRO > MM > Purchasing > Define External Representation of Item Categories

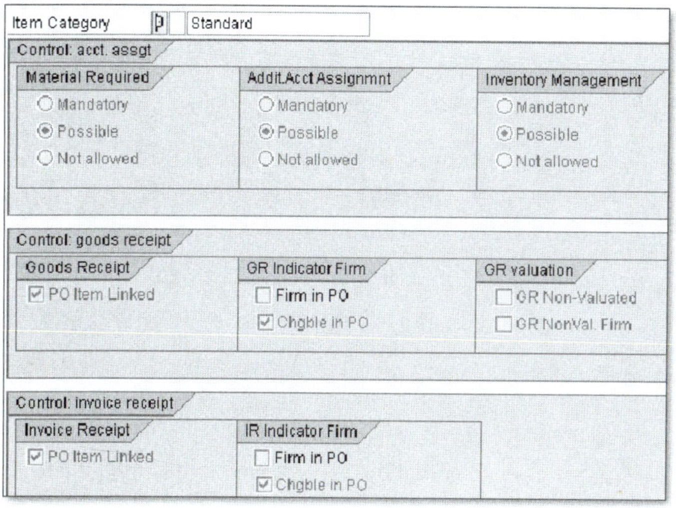

Figure 4.4 Item Category Definitions

Account assignment

First of all, you have to define whether the corresponding purchase order item allows for, enforces, or prohibits specifying a material number or additional account assignments (see MATERIAL REQUIRED field group in Figure 4.4). For materials, you can additionally select whether inventory management is possible (INVENTORY MANAGEMENT field group). This defines whether the material is stock material for which you may want to know at a later stage whether and how much material is in stock.

Goods receipt

Here, you can also specify critical definitions for the goods receipt. You can define whether goods receipt is expected and whether this setting can be changed in the purchase order maintenance. You can also determine whether the goods receipt is non-valuated and also whether this setting can be changed (CONTROL: GOODS RECEIPT field group). For example, for vendor consignments, if the goods receipt is non-valuated, the invoiced value of goods is directly indicated as an expense (and not as stock) in the financial statement.

Invoice receipt

The item category also states whether an invoice is expected and whether this invoice is binding. You can also determine whether this setting can be changed in the purchase order (CONTROL:INVOICE RECEIPT field group).

You cannot configure item categories; that is, you cannot create new or modify existing categories. The only option you have is to assign an external item category (a category that is visible to the user) to the internal item category of the SAP system. Table 4.1 contains a list of the most important item categories.

Item Category		Description	Usage
Int.	Ext.		
0		Standard purchase order	▸ Externally procured goods ▸ GR and IR possible
1	B	Limit purchase order	▸ Definition of a max. value ▸ Neither quantity nor delivery data is defined ▸ IR is mandatory
2	K	Consignment order	▸ Material required ▸ Procurement based on consignment ▸ GR is mandatory
3	L	Subcontracting	▸ Ordering finished products at vendors ▸ Non-valuated GR is mandatory
4	S	Third-party	▸ Purchase order triggered by enterprise, delivery to customer ▸ No GR, but IR mandatory
7	U	Stock transfer	▸ Initiating a stock transfer from plant to plant

Table 4.1 Item Categories with Descriptions

Purchase order item—purchasing info record

A purchaser must also specify the agreed price of the purchase order item. This process can be automated using *purchasing info records*. These records link vendors and materials, and its critical elements are the purchase order and price conditions. A purchasing info record always refers to only one vendor and one material. This enables you to maintain different purchase prices for a material for each vendor. The purchasing info record is additionally characterized by its high level of integration within the SAP system. You can also use it for product cost controlling, for example.

Material group

Because material numbers are not always available, the *material group* is very useful and serves various purposes in materials management. In the basic view, a material group is assigned to a material master; the material group serves to combine materials with similar properties. In reporting, you can then carry out evaluations according to these material groups.

For the integrated value flow, however, the fact that you do not have to enter a material master in the purchase order if you specify a material group in the purchase order item is much more interesting. This option is useful for low-value consumption goods (such as coffee for the employee break room) for which no material master exists.

When the purchaser creates a purchase order without material, he must generally decide to which expense account the purchase order item should be assigned. Using material groups is the solution because they can be linked to MM account determination, which allows for automated assignment of G/L accounts. This means that the purchaser does not have to determine the account manually, a process that often leads to posting errors.

Risk of Incorrect Account Assignments with Manual Input [!]

If the system does not automatically determine the G/L account, the risk of an incorrect account assignment increases considerably! The reason is that you cannot reduce the G/L accounts the system lists for selection.

Purchase order with account assignment

Purchase orders with a material master record in the purchase order items that are not delivered to stock but directly provided for consumption are referred to as *purchase orders with account assignment*. Here, an account assignment category that requires the specification of a respective account assignment for the item is assigned to a purchase order item.

Account assignment categories

The following are the most important *account assignment categories* in a purchase order:

- Internal order
- Cost center

- Project
- Asset
- Production order
- Sales order
- Customer individual stock

The account assignment categories for *internal orders, cost centers, projects, production orders, sales orders*, and *sales order stock* are not unique; they require the specification of the respective account assignment object. This object must exist and be valid when the purchase order is entered. Here, the common rules for the use of Controlling account assignments apply. This means that you can define only one genuine account assignment object.

Asset account assignment category

To assign an account to an *asset*, you need a main asset number and an asset subnumber. This is the problem with this category: The asset number must be available even before the asset is available. There are two solutions to this problem:

- Access via a dummy asset
- The purchaser/creator of the purchase requisition creates the asset

Access via "asset under construction"

When using the access via a dummy asset, you usually work with an *asset under construction* (AuC) with line item settlement to which all asset acquisitions are assigned. Using an AuC has the advantage that line items posted to this asset can be settled individually to a capitalized asset or to an expense account.

Access via capitalized assets

Alternatively, you can also directly use a *capitalized asset* for account assignment. For new acquisitions, this also means that the purchasing department is allowed to create capitalized assets. However, when creating a capitalized asset, you must make decisions regarding the mapping in the financial statement, for example, on the asset class and consequently on the account assignment and on depreciation parameters. If you decide to use this account assignment variant for assets, you should ensure that your employees are able to create the assets properly, for example, by providing training and the corresponding documentation.

You can also have the purchasing department request a new asset number from the asset accounting department in these cases. The asset accounting department would then have the corresponding competence to make a decision about the correct assignment of the asset, create a number, and forward the number to the purchasing department. However, this variant may require time-consuming internal communication, which can be a problem.

When using purchase requisitions, you should create the asset when creating the purchase requisition and not when issuing the purchase order. This way, you reach the highest level of integration. This also means that the creator of the purchase requisition must already possess the know-how to create the asset properly.

Prohibiting the item category

Because these two solutions for the account assignment of assets can lead to specific problems, you can consider prohibiting this account assignment category as a third solution.

Technically, you can easily implement this constraint by simply not providing this category. This is possible because Customizing defines for each order type which account assignment categories are allowed and which are not allowed. You can find this setting in the Implementation Guide under MATERIALS MANAGEMENT • PURCHASING • PURCHASE ORDER • DEFINE DOCUMENT TYPES. If you want to use this variant, post the invoice receipt to a clearing account. Then, the asset accounting department must make manual transfer postings for the values from the clearing account to an asset.

Further definitions in the account assignment category

In addition to the decision of which account assignments can or must be transferred, you can make further decisions under DEFINE DOCUMENT TYPES. Figure 4.5 shows an example.

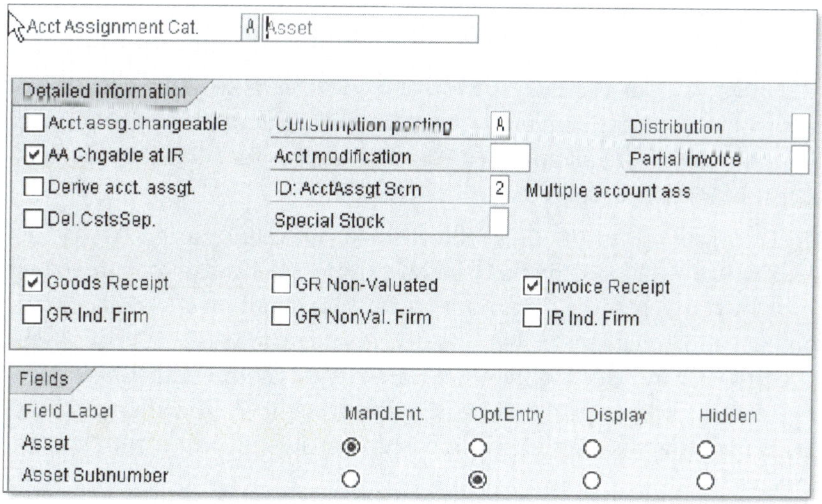

Acct Assignment Cat. A Asset

Detailed information

☐ Acct.assg.changeable	Consumption posting	A	Distribution
☑ AA Chgable at IR	Acct modification		Partial invoice
☐ Derive acct. assgt.	ID: AcctAssgt Scrn	2	Multiple account ass
☐ Del.CstsSep.	Special Stock		

☑ Goods Receipt	☐ GR Non-Valuated	☑ Invoice Receipt
☐ GR Ind. Firm	☐ GR NonVal. Firm	☐ IR Ind. Firm

Fields

Field Label	Mand.Ent.	Opt.Entry	Display	Hidden
Asset	◉	○	○	○
Asset Subnumber	○	◉	○	○

Figure 4.5 Account Assignment Category Definitions

Here, you can see the Customizing for the ASSET account assignment category to which you can also navigate via Transaction OME9 (CHANGE ACCOUNT ASSIGNMENT CATEGORY).

As for the item category, here, you also define whether and what type of goods and invoice receipt is required for the account assignment category. Sections 4.6, Goods Receipt, and Section 4.7, Invoice Verification, describe the corresponding effects of these definitions in more detail. Goods receipt and invoice receipt are the first events in the procurement process that affect Financial Accounting.

Budget monitoring

From the cost accounting perspective, however, it would be negligent to start monitoring the budget only when the invoice has been received. If you determine at this stage that a *budget* has been exceeded, it is too late to take action. Ideally, you therefore start monitoring the budget when you create the purchase requisition or, at the latest, when you create the purchase order. As you could already see in Figure 4.2, the Controlling document for the commitment update is the only document that is already generated when the purchase requisition and purchase order are created.

4.4 Updating Commitments

Commitment

The SAP system provides a *Commitments Management* function. A *commitment* is understood as a scheduled (purchase requisition) or contractual (purchase order) commitment that will result in costs. Costs can be incurred in the form of goods or invoice receipt. This means commitments are prebooked sales that you can check against approved budgets.

Activating Commitments Management

Although you can also integrate *commitment updates* with the general ledger, asset accounting, and funds management, Commitments Management in Controlling is frequently used. You activate this function at the controlling area level (see Figure 4.6).

You can navigate to the Controlling area maintenance using Transaction OKKP. The activation of the COMMITMENTS MANAGEMENT component enables you to manage commitments for cost centers and internal orders. You can also initiate that commitments are updated to sales orders in Transaction OKKP by selecting the W. COMMIT. MGT (With Commitment Management) checkbox in the SALES ORDERS section. These options indicate that commitments can only be updated for purchase orders with account assignment.

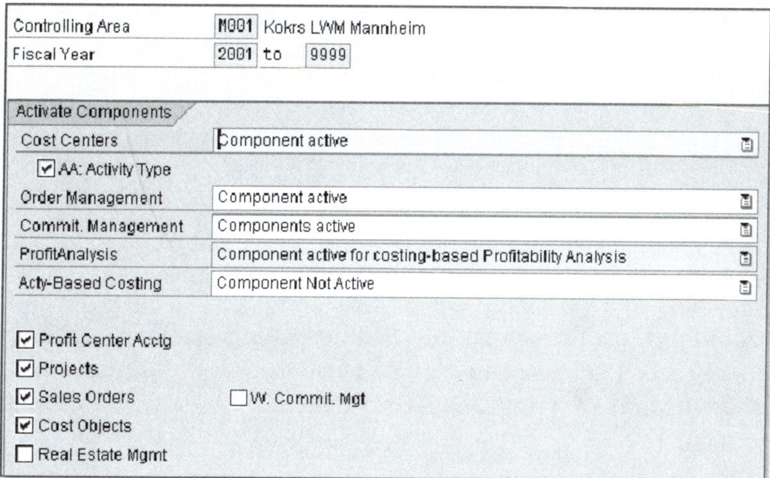

Figure 4.6 Commitments Management Activation

In addition, you have to configure commitment updates for order types and cost center categories.

Commitment update for order types

For internal orders, you can enable these updates by selecting the W. COMMIT. MGT checkbox in the individual order types. To do so, you can use Transaction KOT2_OPA. When the checkbox is selected, this definition immediately applies to all orders of this order type that exist in the system. This is also indicated in the master record of the order in the CONTROL DATA field group. Figure 4.7 displays an example.

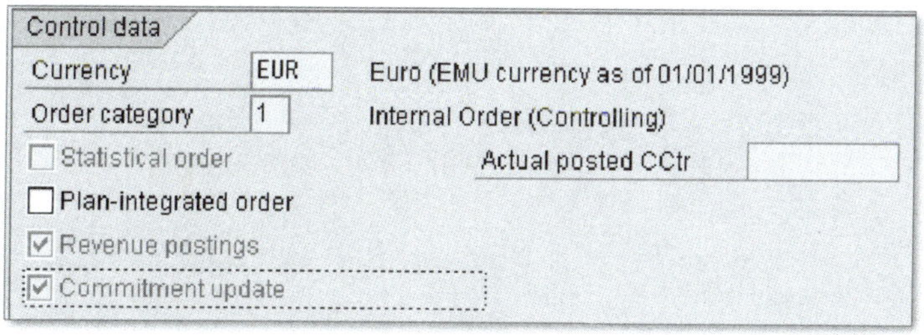

Control data
Currency EUR Euro (EMU currency as of 01/01/1999)
Order category 1 Internal Order (Controlling)
Statistical order
Actual posted CCtr
Plan-integrated order
Revenue postings
Commitment update

Figure 4.7 Order Master for Enabled Commitments Management

Commitment update for cost centers

The logic for cost centers is different. Here, the COMMITMENT block indicator is set for all cost center categories for which *no* commitment update is desired. Commitments are updated for all cost center categories for which this indicator is not set. Figure 4.8 displays the specifications for the two cost center categories 4 (ADMINISTRATION) and 5 (MANAGEMENT). For cost center category 4, commitments should be updated; for category 5, they should not be updated.

Cost center categories

CCtC	Name	Qty	ActPri	ActSec	ActRev	PlnPri	PlnSec	PlnRev	Cmmt	Func
4	Administration	☐	☐	☐	☑	☐	☐	☑	☐	OC-ADM
5	Management	☑	☐	☐	☑	☐	☐	☑	☑	OC-ADM

Figure 4.8 Blocking Commitment Updates for Cost Center Categories

You can implement the commitment update settings for the cost center categories in the Implementation Guide under CONTROLLING • COST CENTER ACCOUNTING • MASTER DATA • COST CENTERS • DEFINE COST CENTER CATEGORIES.

However, because these settings for the cost center categories are only default values for the creation of master data, you can also individually modify Commitments Management in the respective cost center master when creating a new cost center (see Figure 4.9).

[+]

No Effect on Existing Cost Centers

Keep in mind that changes to the Customizing of the cost center category do not affect existing cost centers. Therefore, the SAP system behavior for cost centers differs from the behavior for internal orders.

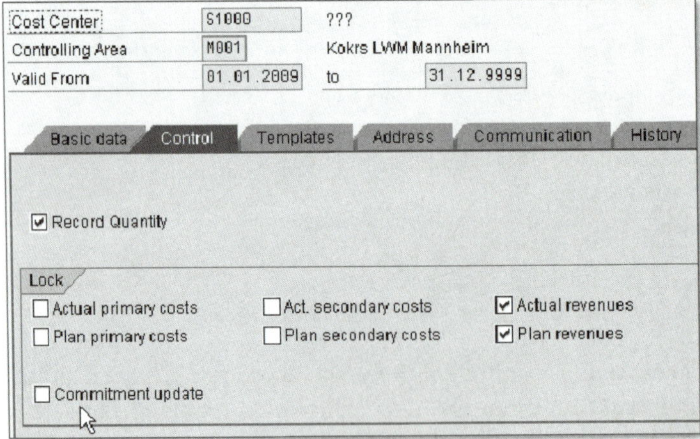

Figure 4.9 Changing the Commitment Update Settings in the Cost Center Master

Reducing commitments

You can reduce commitments in two alternative ways:

- Reduction based on values of the goods receipt
- Reduction based on values of the invoice receipt

Here, the system behavior depends on whether a valuated goods receipt exists. If the goods receipt is valuated, the corresponding goods receipt data is used. and prices are taken from the purchase order.

If there is no goods receipt or if it is non-valuated, the commitment is reduced upon invoice receipt.

[!]

Defining a G/L Account as the Cost Element

To generate commitments, the G/L account to which the purchase order is assigned must be defined as the cost type when the goods or invoices are received.

"Commitment calculation" example

Let's take a look at a budgeted order of Lederwaren-Manufaktur Mannheim and the ordering and budget reduction process. A budget of EUR 1,200,000.00 was assigned to marketing order 400237. A purchase requisition and—based on this—a purchase order with an amount of EUR 5,850.00 were created. Figure 4.10 illustrates the flow and the previous use of the budget.

Orders: Actual/Plan/Commitments   Date: 05.04.2009 23:40:49   Page: 2 / 4

Order/Group   400237   Re-Launch Kelly Bag 1
Reporting period   1 - 12 2009

Cost elements	Actual	Commitment	Assigned	Plan	Available
470000 Marketing Costs	1.170,00	4.680,00	5.850,00	1.200.000,00	1.194.150,00
* Costs	1.170,00	4.680,00	5.850,00	1.200.000,00	1.194.150,00
** Balance	1.170,00	4.680,00	5.850,00	1.200.000,00	1.194.150,00

Figure 4.10 Budget Evaluation for Marketing Order 400237

You can see that an expense of EUR 1,200,000.00 is planned from which EUR 1,194,150.00 are available. At the time the query was issued, the Actual column reads EUR 1,170.00. Where does this value come from? To answer this question, you have to take a look at the development of the purchase order.

Ordered	10	PC	❸	5.850,00	EUR
Delivered	2	PC	❶	1.170,00	EUR
Still to deliv.	8	PC	❹	4.680,00	EUR
Invoiced	3	PC	❷	1.755,00	EUR
Down paymts				0,00	EUR

Figure 4.11 Development of Purchase Order 4500018746

In Figure 4.11, you can see that two pieces were posted as goods receipt. According to the purchase order with EUR 585.00/piece, a total of EUR 1,170.00 ❶ was valuated.

However, three pieces at EUR 585.00 were invoiced; that is, the invoice was EUR 1,755.00 in total ❷. Therefore, in this case, the goods receipt values were used for the budget usage. Because the purchase order is EUR 5,850.00 ❸ in total, but goods of only EUR 1,170.00 were received, a commitment of EUR 4,680.00 ❹ still exists.

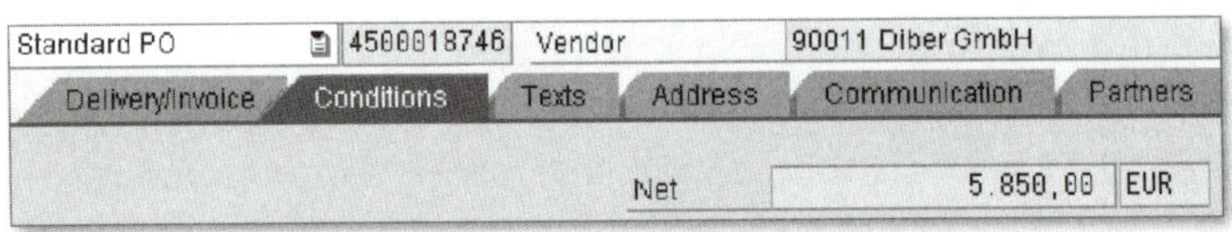

Figure 4.12 Total Value of Purchase Order 4500018746

The budget evaluation (see Figure 4.10) includes the total value in the ASSIGNED column. You can also determine it using the ACTUAL and COMMITMENT columns.

"Commitments Management" tool

This example illustrates that Commitments Management is a simple but powerful tool that enables you to implement cost accounting even before the costs actually incur. Generating the commitment with the purchase requisition allows for an early interaction from the cost accounting side—for example, by blocking the purchase order or increasing the budget.

The topic of reducing a commitment goes beyond the scope of mere budgeting. Only an accounting-relevant document—that is, the valuated goods receipt or invoice receipt—allows for a reduction of the commitment. Section 4.5, Integration of MM and Financial Accounting/Controlling, describes how the system generates accounting documents.

Availability control

However, mapping the budget and commitment flow is only one side of the story. At least as important is the system behavior in the event of a budget overrun or what is called *availability control*. The bad news is that the standard SAP system can prohibit postings because of budget overruns for internal orders or projects only. It does not allow for triggering an error message for account assignments to a cost center.

Availability Control for Account Assignments to Cost Centers [+]

SAP Note 68366 (Active Availability Control for Cost Centers) provides a solution using a substitution.

You can influence the behavior for budget overruns for internal orders and projects using Customizing. You can find the settings for internal orders in the Implementation Guide under CONTROLLING • INTERNAL ORDERS • BUDGETING AND AVAILABILITY CONTROL. Here, you first create a budget profile and then assign it to the order types. Additionally, you determine whether availability control is implemented in the case of an account assignment to a budgeted internal order. You can also define tolerances here.

COAr	Prof.	Tr.Grp	Act.	Usage in %	Abs.variance	Crcy
M001	000001	++	1	80,00		EUR
M001	000001	++	2	90,00		EUR
M001	000001	++	3	100,00		EUR

Figure 4.13 Availability Control Tolerances

Figure 4.13 shows an example of a three-level check. This is controlled via the specification of the budget usage in percentages (USAGE IN %) and absolute amounts for the variance (ABSOLUTE VARIANCE) if necessary. The ACTION column enables you to control the system behavior. In our example, the following control is implemented:

- **Action 1**
  When you reach 80 percent of the budget, the system generates a *warning message* for the goods/invoice receipt.
- **Action 2**
  At 90 percent, the system generates another warning and additionally sends an email to the person responsible.
- **Action 3**
  In the event of a budget overrun, the system generates an error message. You can no longer post a document with account assignment to the budget (for example, via an internal order).

4.5 Integration of MM and Financial Accounting/Controlling

Document flow

Figure 4.2 illustrated which documents are generated during the procurement process. In this context, you learned that value flow-relevant procedures always result in multiple documents:

- Material document
- Financial Accounting document
- Controlling document (optional)

For the goods receipt, it is easy to understand why a document needs to be generated in MM. The MM document posts the receipt and the accounting documents map the corresponding values. The purpose of the MM document for the logistics invoice verification is not clear at first glance. Keep in mind that the logistics invoice verification in SAP has more tasks than simply posting the payables and implementing the respective offsetting account assignment.

The invoice verification is characterized by a high integration with MM. The system can compare the invoice of the purchase order with the goods receipt and can consequently automatically answer the question of whether the existing invoice seems to be justified and correct. For this purpose, however, it requires detailed information from the purchase order and the goods receipt if necessary. Technically, this information is solely available in MM.

Content of the MM document

All stock-relevant processes are therefore first mapped by a material document in the inventory management (MM component). Here, the information flow is generated along the material flow, as you already know from Chapter 2, Section 2.1.1, Value Flow. The material document contains all of the pieces of information you need for proper inventory management and detailed evaluations of goods movement:

- Material number
- Storage data such as storage location or stock type
- Movement type

MM account determination

This information serves as the basis for the structure of the documents in Financial Accounting and Controlling that represent the value flow. The interface from MM to Financial Accounting/Controlling is characterized by a high degree of automation, which can be achieved thanks to what is called *MM account determination*. The MM account determination can be considered complex rules for the derivation of account assignments. It is restricted, however, to the determination of G/L accounts and does not affect Controlling account assignments such as cost centers or orders.

The prospect of newly implementing MM account determination makes most consultants moan. First, you have to configure account determination yourself; then, you have to explain the logic of account determination to the user departments, which are general ledger accounting and cost accounting in this case. The latter is usually quite time-consuming and might require strong nerves. If you look at the steps of MM account determination separately, however, you can see that it is not rocket science. It is complex, but has a logical structure. We will therefore begin with an overview and then go into details.

General structure

As the name implies, the goal of MM account determination is to determine a G/L account in Financial Accounting. As you can see in Figure 4.14, you can categorize the numerous relationships into three groups.

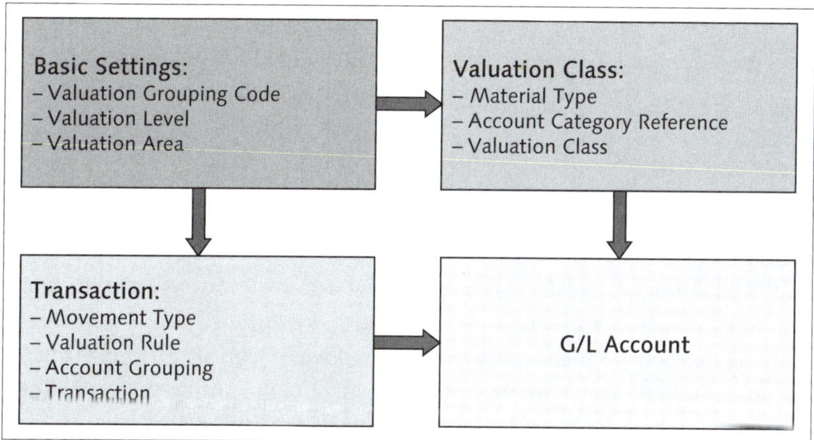

Figure 4.14 Overview of the Settings for MM Account Determination

The basic settings define the valuation class and the transaction, which in turn define the G/L account. The following sections discuss the individual groups in detail.

4.5.1 Basic Settings

Valuation level

Let us start with the basic settings, which enable you to influence the MM account determination behavior as a whole. Here, the central question is at which level you want to influence the account determination and thus the mapping of goods movements in the financial statement. You can choose between plant and company code. The rather simple setting and selection, which are illustrated in Figure 4.15, have far reaching effects.

The *valuation level* defines whether the account determination is identical for all plants of a company code or whether you can set the account determination for each plant individually. After the going-live of the client using standard means, you can no longer change the decision you made. Because this setting applies centrally, you can also find it in the Implementation Guide under ENTERPRISE STRUCTURE • DEFINITION • LOGISTICS – GENERAL • DEFINE VALUATION LEVEL.

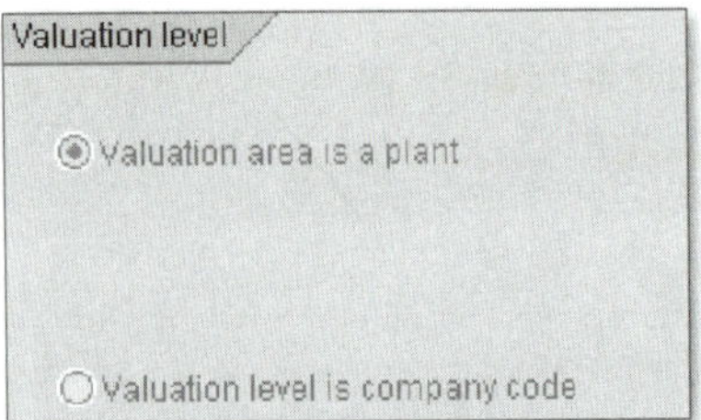

Figure 4.15 Defining the Valuation Level

[!]

Not Reversible and Client-Wide

The valuation level setting is irreversible and applies across all clients.

Plant level recommendation

You should always select the *plant level*, even if no deviating account determination is planned for individual plants at the time of the specification. You have to set the plant as the valuation level if you want to use the PP (Production Planning) component or Product Cost Planning in Controlling. This selection consequently allows for a multitude of options.

Updating the price

In addition to controlling the account determination, the valuation level has further effects. It defines if the accounting view in the material master is maintained per plant or per company code. This is also the level at which the valuated price of a material is updated. The term *accounting view* is therefore misleading.

Valuation area

Accordingly, you usually define the plant as the valuation level. Although multiple plants are defined in your company code, you may still want to specify an account determination at the company code level. One of the reasons for this could be that you want to maintain the account determination specifically for each country, which is a rather common procedure in international enterprises. To map this, the SAP system provides the valuation area classification criterion.

The *valuation area* corresponds to the individual attributes of the selected valuation level. At the "plant" valuation level, each plant corresponds to a valuation area. If you want to work with the "company code" valuation level, the system proposes the company code that exists in the client as the valuation area.

Valuation grouping code

To avoid that you have to assign different account determination to each valuation area, you need to group the valuation areas. For this, you must enable the use of the *valuation grouping code* (VGC). You can do this in the Implementation Guide under MATERIALS MANAGEMENT • VALUATION AND ACCOUNT ASSIGNMENT • ACCOUNT DETERMINATION • ACCOUNT DETERMINATION WITHOUT WIZARD • DEFINE VALUATION CONTROL.

[!]

Missing Connection to the Automatic Transport System

At this point, note that the activation of the VGC, along with the definition of the valuation area, is stored in the TCURM table. This table is not connected to the automatic transport system. Consequently, you enable the VGC directly in the target system. If the target or live SAP system is still initial, for example, in the event of a new system implementation, you can manually bundle the settings in a transport.

For this purpose, you need to include the following entries in the transport request:

- Program ID R3TR
- Object type TABU
- Object name TCURM
- Specify the client as the key.

This missing connection to the transport system is a security measure of the SAP system to avoid that this setting will be overwritten.

Grouping of the valuation areas

You can implement groupings via the MATERIALS MANAGEMENT • VALUATION AND ACCOUNT ASSIGNMENT • ACCOUNT DETERMINATION • ACCOUNT DETERMINATION WITHOUT WIZARD • GROUP TOGETHER VALUATION AREAS Customizing path. Figure 4.16 shows a corresponding example.

The first column, VALUATION AREA (see Figure 4.16) indicates the valuation areas. In this example, these are the plants that exist in the client because here, plants serve as the valuation area (see Figure 4.15). The next two columns, COMPANY CODE and COMPANY NAME, display the ID and the name of the company code to which the respective plant is assigned. SAP uses the company code to determine the operating chart of accounts that is valid for the account determination for goods movements. Accordingly, the account determination is specific to the charts of accounts.

Val. Area	CoCode	Company Name	ChrtAccts	Val.Grpg Code
M100	M100	LWM Belgium	M001	BE01
M200	M200	LWM France	M001	FR01
M300	M300	LWM Italia	M001	IT01
PL01	0006	IDES Warszawa	INT	PL01
PL02	0005	IDES AG Lublin	INT	PL01

Figure 4.16 Grouping of the Valuation Areas

Assigning the VGC

In the last column, VALUATION GROUPING CODE (see Figure 4.16), you can view the valuation grouping code. Here, the entries can be freely selected. You should use clear logic, for example, the country code at the first two places and then ascending numbers.

As our example illustrates, Lederwaren-Manufaktur Mannheim has created specific plants for logistics processing in Belgium, France, and Italy. Each plant of Lederwaren-Manufaktur Mannheim you can see in Figure 4.16 is located in another country. Because you work with country-specific VGCs, each plant has its own VGC: plant M100 in Belgium uses BE01, M200 in France uses FR01, M300 in Italy uses IT01. The two plants that are located in Poland, PL01 and PL02, of the 0006 and 0005 company codes both use the PL01 VGC and are thus treated identically in the MM account determination. The figure is therefore an example of how you should define the VGC: The numbering consists of a country code and a counter.

You will then implement all account determination settings at the VGC level only. The settings will apply to all assigned valuation areas.

VGC Assignment

You should only assign company codes with the same chart of accounts to a common VGC to avoid unnecessary complexity for the account determination.

At first, it does not seem to be useful to work with VGCs for, for example, SAP implementations with a single plant/company code. However, for future-oriented project approaches and if the enterprise might continue to grow, you should work with VGCs right from the start. This does not involve much additional effort but considerably facilitates expansion.

You are now familiar with the basic settings for MM account determination, which are summarized in Figure 4.17. This schematic illustration shows that the basic settings are complex only at first glance.

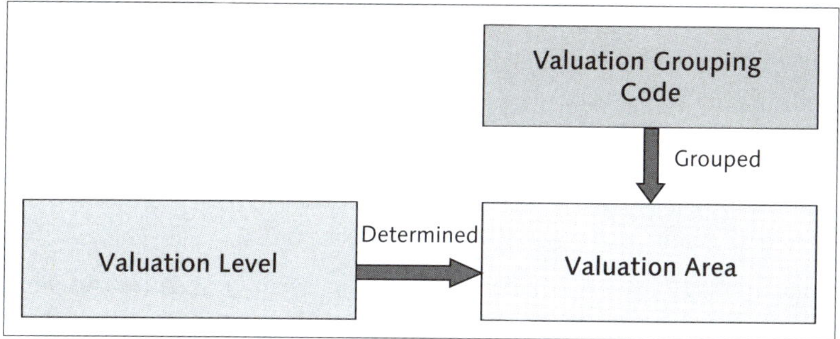

Figure 4.17 Schematic Illustration of Basic MM Account Determination Settings

Split valuation

For the sake of completeness, the option of split valuation should also be mentioned. This enables you to further divide the valuation areas for a material. A common criterion for the division of prices and account determination for a material and its stock is the batch. Batches of a material can have different prices and can be mapped in different ways in the financial statement. This is the case, for example, if the product quality at the end of a production process cannot be absolutely defined and the batches cannot be compared or exchanged. Because this is a topic that is critical in individual industries but not relevant to the majority of enterprises that use SAP, it is not further discussed here.

Instead, we will take a step forward in the MM account determination and turn to the categorization of materials. Because not all materials should be managed in one material stock account in the financial statement, a distinguishing criterion is required for the account determination. SAP provides the *valuation class* for this purpose.

4.5.2 Valuation Class Settings

Valuation class

From the MM account determination view, you can consider the valuation class a grouping of materials. It is defined in the accounting view of every material that is managed on a value basis. Materials with the same valuation class are subject to the same account determination. When designing the account determination, you can define a separate valuation class for each material stock account you want to map in the financial statement. Usually, the following materials are mapped separately:

- Raw materials
- Semi-finished products
- Finished products
- Trading goods
- Operating supplies

In addition, you may want to evaluate certain materials or goods—especially valuable raw materials or goods with high price fluctuations—separately.

Customizing enables you to define which valuation classes are provided for selection in the maintenance of a material. This way, you can reduce the risk of incorrect entries in the material master.

Account category reference

For this purpose, you can group the valuation classes into what are called account category references. For example, if you use multiple valuation classes to map raw materials, you can combine them in the "raw materials" account category reference. When you then create a new material master for a raw material, you can select from all of the valuation classes for raw materials. Every valuation class is assigned to exactly one account category reference; that is, it is an n:1 relationship.

Assignment to the material type

The account category references, in turn, are assigned to the *material types*. Every material type is assigned exactly one account category reference; that is, it is a 1:n relationship. If you use account category references, not all of the materials of one material type have to use the same account determination. Moreover, materials of different material types can be subject to the same account determination.

Figure 4.18 again illustrates the relationships between material type, account category reference, and evaluation class.

Valuation class Customizing

SAP combined the entire Customizing of the valuation class in one Customizing item. You can find it in the Implementation Guide under MATERIALS MANAGEMENT • VALUATION AND ACCOUNT ASSIGNMENT • ACCOUNT DETERMINATION • ACCOUNT DETERMINATION WITHOUT WIZARD • DEFINE VALUATION CLASSES. From there, you can navigate to the three necessary operations: the editing of ACCOUNT CATEGORY REFERENCE, VALUATION CLASS, and MATERIAL TYPE. Figure 4.19 shows the initial screen.

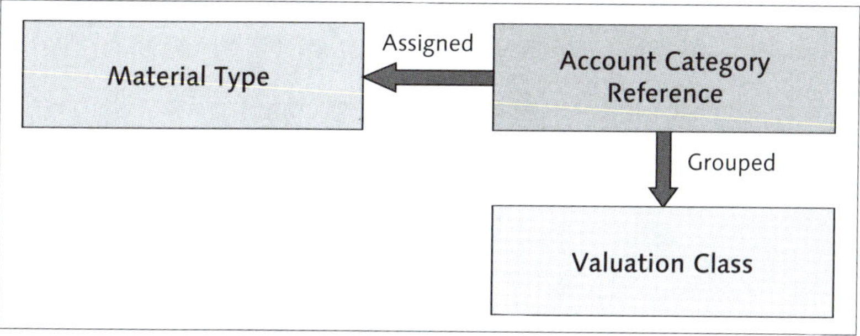

Figure 4.18 Schematic Illustration of the Valuation Class Determination

Account Category Reference/Valuation Classes

Process the objects in the specified sequence

Account category reference

Valuation Class

Material type/account category reference

Figure 4.19 Customizing of the Valuation Classes

Using the ACCOUNT CATEGORY REFERENCE/VALUATION CLASS view, first define the ACCOUNT CATEGORY REFERENCES, that is, the link between valuation classes and material type (see Figure 4.20).

Account Category Reference

ARef	Description
0001	Reference for raw materials
0002	Ref. for operating supplies
0003	Reference for spare parts
0004	Reference for packaging
0005	Reference for trading goods
0006	Reference for services
0007	Ref. for non-valuated material
0008	Ref. for semifinished products
0009	Ref. for finished products
0010	Ref. for NLAG
0600	Ref for empties fixed
0700	Ref for empties current

Figure 4.20 Definition of the Account Category References

Then, you can create the VALUATION CLASSES and immediately assign them to an account category reference. This is illustrated in Figure 4.21.

Valuation Classes			
ValCl	ARef	Description	Description
M100	0009	LWM - finsihed products	Ref. for finished products
M200	0008	LWM - semifinished pro.	Ref. for semifinished products
M300	0005	LWM - trading goods	Reference for trading goods
M400	0002	LWM - operating supplies	Ref. for operating supplies
M500	J001	LWM - model	
M600	0001	LWM - raw materials	Reference for raw materials
M610	0001	LWM - raw material GOLD	Reference for raw materials
M700	0004	LWM - packaging	Reference for packaging

Figure 4.21 Creating and Assigning Valuation Classes

In the third and last step, you assign the account category references to the MATERIAL TYPES (see Figure 4.22).

Account Category Reference/Material Type			
MTyp	Material type descr.	ARef	Description
MFER	Finished product	0009	Ref. for finished products
MHAL	Semi-finished product	0008	Ref. for semifinished products
MHAW	Trading goods	0005	Reference for trading goods
MHBS	Operating supplies	0002	Ref. for operating supplies
MMUS	Samples	0005	Reference for trading goods
MODE	Apparel (seasonal)	0009	Ref. for finished products

Figure 4.22 Assigning the Account Category Reference to the Material Type

Material type

For the inventory management of the materials in the SAP system, the material type assumes a major role. Chapter 3, Section 3.4.3, Material Master, already discussed some material master settings that are essential for the value flow. The material type was not mentioned there, because it does not directly affect the value flow. But as you know now, the material type is a critical MM account determination element.

Customizing of the material type

You can find the material type Customizing in the Implementation Guide under LOGISTICS – GENERAL • MATERIAL MASTER • BASIC SETTINGS • MATERIAL TYPES • DEFINE ATTRIBUTES OF MATERIAL TYPES.

Quantity update and value update

The material type also defines whether quantities and/or values are updated for the materials that are assigned to the material type. You can generally activate or deactivate quantity and value updates or even make this decision at the valuation area level. There are certainly reasons for controlling the quantity and value updates of the material types in the individual valuation areas in different ways. In real life, however, this is an exception.

Figure 4.23 displays the corresponding settings for the MFER material type (LWM – finished products), which you can find in the Implementation Guide under LOGISTICS – GENERAL • MATERIAL MASTER • BASIC SETTINGS • MATERIAL TYPES • DEFINE ATTRIBUTES OF MATERIAL TYPES.

Quantity/value updating

Quantity updating	Value updating
○ In all valuation areas	○ In all valuation areas
○ In no valuation area	○ In no valuation area
◉ By valuation area	◉ By valuation area

Figure 4.23 Quantity/Value Updates of the Material Type

As you can see in Figure 4.23, our material type does not clearly define whether quantities or values are updated. It depends on the settings in the individual valuation areas, which are shown in Figure 4.24.

This figure also indicates that a decision about the quantity and value update at the valuation area level actually means that the materials in the individual plants/company codes behave differently. Based on our example, this means that quantities and values are updated for MFER in all valuation areas, except for valuation area QMTR.

Quantity/value updating

Val.	Matl	Qty updating	Value Upda
M001	MFER	☑	☑
MT00	MFER	☑	☑
PL01	MFER	☑	☑
PL02	MFER	☑	☑
QM01	MFER	☑	☑
QM02	MFER	☑	☑
QMTR	MFER	☐	☐

Figure 4.24 Quantity/Value Updates for Every Valuation Area

New material types

MM account determination is only relevant for materials that are subject to value updates. However, you should trust in the SAP standard and only create new material types by copying a standard material type and changing it according to your requirements.

Usually, the MM component administrators/consultants design and implement the material types. Afterward, the material types should be assigned to the account category references by the persons who are responsible for the MM account determination.

Regarding the account category references, this section introduced the standard-related solution. In this context, the system only provides a part of the valuation classes (namely, the account category reference) when you create a material.

Alternative assignment

Alternatively, you can also assign all valuation classes to one account category reference. As a result, the material maintenance then provides all classes of the client for the valuation class selection. One of the benefits of this method is that you can decide for each material how it should be mapped in the financial statement. The disadvantage is that a wrong valuation class may be selected due to the large number of options. If the wrong valuation class is selected, all movements of this material will be mapped incorrectly in accounting and cost accounting.

You now know that the definition of valuation classes is no problem at all. All that remains is the last subject area: determining transactions and modifying accounts. Unfortunately, this subject area is also the area with the highest complexity within MM account determination.

4.5.3 Determining Transactions

Because the MM account determination reflects the goods movements in inventory management, the properties of each movement play an essential role in account determination: Is it merely an internal transaction or perhaps a delivery to a customer? Is the enterprise the owner or is it vendor stock?

Transactions and account groupings

The most apparent element that can provide important information is the *movement type*. Because the standard version already contains numerous movement types, it would be very time-consuming to directly link the movement types to G/L accounts. You also have to consider additional influencing factors such as the stock type (e.g., special stock) and quantity or value updates of the material. Consequently, SAP developed comprehensive rules according to which you can specify and classify goods movements for the account determination. In the end, the account determination is configured based on what are called *transactions* and *account groupings*.

Figure 4.25 illustrates how the SAP system determines these two objects. The following sections describe in detail how this determination is implemented.

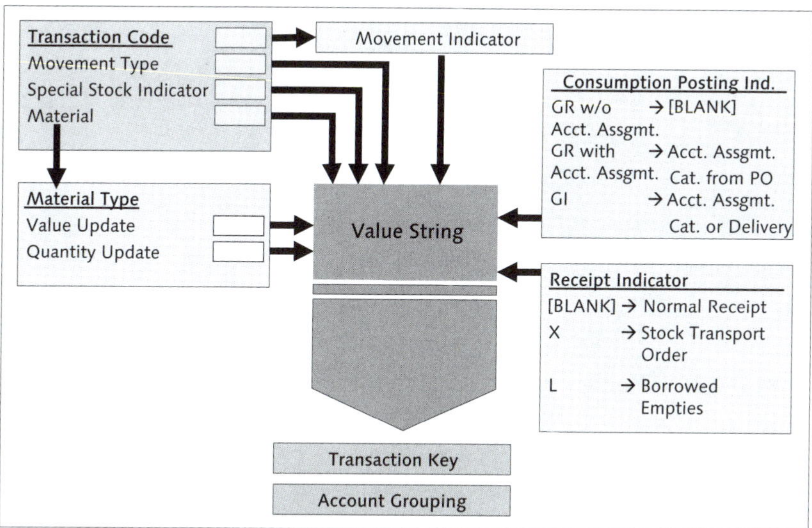

Figure 4.25 Determining the Transaction Key and Account Grouping

Movement indicator

To record goods movement in materials management, the SAP system provides a wide range of special transactions. Within the SAP system, these transactions are linked to what are called movement indicators. The following attributes are available for movement indicators:

- B goods movement for purchase order
- F goods movement for order
- L goods movement for delivery note
- O subsequent adjustment of stock of material provided/material provided

The link between transaction and movement indicator is established in table T158 (Inventory Management Transaction Control). Table 4.2 shows six transactions for posting goods movements.

The names of the transaction codes already imply whether the system can determine which transaction is posted. For Transactions MIGO and MIGO_GR, the SAP system assumes that a goods movement is recorded for a purchase order. MIGO_GO is a goods movement for an order. Transactions MIGO_GI and MIGO_TR do not indicate what kind of movement is posted. Consequently, no movement indicator is defined for these transactions. Although this indicator affects MM account determination, you will rarely come across it.

Transaction	Description	Value Assignment Indicator
MIGO	Goods Movement	B
MIGO_GI	Other Goods Movement	
MIGO_GO	Goods Movement for Order	F
MIGO_GR	Goods Movement for Purchase Order	B
MIGO_GS	Subsequent Adjustment of Material Provided	O
MIGO_TR	Other Transfer Posting	

Table 4.2 Link Between Transaction and Movement Indicator

Movement type

This is different for the movement type, which is another important account determination element. Its primary task is the presentation of the material flows in the enterprise.

Reduced to its key aspects, every goods movement leads to a goods receipt, a goods issue, or—for stock transfers—both. However, to control the numerous goods movements, this information is not detailed enough. Therefore, the movement type supports you because it is responsible for a more detailed specification of the movement.

To perform this task, you have to implement various definitions for each movement type. You define individually which transactions provide the movement type and which fields can or have to be populated. The movement type also specifies whether the incident leads to quantity and/or value updates. The system proposes movement types in many MM transactions. If the SAP system does not propose a movement type, you can also enter one manually.

Special stock indicator

When entering a goods movement, you also define whether the transaction affects *special stock*. If so, a special stock indicator is required. This indicator enables you to manage certain stock separately from normal stock for a material. Common examples include customer stock (goods are reserved for the customer) or consignment stock (goods are received by you, but are still the property of the vendor). The consignment stock topic in particular affects value updates to a large extent: As long as the goods are still the property of the vendor, you are not allowed to map the goods as values in the financial statement.

Consumption posting

Another indicator you usually cannot influence is the *consumption posting* indicator. The system sometimes sets this indicator automatically and sometimes has to determine it. For example, movements with purchase order reference are provided with a value of this indicator from the account assignment category of the purchase order item. The SAP system offers the following values for the consumption posting indicator:

- A asset
- V consumption
- E settlement through sales order
- U unknown
- P settlement for project

Receipt indicator

Finally, there is the *receipt indicator*, which is used for MM account determination. It specifies the type of the goods receipt or of the stock transfer but can only adopt one of the following three values:

- [BLANK] normal receipt
- X stock transport order
- L borrowed empties

Value string

From the combination of all of these indicators—movement indicator, movement type, special stock indicator, quantity and value update, consumption posting, and receipt indicator—the SAP system determines what is called a *value string*. You can consider this string a posting rule that defines how you have to transfer a material document to Financial Accounting/Controlling. This context can be best understood at the table level.

PstgStrRef	Val.Update	Qty update	S	Mvt	Rec	Cns	Value str.
101	X	X		B			WE01
101	X	X		B		A	WE06
101	X	X		B		V	WE06

Figure 4.26 Excerpt of Table T156SY
(Quantity/Value Update Movement Type: System Table; as of Rel. 4.6A)

Figure 4.26 shows an example of movement type 101 ("Goods receipt for purchase order in stock"). In all three rows, both the value and quantity are updated. They are not special stock movements, as you can see from the missing entries in the S column (special stock indicator). The B movement indicator in the MOVEMENT column indicates that this transaction is a goods movement for a purchase order. The fact that the receipt indicator (RECEIPT column) is missing means that it is a usual receipt. Up to this point, the three rows are identical.

The only difference occurs in the CONSUMPTION column (consumption posting). You can see that it is not relevant whether it is a consumption or a consumption for an asset because both cases refer to the WE06 value string. Only the fact that the first entry does not include a consumption posting leads to a deviating value string (WE01).

You can then use the value string to determine a transaction. Because some transactions require a more detailed subdivision of the account determination, the SAP system provides account grouping.

Transaction and account grouping

Account grouping enables you, for example, to further break down the "Offsetting entry for inventory posting" transaction (GBB transaction key). Various account groupings enable you, for example, to control goods issues for cost centers (movement type 201) and goods issues for sales orders (movement type 231) for different consumption accounts. In addition to the "Offsetting entry for inventory posting" transaction, you can also use account groupings for price differences (PRD) and consignment liabilities (KON). Transaction OMWN enables you to customize the account grouping.

Creating custom account groupings

You can also define your own account groupings. This is useful if your reporting requirements are specific. A common example can be that you are unsatisfied with the VBR (consumption) account grouping because you want to display withdrawals for orders separately from withdrawals for cost centers. In this context, MM uses two different movement types anyway: 201 for withdrawals for cost centers, and 261 for withdrawals for orders. This means that you have to create only two additional account groupings. Afterward, you must adapt the mapping of the 201 and 261 movement types to the new entries.

Transactions in the SAP standard

OBL1

The standard SAP system already provides numerous *transactions*. The documentation prepared by SAP has considerably improved over the last years but is still rather confusing. Therefore, the following sections detail the most critical default transactions:

- **Expenditure/income from consignment material consumption (AKO)**
  Transaction AKO is used when material is withdrawn from consignment stock. The withdrawal can be due to consumption or due to a transfer to your own stock.

- **Expenditure/income from transfer posting (AUM)**
  Transaction AUM is used for transfer postings of material to material. If the price of the issuing material is different from the price of the receiving material, this results in price differences. These price differences are posted with AUM.
- **Stock change (BSV)**
  Transaction BSV is only possible for materials that are produced externally using subcontracting. You use BSV for goods receipt or subsequent allocations to subcontract orders.

  This is one of the situations where the SAP system cannot derive useful Controlling account assignment. If you still want to define the assigned account as a cost element, you have to define standard account assignments, for example, using Transaction OKB9.

Defining Standard Account Assignments [+]

Postings always exist that you cannot provide with useful Controlling account assignments or that always have to be assigned to the same cost center/order. In these situations, you have two options to link a cost element to a fixed cost center or order:

- You can enter the Controlling account assignment in the cost element master record itself.
- You can use Transaction OKB9, which enables you to define a fixed cost center, order, business area, or profit center for a cost element.

The advantage of Transaction OKB9 is that it displays an overview of all standard account assignments. However, you should ensure that you select one of these two methods to be able to understand how a Controlling account assignment has been determined.

- **Stock posting (BSX)**
  Transaction BSX addresses the material stock accounts in the financial statement. It is always relevant when the material stock changes. Examples of this are goods receipts or issues in your own stock or an update of the moving average price when price differences occur in invoice verification.

  The specifications for reconciliation accounts also apply to material stock accounts: You should not post them manually. This is the only way to ensure that the MM inventory management corresponds to accounting regarding values.

- **Mapping of delivery costs**
  In orders, you can specify different kinds of delivery costs. To post these costs for the goods or invoice receipt, different transactions are available:
  - Freight clearing (FR1)
  - Provisions for freight charges (FR2)
  - Customs clearing (FR3)
  - Provisions for customs clearing (FR4)
- **Offsetting entry to the stock posting (GBB)**
  Transaction GBB is the most important and comprehensive transaction in the standard SAP system. Both from an accounting and controlling view, it is not sufficient to say that a posting item is the offsetting entry to the stock posting. Consequently, Transaction GBB in particular is further structured through the intensive use of account groupings.

  The standard version provides the account groupings shown in Table 4.3.

Account Grouping	Usage
AUA	Settlement of orders
AUF	Goods receipts for orders if no genuine Controlling account assignment is provided and for order settlement if the AUA account grouping is not maintained
BSA	Initial entries of stock balances
INV	Expenditure or income from inventory differences
VAX	Goods issues for sales orders without account assignment object (the account is not a cost element)
VAY	Goods issues for sales orders with account assignment object (the account = cost element)
VBO	Consumption from stock provided to vendor
VBR	Internal material withdrawals, for example, for internal order/cost center
VKA	Sales order account assignment
VKP	Project account assignment
VNG	Scrapping or destruction
VQP	Sample without account assignment

Table 4.3 Account Groupings for Transaction GBB

Account Grouping	Usage
VQY	Sample with account assignment
ZOB	Goods receipts without purchase order (movement type 501)
ZOF	Goods receipts without production order (movement types 521, 531)

Table 4.3 Account Groupings for Transaction GBB (Cont.)

- **Purchase order with account assignment (KBS)**
  Transaction KBS is an entry that is required for technical reasons only. In purchase orders with account assignment, the MM account assignment does not have to identify a G/L account because the account assignment is already defined in the purchase order. Transaction KBS therefore only serves to specify the posting keys for the goods receipt posting.
- **Exchange rate rounding differences for Materials Management (KDR)** P&L
  An exchange rate rounding difference can occur when an invoice in foreign currency is received. If a balance is created when the invoice is converted to the local currency, the system automatically generates a posting line for exchange rate rounding differences.
- **Small differences in Materials Management (DIF)** P&L
  Transaction DIF is used in invoice verification when you define a tolerance limit for small differences and the balance of the invoice does not exceed the tolerance.
- **Price differences (PRD)** P&L
  Price differences occur for materials with a standard price for all movements and invoices that are valuated at a price other than the standard price. You will face price differences in the following examples:
  - Goods receipts for purchase orders if the purchase order price differs from the standard price
  - Goods issues if an external amount is entered
  - Invoices when the invoice price differs from both the purchase order price and the standard price

  Price differences can also occur for invoices for materials with a moving average price when there is insufficient stock coverage for the quantity invoiced. For goods movements that would result in negative stock balances, the moving average price does not change; instead, possible price variances are posted to a price difference account.

Depending on the settings for the posting rules for Transaction PRD, you can work with or without account grouping. If you work with account grouping, the standard SAP system uses the groupings shown in Table 4.4.

Account Grouping	Usage
[BLANK]	Goods/invoice receipts for purchase orders
PRF	Goods receipts for production orders and order settlement
PRA	Goods issues and other movements
PRU	Price differences in the context of transfer postings

Table 4.4 Account Groupings for Transaction PRD

- **Delivery cost provisions (RUE)**
  Provisions for delivery costs are created when a condition type for provisions is entered in the purchase order.

  Unfortunately, the SAP system does not support provision clearing against actual costs; therefore, this has to be done manually.
- **Income/expenditure from revaluation (UMB)**
  Transaction UMB is used both in inventory management and in invoice verification when the standard price of a material has changed and a goods movement or an invoice is posted to the previous period (at the previous price). You can only post in previous periods if period closing for material masters is set accordingly. For more information on this topic, refer to Chapter Section 7.5.1, Period Closing for the Material Master.
- **Unplanned delivery costs (UPF)**
  In the ideal case, the purchasing department has already entered the conditions for the delivery costs in the purchase order. Unplanned delivery costs are costs that are included in the vendor invoice (such as freight or duty costs) but not specified in the purchase order. You can either distribute these costs across the invoice items or post them to a separate account. For the second variant, Transaction UPF must be maintained in account determination.
- **GR/IR clearing (WRX)**
  Postings to the GR/IR clearing account occur when goods and invoices are received for purchase orders. For more information on the GR/IR account, refer to Section 4.8, GR/IR Account.

Additional transactions are available, for example, regarding the material ledger. However, the transactions listed here are the transactions you will use most often.

To understand how MM account determination works is only one side of the coin. It is just as important to understand what to do to rebuild account determination.

4.5.4 Rebuild Process for Account Determination

If you want to rebuild account determination in a result-oriented way, you should perform the following steps:

1. Define the a company code or plant as the valuation level.
2. Create a valuation grouping code and link it to the valuation areas.
3. Define and assign valuation classes.
4. Define G/L accounts and check whether cost elements are created for the relevant transactions.
5. Correct reported errors for the goods movements.

Defining the valuation level

The first step, defining the valuation level, involves an easy decision: If you use PP or want to calculate products in Controlling, you must use the plant as the valuation level.

Defining the valuation class

The valuation classes are also usually not a problem. The critical question is: Which material stock accounts does the accounting department want to map in the financial statement? One valuation class is required for each material stock account. The resulting list of valuation classes should then also be discussed with the cost accounting department because it may want to be able to evaluate specific materials separately, for example, because high stock values are expected for these materials or because extreme price fluctuations are likely, which are supposed to be analyzed separately. Tracking becomes easier if you use separate accounts for the mapping of stock, expenditure, and income.

Defining G/L accounts for critical transactions

Afterward, you should define a G/L account for the most important transactions. Which transactions are critical depends on the business activities of your enterprise. In a first step, you could maintain the following transactions and account groupings, for example:

- Transaction BSX
- Transaction GBB
  With the AUA/AUF, VAX/VAY, and VBR account groupings

- Transaction DIF
- Transaction PRD
- Transaction WRX

[+]

Learning by Mistakes

When rebuilding the MM account determination, you can spend a lot of time with theoretical discussions about transactions, valuation classes, and accounts in advance. Alternatively, you can deploy the "learning by mistakes" method and directly start with the implementation.

This means: Configure the basic account determination that covers the material stock accounts, the critical offsetting account assignments, and the GR/IR accounts. All transactions of which you are not sure whether they are needed or how they should be mapped in accounting are not maintained.

You then have to wait for error messages in Logistics. With each message on a missing account determination, you can enhance the account determination. However, for this procedure, short response times in the event of error messages are essential. Otherwise, you cannot test the Logistics components.

Usually, this procedure is of interest for everyone involved, because it shows which transactions are posted in Logistics. Sometimes interesting technical discussions about how to handle materials and their mapping in the financial statement may arise in this context.

Tabular mapping of the MM account determination

Experience has shown that tables are best suited for the mapping of the *MM account determination*. Among other things, the horizontal axis shows the valuation classes. The vertical axis can list the movement types and transaction keys with possible account groupings. In the matrix data area, you can then define the corresponding G/L accounts, separated by debit and credit if required. If you need to map several parallel account determinations, you should create a table for every VGC. Table 4.5 shows an example.

Transaction	Movement Types	Transaction/ Account Grp.	VGC	Valuation Classes			
				Raw	Semi	Finish	Pack.
Goods receipt	101, 102, ...	BSX	0001	39000	39100	39200	39300
Inventory difference	701, 702	GBB INV	0001	35000	35000	35020	35010
Inventory difference	701, 702, ...	GBB INV	0002	35040	35020	35020	35010

Table 4.5 Structure of a Microsoft Excel Table for the MM Account Determination (Excerpt)

Finally, you have to clarify who is responsible for maintaining the MM account determination. As with all interface topics, you can only achieve the goal to set up reasonable account determination if the logistics, accounting, and cost accounting departments work in close coordination. Nevertheless, the accounting and/or cost accounting departments should be responsible for maintaining the account determination because they receive the data and have to meet the requirement that the material stock and income statement accounts are correctly debited and credited for goods movements.

MM account determination simulation

You may not always be sure which posting is generated for an MM movement type. For these situations, SAP provides an *MM account determination simulation* for experts. You can navigate to this simulation using the SIMULATION button in Transaction OMWB.

In the SIMULATE INVENTORY MANAGEMENT: ENTRY OF SIMULATION DATA input screen, you must enter the plant, the material, and a movement type (see Figure 4.27).

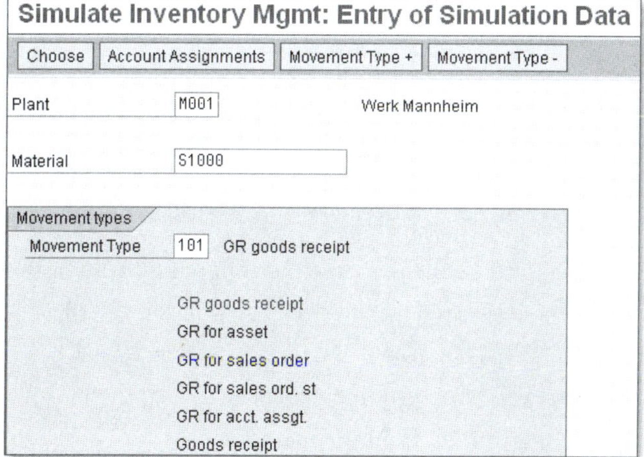

Figure 4.27 Simulation of the MM Account Determination—Selection

In Figure 4.27, 101 is specified for the MOVEMENT TYPE in the selection field. The system displays or updates the list below this field, which shows the different goods receipts, when you confirm the entry of the movement type with [Enter]. Select a variant from the list by double-clicking on it. It is then highlighted in blue. The ACCOUNT ASSIGNMENTS button takes you to the evaluation of the simulation (see Figure 4.28).

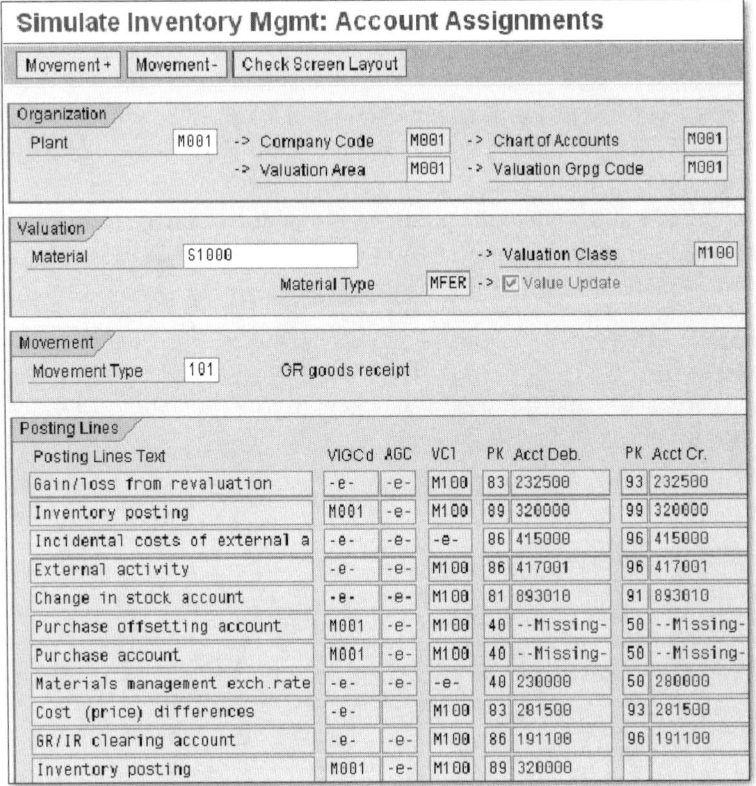

Figure 4.28 Simulation of the MM Account Determination—Evaluation

The top field groups in Figure 4.28 show that the following information has been derived from the plant:

- Company code and thus chart of accounts.
- Valuation area and thus valuation grouping code.
- The valuation class is determined from the material.
- The system uses the material type to check whether value updating is enabled in this case.

The lower part of the screen displays all transactions that could be relevant for the selected movement type. The list ranges from inventory management to GR/IR account and purchase account determination. It indicates which account is determined or if—as in this example—the account determination is not maintained for the purchase account and purchase offsetting account.

Comparing the field control

The Check Screen Layout button (see Figure 4.28) enables you to navigate to additional useful functions, namely, the comparison of the field groups of movement type and G/L account. Both elements—movement type and G/L account—individually define which fields are ready for input or even which fields are mandatory entry fields. However, it is possible that the movement type in MM does not allow for transferring a cost center in the material posting and at the same time, the cost center is a mandatory entry for a G/L account that has been determined for the movement type in the account determination. In this situation, the system outputs an error message because the G/L account does not receive all necessary information. The reconciliation function enables you to compare the field controls of movement types and of the G/L accounts that have been determined in the MM account determination.

Figure 4.29 shows this kind of comparison. A yellow minus indicates that the field is hidden. A circle stands for an optional entry. Mandatory fields are illustrated by a plus.

```
Mvmt Type 101   GR goods receipt
Field Status Group G001
G/L Accounts
 0000230000 0000280000 0000417001

  Field Group FI                  Fld
     Field Description              MvT  A/c  Different Field Group MM

  No MM group assigned            G001
     Bank charges                    -    -

  General data                    G001
     Assignment number               -    o
     Text                            -    o
     Invoice Reference               -    -
     Hedging                         -    -
     Collective Invoice              -    -

  Additional account assignments  G001
     Settlement period               -    -
     Material number                 -    -
     Cost center                     -    o
```

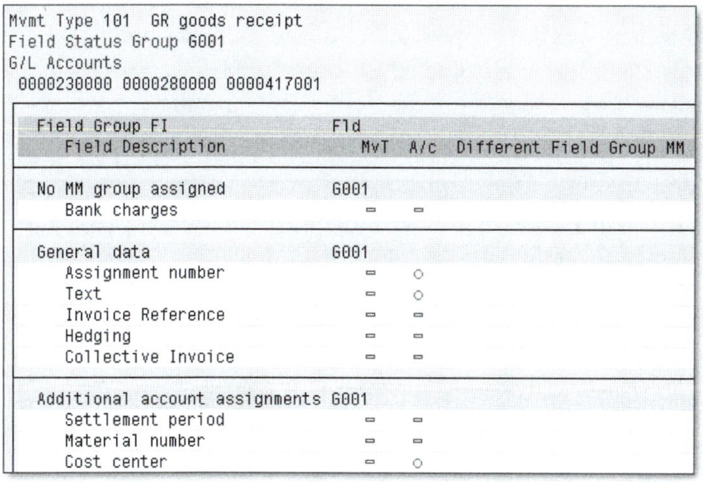

Figure 4.29 Comparing the Field Controls of Movement Type and G/L Account

You only need these two functions—simulation and field comparison—when the system outputs an error message. In that situation, however, they are very useful.

You have now met all requirements for a smooth integration of logistics and accounting. All MM transactions that are relevant for the value flow should now be transferred without any problems. Let us recall Figure 4.1 with the illustration of the adapted SCOR model. According to this model, the goods receipt is the next process step after the purchase order.

4.6 Goods Receipt

Are goods receipts necessary?

The decision whether *goods receipts* are necessary is already made in the purchase order. The system generates a proposal on this using the account assignment category, which you already know from Section 4.3, Purchase Order as the Basis of the Procurement Process. The item category controls whether you can overwrite this proposal.

The first decision—whether the goods receipt should be posted in the system—is rather easy. For stock material that is delivered at the gate with a delivery note, you expect a goods receipt and can also post it accordingly. For a drop shipment, the vendor delivers the goods directly to your customers. This means that you do not post a goods receipt.

Valuated/ non-valuated goods receipt

More complicated is the decision about whether the goods receipt should be *valuated* or *non-valuated*. If you define in the purchase order that the goods receipt should be non-valuated, the valuation does not take place until the invoice is received.

"Asset acquisition"

The best example of consequences of a decision about a valuated or non-valuated goods receipt is the acquisition of an asset. This is an example that is also frequently discussed in day-to-day work. For an asset acquisition, the time of the valuation defines when the asset is posted for the first time.

For a non-valuated goods receipt, the goods value is initially posted to a clearing account only. When the invoice is received, the clearing account is credited against the capitalized asset. This means that the relevant event for the asset capitalization is not the goods receipt but the invoice receipt.

For a valuated goods receipt, the goods value is directly posted to the asset when the goods are received. If it is a capitalized asset, the depreciation calculation begins when the goods are received. This is the common method.

We will now take a look at an example with a purchase order for an asset. For this purpose, a valuated goods receipt and an invoice receipt were posted, as you can see in the purchase order status in Figure 4.30.

Standard PO	4500018847	Vendor	K1100 Maschinen Silfer	
Delivery/Invoice	Conditions	Texts	Address	Communication / Partners / Additional Data

Active	Ordered	1	PC	25.000,00	EUR
Not Yet Sent	Delivered	1	PC	25.000,00	EUR
Fully Delivered	Still to deliv.	0	PC	0,00	EUR
Fully Invoiced	Invoiced	1	PC	25.000,00	EUR

Figure 4.30 Purchase Order Status—Valuated GR for an Asset

The fact that both a quantity and an amount are specified in the DELIVERED line (see Figure 4.30) also indicates that this is a valuated goods receipt. This means that the purchase order has been delivered completely and invoiced in the meantime. To view the date on which the goods and invoice receipt were posted, you have to look at the history of the purchase order item (see Figure 4.31).

Sh...	MvT	Material Do...	Item	Posting Date	Σ Quantity	OUn	Σ	Amount	Crcy
WE	101	5000014078	1	01.04.2009	1	PC		25.000,00	EUR
Tr./Ev. Goods receipt					**1**	**PC**		**25.000,00**	**EUR**
RE-L		5105609189	1	26.04.2009	1	PC		25.000,00	EUR
Tr./Ev. Invoice receipt					**1**	**PC**		**25.000,00**	**EUR**

Figure 4.31 Purchase Order History for the Asset Item

Here, you can see that the goods receipt was posted on 04/01/2009 while the invoice was entered much later, on 04/26/2009. For a valuated goods receipt, the asset has to use the date of the goods receipt. This is indicated by the CAPITALIZED ON field in the asset master in Figure 4.32.

Stock material receipt

From the value flow perspective, the goods receipt does not include further special aspects. For materials that are managed on a quantity and value basis, the stock is built-up at this point and thus the stock value in the financial statement increases.

Vendor consignment stock

The stock value may not be increased if you are not the owner of the goods. An example of this is the vendor consignment stock. In this case, only an MM document but no Financial Accounting document is generated when the goods are received. Moreover, the goods are still the property of the vendor. Regarding quantity, you have to enter the stock for your plant so that you can include it in your production process.

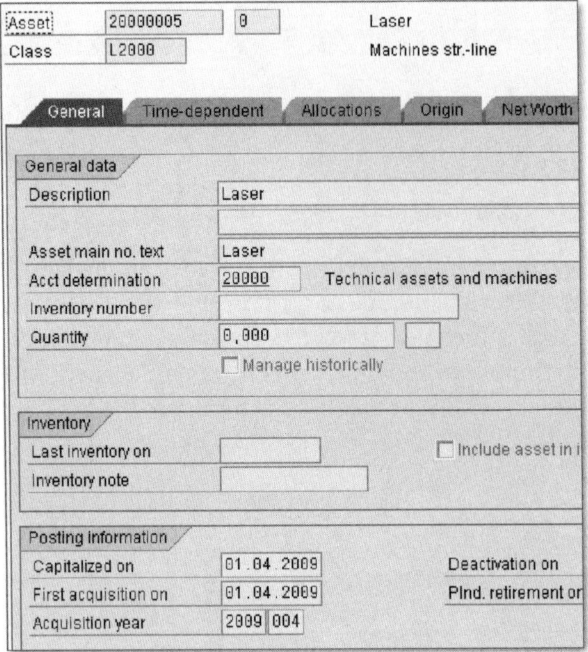

Figure 4.32 Capitalization Date in the Asset Master

4.7 Invoice Verification

Formal invoice verification

The term *invoice verification* can refer to different processes: to the technical verification and to the formal verification of an incoming invoice. This ensures that a vendor invoice meets the legal requirements and can be posted. An incoming invoice must include the following specifications, for example, to pass the invoice verification:

- Name and address of the providing enterprise and of the debiting party
- Tax number of the providing enterprise
- Unique sequential invoice number
- Issue date of the invoice (invoice date)
- Quantity and standard description of the delivery or type and scope of the service provided
- Net amount for the delivery or service
- Tax rate and amount (if the delivery or service is tax-exempt, this needs to be specified explicitly)

- Any reduction of the amount to be paid that was agreed in advance, such as discounts
- Time of the delivery and service

[+]

Invoice and Delivery Date are Identical

You have to identify both dates, even if the invoice and delivery date are identical. In this case, it is usually sufficient to refer to the delivery note number or make a note that the invoice and delivery dates are identical.

The goal here is not to check whether the invoice is factually justified but whether it meets all legal requirements.

Factual invoice verification

In addition to the formal verification, incoming invoices also need to be factually verified. In this context, you should primarily clarify whether the invoice amount is correct and whether the vendor has correctly provided or delivered the agreed service or goods.

System support

SAP systems cannot support formal invoice verification. Instead, software solutions with handwriting recognition and the respective check routines can be used instead. The problem is that vendor invoices have different structures so that the support of a third-party system often does not have the desired result. Enterprises with a high volume of incoming invoices tend to outsource this schematic verification to countries with low wage levels.

Logistics Invoice Verification

For factual invoice verifications, however, the SAP system provides a very good tool: Logistics Invoice Verification. It is characterized by a high integration with MM and Financial Accounting/Controlling. Posting invoices with Logistics Invoice Verification should be a standard process and is therefore discussed in detail in this section.

Invoice Verification also Includes Credit Memos

At this point, it should be mentioned that we are still referring to invoices and that the function is called *Logistics Invoice Verification*. However, you can, of course, also post credit memos.

4.7.1 Invoice Verification Process

Whether the system expects an invoice is defined by the account assignment category in the purchase order—as is the case for the goods receipt. If you define here that you do not expect an invoice for an external purchase order—that is, a purchase order that is provided to an external vendor—the system assumes that the delivery is free of charge. Usually, however, an invoice receipt is defined in the purchase order.

GR-based invoice verification

Another critical specification for invoice verification is made in the purchase order. You define against what the invoice is checked: the purchase order or the goods receipt (GR). You make this decision via the GR-BASED INVOICE VERIFICATION checkbox. You can find this checkbox in the detail view of the purchase order item on the INVOICE tab (see Figure 4.33).

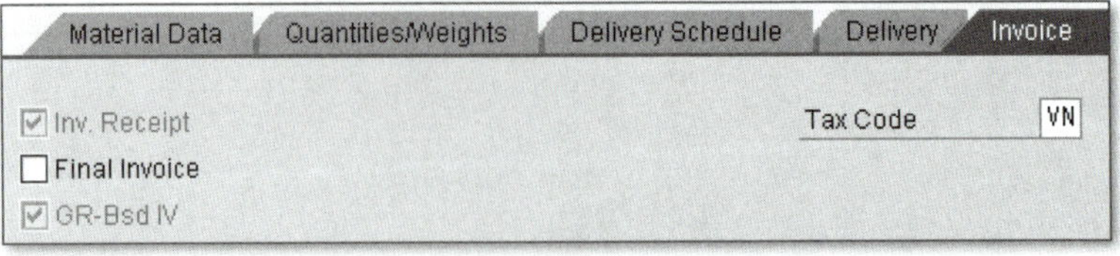

Figure 4.33 Invoice Receipt Specifications in the Purchase Order

"Invoice receipt specifications" example

Let us take a closer look at the consequences of this decision using two examples:

- The invoice is received before the goods are received.
- A partial delivery is received and the invoice is received afterward.

In the example, two purchase orders with 10 m2 of box calf leather are created. In the first purchase order, the indicator for the GR-based invoice verification is not selected; in the second purchase order, the indicator is selected.

IR before GR

Let us assume that the vendor issues the invoice faster than delivering the goods. The following section details what happens next.

Purchase Order Without GR-Based Invoice Verification

The invoice is checked against the purchase order. The SAP system generates a warning that no quantities have been posted yet (see Figure 4.34).

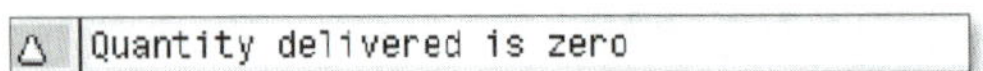

Figure 4.34 Message if the Invoice is Received Before the Goods are Received—Without GR-Based Invoice Verification

However, this message is only a warning and does not prevent you from posting the document. Nevertheless, in this case, the system automatically blocks the document for payment because there is a quantity variance because of the missing goods.

Purchase Order with GR-Based Invoice Verification

The system behaves differently with GR-based invoice verification. Because no goods receipt has been posted yet, the SAP system cannot verify the invoice. It therefore prevents you from entering the invoice (see Figure 4.35).

```
No (suitable) item found for purchase order 4500018819
No goods items found
```

Figure 4.35 Message for GR-Based Invoice Verification and Invoice Receipt Before Goods Receipt

Although these messages are not actual error messages, they make it impossible to enter the invoice with reference to the purchase order.

This system behavior indicates the first consequence of the GR-BASED INVOICE VERIFICATION indicator: If it is selected, you cannot enter the invoice until the goods receipt has been posted. For purchase order items for which you do not expect timely postings of the goods receipt—for example, for the weekly beverage delivery for the office—you should avoid using GR-based invoice verification. Alternatively, you have to considerably increase the discipline applied for posting the goods receipts.

GR with partial delivery before IR

Let us take a different situation as an example: First, the goods receipt and then the invoice is posted. Because real life is not always as ideal as we would like it to be, let us add another detail. According to the principle "trust is good, control is better," a proper incoming inspection also entails counting the actual quantity and it is possible that only a partial delivery is received instead of the entire ordered quantity. It is also possible that the vendor is honest and has made a partial delivery due to delivery problems on his end, for example. Therefore, let us assume that the vendor in the example has production problems and can therefore only deliver 8 instead of 10 m2 of leather. Unfortunately, the ordered 10 m2 were invoiced.

In both cases—with and without GR-based invoice verification—the system provides only a quantity of 8 m2 for selection when you want to enter the invoice using Transaction MIRO (see Figure 4.36).

Item	Amount	Quantity	Or...		Purchase ...	Item
1	1.600,00	8,00	M2	☐	4500018823	10

Figure 4.36 Item Proposal in the Invoice Receipt for Partial Delivery

We will overwrite this proposal and post 10 m2 of our material at a net price of EUR 2,000.00. The only consequence is an automatically set payment block due to the quantity variance between invoice and goods receipt. As an alternative to the purchase order history, you can also have the system display the status of the purchase order (Figure 4.37).

Ordered	10,00	M2	2.000,00	EUR
Delivered	8,00	M2	1.600,00	EUR
Still to deliv.	2,00	M2	400,00	EUR
Invoiced	10,00	M2	2.000,00	EUR
Down paymts			0,00	EUR

Figure 4.37 Purchase Order Status for Partial Delivery and Complete Invoice Receipt

It is obvious that the vendor has invoiced more than delivered. You can also see that it makes little difference whether you work with or without GR-based invoice verification. Only the case where the invoice is received before the goods receipt is posted is handled more restrictively for GR-based invoice verification.

Customizing of the Logistics Invoice Verification

You were already introduced to the Logistics Invoice Verification settings that are implemented by the purchasing department in the purchase order. These settings include the definition whether an invoice is expected at all and against which material document—purchase order or goods receipt—the invoice is checked. Let us take a step back and have a look at the parameters that the invoice verification itself provides. You can find all corresponding settings in the Implementation Guide under MATERIALS MANAGEMENT • LOGISTICS INVOICE VERIFICATION.

Document number assignment

The fact that Logistics Invoice Verification also creates both an MM document and a Financial Accounting document often leads to discontent among invoice verification clerks, particularly in the event of SAP implementations. One of the reasons for this is an admittedly unfavorable procedure in the SAP standard: When an invoice is posted, the SAP system initially only displays the MM document number. However, this document number is usually rather uninteresting because—as for any other Financial Accounting transaction—the system shows the Financial Accounting document number in the line item display of the vendor account. There are two solutions to this situation:

- The MM document number is also used as the Financial Accounting document number.
- In the message that indicates that a document has been posted, the system displays the Financial Accounting document number in addition to the MM document number.

Buffering deactivation

In the early Logistics Invoice Verification years, only the first variant was available. You had to provide external number assignment for the Financial Accounting number range to have the system use the MM document number. Additionally, you had to deactivate the buffering of the MM number assignment, which also leads to an improved posting performance. However, because the buffer is rebuilt regularly, independently of whether it has been used to its full extent, gaps between the numbers occur. These gaps also continue to exist in the Financial Accounting component, which is not permitted regarding revision.

Procedure for Deactivating the Buffering

SAP Note 62077 (Info: Internal Number Assignment is Not Continuous) describes the detailed procedure for deactivation of buffering. This is a modification of the system, which should usually be avoided, because modifications entail additional work in the event of release changes.

In this case, however, the modification is not critical and therefore also justifiable from the point of view of the IT.

Adapting the information message

In the meantime, SAP has developed an easier solution, which you can completely implement in the standard SAP system. For this purpose, you only have to expand the parameters in the user master. Users can maintain their master using the System • User Profile • Own Data menu path (see Figure 4.38).

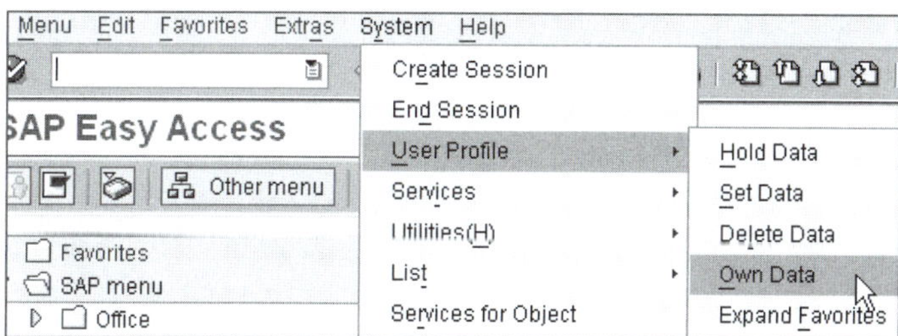

Figure 4.38 Changing the User Profile for Logistics Invoice Verification

Next, you have to specify the IVFIDISPLAY entry on the Parameter tab and add a large X. After you have saved the settings, the system reports both document numbers when you post incoming invoices (see Figure 4.39).

Invoice document 5105609181 was posted and blocked for payment (Accountng Documnt: 5100000014)

Figure 4.39 Display with MM and Financial Accounting Document Number

With this information, you considerably facilitate the work of invoice verification clerks without having to implement modifications.

[+]

Material Document Number in a Reference Field

The standard SAP system writes the number of the material document to the REFERENCE KEY field in the accounting document header. Therefore, if you want to view Financial Accounting and MM document numbers in the line item display of accounts payable accounting, you have to permit the BKPF-AWKEY field in the line item display.

You can initiate this in the Implementation Guide, for example, under FINANCIAL ACCOUNTING (NEW) • ACCOUNTS RECEIVABLE AND ACCOUNTS PAYABLE • VENDOR ACCOUNTS • LINE ITEMS • DISPLAY LINE ITEMS • DEFINE ADDITIONAL FIELDS FOR LINE ITEM DISPLAY.

We will now proceed with the Logistics Invoice Verification posting technologies.

Unplanned delivery costs

Logistics Invoice Verification uses MM account determination. Section 4.5.3, Determining Transactions, already described that there is a specific transaction key for unplanned delivery costs and that there are two posting options. You can make the following decisions:

- Whether you divide the additional costs between the purchase order items
- Whether you want to post a special G/L account line

For materials with moving average price, the first variant ensures that the price will be adjusted. For materials with a standard price, a posting is made in the price variances. You cannot make this decision for each case individually because it is a permanent specification at the company code level. You implement the corresponding setting in the Implementation Guide under MATERIALS MANAGEMENT • LOGISTICS INVOICE VERIFICATION • INCOMING INVOICE • CONFIGURE HOW UNPLANNED DELIVERY COSTS ARE POSTED. Unplanned delivery costs are a special invoice verification case. They are posted at the header level and not at the posting item level to allow for a cost distribution across the purchase order items if required (see Figure 4.40).

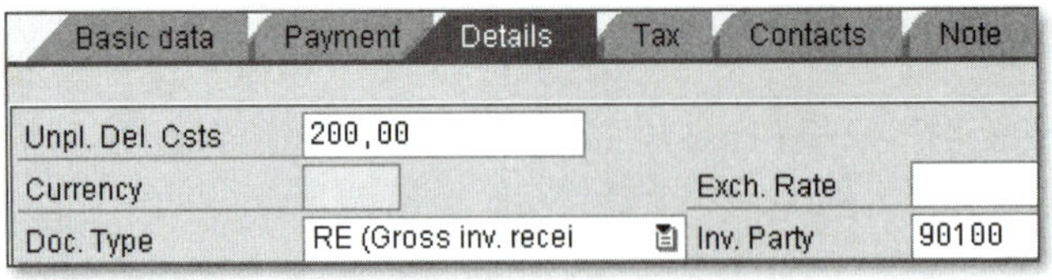

Basic data | Payment | Details | Tax | Contacts | Note

Unpl. Del. Csts	200,00		
Currency		Exch. Rate	
Doc. Type	RE (Gross inv. recei	Inv. Party	90100

Figure 4.40 Posting Unplanned Delivery Costs

You have to post unplanned delivery costs on the DETAILS tab. The following sections describe two posting examples.

Posting Unplanned Delivery Costs with Distribution

Figure 4.41 displays the Financial Accounting document of an invoice receipt.

C...	Itm	PK	S	Account	Description		Amount	Curr.	Tx
M001	1	31		90100	Leder Greiner		2.975,00-	EUR	VN
	2	86		191100	Goods Rcvd/Invoice R		1.000,00	EUR	VN
	3	89		300000 ❶	Inventory - Raw Mat		86,96	EUR	VN
	4	86		191100	Goods Rcvd/Invoice R		1.300,00	EUR	VN
	5	89		300000 ❷	Inventory - Raw Mat		113,04	EUR	VN
	6	40		154000	Input tax		475,00	EUR	VN

Figure 4.41 Distribution of Unplanned Delivery Costs

This document contains two purchase order items that were posted to the GR/IR account (items 2 and 4). Furthermore, you can also see that a posting to the raw materials account was made twice (see ❶ and ❷ in Figure 4.41). This indicates that the ordered materials have a moving average price because materials with a standard price would be posted to a price difference account. The unplanned delivery costs of EUR 200.00 are therefore directly added to the stock value of the two materials.

Posting of Unplanned Delivery Costs in a Separate Line

This is different for the Financial Accounting document when you do not distribute the unplanned delivery costs but instead post them in a separate line (see Figure 4.42).

C...	Itm	PK	S	Account	Description	Amount	Curr.	Tx	Cost Center	Order	Profit Center	Segment
M001	1	31		90100	Leder Greiner	2.975,00-	EUR	VN				
	2	86		191100	Goods Rcvd/Invoice R	1.000,00	EUR	VN				
	3	86		191100	Goods Rcvd/Invoice R	1.300,00	EUR	VN				
	4	40		231600	Unpl. delivery costs	200,00	EUR	VN			DUMMY	M_ZZZ
	5	40		154000	Input tax	475,00	EUR	VN				

Figure 4.42 Special Posting of Unplanned Delivery Costs

Here, you can see that the EUR 200.00 of unplanned delivery costs were posted in their entirety to account 231600. The prices of the two ordered materials are consequently not increased, and the entire amount is posted as expenditure. However, you can easily recognize the problem with this posting: The system cannot derive a useful Controlling account assignment. This means you can either treat account 231600 as a neutral account by creating no cost elements for it or, alternatively, define a standard account assignment, for example, via Transaction OKB9.

Posting without purchase order reference

In real life, you will often come across invoices that do not refer to a purchase order. In these cases, you can post the invoice without integration with MM, which is discussed in Section 4.9.1, Invoice Receipt Without MM Integration. Or you can use Logistics Invoice Verification. For this purpose, however, you have to enable this kind of posting first. You can find the corresponding Customizing in the Implementation Guide under MATERIALS MANAGEMENT • LOGISTICS INVOICE VERIFICATION • INCOMING INVOICE • ENABLE DIRECT POSTING TO G/L ACCOUNT AND MATERIAL ACCOUNTS. Transaction MIRO provides the corresponding tabs only when you enable the functions here.

4.7.2 Considering Tolerances

Acceptable variances

The procurement process can include numerous variances. Some of them can be tolerated such as differences of a few cents in an invoice due to the summation of all invoice items.

Individual tolerance limits

Other variances are not acceptable such as an obvious price difference between purchase order and invoice. To set a limit for variances you are willing to accept, you have to define tolerance limits in Customizing.

Depending on your individual situation, you can maintain various tolerances. The standard SAP system provides the following tolerances:

- AN amount for item without purchase order reference
- AP amount for item with purchase order reference
- BD form small differences automatically
- BR percentage OPUn variance (IR before GR)
- BW percentage OPUn variance (GR before IR)
- DQ exceed amount: quantity variance
- DW quantity variance when GR quantity = zero
- KW variance from condition value
- LA amount of blanket purchase order
- LD blanket purchase order time limit exceeded
- PP price variance
- PS price variance: estimated price
- ST date variance (value * days)
- VP moving average price variance

You cannot add custom tolerances to this list of what are called *tolerance keys*.

Normally, all tolerance settings have the same structure. You can define an upper and a lower limit for the variance; additionally, the variance is defined in absolute amounts and in percentages.

Definition of upper and lower limits

The definition of upper and lower limits enables you, for example, to prevent vendors from considerably exceeding or going below the price that has been agreed in the purchase order. By setting an absolute tolerance in amounts and additionally a tolerance in percentages, you avoid that you define unwanted high tolerance limits.

[Ex]

Specifying Tolerance Limits in Absolute Amounts and in Percentages

If you define the percentage for the price overrun at five percent, this would be EUR 5.00 for an invoice item of EUR 100.00. For an invoice item of EUR 100,000.00, the tolerance would be EUR 5,000.00, which is probably not what you want.

You can prohibit this system behavior by defining that a maximum of EUR 10.00 variance is allowed. With this setting, you would tolerate a price variance of EUR 5.00 in the first case and of EUR 10.00 in the second case.

You implement the Customizing of tolerance limits in the Implementation Guide under MATERIALS MANAGEMENT • LOGISTICS INVOICE VERIFICATION • INVOICE BLOCK • SET TOLERANCE LIMITS. Figure 4.43 displays the definition of the tolerance limits for price variances in the Lederwaren-Manufaktur Mannheim company code as an example.

AN and AP tolerance keys

As you already know, there are numerous tolerance limits that can be checked, however, you do not have to use them all. For example, the AN and AP tolerance keys are often deactivated for the check of the permitted maximum amount for each document item.

The BD tolerance key

The BD tolerance key enables you to accept that an invoice document initially does not balance to zero. This can happen especially if the taxes for the individual items lead to a smaller amount than the tax calculation for the total net amount. To be able to post the invoice without problems in such situations, you should allow for a small tolerance of approximately EUR 2,00.

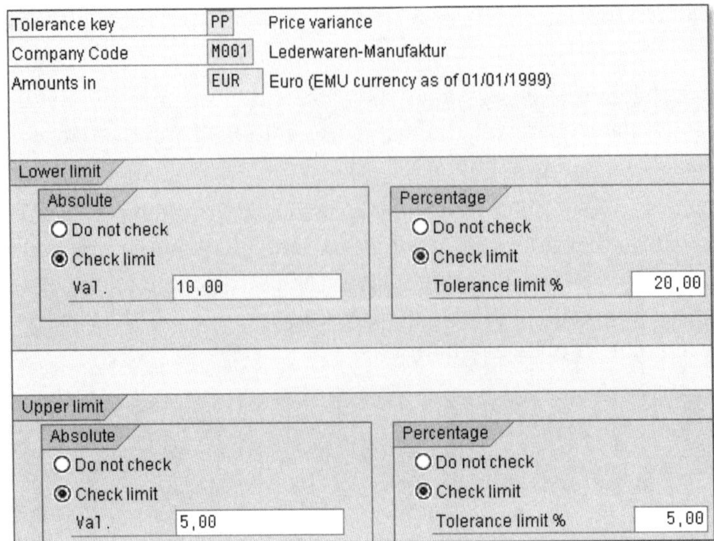

Figure 4.43 Tolerance Limits for Price Variances

PP, KW, and PS tolerance keys

Figure 4.43 displayed the PP tolerance keys for basic price variances. However, there is also a specific tolerance key (the KW tolerance key) for price variances for delivery costs.

Furthermore, there is the PS key for price variances for estimated prices. With this, the purchasing department can insert a note in the purchase order if the purchase order price is estimated. In this case, you would allow for larger variances than for normal purchase orders with fixed prices/prices agreed upon with the vendor.

[!]

Setting the PS Tolerance Key by Default

Unfortunately, some purchasers set the "estimated price" indicator regularly because they know about higher tolerance limits. This reduces the number of questions the purchaser receives from the invoice verification department. Thus, you should think twice before setting higher tolerance limits.

LA and LD tolerance keys

Finally, SAP also supports you in verifying blanket purchase orders by enabling you to define tolerances for the amount (LA key) and schedule fulfillment (LD key).

The VP tolerance key

The VP tolerance key is also quite interesting. It compares the moving average price before the invoice receipt with the moving average price after the invoice receipt. If the difference is too large, the system blocks the invoice for payment.

Outside of tolerances

If the amount exceeds or falls below all mentioned tolerances, the SAP system indicates the reason for the variance in the document and blocks the open vendor item for invoice. The system also supports you in releasing blocked invoices as you will see next.

4.7.3 Automatically Releasing Blocked Invoices

Automatic release

To automatically release blocked invoices, you use Transaction MRBR (Release Blocked Invoices). If you start the report with the automatic invoice release option, the system checks for every automatically blocked invoice if the invoice blocking reason still exists. If not, the system releases the payment block.

[Ex]

Releasing the Payment Block

For example, if no goods have been received, the system blocks the invoice due to quantity variances. After the respective goods receipt has been posted, you can pay the invoice.

If there is a price difference, you have to inform the purchasing department after having entered the invoice. This can be done manually or automatically using a workflow. If the purchasing department adapts the purchase order after having clarified the price issue, the invoice can be released for payment.

Manual release

Regardless of the elimination of the invoice blocking reason, you can also delete the invoice blocking reason manually using Transaction MRBR. For this purpose, you have to start the report using the RELEASE MANUALLY option.

[+]

Scheduling Transaction MRBR

Schedule the transaction every night using the AUTOMATIC RELEASE option and send the result list to the printer of the responsible accountant. This ensures that all invoices are released as soon as the reason for the payment block is eliminated.

This concludes our discussion of entering incoming invoices. In this context, we also came across the GR/IR account, which is described in further detail in the following section.

4.8 GR/IR Account

You already know that the goods receipt and the invoice receipt involves the *GR/IR account* if the corresponding goods receipt and the invoice receipt refers to an invoice.

4.8.1 Posting to the GR/IR Account

The WRX transaction

To allow for high automation, GR/IR accounts are also defined in the MM account determination. This was explained in detail in Section 4.5.3, Determining Transactions. You normally use the GR/IR account independently of valuation classes. Many times, only one GR/IR account is used.

Purpose of the GR IR account

From the accounting perspective, the GR/IR account is a balance sheet account that is not mapped in the financial statement because it is just a clearing account. This is discussed in more detail later on. Then what is the reason for this account?

In college, you learned the following posting record:

Material Stock		
Tax	to	Payables

In real business life, however, you will have noticed that this posting record does not exist in this form. In this posting record, the goods movement and the accrual of the payables are posted simultaneously. From the business perspective—and also according to the SCOR model—these are two different transactions: first goods receipt and then invoice receipt.

This separation of goods and invoice receipt is implemented using the GR/IR account. Figure 4.44 shows a posting example.

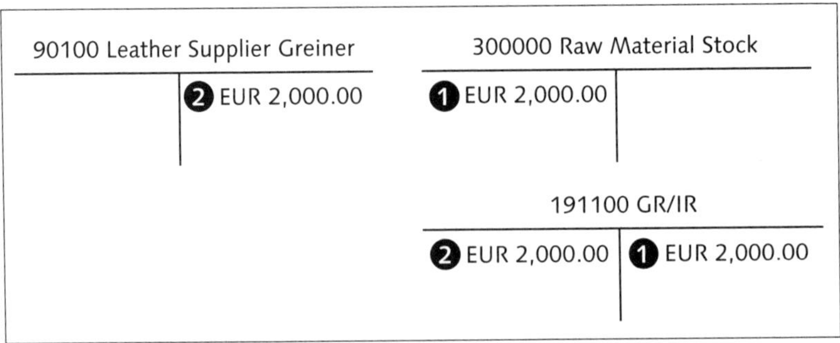

Figure 4.44 Posting Example—GR/IR Account

Let us take the previous purchase order of 10 m2 of box calf leather with EUR 200.00 each as an example—you can find the goods receipt (10 m^2) of EUR 2,000.00 and the invoice receipt (10 m^2) of EUR 2,000.00.

As agreed, the vendor delivered 10 m^2 of leather. These are posted to the material stock account for raw materials. The GR/IR account is the offsetting account. The value can be derived from the price according to the purchase order, multiplied by the actual quantity of goods received.

With the invoice receipt, the vendor account is debited. For the offsetting account assignment, the GR/IR account is used. The following is the ideal situation: The purchase order was delivered in full and invoiced and there are no quantity or price variances. Therefore, the GR/IR account is cleared for this purchase order. But the clearing cannot be implemented directly, neither through the goods nor through the invoice receipt. Instead, it is part of the GR/IR account maintenance, which must be done with urgency and on a regular basis—at the latest, when preparing closing operations.

4.8.2 Clearing the GR/IR Account

Automatic clearing

For clearing, use the function for automatic clearing of G/L accounts in Financial Accounting. You can find this function in the user menu under ACCOUNTING • FINANCIAL ACCOUNTING • GENERAL LEDGER • PERIODIC PROCESSING • AUTOMATIC CLEARING • WITHOUT SPECIFICATION OF CLEARING CURRENCY (or directly via Transaction F.13). In this case, the system tries to clear open items on the account according to defined rules. You define the rules in Customizing under FINANCIAL ACCOUNTING (NEW) • GENERAL LEDGER ACCOUNTING (NEW) • BUSINESS TRANSACTIONS • OPEN ITEM CLEARING • PREPARE AUTOMATIC CLEARING. Here, you can specify which fields of the open items have to match so that the items can be grouped. Figure 4.45 displays the default settings.

OB74

ChtA	AccTy	From acct	To account	Criterion 1	Criterion 2	Criterion 3	Criterion 4
	D	A	Z	ZUONR	GSBER	VBUND	
	K	A	Z	ZUONR	GSBER	VBUND	
	S	0	999999	ZUONR	GSBER	VBUND	

Figure 4.45 Default Settings—Automatic Clearing

The definitions are made for each account type and at intervals if required. In our case, the ZUONR (assignment number), GSBER (business area), and VBUND (trading partner number) fields must match. In our small sample enterprise, the check whether these three fields match is sufficient. In real life, however, you should additionally define the purchasing document number (EBELN) and item (EBELP) for the GR/IR account. The system groups all documents that contain identical entries. If the grouped documents balance to zero, the system proposes or implements automatic clearing.

Clearing transaction

Let us have another look at the example from Section 4.7.1, Invoice Verification Process, and consider this situation for clearing via Transaction F.13. Three items are found on the GR/IR account of which two match in the relevant fields (according to the Customizing shown in Figure 4.45) so that the system identifies that they belong together. Because the group balances to zero, the system clears the open items (see Figure 4.46).

Company Code M001
Account Type S
Account number 191100
G/L 191100

DocumentNo	Itm	Clearing	Clrng doc.	SG	Crcy	Amount	Assignment	Business Area	Trading Partner
5000000007	002				EUR	400,00-	450001882200010		1000
*					EUR	400,00-	450001882200010		1000
5100000009	002	19.04.2009			EUR	2.000,00	450001883300010		1000
5000000008	002	19.04.2009			EUR	2.000,00-	450001883300010		1000
*		19.04.2009			EUR	0,00	450001883300010		1000

Figure 4.46 Clearing the GR/IR Account Using Automatic Clearing

Clearing document

The two document items highlighted in green are cleared. The system also displays the number of the resulting clearing document. Due to the SAP General Ledger and the activation of document splitting, there is one essential innovation for the clearing document (see Figure 4.47).

Data Entry View

Document Number	100000005	Company Code	M001	Fiscal Year	2009
Document Date	20.04.2009	Posting Date	20.04.2009	Period	4
Reference		Cross-CC no.			
Currency	EUR	Texts exist	☐	Ledger Group	

C...	Itm	PK	S	Account	Description	Amount	Currenc
M001	1	40		191100	Goods Rcvd/Invoice R	2.000,00	EUR
	2	50		191100	Goods Rcvd/Invoice R	2.000,00-	EUR

Figure 4.47 Clearing Document from the GR/IR Account Maintenance

As you can see in Figure 4.47, the document now includes line items. Prior to the introduction of the SAP General Ledger and its document splitting, the document consisted of a document header only and no document items were posted.

Transaction F.13

Transaction F.13 provides two additional functions we used in our example: You can consider implementing tolerance limits and reduce the criteria for the grouping of documents on the GR/IR account.

- **Considering implementation of tolerances**
  Considering the implementation of tolerances for exchange rate differences and rounding differences enables you to clear documents despite small variances in the amount. The system then posts the difference to the respective expense or revenue account.
- **Reducing criteria for the grouping of documents on the GR/IR account**
  Alternatively, you can also reduce the rules for the grouping of documents. In the standard, the link is implemented via the purchase order number and item. For GR-based invoice verification, you can also implement the grouping via the material document. This is only useful if the link via the purchase order is not meaningful for, for example, scheduling agreements.

GR/IR Account Maintenance with MR11

However, Transaction F.13 does not provide support for deviating goods or invoice receipts—for example, if no goods or invoice receipts are expected for a purchase order or if the existing documents cannot be cleared due to quantity variances. You can clear them in the GR/IR account maintenance using Transaction MR11. You can find this transaction in the user menu under Logistics • Materials Management • Logistics Invoice Verification • GR/IR Account Maintenance • Maintain GR/IR Clearing Account.

Automatic or manual start

You can start the program automatically or manually. In automatic operation, the system can write off open items for which the delivery quantity is larger than the quantity invoiced or for which the quantity invoiced exceeds the delivery quantity. If all expected goods and invoices have been received but the purchase order quantity has not been reached, you have to clear the items manually.

Posting configurations

For these transactions, you do not have to configure a specific account determination. The system works with the settings that are also used for the invoice receipt. The possible posting records depend on the price control of the materials or on the purchase order. The following posting configurations are likely:

- **Purchase orders with account assignment**
  The offsetting entry is posted to the account assignment that is defined in the purchase order.
- **Material with standard price**
  The offsetting entry is posted to the price difference account.
- **Material with moving average price**
  If the stock level is greater than/equal to the difference quantity, the posting is made to the material stock account (this corresponds to a revaluation). If the stock level covers the difference quantity, the offsetting entry is posted to the price difference account, as is the case for materials with a standard price.

Mapping in the financial statement using F.19

It has already been mentioned that the GR/IR account is not mapped in the financial statement. However, to ensure that the financial statement is correct, all values on the GR/IR account that exist at the time the financial statement is created need to be reposted to other accounts. This reposting is implemented at the period key date and reversed in the subsequent period. Both is done using Transaction F.19. When the posting is made, however, the GR/IR account is not addressed directly to set a zero balance. Rather, the zero balance is set using an adjustment account, which is mapped in one item in the balance sheet structure together with the GR/IR account. This means that the zero balance is not set on the GR/IR account but on the corresponding balance sheet item. The repostings are usually implemented on two accounts:

- An account that maps invoice receipts for which no goods have been received
- An account for goods receipts for which the vendor has not yet issued an invoice

The account determination here is not part of the MM account determination, because the postings are exclusively made in the G/L. You can find the corresponding settings in the Implementation Guide under FINANCIAL ACCOUNTING (NEW) • GENERAL LEDGER ACCOUNTING (NEW) • PERIODIC PROCESSING • RECLASSIFY • DEFINE ADJUSTMENT ACCOUNTS FOR GR/IR CLEARING. Figure 4.48 shows an example.

Chart of Accounts	M001	Lederwaren Manufaktur, Mannheim
Transaction	BNG	Invoiced but not yet delivered

Account assignment

Reconciliati...	Adjustment...	Targ.acct
191000	191099	191101
191100	191199	191101

Figure 4.48 Account Determination for the Reclassification of the GR/IR Account

Here, you can see Transaction BNG (INVOICED BUT NOT YET DELIVERED). For our 191100 GR/IR account, the 191199 adjustment account has been defined as the account to which the posting is made instead of the GR/IR account. The 191101 account is the target entry, which is mapped along with the stocks in the financial statement. It should be mapped in the financial statement because goods have been received for the received invoice, which means that a material value exists. In the other case—material has been delivered, but not invoiced—Lederwaren-Manufaktur Mannheim makes the posting to the 191102 account (DELIVERED BUT NOT YET INVOICED). Here, you have to maintain Transaction GNB. The financial statement maps the 191102 account in other provisions. The GR/IR account and the 191199 adjustment account balance to zero, which means that the adjustment account must be mapped in the not assigned accounts, along with the GR/IR account.

Account Control of the GR/IR Account [!]

For GR/IR accounts, the balance indicator must only be set for the local currency. Otherwise, there may be problems when you clear open items with foreign currencies.

From a business perspective, this is not a problem because foreign currencies are not relevant for GR/IR accounts.

Let us now turn our attention from general ledger accounting to the subsidiary ledger—that is, accounts payable accounting.

4.9 Integration of Accounts Payable Accounting

In accounting, the FI-AP subcomponent (Accounts Payable) maps all transactions that affect vendors. FI-AP is accounts payable accounting with an integration into general ledger accounting, and its account assignment object is the vendor master. In addition to the entry of incoming invoices via Logistics Invoice Verification, which was described in Section 4.7.1, Invoice Verification Process, you can also directly enter invoices and credit memos in *Accounts Payable*.

4.9.1 Invoice Receipt Without MM Integration

Lack of integration

The lack of integration with MM and Purchasing is a problem when the data should be directly entered in FI-AP. It means that you cannot access purchase orders. You also cannot post materials that are subject to inventory management. This method is particularly suited for "minor" invoices, such as for the flower pot that is paid from the department's kitty. These transactions are often called *secondary businesses*.

Deviating document type and number

These kinds of documents are usually not posted with the RE document type, but—if you use the standard SAP system—with the KR document type for invoices and the KG document type for credit memos. Unlike the document types from Logistics Invoice Verification, these document types do not use the same number range. This—as well as the necessity of an additional input screen and the missing verification against a purchase order or goods receipt—is often the reason why invoice verification clerks do not fully accept this screen variant. You can address this by providing an option in Logistics Invoice Verification for postings to G/L accounts. This enables invoice verification clerks to enter all incoming invoices with a standardized transaction. For more information, you can also refer to the descriptions in the context of Logistics Invoice Verification in Section 4.7, Invoice Verification.

Recurring entries

The direct posting of invoices to Accounts Payable is useful, however, if you have to enter recurring documents at regular intervals. A prominent example of this is rent. In this case, the amount, account assignment, and due dates are known over a longer period and normally stay the same. To facilitate the regular posting of such documents for user departments, the SAP system provides what are called recurring entries. They work exactly like standing orders at a bank. You define the posting with the complete account assignment, the amounts, the start date, and the end date as well as the desired cycle (for example, monthly, weekly). This information is then stored in a recurring entry original document, which is an accounting document that does not trigger updating the transaction figures. You can consider it a template for the actual postings. At regular intervals, usually monthly, the system starts a job that checks all original documents and generates the respective posting if required.

This tool has the following advantages:

- Reduction of the work involved in accounting because you do not have to re-enter documents every time they recur
- Reduction of error sources because the number of manual entry operations has been reduced

The "Recurring Entries are Selected Incorrectly" Error Message [+]

At the beginning of a new fiscal year, the Financial Accounting component administrators are frequently addressed even by experienced colleagues with the following cry for help: "I've entered a new original document, but the system does not post it! The job does not select our recurring entries correctly!"

The solution to this is usually quite simple: In the selection criteria of the processing program, a fiscal year or a variable has been defined. As a result, the system verifies the fiscal year of the original document, but not the fiscal year of the documents that are supposed to be posted. The simple solution is to not enter a fiscal year at all!

Regardless of how invoices get into an SAP system—they have to be paid sometime. This is the task of the payment run.

4.9.2 Outgoing Payments

Functional scope of the payment run

The *payment run* is an accounting tool that enables you to trigger all existing payments automatically. In many enterprises, the majority of payments refer to due vendor invoices. However, you can also pay credit memos to customers or fulfill other payment obligations. SAP supports the common methods such as payments via bank transfers, checks, bills of exchange, or lockbox procedures. These procedures are called payment methods in the SAP world.

The behavior of an individual payment run depends on different factors such as the Customizing of the payment program, the information from vendor master and single document, or the parameters of the current payment run (see Figure 4.49).

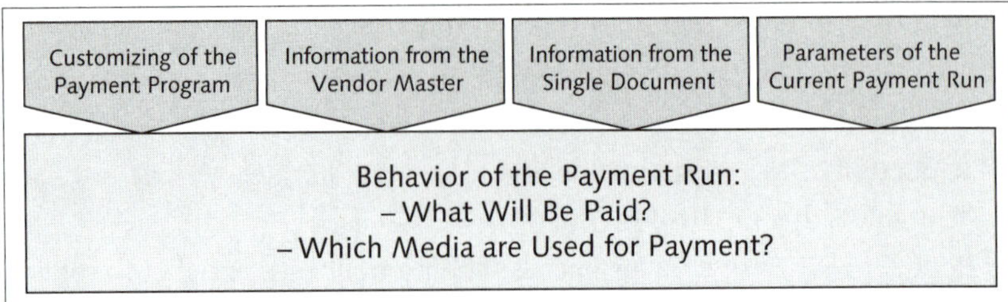

Figure 4.49 Influencing Factors of a Payment Run

Customizing of the payment program

You can find the Customizing of the payment program in the Implementation Guide under FINANCIAL ACCOUNTING (NEW) • ACCOUNTS RECEIVABLE AND ACCOUNTS PAYABLE • BUSINESS TRANSACTIONS • OUTGOING PAYMENTS. Here, for every company code that should map outgoing payments, you have to define the valid *payment methods*. For each payment method, you specify a minimum and a maximum amount, for example. Additionally, you define whether payments in foreign currencies or to foreign banks are allowed and, if required, which forms have to be printed. Furthermore, you define for each payment method which information is required, for example, the vendor address for payments by check or the bank details for bank transfers.

Bank determination

Because enterprises today typically have more than one bank account and often at different banks, bank determination needs to be configured. Here, depending on the payment methods and currencies, you can define a ranking of the *house banks* and accounts. In the standard SAP system, the bank determination is part of Customizing. An option for changing the ranking of house banks and accounts in the course of day-to-day operations is not provided. However, many users want to keep the option for possible short-term adjustments open. You can meet this user department requirement by defining tables T042A and T042D as *current settings*.

[+]

SAP Notes on Bank Determination

For further information on the exact procedure for bank determination, refer to SAP Notes 77430 (Customizing: CURRENT SETTINGS), 69642 (Planned Amounts [T042D] Cannot be Maintained), and 81153 (Bank Selection as a Current Setting).

Information from the vendor master and single document

You have two options for selecting the payment method that should be used for an individual open item: by definition in the company code-specific data of the vendor master or directly in single documents. Normally, the payment method is defined in the vendor master. You should select the option of assigning the payment method at the document level only if you want to use a specific payment method for individual documents. If a payment method is specified twice, the more specific definition wins; that is, the single document. You can always define more than one payment method in the PAYMENT METHODS field. If there are several entries, the priority of the entries decreases from the left to the right—that is, the first entry from the left usually wins.

Figure 4.50 shows an example. Here, three entries are maintained in the PAYMENT METHODS field: U for domestic bank transfer, S for payment by check, and L for foreign bank transfer. A payment run that provides for all three payment methods pays open items of vendor K1100 via domestic bank transfer because this payment method comes first. A payment run that only allows for payment by check or foreign bank transfer, in contrast, would pay the vendor invoices with a check.

The vendor master also contains the bank details.

Using the Partner Bank Type [+]

Lederwaren-Manufaktur Mannheim has a leather supplier that supplies both the German and the Belgian production. The invoices of the supplier are directly paid by the respective branch office. Let us assume that the supplier has a German and a Belgian bank account. To minimize costs, the transfers should be made nationally: Brussels makes it payments to the Belgian vendor bank account and Mannheim to the German vendor bank. You can implement this using the partner bank type.

First, create the two bank accounts in the general vendor master view. For example, the Belgian account obtains the BE partner bank type and the German account the DE partner bank type. All invoices of this supplier that specify the BE partner bank type are now paid against its Belgian bank account and all with the DE partner bank type against the German account.

If the document does not define a partner bank type, the system always uses the first bank in the vendor master.

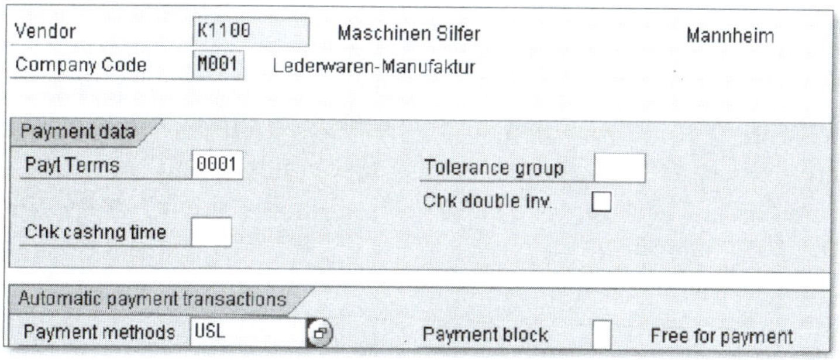

Vendor K1100 Maschinen Silfer Mannheim
Company Code M001 Lederwaren-Manufaktur

Payment data
Payt Terms 0001 Tolerance group
Chk double inv.
Chk cashng time

Automatic payment transactions
Payment methods USL Payment block Free for payment

Figure 4.50 Payment Methods in the Vendor Master

Payment run parameters

The payment run also allows you to set parameters you can use to configure the payment of open items. To do so, navigate to the payment run using Transaction F110 or in the user menu via ACCOUNTING • FINANCIAL ACCOUNTING • ACCOUNTS PAYABLE • PERIODIC PROCESSING • PAYMENTS. Here, you have to specify a scheduled execution day as well as an alphanumeric ID. It is important to know that the day of the execution is not relevant for the open items that are supposed to be selected or the value date of the payment. These are defined in the payment run.

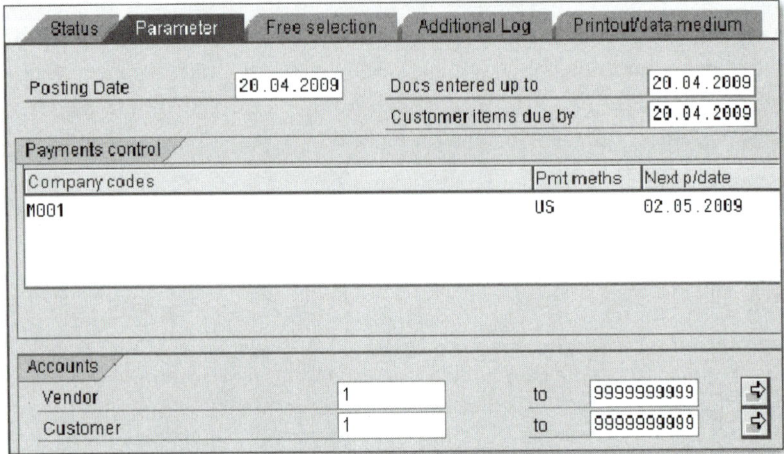

Figure 4.51 Definition of the Parameters in the Payment Run

Figure 4.51 shows an example of the *parameter definition* in a payment run. Here, you can find the posting date that is used for the accounting documents. You use the DOCUMENTS ENTERED UP TO and CUSTOMER ITEMS DUE BY fields to define which documents should be considered. In addition, you must enter various vendor and/or customer accounts that the payment run should take into account.

The payment run defines for which COMPANY CODES payments are made and which PAYMENT METHODS are considered. In this case also, the rule applies that the payment method on the very left has a higher priority than the one on its right. Via the date in the NEXT POSTING DATE field, the SAP system determines which open items that are not yet due have to be paid. Let us look at an example of an open item that is due on 08/15 (see Table 4.6).

Payment Run Date	Next Posting Date	Behavior
08/10	08/12	The document is not paid because the next payment run takes place before the due date (08/15).
08/10	08/18	The document is paid because it would be overdue for three days in the next payment run (08/18).

Table 4.6 Due Date and Payment

Grace days

However, you can also set grace days for yourself in Customizing. For example, if you define three grace days for this example, the open item will not be paid on 08/10 in the second case.

[+]

Activating the Additional Log

The SAP system allows for easy logging of the payment run, which enables you to easily track why the SAP system has (or has not) paid an open item or why a discount is used (or not).

For this purpose, you need to activate enhanced logging for the payment run on the ADDITIONAL LOG tab. This is strongly recommended for all vendors and customers considered in the payment run.

Payment proposal

During the further course of the payment run, the system creates a payment proposal. You can modify it by blocking items for payment or releasing blocked items for payment. However, this blocking (or releasing) of invoices applies only to this specific payment run. If you want to permanently block an invoice payment, you have to directly navigate to the document using Transaction FB02 and set a permanent payment block there.

Permanent Payment Block Overrides Bank Account Determination

Especially in medium-sized enterprises, the decision of which invoices will be paid and which will not be paid is made without system support. The enterprises often suspect that invoices could be paid "by mistake." However, you cannot block all invoices for payment by default because a payment block in the document prevents the system from determining the paying bank in the payment run. This means that if you release the payment block when modifying the payment proposal, you have to manually select the bank account from which you want to make the payment.

It is only during the update run that the system makes a posting "vendor to bank clearing" and thus clears the open item. In the last step, you can send a payment medium file to the bank or print payment advices, checks, bills of exchange, and so on.

After your bank has executed the payment request, the purchasing process is complete from the accounts payable accounting view. But there is still another leg of the value flow, which leads you from the invoice receipt directly to G/L accounting and maps the taxation of purchases.

Although numerous tax types are involved when purchasing goods or services, we want to focus on a widely used type: the tax on sales/purchases.

4.10 Mapping the Tax on Sales/Purchases

Tasks of the tax code

In the SAP system, the tax code is the central object for mapping tax on sales/purchases. It defines the type as well as the calculation and posting of taxes.

Tax codes enable you to map the input and output tax. There are also tax codes for the handling of withholding taxes, which are particularly critical in Southern Europe. They will not be discussed in further detail here.

Attributes of a tax procedure

You can find the settings for the tax on sales/purchases centrally in the Financial Accounting component. Customizing takes place in the Implementation Guide under FINANCIAL ACCOUNTING (NEW) • FINANCIAL ACCOUNTING GLOBAL SETTINGS (NEW) • TAX ON SALES/PURCHASES. The standard SAP system provides country-specific pricing procedures, called tax procedures, which meet country-specific basic taxation conditions. However, you should always check the settings for any new SAP system implementation.

Scope of tax procedures

You need to assign a tax procedure to every country in which you perform business transactions that are subject to taxes on sales/purchases. In turn, the tax procedure is assigned a tax code. This means that tax procedures must include all required tax types and rates in the form of tax codes. For example, if accounts need to be assigned for Belgian taxes on sales/purchases for an incoming invoice in Germany, a code is required that enables you to determine the Belgian tax correctly and clearly identify it for the tax return later on.

Maintaining tax codes

You maintain the tax codes using Transaction FTXP. The system indirectly determines which tax code is used by initially querying the country. Let us continue with the VN tax code, which was already used in the sample postings (see Figure 4.52).

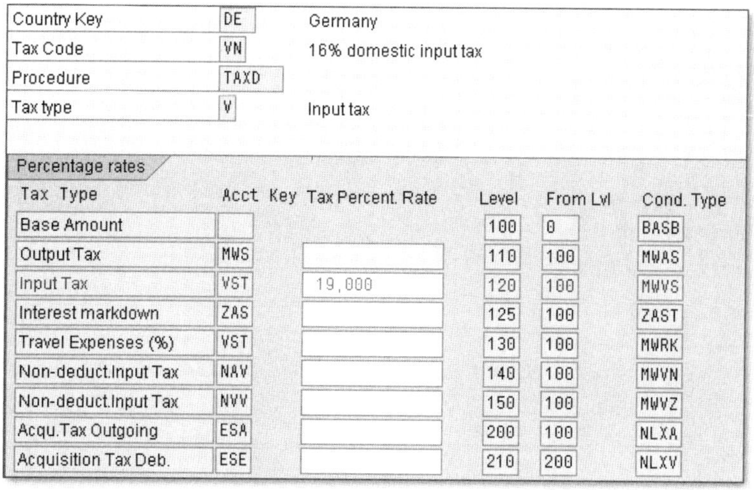

Country Key	DE	Germany
Tax Code	VN	16% domestic input tax
Procedure	TAXD	
Tax type	V	Input tax

Percentage rates

Tax Type	Acct Key	Tax Percent. Rate	Level	From Lvl	Cond. Type
Base Amount			100	0	BASB
Output Tax	MWS		110	100	MWAS
Input Tax	VST	19,000	120	100	MWVS
Interest markdown	ZAS		125	100	ZAST
Travel Expenses (%)	VST		130	100	MWRK
Non-deduct.Input Tax	NAV		140	100	MWVN
Non-deduct.Input Tax	NVV		150	100	MWVZ
Acqu.Tax Outgoing	ESA		200	100	NLXA
Acquisition Tax Deb.	ESE		210	200	NLXV

Figure 4.52 Maintaining the VN Tax Code

This example shows the input tax code for a taxation of 19 percent. To determine the tax amount, the system uses only active lines of the procedure. You can identify them because they are highlighted in blue writing. In this example, it is level 120.

Account determination

The account determination is also defined at the tax code level. This means that you only have to specify the tax code in the posting process. The system can then assume the determination and posting processes. Both in the procurement process and in the sales and distribution process, this provides for significant advantages for the upstream MM and SD components. They only have to identify the correct code; the Financial Accounting component then assumes further processing. The tax procedure also defines the basic screen, including the lines

Figure 4.53 provides a schematic overview of the Customizing.

[+]

Transferring the Sales Tax Code

Sales tax codes have the disadvantage that they may not be correctly transferred to the target system. The SAP system therefore provides a download and upload function for which the target client needs to be modifiable. When you create individual codes, the direct maintenance is usually less time-consuming in the target system.

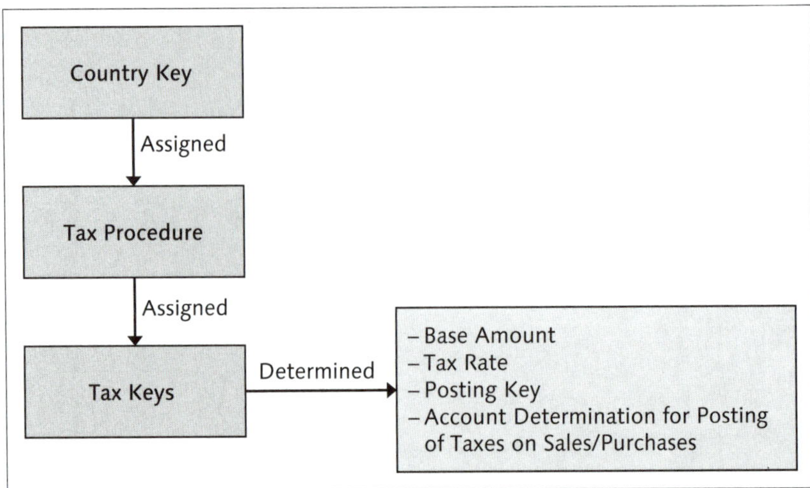

Figure 4.53 Schematic Illustration of the Customizing for the Tax on Sales/Purchases

Enjoy transactions

When creating new sales tax codes, there is an additional step you need to perform. You have to permit the new code for what are called Enjoy transactions. In contrast to older transactions, for example FB01 (General Posting), these transactions—such as FB50 (Enter G/L Account Document) and FB60 (Enter Invoice)—enable you to enter all specifications in one screen. You register the tax codes using Transaction OBZT (Tax Code Selection for Transactions), which you can find in the Implementation Guide, for example, under Financial Accounting (New) • Accounts Receivable and Accounts Payable • Business Transactions • Incoming Invoices/Credit Memos • Incoming Invoices/Credit Memos - Enjoy • Define Tax Code per Transaction.

Here, depending on the country keys (required for determining the tax procedure) and tax codes, you can define for which posting procedures a code is available in the Enjoy transactions. The following posting procedures are available:

- (Logistics) invoice verification
- Invoice receipt for financial accounting
- Invoice issue for financial accounting
- All transactions

You usually should not use the "all transactions" selection because this way, for example, you also provide tax codes for the output tax to users who want to enter incoming invoices. You must assign the input tax codes both to the invoice verification and to the invoice receipt in Financial Accounting to allow for the use in Logistics Invoice Verification and within Accounts Payable.

If you forget this setting, you created the sales tax code but the system cannot use it in operational business.

4.11 Summary

This chapter explained that the purchasing process is characterized by high integration of inventory management in the MM component with Financial Accounting and Controlling. You already have to define many aspects in a purchase requisition or purchase order that control the remaining value flow.

If commitments management is enabled, Controlling is already supplied with information when a purchase requisition or purchase order is created. By creating a commitment, you can identify potential budget overruns before the actual value flow—that is, when the goods or invoices are received.

MM account determination is the central element for controlling the value flow in the purchasing process. It is quite complex but also ensures high automation in the process flow. If you do not want to configure account determination manually, you can use the account determination wizard. This wizard asks the most important questions, which were also introduced in this context. While the goods receipt usually does not pose any problems regarding the integration, the invoice receipt covers special cases. MM account determination is used here as well, for example, to map exchange rate differences or small price differences. Invoice verification enables you to set tolerances to block factually incorrect invoices for payment.

You usually link the goods receipt and the invoice receipt via a GR/IR account. Its maintenance is critical for correct mapping in the financial statement but is often neglected in real life.

However, the invoice receipt ensures the integration with accounts payable accounting by creating an open item on the vendor account that can be paid later on.

Except for commitments management, MM account determination, and goods receipts for purchase orders with account assignment, the topic is driven by accounting rather than cost accounting and the focus will probably be on invoice verification.

Businesses are not built, managed, and run for their own sake but with the goal to make profits. The most straightforward option for generating profits is to sell goods as profitably as possible.

5 Sales and Distribution Process

In the overall logistics process, there are two areas that are characterized by a high percentage of interaction with external business partners. Chapter 4 has already introduced the first area, the procurement process. This chapter now describes the sales and distribution process.

This process includes the sales of generated or traded products and services rendered and the SAP system provides a wide range of tools to map the sales and distribution activities. These activities range from classical SD (Sales and Distribution), to CRM (Customer Relationship Management), to industry-specific sales and distribution enhancements. This chapter also uses the example of Lederwaren-Manufaktur Mannheim and therefore focuses on the sales of products and trading goods that were manufactured in-house. The SD component is the technical utility used for mapping all value flow-relevant processes.

For many customers, the revenue achieved is the focus of the sales process. Additionally, there are further value flows that you must map in accounting and cost accounting. The chapter begins with an overview of the value flows that arise in the sales and distribution process. These value flows usually originate from the price determination of Sales and Distribution. Therefore, you need to know the structure and functioning of a price determination to understand the development of values.

Next, you will get to know the value flows in detail. Following the value flows, this chapter then discusses the individual value flows and their mapping in accounting and cost accounting. Here, the primary focus is on the integrated description of value flows.

5.1 Sales and Distribution Process in the SCOR Model

In the SCOR model, we are now in the sales and distribution section (deliver), which comprises the warehouse, sales order, and transport management. Here, you can distinguish four basic types of the process. Figure 5.1 illustrates this with a presentation of the design level in the adapted SCOR model.

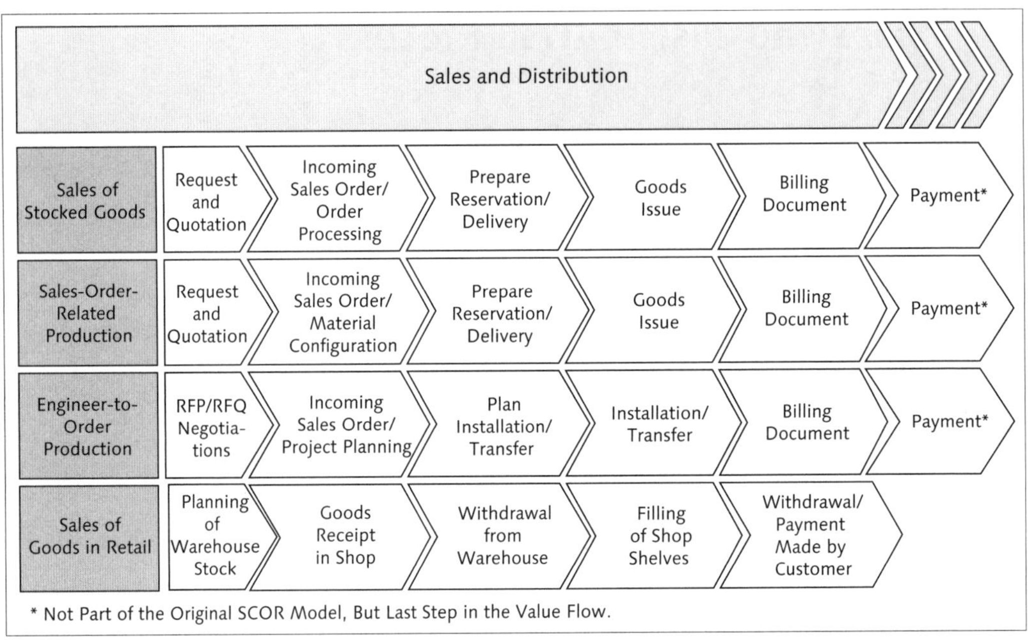

Figure 5.1 Sales Process in the Adapted SCOR Model

Because this book focuses on manufacturing enterprises, retail sales of goods is not further discussed.

The other three types of sales—*stocked goods, sales-order-related production*, and *engineer-to-order production*—differ only slightly at first glance. In fact, it is not really relevant for accounting whether it is the sales of standardized stocked goods or of an *engineer-to-order production* (e.g., the construction of a dam), even if the latter would presumably lead to deferral items in the financial statement due to the long runtime. Chapter 7, Closing and Reporting in SAP ERP, provides more detailed information on this topic.

Process category

The orientation of controlling is influenced by the *process category*. For an engineer-to-order production, the sales order is often used as a central cost object so that the real expenses are updated in addition to the revenues. This is not possible for an anonymous or customer-neutral stockholding. In cost accounting, it is of particular interest that at most, only the calculated costs incur in production and that the goods are not sold at a price that is too low. Chapter 6, Production Process, provides more information on this subject.

Moreover, not all process steps shown in Figure 5.1 are relevant for the value flow.

Account origination

In the account origination phase—that is, during inquiries, quotations, or negotiations with the customer—no relation develops between the enterprise and the customer that has to be mapped in accounting or cost accounting.

Start of the value flow—sales order

You therefore define the receipt of a *sales order as the start of the value flow.* This sales order is processed in SD. The entered sales order can be transferred to CO-PA, which enables controlling of the sales order stock. Initially, from the balance sheet perspective, this sales order is not relevant.

Delivery

The goods issue is the first point in the sales process that has an effect on the balance sheet. It is part of the logistics delivery. The concept of *delivery* combines activities such as picking of the goods in the warehouse, packaging, or printing of the delivery notes. The last steps include posting the goods issue in inventory management and mapping the transaction in the financial statements and the profit and loss statement. The transaction can—but does not have to be—transferred to overhead cost controlling. A transfer to costing-based CO-PA does not take place.

Billing document

Costing-based CO-PA receives the values of stock changes only with the *billing document*. In financial accounting, receivables, (forecasts of) revenues, and taxes (if applicable) are posted. This results in the open item in accounts receivable accounting.

Incoming payment

The clearing of this open item through an *incoming payment* concludes the sales process. With this step, you exit SD as the triggering component because this is a transaction in Financial Accounting. Integration is now only with cost accounting—and only if the transaction is designed accordingly.

Thus, values emerge in Financial Accounting and Controlling at different points in the sales process. Figure 5.2 shows an overview of the documents that are required respectively.

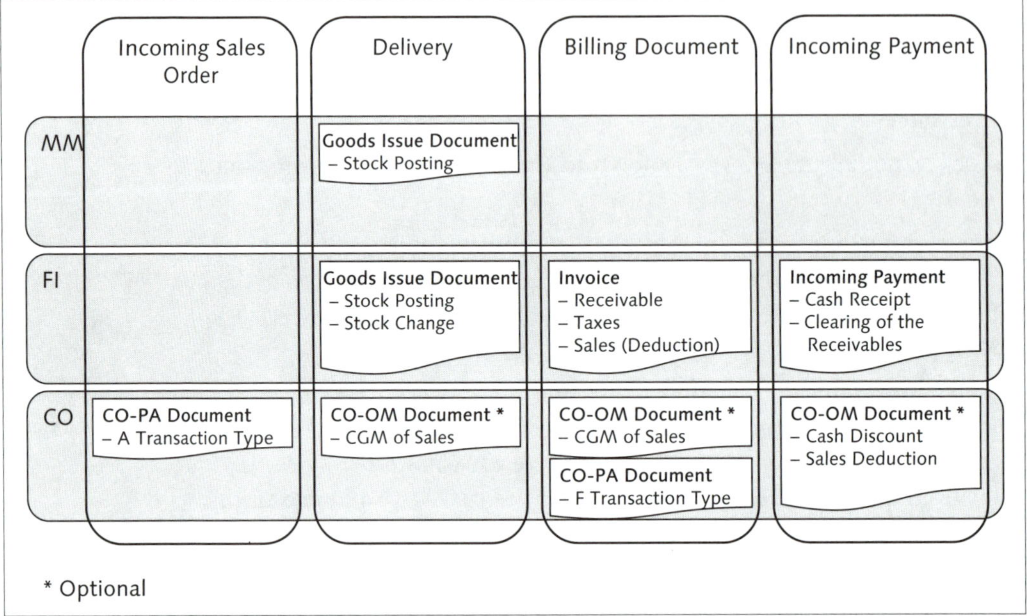

Figure 5.2 Value Flow of the Sales Process

The following sections discuss the individual steps and phases of the sales process in more detail. We will start with the sales order.

5.2 Sales Order as the Basis of Further Account Assignment

Even though the *sales order* itself has no relevance for accounting and can be displayed in CO-PA only optionally, important specifications are made here for the subsequent posting in Financial Accounting and Controlling. Financial Accounting and Controlling account assignments are made, and the value for the subsequent billing document is defined for the first time.

For the account assignments, the determination of profit centers and segments are particularly important aspects.

This section initially considers derivation options for the *profit center account assignment*. Various options are available to do this in the sales process. This forms the basis for segment derivation.

Source of Controlling account assignment

In the standard SAP system, the profit center and segment account assignment is derived when the sales order is saved for the first time. All documents in the remaining document flow take their account assignment from the sales order.

5.2.1 Profit Center Derivation

Profit center derivation from the material master

The easiest method of derivation is to copy the profit center from the plant level of the material master. There, you can find the profit center both on the SALES: GENERAL/PLANT tab and on the COSTING 1 tab, depending on the plant. Figure 5.3 shows an example. This procedure corresponds to the SAP standard.

The derivation from the material master is sufficient for the product-oriented profit center structure of Lederwaren-Manufaktur Mannheim.

Matrix organization with profit centers

However, many enterprises map a matrix organization in profit center accounting—for example, a combination of division and customer grouping. This often necessitates sales-oriented derivation of the profit center. This would enable Lederwaren-Manufaktur Mannheim to distinguish whether a bag is sold to a key account or to medium-sized retailer. Consequently, this requires you to take the customer into account when you derive the profit center.

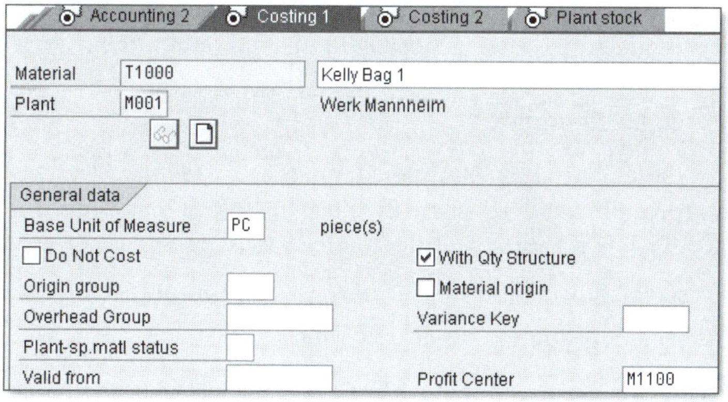

Figure 5.3 Profit Center Assignment in the Material Master

Using a substitution

SAP provides a substitution for this purpose. It enables you to find a constant profit center, depending on various fields of the sales order item. An example is the definition of Profit Center K1000 (Key-Accounts) if the sales order is implemented via Distribution Channel M1 (Key-Accounts).

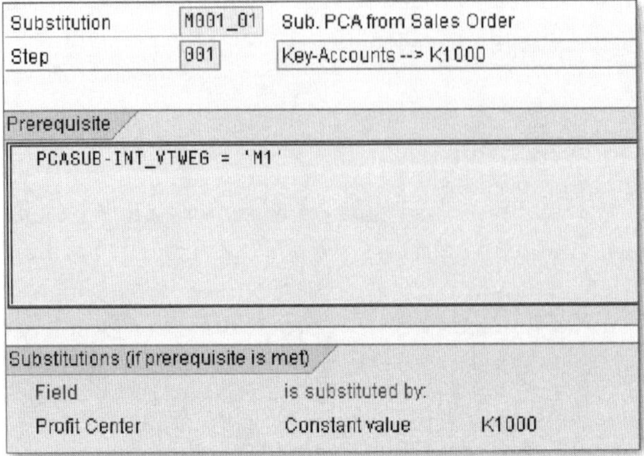

Figure 5.4 Profit Center Derivation via Substitution

You can maintain the substitution via Transaction OKEM. You can find the corresponding setting in the Implementation Guide under FINANCIAL ACCOUNTING (NEW) • GENERAL LEDGER ACCOUNTING (NEW) • TOOLS • VALIDATION/SUBSTITUTION • SUBSTITUTION OF PROFIT CENTERS IN CUSTOMER ORDERS • DEFINE SUBSTITUTION RULES.

Derivation options

Using the substitution, you can define constant values, assign a table field, or map complex facts. Then, it often makes sense to use a user exit. You can also transfer the profit center manually in the sales order item.

5.2.2 Deriving a Segment

Because only the Financial Accounting component knows the SEGMENT field, it is not possible in SD to manually transfer the segment. Thus, the segment must be derived automatically. You have two options:

- Derive the segment using the `FAGL_DERIVE_SEGMENT` BAdI
- Derive the segment from the profit center master record

When you create the document in the SAP General Ledger, the system initially checks whether the `FAGL_DERIVE_SEGMENT` BAdI is active and whether it can be used to derive the segment. If this is not possible, the derivation is carried out using the profit center.

Advantages and Effort for the Use of BAdIs [+]

The use of BAdIs considerably increases the level of freedom for segment reporting but nevertheless, you should not underestimate the implementation effort.

Mapping in CO-PA

In projects implementing Profitability Analysis, a lot of time is consumed answering the question of whether sales orders should be transferred to CO-PA. The answer depends on the industry and on the general controlling philosophy of an enterprise.

Meaning of industry and delivery times

In principle, the transfer of a received sales order to CO-PA lets you determine the result to be expected at a very early stage of the sales process. The entering of sales orders in CO-PA is interesting particularly for industries and enterprises in which a long period of time elapses between the incoming sales order and the billing document. Classic examples are the construction of a power plant or dam.

Transfer for long delivery times

Considering the model of Lederwaren-Manufaktur Mannheim, you can expect a *delivery time* of approximately three months for made-to-order shoes. Here, sales order controlling makes sense. For the mass production of belts in stock, however, it is not very useful because only a few days elapse between the incoming sales order and the billing document and the added value of information is low. Due to the short period of time involved, you have no option to take corrective action.

As you can see, the transfer of sales orders to CO-PA makes sense for make-to-order production and long delivery times. Thanks to early costing of the results to be expected, you can still take corrective measures in case of imminent losses. You cannot, however, initiate counter-measures for delivery times of only a few days. The assessment of sales order data in Controlling offers no benefits in this situation.

No Duplicated CO-PA Records in Sales Order Controlling [+]

An argument against the transfer of sales orders to CO-PA is to avoid "duplicated entries." It is correct that in addition to the sales order, you also transfer the corresponding billing document to CO-PA later on. However, you can differentiate the records using the TRANSACTION TYPE field. The transaction type for sales orders is A; billing documents are indicated with F.

An important element of sales orders is the costing of the sales price.

5.3 Price Determination as the Basis of Value Determination

Providing values for Financial Accounting and Controlling

Both accounting and cost accounting utilize the values of the price determination for the posting. Therefore, close cooperation of SD, Financial Accounting, and Controlling consultants is required, where the majority of requirements originate from cost accounting and not from financial accounting. With regard to the SD component, you must display a market-driven price determination, which represents a balancing act because many market requirements are contrary to the requirements of Controlling. In most cases, it is not sufficient to display a price for the goods and to add the corresponding taxes; usually, you are expected to provide detailed price costing.

Elements of price determination

You are provided with the following elements to determine the prices to be cost (see Section 5.3.2, Price-Determining Elements):

- Prices
- Surcharges and discounts
- Freights
- Shipping costs
- Tax

Costing-based elements

Additionally, there are elements that are not used for price determination but are used for costing (see Section 5.3.3, Costing-Based Elements), for example:

- Commissions (internal)
- Rebates (settled separately in the subsequent periods)
- Costing-based freights

All of these price elements are summarized in a *costing sheet*, which represents the price calculation in the system. The following sections first discuss the costing sheet and then the elements of price determination and costing.

5.3.1 Conditions and Costing Sheet

Costing sheet

You can maintain multiple price calculations (costing sheets) in parallel. Which costing sheet must be used for the sales order depends on the sales area, the sales document type, and the customer. Figure 5.5 shows an example of a *costing sheet*.

Procedure ZM1000 Standard

Control

Reference Step Overview

Step	Co	CTyp	Description	Fro	To	Ma	R	Stat	P	SuTot	Reqt	CalTy	BasTy	AccK	Accru
11	0	PR00	Price			☐	☐	☐			2			ERL	
13	0	PB00	Price (Gross)			☑	☐	☐			2			ERL	
14	0	PR02	Price Increased			☐	☐	☐			2			ERL	
15	0	ZK01	Variant Costs			☐	☐	☐	X		2			ERL	
100	0		Gross Value			☐	☐	☐	X	1		2			
101	0	KA00	Sales Promotion			☐	☐	☐	X		2			ERS	
102	0	K032	Price Group/Material			☐	☐	☐	X		2			ERS	
103	0	K005	Customer/Material			☐	☐	☐	X		2			ERS	
104	0	K007	Customer Discount			☐	☐	☐	X		2			ERS	
105	0	K004	Material			☐	☐	☐	X		2			ERS	
106	0	K020	Price Group			☐	☐	☐	X		2			ERS	
107	0	K029	Mat.Pricing Group			☐	☐	☐	X		2			ERS	
108	0	K030	Customer/Mat.Pr.Grp			☐	☐	☐	X		2			ERS	
109	0	K031	Price Grp/Mat.Pr.Grp			☐	☐	☐	X		2			ERS	
110	1	RA01	% Disc.from Gross	100		☑	☐	☐	X		2			ERS	
110	2	RA00	% Discount from Net			☑	☐	☐	X		2			ERS	

Figure 5.5 Pricing Costing Sheet

The structure of the SD costing sheet is similar to Microsoft Excel. You can carry out calculations in the individual rows and, in doing so, access any other rows. You implement the settings in Transaction V/08 or alternatively in the Implementation Guide under SALES AND DISTRIBUTION • BASIC FUNCTIONS • PRICING • PRICING CONTROL • DEFINE AND ASSIGN PRICING PROCEDURES • DEFINE PRICING PROCEDURE DETERMINATION.

Condition type

Each element (row) of the costing sheet is represented by a *condition type*. The condition type defines the *type*, for example, *price* or *discount/surcharge*, as well as its calculation base (absolute or percentage).

Customizing of condition types is very complex. You can find it in the Implementation Guide under SALES AND DISTRIBUTION • BASIC FUNCTIONS • PRICING • PRICING CONTROL • DEFINE CONDITION TYPES. Figure 5.6 shows PR0O, which is one of the default condition types in the SD component. Here, you can define many basic settings. For example, the CALCULATION TYPE specifies whether the pricing row is a fixed amount, a percentage, or a quantity-dependent price element.

Condition records

In the upper right corner of Figure 5.6, you can see the RECORDS FOR ACCESS button. You can use this button to maintain the *condition records* for condition type PR00. Figure 5.7 shows an example.

Condit. type PR00 Price
Access seq. PR00 Price
Records for access

Control data 1
Cond. class B Prices
Plus/minus positive a
Calculat.type C Quantity
Cond.category
Rounding rule Commercial
StrucCond.

Group condition
Group cond.
GrpCond.routine
RoundDiffComp

Changes which can be made
Manual entries C Manual entry has priority
Header condit.
Amount/percent
Qty relation
Item condition
Delete
Value
Calculat.type

Master data
valid from Today's date
PricingProc PR0000
Valid to 31.12.9999
delete fr. DB Do not delete (set the deletion
RefConType
Condition index
RefApplicatio
Condit.update

Figure 5.6 Condition Type Customizing (Excerpt)

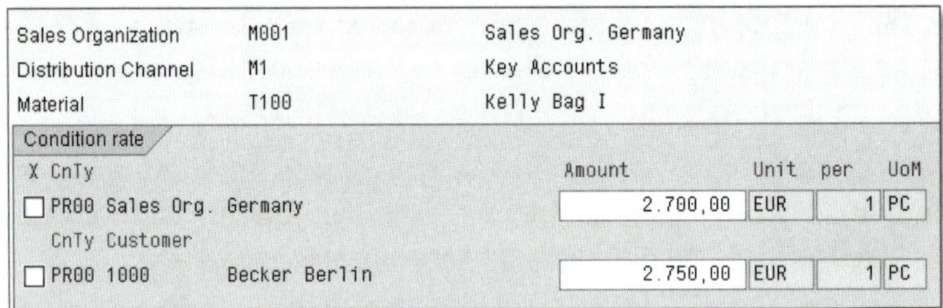

Figure 5.7 Condition Records for Condition Type PR00, Material T100

You can see that two prices (*condition records*) have been maintained for Material T100 because two entries were made with different prices. A customer is specified for the second entry but not for the first one. It is clear that maintaining different prices is common practice; for example, key accounts may get lower prices than new customers. But how does the system know which price should be used?

Access sequence

For this, you must maintain an *access sequence* that defines the sequence in which the system searches for prices. If you go back to Figure 5.6, you can see that Access Sequence PR 00 (shown in Figure 5.8) is assigned to the condition type.

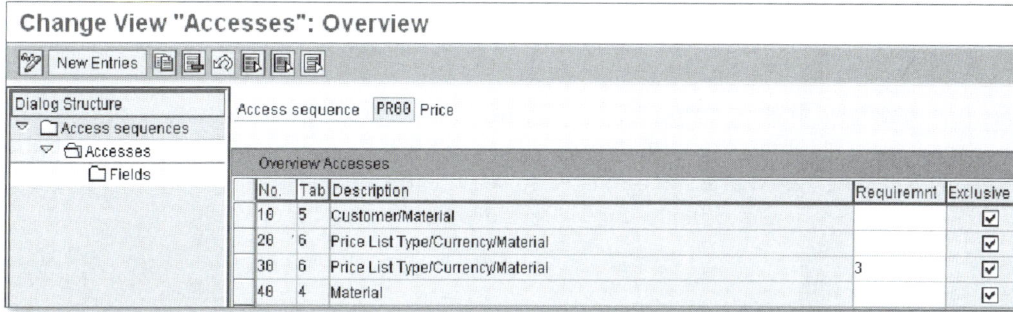

Figure 5.8 Overview of Access Sequence PR00

The condition type and the access sequence have the same name in the example. This makes it easier to understand the relationships; however, it is not necessary from a technical perspective.

The access sequence determines the order in which the maintained prices must be considered and the system searches each step for defined prices/information until the first valid entry is found. If you create a large number of steps, this may result in long runtimes as well as in lower transparency for the user.

[+]

Rule of Thumb: From Specific to General

The system goes through the access sequence until it finds a valid entry. It is therefore important to maintain entries with the greatest limitations at the beginning of the access sequence. Very general entries that are almost always valid (e.g., only material number) should be at the end of the derivation.

This ensures that special prices are applied. For example, you can assign a standard sales price to a material. If you maintained this price, which depends only on the material, at the first position of the access sequence, the other prices—for example, those that depend on the material and customer—would not apply.

Because the *access sequence* is often riddled with special cases, you can use conditions (ABAP-programmed exit structures) to regulate the relevance for each step of the access sequence.

Costing sheet

The *costing sheet* is also processed starting with row 1. The arrangement of the condition types follows the sequence of their calculation.

Table 5.1 maps Condition Type RA01 as an example. Row 110 refers to row 100 and calculates a surcharge or discount of 10 percent.

These settings for the costing sheet are part of Customizing. Thus, a user cannot intervene in the calculation pattern when a sales order is created or changed.

Subtotals

In this example you can also see that *subtotals* can be integrated. You can apply condition types to these subtotal rows. Row 100 is used to map the gross price accumulated so far, where gross must be understood not in the sense of "including value-added tax," but as "not reduced price."

Row	Condition Type		At Step	Value of Condition	Value of Row	Accumulated Value
11	PR00	Price		EUR 100.00	EUR 100.00	EUR 100.00
100		Gross				EUR 100.00
103	K005	Discount "Customer"		–10%	EUR -10.00	EUR 90.00
105	K004	Discount "Material"	103	–10%	EUR -9.00	EUR 81.00
110	RA01	Discount "Gross"	100	–10%	EUR -10.00	EUR 71.00

Table 5.1 Application Example for Surcharges and Discounts

Whether a step in the costing sheet should be processed within the framework of pricing can be additionally restricted using the conditions (ABAP-programmed exit structures).

First, you always position the item-based price elements and then the superordinate conditions such as freights.

The SAP system provides a complex tool for an equally complex topic as this brief discussion on pricing already indicates. We will now detail the elements of pricing, which were mentioned earlier.

5.3.2 Price-Determining Elements

Price

Initially, the *price* must be mentioned as a price-determining element.

The influencing information for a price can originate from the *article*, including its grouping characteristics, and from the *customer*, including its grouping characteristics, as well as from all organizational elements of *sales and distribution*.

- **Article**
  Product hierarchies or material groups are examples of typical groupings of articles in the SAP system. You can also use elements of classification. An extreme example would be the variant pricing.
- **Customer**
  On the customer side, customer hierarchies, which are mapped via partner roles or customer groups, can be used.

You can use these means to define prices based on a combination of customer and article. It is not necessary to define the price on a common level for all salable articles; a valid price is determined respectively via the access sequence.

Additionally, you can define price list types and assign them to customers. For example, Lederwaren-Manufaktur Mannheim can define a *key accounts* type and a second type, *private persons*, and provide different prices respectively. In each price list type, a price is defined for each material number.

Surcharges and discounts

The prices found can then be changed with any number of surcharges and discounts. A typical *discount* is a customer-specific discount. However, there are also article-specific discounts. If multiple discounts are granted, you must specify in the costing sheet whether a discount is granted for the initial value for the value that has accumulated so far (already reduced). The former case is referred to as *net discount*. If the discount is applied to a higher step, this is referred to as *gross discount*. The price changes according to this pattern.

Table 5.1 includes both variants. Row 105 is a net discount that calculates 10 percent of the preceding row 103. The discount in row 110, however, calculates from row 100; consequently, it does not consider the price changes in rows 103 and 105.

Changing the values manually

It must also be defined whether the values found may be changed manually or whether manual changes of the price calculation is only permitted via additional condition types. The advantage of the second variant is that you can determine at any time which changes have been made by the user. This is often a requirement from reporting.

Condition exclusion

In addition to pricing with a tabular structure, you can also work with *condition exclusions*. An example is the *best price determination*, which is particularly common in the retail environment. In this procedure, you have several options for price calculation. For example, you can determine general prices according to the catalog and additionally implement customer-specific pricing.

All calculation variants are stored in the costing sheet. You can use the *condition exclusion procedure* to determine that the lowest price for this order is set as the active value. The other condition types and their values then only have statistical character.

With condition exclusion, you can also specify that no further discount is granted if a specific discount has already been found. You would use this, for example, if you want to grant a discount due to a clearance sale but want to exclude that additional quantity discounts are granted.

Financial Accounting interface

Each row of the costing sheet relevant for accounting must be provided with an *account key* that is responsible for transferring the value to Financial Accounting (see Figure 5.9). Section 5.7.3, Presentation of the Sales Revenues, provides further information on this topic.

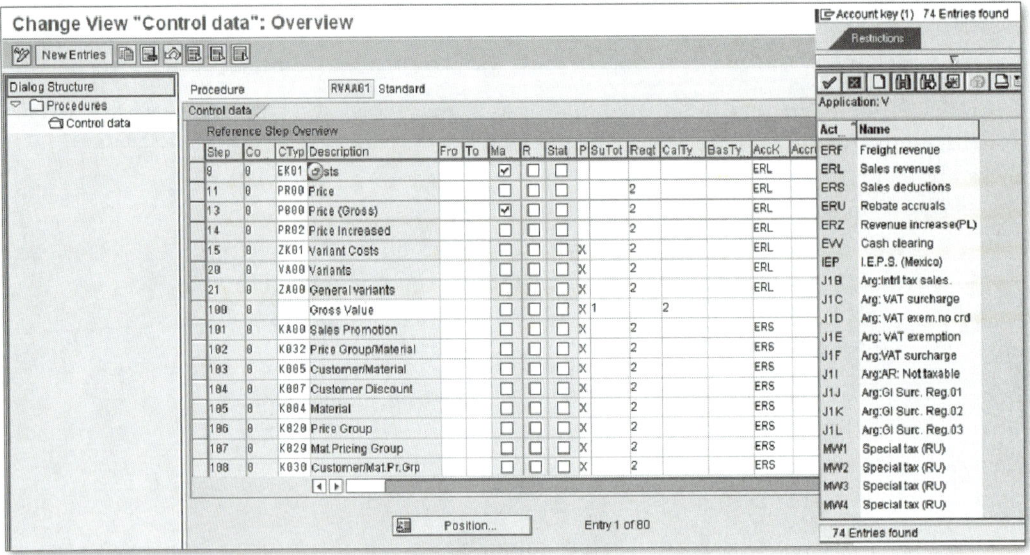

Figure 5.9 Assigning Account Keys

Controlling interface

For updating CO-PA, you must assign the condition types to the value fields of CO-PA (see Figure 5.10).

Each condition type used that is not statistical must refer to a value field. Here, it is possible that multiple condition types refer to a common value field. For example, discounts are often calculated in a differentiated manner but are controlled using a single value field, the PRICE REDUCTION value field. Statistical conditions can also refer to value fields.

Change View "CO-PA: Assignment of SD Conditions

New Entries

Op. concern LWA6 Lederwaren-Manufaktur EUROPE

CTyp	Name	Val. fld	Description	Transfer +/-
HA00	Percentage Discount	VV920	Sales deductions	☐
HD00	Freight	VV100	Outgoing freight	☐
K004	Material	VV095		☐
K005	Customer/Material	VV030	Customer discount	☐
K007	Customer Discount	VV030	Customer discount	☐
K020	Price Group	VV095		☐
K029	Mat.Pricing Group	VV095		☐
K030	Customer/Mat.Pr.Grp	VV030	Customer discount	☐
K031	Price Grp/Mat.Pr.Grp	VV095		☐
K032	Price Group/Material	VV095		☐
KA00	Sales Promotion	VV095		☐
KF00	Freight	VV100	Outgoing freight	☐
NETP	Price	ERLOS	Revenue	☐
PDIF	Diff.value (own)	VV095		☐
PN00	Net Price	ERLOS	Revenue	☐
PR00	Price	ERLOS	Revenue	☐

Figure 5.10 Assignment of SD Conditions to Value Fields

Generate Comparable Values [+]

It is important that the values are "comparable;" that is, there cannot be a mix of tax-exempt and taxed values! Otherwise, you would literally be comparing apples and oranges.

5.3.3 Costing-Based Elements

Costing-based elements and other elements initially only differ in their "statistical" selection in the costing sheet. All controls and settings for condition type, condition table, and access sequence are identical. The only exception is rebate conditions.

When an element is selected as statistical, the system determines the value. However, the row is not included in the summation of the value to be invoiced. Costing-based elements can be "added" at every step. They are preferably used to provide additional line item-related values for CO-PA.

Commission

Costing-based elements are often used for the statistical determination of *commissions*, which are internal payments based on the sales or implemented prices per customer/article. Usually, they are not provided globally so that no uniform percentage applies for all sales invoiced. Instead, the payment depends on specific article spectrums and often also the implemented prices. For this purpose, you define your own conditions that are set in the costing sheet. The value determined using these conditions is provided to a separate field during the transfer to CO-PA.

[!]

No Automatic Posting and Payment to the Commission Recipient

With the implementation of statistical elements for calculating commissions, you neither implement automatic posting nor payment to the commission recipient. You use this option to directly supplement the presentation of CO-PA line items.

Rebate

Rebates are a special form of pricing. You map rebates using standard pricing means. However, the difference with rebates is that they update their values in rebate agreements from which you then generate a rebate settlement retroactively (see Figure 5.11).

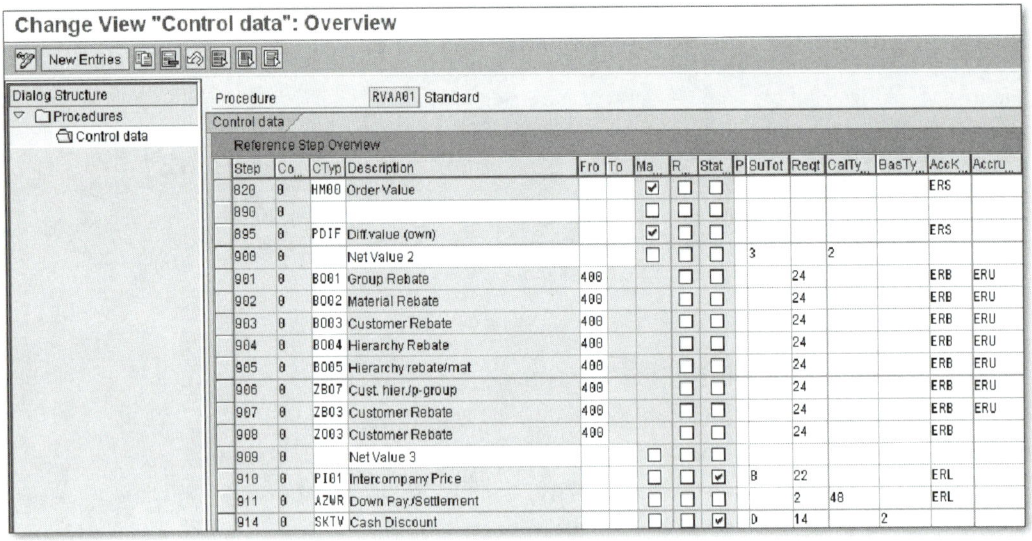

Change View "Control data": Overview

New Entries

Dialog Structure
- Procedures
  - Control data

Procedure RVAA01 Standard

Control data

Reference Step Overview

Step	Co	CTyp	Description	Fro	To	Ma	R	Stat	P	SuTot	Reqt	CalTy	BasTy	AccK	Accru
820	0	HM00	Order Value			☑	☐	☐						ERS	
890	0					☐	☐	☐							
895	0	PDIF	Diff.value (own)			☑	☐	☐						ERS	
900	0		Net Value 2			☐	☐	☐		3		2			
901	0	B001	Group Rebate	400			☐	☐			24			ERB	ERU
902	0	B002	Material Rebate	400			☐	☐			24			ERB	ERU
903	0	B003	Customer Rebate	400			☐	☐			24			ERB	ERU
904	0	B004	Hierarchy Rebate	400			☐	☐			24			ERB	ERU
905	0	B005	Hierarchy rebate/mat	400			☐	☐			24			ERB	ERU
906	0	ZB07	Cust. hier./p-group	400			☐	☐			24			ERB	ERU
907	0	ZB03	Customer Rebate	400			☐	☐			24			ERB	ERU
908	0	Z003	Customer Rebate	400			☐	☐			24			ERB	
909	0		Net Value 3			☐	☐	☐							
910	0	PI01	Intercompany Price			☐	☐	☑		B	22			ERL	
911	0	AZWR	Down Pay./Settlement			☐	☐	☐			2	48		ERL	
914	0	SKTV	Cash Discount			☐	☐	☑		D	14		2		

Figure 5.11 Controlling the Rebate Settlement

In the costing sheet, rebates are considered statistical elements and are not included in the direct billing document determination; however, they are not labeled as statistical.

Moreover, rebates can be supplemented with two account keys, ERU and ERB. With ERU, you post the determined value as an accrual directly in Financial Accounting. With ERB, you can then close the provision account for the settlement of the rebate agreement.

5.3.4 Special Business Transactions

Sale to business and private customers

Special requirements arise if enterprises such as Lederwaren-Manufaktur Mannheim sell the same article both to business and private customers. Let us recall: Lederwaren-Manufaktur Mannheim also sells matching accessories for shoes to private customers.

Gross/net schema

For private customer sales, the invoiced values must be presented as gross values, that is, in what is called a *net schema*. Additionally, the tax amount contained in the billing document value must be indicated. To meet this requirement, you must work with two costing sheets:

- Standard
- Standard including value-added tax

For the second schema, standard including value-added tax, all prices must be duplicated: Each price must be presented with and without tax. This, however, has the disadvantage of more complex master data maintenance.

Standard SAP system

The standard SAP system suggests to process the gross schema completely and then "de-tax" the complete, accumulated value for the transfer to Financial Accounting, transferring the two values in differentiated form.

Problems arise with this process because no sales deductions and/or proportions of freight charges can be transferred. Moreover, the transfer to CO-PA is only possible as gross on the other conditions. Consequently, comparability or shared reporting of these business transactions is not possible.

Detailed de-taxation

A better alternative is detailed de-taxation. The level of detail is determined by the value fields in CO-PA. This means that the gross value is summarized for each value field and then de-taxed by Condition MWS* (copy of MWSI). This enables de-taxed transfer to the value fields in CO-PA.

Table 5.2 shows that the VAT share and net value is calculated for each gross value. In this example, the calculation is carried out for row 10, the original gross value, and for row 110, a discount. Now, the tax amount must be rounded up or down to the nearest whole number in each calculation. The more calculations—and thus roundings—a price determination includes, the more rounding differences cumulate. If you calculated the tax once at the end of the determination, this would result in the identical tax value in a small example like the one in Table 5.2. With more calculation rows, however, the tax that is determined in many individual steps deviates from the tax that is determined in a single step.

Row	Condition Type		Value of Condition	Tracing Factor	Accumulated Value
10	PB00	Gross Price	EUR 100.00		EUR 119.00
20	ZMWP	*VAT Share Price*	19%		EUR 19.00
100		*Net price*			EUR 100.00
110	K005	*Gross Discount*	–10%	for EUR 100.00	EUR -11.19
120	ZMWR	VAT Share Discount	19%		EUR -1.19
200		*Net Discount*			EUR -10.00
400		*End Value Gross*			EUR 107.81
410	MWST	VAT included			EUR 17.21
420	NETW	*Net Value*			EUR 90.60

Table 5.2 Example of a Gross Schema

Now, the trick is to minimize the differences to the components and levels that are required by reporting in Controlling by reducing the taxation.

Net schema

You must then determine the differences for the gross schema and assign them proportionally to the origin. Table 5.3 shows the corresponding process for the *net schema*, in which you must set Condition DIFF for the rounding differences.

Row	Condition Type		Value of Condition	Tracing Factor	Accumulated Value
10	PR00	*Price*	EUR 100.00		EUR 100.00
110	K005	*Discount*	–10%	for EUR 100.00	EUR -10.00
400		End Value Net			EUR 90.00
410	MWST	*with VAT*			EUR 17.10
		Gross			EUR 107.10

Table 5.3 Example of a Pure Net Schema

Compared to the gross schema in Table 5.2, the difference of 60 cents in the net schema is distributed on a value basis respectively—that is, proportionately according to values, price, and discount portion. The distribution is displayed using the additional difference conditions (DIFF).

The entire pricing is passed through during the creation of the sales order. Later, when the billing document is created, you can either copy the price from the order on a quantity basis or trigger completely new pricing during invoice creation.

Trigger New Pricing During Invoice Creation [Ex]

This variant is often used if precious metals were processed in the product sold because this way, the precious metal is valuated with the current price.

Price fluctuations between the receipt of the sales order and invoice creation are not for the account of the seller.

However, the goods issue occurs between these two transactions in the sales process (see Section 5.4). Before you learn more about this topic, we will first discuss the transfer to CO-PA.

Assigning value fields

The condition types of the price determination are the basis for populating CO-PA from SD. As already discussed in Chapter 3, Section 3.5, CO-PA as a Central Reporting Tool, you can link condition types with *value fields* in CO-PA. Depending on the Controlling approach, you can then transfer the values of the conditions to CO-PA when the sales order is received and/or when the invoice is created.

Definitions for the transfer must be made in the Implementation Guide under CONTROLLING • PROFITABILITY ANALYSIS • FLOWS OF ACTUAL VALUES • TRANSFER OF INCOMING SALES ORDERS or TRANSFER OF BILLING DOCUMENTS.

Initially, you assign the value fields to the condition types. Figure 5.12 shows an excerpt of the settings for Lederwaren-Manufaktur Europe.

In the figure, you can see that several condition types point to one value field. Because the evaluation in CO-PA is possible at the value field level only, you should ensure that you do not compress too much. However, it also does not make sense to create a separate value field for each condition type, especially because a maximum of 120 value fields are allowed in CO-PA and because values from overhead cost controlling and production must be mapped in addition to the sales order or the billing document.

Assigning quantity fields

In addition to values, you usually also want to present sales quantities in CO-PA. You must therefore establish a connection between the SD *quantity fields* and the CO-PA quantity fields.

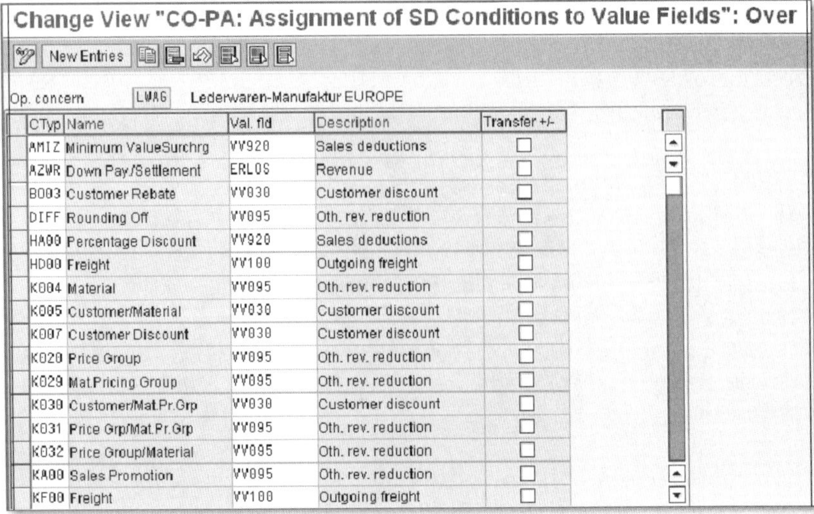

CTyp	Name	Val. fld	Description	Transfer +/-
AMIZ	Minimum ValueSurchrg	VV920	Sales deductions	☐
AZWR	Down Pay./Settlement	ERLOS	Revenue	☐
B003	Customer Rebate	VV030	Customer discount	☐
DIFF	Rounding Off	VV095	Oth. rev. reduction	☐
HA00	Percentage Discount	VV920	Sales deductions	☐
HD00	Freight	VV100	Outgoing freight	☐
K004	Material	VV095	Oth. rev. reduction	☐
K005	Customer/Material	VV030	Customer discount	☐
K007	Customer Discount	VV030	Customer discount	☐
K020	Price Group	VV095	Oth. rev. reduction	☐
K029	Mat.Pricing Group	VV095	Oth. rev. reduction	☐
K030	Customer/Mat.Pr.Grp	VV030	Customer discount	☐
K031	Price Grp/Mat.Pr.Grp	VV095	Oth. rev. reduction	☐
K032	Price Group/Material	VV095	Oth. rev. reduction	☐
KA00	Sales Promotion	VV095	Oth. rev. reduction	☐
KF00	Freight	VV100	Outgoing freight	☐

Figure 5.12 Assignment of Condition Types to Value Fields

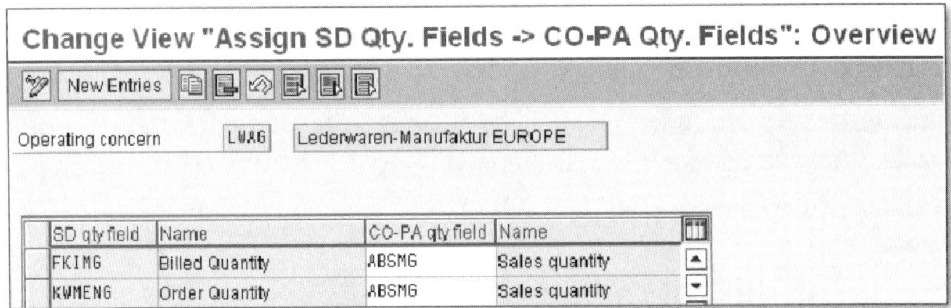

SD qty field	Name	CO-PA qty field	Name
FKIMG	Billed Quantity	ABSMG	Sales quantity
KWMENG	Order Quantity	ABSMG	Sales quantity

Figure 5.13 Assigning Quantity Fields

Figure 5.13 shows an example for Lederwaren-Manufaktur Europe. In this case, different quantities are shown, for example, the order quantity and the billed quantity. This way, you can evaluate in CO-PA whether you can deliver the sales orders completely—an important factor for customer satisfaction.

5.4 Goods Issue

As already described in Section 5.1, Sales and Distribution Process in the SCOR Model, the goods issue posting is the last step in the subprocess of logistics delivery. The processing of the goods issue posting can be carried out for each individual delivery or as mass processing, for example, for all deliveries on a given day.

In accounting, the goods issue process affects the financial statement and the profit and loss statement. In the financial statement, you must reduce the stock values, which results in a reduction of the assets. The changes in stock are posted as an offsetting item in the profit and loss statement.

Effect on financial statement and profit and loss statement

This posting of the change in stock can be forwarded to overhead cost controlling. If a transfer should take place, you must clarify to which Controlling object the account assignment should be done.

Defining a *fixed account assignment* is a simple method to accomplish this; however, with little informative value. You can define a fixed value using Transaction OKB9. However, the grid is very large because the defined cost center or internal order is defined only depending on a company code and a cost element, possibly in combination with the business area or profit center. You can use Transaction OVF3 to define a default cost center for each sales organization, distribution channel, division, and order reason.

Fixed account assignment and default account assignment

Of course, the variants via a Controlling substitution or a default account assignment in the cost element master are always available. However, at this point, you should ask yourself whether it really makes sense to transfer the stock changes of goods issue to overhead cost controlling. As an alternative, you can also transfer the goods value—that is, the stock change—to CO-PA, together with the billing document.

The valuation of material stocks was already mentioned in Chapter 3, Basic Principles of Integration in SAP ERP, and is discussed in detail in Chapter 6, Production Process. Goods issue uses the respective current *valuation price of the material*. In this process, price control of the material using the floating average price or the standard price is also considered.

Valuating according to the current valuation price of the material

[+]

Account-Based Value of the Goods Issue Posting

For goods issue posting, the total value results from the current valuation price of the material, multiplied by the posted quantity.

The delivery is created in SD. For stock materials, this process results in a goods issue posting in Material Management (MM). If the material is managed not only on a quantity basis but also on a value basis, a corresponding posting is carried out in Financial Accounting. Figure 5.14 shows the document flow. You can view the document flow by displaying the sales order via Transaction VA03 and then selecting the icon.

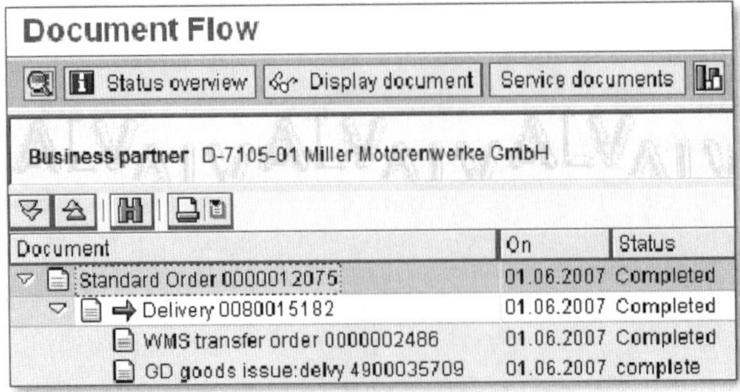

Figure 5.14 SD Document Flow up to Goods Issue

Quantity flow in MM

Select the last line with the goods issue and click on the DISPLAY DOCUMENT button. The system takes you to the material document, which shows only the material, quantity, and movement type (see Figure 5.15).

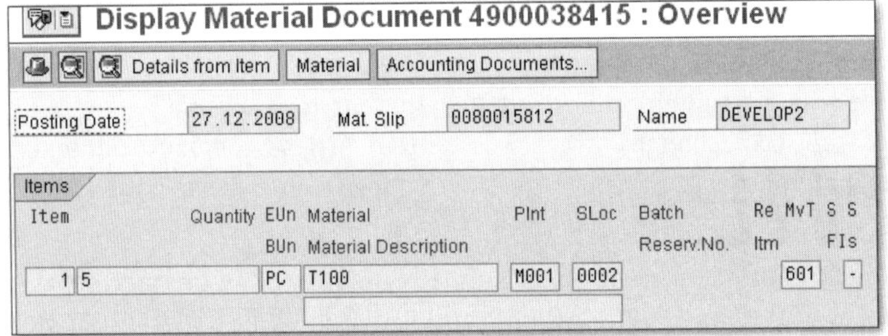

Figure 5.15 Material Document for Goods Issue

Value flow in Financial Accounting

The value flow is only visible in the documents of Financial Accounting. Because you are working with the SAP General Ledger and have activated Profit Center Accounting and Sales Accounting, you now receive a Financial Accounting document in ledger 0L (see Figure 5.16).

Data Entry View

Document Number	4900000002	Company Code	M001	Fiscal Year	2008
Document Date	27.12.2008	Posting Date	27.12.2008	Period	12
Reference	0080015812	Cross-CC no.			
Currency	EUR	Texts exist	☐	Ledger Group	

C...	Itm	PK	S	Account	Description	Amount	Curr.	Profit Center	Segment	Billing Doc.
M001	1	99		320000	Finished goods	17.500,00-	EUR	M1100	M_BAGS	80015812
	2	81		892000	Inventory change - f	17.500,00	EUR	M1100	M_BAGS	80015812

Figure 5.16 Financial Accounting Document for Goods Issue

Valuation of goods issue

The value of the goods issue results from the delivered quantity and the valuated price of the material based on the material master. In this example, this entails five bags with a value of EUR 3,500.00 each. You can see the total value of EUR 17,500.00 in the AMOUNT column.

Account determination for stock issue

The accounts result from the *MM account determination*. The reduction of stock in line 1 derives from the BSX transaction (stock posting) and the valuation class M100 for finished goods.

The second document item determines the account from the GBB transaction (offsetting entry for inventory posting) in combination with the general modification constant VAX (goods issues without Controlling account assignment) and again valuation class M100 for finished goods. The defined account 892000 INVENTORY CHANGE - FINISHED GOODS is not created as a cost element, which is why in this case, no document is created in overhead cost controlling. Lederwaren-Manufaktur Mannheim decided against the presentation of changes in stock in Controlling.

Profit center account assignment from sales order

Section 5.2, Sales Order as the Basis of Further Account Assignment, already discussed that the profit center determined in the sales order is forwarded to the subsequent documents and therefore also to the goods issue. To ensure that the system posts the change to stock to the profit center of the sales order during the goods issue, this account must be defined as a profit and loss account but must not be a cost element.

If the stock change account is created as a cost element (for example, for account-based Profitability Analysis), this account must have a "real" Controlling account assignment and therefore derives the profit center from the Controlling account assignment.

Do Not Create the Stock Change Account as a Cost Element [+]

If you use profit center accounting and costing-based Profitability Analysis, it is recommended to not create the stock change account as a cost element. This way, no transfer is carried out to overhead cost controlling and, above all, the profit center is not taken from the material of the goods issue but from the sales order.

No effect on CO-PA

A document is also not created in costing-based CO-PA. This is because the update in CO-PA is carried out according to cost of sales accounting. Therefore, the transaction is not relevant for Profitability Analysis until the creation of the billing document and the resulting sales. The goods usage indicated in the Financial Accounting document can then be updated in CO-PA within the framework of billing.

Because the delivery and billing document creation are implemented in two technically separate steps, it is important—especially at the end of the period—that all deliveries relevant for billing are billed and transferred to accounting.

After the account determination has been clarified, the goods issue posting usually runs without problems from the accounting and controlling perspective.

5.5 Presentation of Receivables

When you assess the performance of an enterprise, the main focus is on the EBIT (*Earnings Before Interests and Taxes*). But you should not forget that the highest sales and the best EBIT cannot ensure the continued existence of an enterprise if no consistent receivables management is applied. This includes, on the one hand, a prompt *billing document* that is sent to the customer so that a legally effective *receivable* is created, and, on the other hand, regular *monitoring* of unpaid items and collection of overdue items.

Laws

In international law, there are no detailed specifications for presenting receivables in the financial statement. In general, receivables must be subdivided in *receivables from goods and services* and other receivables. Moreover, it must be communicated which share accounts for affiliated or associated companies.

Created during billing

Regarding the time of receivable creation, international accounting principles also agree to a large extent: the time of billing the customer is what is relevant. This complies with the common procedure in the SAP system: Immediately after the creation of the billing document in SD, the data and the billing date are transferred to financial accounting.

Dunning history of smaller enterprises

Especially small enterprises are frequently affected by liquidity problems because they create outgoing invoices too late and respond too late or too kindly to their customers' delays in payment. In such cases, the functions of *Accounts Receivable* (FI-AR) can provide great support.

Accounts Receivable (FI-AR)

FI-AR is the most commonly known component for mapping receivables in SAP. It is part of the standard components in external accounting. Additionally, SAP provides *Contract Accounts Receivable and Payable* (CA) with mass processing in Accounts Receivable. For example, it is a central component of industry solutions for industries such as telecommunication, insurance, and energy supply. Because most SAP installations work with A/R and not with CA, this book focuses on A/R.

FI-AR is characterized by a high level of integration both with G/L Accounting and SD, which results in a high degree of automation in the maintenance of customer accounts and the processing of customer receivables. Usually, the relevant documents are automatically transferred from SD to Financial Accounting. The posting in Financial Accounting includes the G/L account items—for a bill, usually revenue and sales tax—and the open items in the customer account.

5.5.1 Customer Account

Structure of customer master

The *customer account*, abbreviated as customer, is the account assignment object of Accounts Receivable. Regarding the vendor, Chapter 4, Section 4.2, Vendor Master as an Integrative Element, already informed you that a master record can be subdivided into different areas. This also applies to the customer master that essentially consists of the following three sections:

- General part (A segment)
- Sales and distribution data (C segment)
- Company code data (B segment)

With this structure, SAP supports both the integration and the division of responsibilities.

General Part

Account group

In the *general part*, you initially maintain the account number as well as the name and contact data. When you create a new customer, you must decide on an account group. The account group controls the screen layout and the number interval when a master record is created. Later, when the customer is used, the partner determination is influenced by the account group.

General information

The independence of the general view from further organizational units such as company code or sales organization, enables company-wide, shared use of the company masters. You therefore define information in the general part of the master record that is equally valid for all users of the enterprise. For example, a customer always has the same name, the same tax number, or the same bank details—regardless of whether an accounts receivable accountant or a sales employee in Germany or Italy views the information.

Data for the sales area

Aside from the general data, there are different pieces of information about the customer that change, depending on the perspective of the user. Sales data is an example of this user-dependent, changing information.

Sales Data

We will start the description of sales data with an example.

[+]

Data in the Sales Area

Imagine a German customer that Lederwaren-Manufaktur Mannheim supplies from both Germany and Italy. This can mean that the German SD grants a payment target of 30 days net, while the Italian subsidiary applies the national conditions and agrees to payment by bill of exchange with the customer. Moreover it is likely that different Incoterms are agreed with the customer in Germany and Italy.

You can map such differences in the customer master because you can maintain this and other information depending on the sales area. Thanks to this method, a single customer master can have multiple sales area views.

Figure 5.17 shows an extract of the sales area data of a customer.

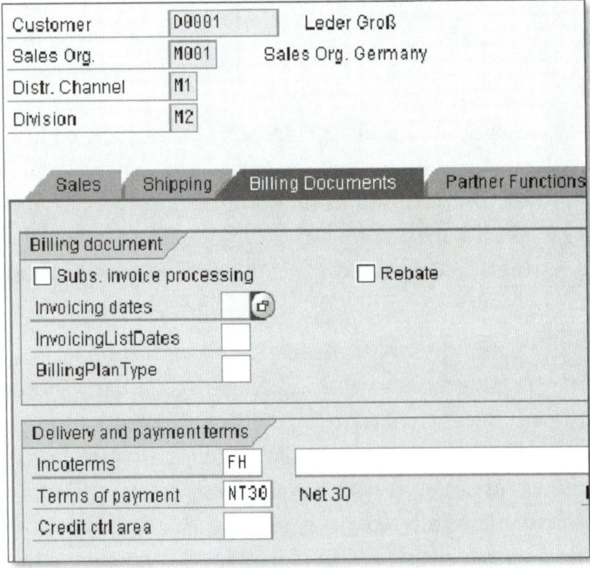

Figure 5.17 Sales Area Data for Customer D0001

Company Code Data

Company code-specific data

The same technology is also used for the information that is relevant for Accounts Receivable or that influences the posting in Financial Accounting. It is maintained depending on the company code. You can maintain many fields in the company code data. Because they touch and influence the value flow, we will take a closer look at the following fields:

- Head office
- Terms of payment
- Reconciliation account

"Head office" field

The HEAD OFFICE field is used to map customers' relationships of head offices and branch offices. Here, you specify whether a customer has a head office and multiple branch offices. Using the HEAD OFFICE field, you cannot influence the value flow itself but you can map the values (see Figure 5.18).

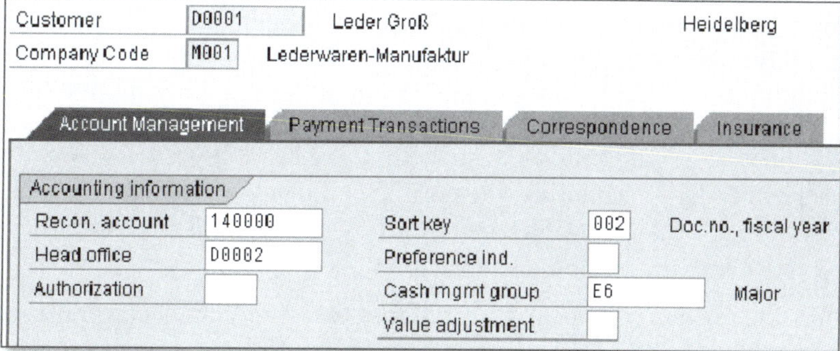

Figure 5.18 Defining a Head Office in the Customer Master

Occasionally, branch offices order directly from the supplier and open items are handled via the head office. It is then useful if all open items are shown only in the customer account of the head office. For this, you must initially create the head office and all required branch offices as customers with the company code segment.

Then, you enter the customer number of the head office in the HEAD OFFICE field of all branch master records. As a result, all items that are assigned to the account of a branch office are displayed exclusively in the head office account. For the branch accounts this means they contain neither items nor balances although the branch office was addressed in the documents. Thus, open items are displayed for the customer from which you expect the payment—the head office.

"Terms of payment" field

The TERMS OF PAYMENT field is often a cause of irritation in the company code data. Because a term of payment is also defined in the sales data, it is not completely clear to many SAP users when they must use which entry. The rule, however, is simple: Each component uses "its" term of payment. Therefore, if a sales order is created in SD, the SAP system automatically retrieves the term of payment from the sales part of the customer master. If you entered an A/R invoice directly in Financial Accounting, the system would use the term of payment from the company code data of the customer master. Consequently, the term of payment of Financial Accounting is usually of little significance.

"Reconciliation account" field

The RECONCILIATION ACCOUNT field provides the most important information in the company code data. This G/L account, defined in the customer master, forms the connection between accounts receivable accounting and general ledger accounting. You must declare as reconciliation accounts all receivables accounts that are posted to not only manually but also via automatic postings to customers.

5.5.2 Determining the Reconciliation Account

In General Ledger Accounting, the posting of the billing document is completed through the receivables item. Usually, the *reconciliation account* in the customer master is used as the account.

Reconciliation account in the customer master

When you create G/L accounts, you decide which accounts are available as reconciliation accounts in the maintenance of customer masters. For this purpose, you are provided with the RECONCILIATION ACCOUNT FOR ACCOUNT TYPE field at the company code level. Each G/L account that is defined as a reconciliation account for customers is then provided in a selection list in Accounts Receivable (see ❶ in Figure 5.19).

Receivables item in General Ledger Accounting

When you define the required reconciliation accounts, you must remember that this is only the mapping of the receivables item in G/L Accounting. Therefore, only the account balance is of interest in normal business activity. A detailed examination of the individual items in the reconciliation accounts only makes sense for deviations between the G/L and the subsidiary ledger—a possible worst case scenario in Financial Accounting.

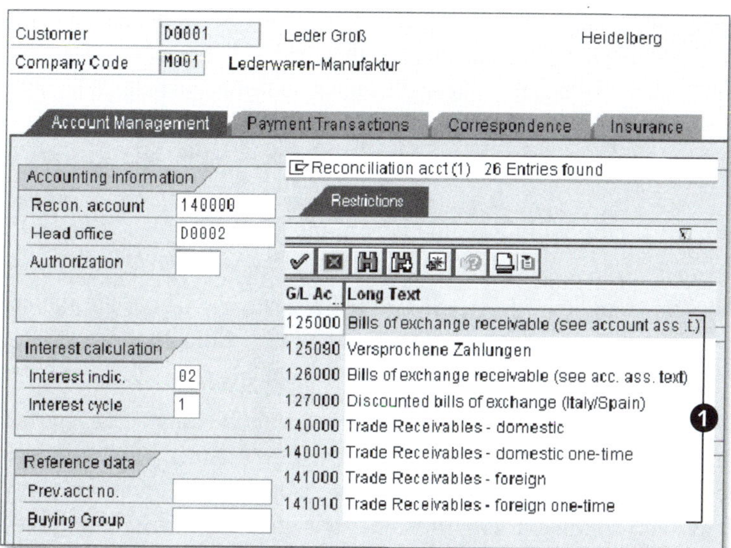

Figure 5.19 Defining the Reconciliation Account

New SAP implementation

Particularly during new SAP implementations, G/L accounts sometimes request a very differentiated presentation of receivables. Frequently, separate receivables accounts are requested for each tax rate. However, the accounts to which postings have been made are not relevant to determine the sales/purchases tax payable in the SAP system. In most cases, you can avoid this user department request by describing the tax determination logic in SAP.

Usually, a categorization by home country, EU, and third countries as well as by affiliated companies and external third parties is sufficient. For detailed analyses, you are provided with the information system of Accounts Receivable or SD and frequently a BI/BW system.

[+]

Restrict the Selection of Reconciliation Accounts on the Customer Side

Reduce the number of reconciliation accounts on the customer side to the minimum that is required from the financial statement perspective. The greater the number of accounts, the higher the risk of entering wrong data in the master data maintenance.

Changing the reconciliation account

You must define the reconciliation account when you create the company code view of the customer master. Whether and by who changes can be made later on depends on the working method of accounting. Both variants—reconciliation account is changeable or reconciliation account is no longer changeable after posting of the customer—can be plausibly justified. A change of the reconciliation account can be indicated by an incorrect entry during the creation of the customer account or by the sale of an affiliated enterprise. For these situations, you should have a procedure at hand. We will provide different suggestions for this in the next section.

Procedure for Changeable Reconciliation Accounts

Change after posting of the customer

If the reconciliation account is changeable after posting of the customer, you can simply change the master record of the customer. This way, all new postings to the customer are also posted to the new reconciliation account. Items that might still exist remain in the old reconciliation account.

Effects at period end

This way, however, the display of receivables would be incorrect at period end because all items must be displayed in the new reconciliation account. To address this, the SAP system provides you with a function to reclassify receivables and payables. Using this function, open items are temporarily displayed in the new financial statement item for reporting. Chapter 7, Section 7.7, Reclassification of Receivables and Payables, provides more details on this topic.

Procedure for Non-Changeable Reconciliation Accounts

Creating a new account

Many accounting departments reject or do not use the change of the reconciliation account after posting of the customer. As a result, instead of changing the master record, the existing customer account for posting must be blocked and a new account—with a new number—must be created. This is problematic in reporting, however, because the order history cannot be transferred from the old customer to the new one.

Periodic business transactions

However, there may also be periodic business transactions in Accounts Receivable that you want to display in a separate account in the G/L.

Special G/L transactions

An important example is the *down payment received*. IAS 1 also requires a separate display of down payments received.

Special G/L transactions

In the SAP system, this process can be displayed using *special G/L transactions*. The standard system provides many common preconfigured special G/L transactions. Aside from this, you can also set your own business transactions. In addition to down payments, you can also map payments by bill of exchange, guarantees of payment, interests, and other transactions.

The goal of using special G/L transactions is having the option of a separate evaluation. For this purpose, you flag the posting with a *special G/L indicator* and additionally redirect the posting from the reconciliation account to a separate G/L account.

For better understanding, we will first discuss the settings for a special G/L transaction.

Settings of the special G/L indicator

The special G/L indicator is a central characteristic. It is a one-digit field that can be transferred for postings and evaluated in various reports. Special G/L indicators can be used for transactions in either accounts receivable accounting or accounts payable accounting. This restriction is due to the fact that the creation of the indicator relates to an account type, as shown in Figure 5.20.

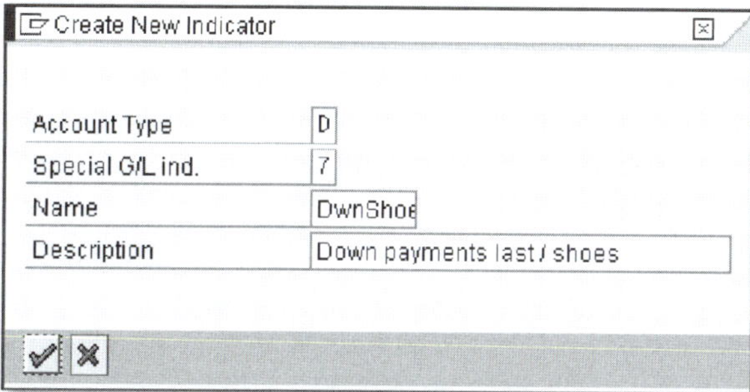

Figure 5.20 Creating a Special G/L Indicator

During the maintenance of the special G/L indicator, you configure certain critical specifications (see Figure 5.21).

"Noted items" checkbox

You can use the NOTED ITEMS checkbox to determine whether a posting to the G/L is actually made upon entering the special G/L indicator or whether you only want to set a note in Accounts Receivable. Down payment requests are typical noted items.

Figure 5.21 shows the settings for a special G/L indicator for down payments ❶. You must post a down payment directly with incoming payments for a down payment request. In the financial statement, the down payment is displayed as a payable toward the customer but as long as the payment has not been received, you have no reason for a posting in the G/L. In Accounts Receivable, however, you will want to know that you have requested a down payment from the customer. It is therefore posted as a noted item only.

Account Type D Customer
Special G/L ind. 7 Down payments last / shoes
Properties
Noted items
Rel.to credit limit
Commitments warning
Target sp.G/L ind.
Special G/L transaction types
1 Down payment/Down payment request
Bill of exchange/Bill request
Others
Posting Key
Debit
09 Reverse down payment
Credit
19 Down pmnt received

Figure 5.21 Properties of a Special G/L Indicator

Relevance to the credit limit calculation

Via the RELEVANT TO CREDIT LIMIT checkbox, you can determine whether the posting procedure should be considered for calculating the credit limit used by the customer.

Let us stay with the example of a down payment request and the down payment received later on: A down payment request could be defined as a request toward the customer. So far, however, no financial risk has arisen. If the customer does not pay, you might refrain from delivery. An interesting situation evolves if the customer makes a down payment. In this case, it seems justified to reduce the used credit limit by the incoming payment.

Message in case of commitment

Usage of the COMMITMENTS WARNING depends on the working method in Accounts Receivable. If you set this indicator, the system generates a message about existing special G/L sales (see Figure 5.22).

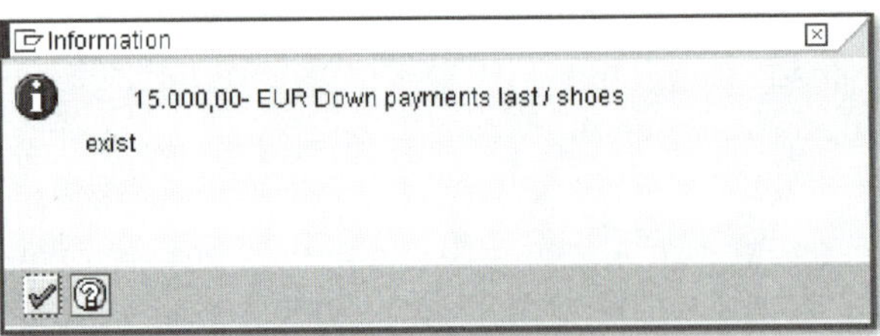

Figure 5.22 Message about Existing Special G/L Sales

This message can be particularly useful for posting payment transactions. Because it is only an information message, you can confirm it with [Enter].

Select "Commitments warning" Checkbox?

If special G/L transactions are frequently used in accounting, you should ask yourself whether this message still draws attention or whether it "annoys" and is therefore confirmed without further attention paid to it. If this is the case, you should dispense with setting the COMMITMENTS WARNING indicator.

Special G/L indicators for down payment request

If you create a special G/L indicator that maps a down payment request, you must also specify at least one Target special G/L indicator. In other words, if the incoming payment for a down payment request is posted, the system deactivates the special G/L indicator for the down payment request. In turn, the target special G/L indicator is activated when the down payment is made.

Because you can enter more than one target special G/L indicator in Customizing, you do not have to define the special G/L indicator for the request when a down payment request is posted but only the specific indicator for the down payment.

The complete posting data from the down payment request to the clearing, with final billing, looks as is shown in Figure 5.23.

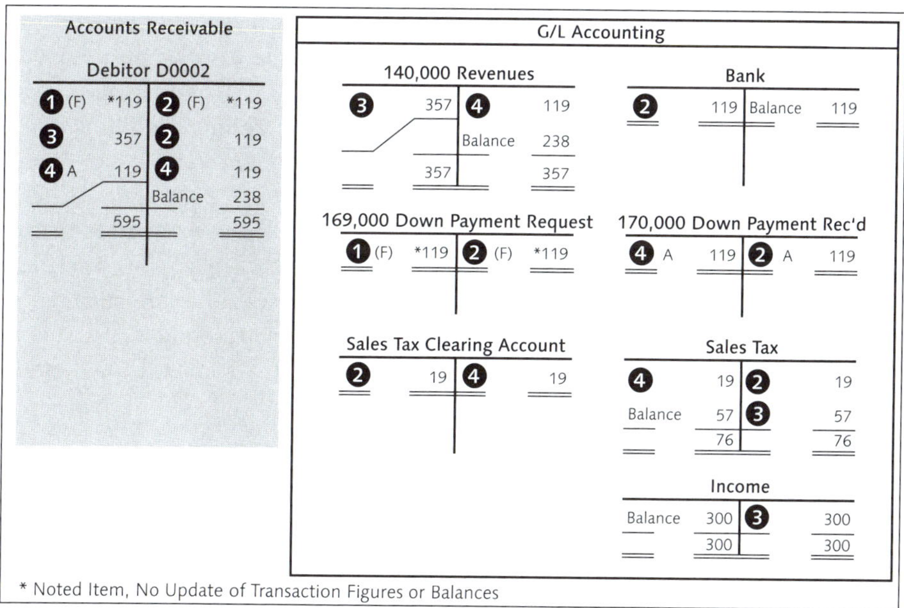

Figure 5.23 Posting Procedure for Down Payment Received

Posting procedure for down payment received

In the first step of the process, you request the customer to make a down payment. This transaction is mapped via a down payment request in the system. The down payment request triggers a posting in general ledger accounting and accounts receivable (see ❶, posting of a down payment request). However, this is only a noted item (special G/L indicator F), comparable with statistical postings in Controlling.

When the payment is received (see ❷, incoming payment and posting of down payment), the posting of the down payment request is canceled. The incoming payment is posted in the customer account with special G/L indicator A. As a result, the posting in the G/L is not made in reconciliation account 140 000 (receivables) but in down payment account 170 000 (see ❸, down payments received).

When the service has been performed completely, the customer receives a final billing document, the *final settlement* ❹, which is posted like any other billing document. However, this is now followed by another step in which the down payment and the billing are cleared against each other (see ❺, clearing of down payment and billing). Thus, only one open item remains in the customer account, which results from the difference of final settlement less down payment received.

Integration of special G/L transactions with SD

Even if postings of special G/L transactions are primarily implemented in accounting, the integration with SD is still possible. For this purpose, you are provided with a separate Customizing item in SD, which you can use to determine and post deviating reconciliation accounts for billing documents. You can find the corresponding Customizing item in the Implementation Guide under SALES AND DISTRIBUTION • BASIC FUNCTIONS • ACCOUNT ASSIGNMENT/COSTING • RECONCILIATION ACCOUNT DETERMINATION. This option is interesting for mapping down payments and their requests; in real life, however, it is also problematic. The implementation is only possible in the context of billing plans. Furthermore, if the final settlement deviates from the down payments, the standard SAP system reaches its limits.

[+]

Further Information on the Integration with SD

You can use SAP Note 213444 (Consulting Note Down Payment Processing SD/FI) as a starting point for detailed information on the integration of special G/L transactions in SD.

Bills and credit memos are transferred from SD to accounting more frequently than down payments. Because each bill or credit memo contains a customer number, Accounts Receivable is addressed here as well.

5.5.3 Integration of SD and Accounts Receivable

The partner role principle

To understand how the SAP system finds the correct customer account, you must also understand the principle of partner roles in SD. A partner role defines which function a customer created in the SAP system assumes in the sales and distribution process. The most important partner roles a customer can assume are as follows:

- Sold-to party that assigns a sales order
- Ship-to party to whose address the delivery is made
- Bill-to party to whose address the billing document is sent
- Payer from which payment is expected

Payer

From an accounting perspective, only the payer is relevant. This is the party from which you expect payment. Accordingly, you must keep a customer account for managing open items for this party.

[Ex]

Example to Illustrate the Partner Role

NIMAAR, a customer of Lederwaren-Manufaktur Mannheim, is an international fashion label with stores in various European cities. The customer's head office in Madrid always places orders from the Mannheim branch office. The goods should be delivered to the Munich branch office but the bill is paid by NIMAAR Germany in Cologne. The partner role definition is as follows:

- Central purchasing department in Madrid is the sold-to party; it must at least be created in SD.
- The branch office in Munich receives only a customer master with an SD view and is defined as the ship-to party in the sales order.
- Thus, the regional subsidiary in Cologne is the bill-to party and payer in this case. This customer master record must be created both in SD and in Financial Accounting.

To transfer an open Accounts Receivable item automatically to G/L Accounting, you must define a reconciliation account in each master record with a Financial Accounting view.

[+]

Use Different Document Types from SD

In older SAP releases, SD documents were transferred by default to accounting with only the RV document type. This restriction has since been removed so that different Financial Accounting document types can be used, depending on the billing type. Use Transaction VOFA in the billing type to maintain the DOCUMENT TYPE field as desired.

For example, a differentiation between bills and credit memos is convenient from the Accounts Receivable perspective.

5.5.4 Mapping of Secondary Businesses

Posting of bills in Accounts Receivable

So far, this chapter has only considered the normal sales process scenario: the sale of one's own products and trading goods. However, there are also what are called *secondary businesses*. This involves sales that are not implemented within the actual business activity (such as sales of fixed assets or the occasional sale of waste or raw materials). In projects, the general tendency is to not map these transactions in the SD component but in Financial Accounting. The posting is implemented directly via Accounts Receivable. In this procedure, you can focus on the main processes in SD and avoid extended costing sheets.

Weaknesses of this approach

In real life, however, this approach reveals considerable weaknesses:

- **Difficult integration with CO-PA**
  The integration with CO-PA is more difficult because an automatic derivation of characteristics and value fields is only possible to a very limited extent.
- **No integrated evaluation possible**
  An integrated evaluation of these transactions is not possible because the data is only available in Financial Accounting but not in SD.
- **No support of billing document print in the standard SAP system**
  Therefore, you must develop your own corresponding function, or—which is more frequently the case—you must switch to Microsoft Word and manual creation.

Therefore, you should carefully check how often you must process secondary businesses. It is recommended to use the mapping via credit memo and debit memo imitation in SD. For this purpose, you use a non-inventory item (dummy item) that contains all required conditions.

Incoming payment from customer

Regardless of how a receivable is posted in the SAP system, you as the invoicing party hope that no further activities are necessary until the correct incoming payment. In real life, however, this wishful thinking remains unmet on occasion and the customer makes only a partial payment or does not pay at all. Initially, your only option to act is to send a request to the customer informing them that an incoming payment is expected.

In the system, you can process the entire correspondence via the dunning of Accounts Receivable.

5.5.5 Dunning

Ideal case vs. reality

The following section discusses *dunning* only briefly, for the sake of completeness. In the ideal case, the customer supports your internal value flow by paying punctually and in the correct amount. In reality, however, open items are often not paid punctually. In this case, all you as the creditor can do is use dunning notices and, in the worst case, the legal dunning procedure.

Although the Customizing of the dunning procedure can be regarded as basic knowledge of a Financial Accounting consultant, this topic is often the cause of vehement discussions. This may be caused by the many options the SAP system provides that lead to high expectations among accounts receivable accountants.

Dunning charge

Dunning charges are an excellent example. You should ask yourself which procedure customers expect from you. If your enterprise has dunned only reluctantly and cautiously, it will be difficult for your customers to understand why they are suddenly dunned regularly and are supposed to pay dunning charges. The reason that you have implemented SAP and everything has changed will probably not make sense to them.

Dunning Interests

The billing of dunning interest seems to be easy money. In the SAP system, the posting of charges or interests directly in the dunning process is only available if you use the CA component. This is not possible in the dunning process of regular Accounts Receivable.

[+]

Billing of Dunning Charges and Dunning Interests

You do not want to omit the billing of dunning charges and/or interests.

Only indicate the corresponding amounts in the forms. Do not create postings if you can foresee that a majority of dunned customers is not going to pay these additional amounts. This saves account receivables accountants the work of manually clearing these open items.

If you have not generated open items for charges or interests and the customer pays them, you can always post the difference of the incoming payment as other revenue.

Even though dunning of overdue items is part of daily business in most enterprises, we hope that customers pay their open items punctually and in full. This brings us to the next topic of incoming payment.

5.5.6 Incoming Payment

End point of the sales value flow

Incoming payments represent the end point of the value flow in the sales process. There are different ways how incoming payments can reach you. Examples include payments via check, bill of exchange, automatic debit, or bank transfer.

Preferences of payment methods

You cannot make any general statement on the preferred payment method. The distribution also depends on the industry, enterprise size, and country. For example, in Central Europe, bank transfer is an important method of payment, whereas payments via bills of exchange are hardly used. In countries such as France, Spain, or Italy, bills of exchange are quite common. Checks, in contrast, are used more often by medium-sized enterprises than by large enterprises. This is supposed to extend the date of required payment because a bank transfer would lead to an immediate liquidity loss; a check must first be sent to the vendor and then be submitted at the bank. Thus, you must calculate a delay of at least two days.

Electronic Bank Statement

Customizing

The best way to be informed about an incoming payment is an *electronic bank statement*, which you can import to the SAP system and thus trigger automatic postings in the G/L and subsidiary ledger. This, however, requires Customizing and possibly also programming in a user exit. In many countries, there are standards for files provided by the bank.

Collaboration with banks

Experiences in real life have shown that not all banks interpret these standards in the same way. Consequently, you must configure the processing of electronic bank statements specifically for each bank. To reduce the implementation and maintenance effort as much as possible, you should try to minimize the number of connected banks. Unfortunately, this idea, which is quite useful from the IT perspective, does not always meet a positive response in user departments. They usually do not want to be dependent on one bank and thus distribute the bank assets.

At first glance, the Customizing of electronic bank statements is very complex. However, if you take a closer look, the interrelationships quickly become clear.

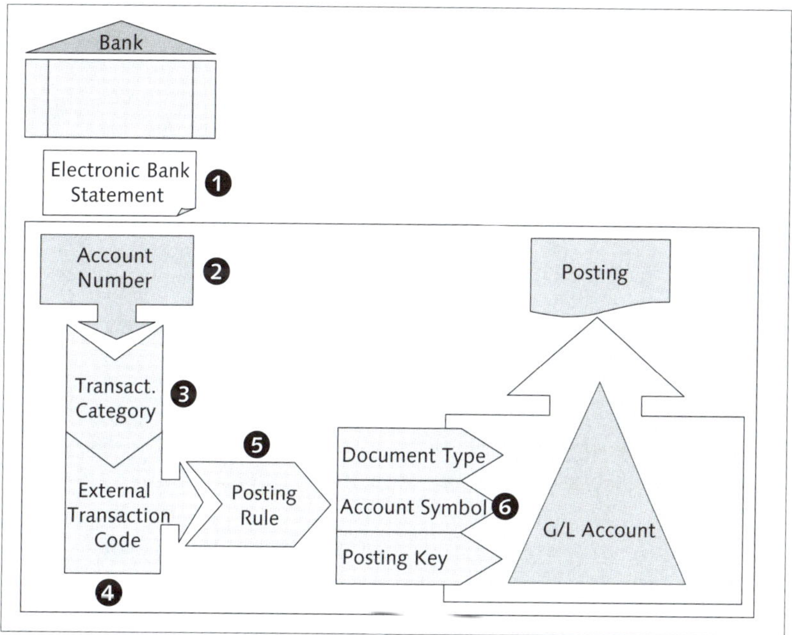

Figure 5.24 Customizing of Electronic Bank Statements

How can you read Figure 5.24? When you receive an electronic bank statement from the bank, the file contains the bank routing number and the account number. Consequently, you know which of your house banks sent the file.

MT940 standard

Usually, the house bank can provide you with a list that explains the structure and content of the bank statement. The *MT940 standard*, for example, contains your account number and the bank routing number as general information. Furthermore, the standard provides information on the account balance with and without the payment transactions mentioned in the file.

External Transaction Codes

Additionally, for each item, the electronic bank statement states the bank details (for example, account, bank routing number, and IBAN) and the name of the party that made the incoming/outgoing payment. You can also view the amount and reference. An *external transaction code* ❹ that specifies to which payment transaction the corresponding item refers is critical in this context: incoming or outgoing payment via bank transfer/check, returns of an outgoing payment (for example, if the wrong bank details are maintained in a vendor master), bank charges, or interests.

Transaction category

You have to enter all external transaction codes a bank uses and that are relevant for you in your system. The *transaction category* (see Figure 5.24) incorporates all transaction codes of a bank or a standard.

External trans	+/-	Posting	Interpretation Algorithm	Planning	Processing Type
051	+	0001	001: Standard algorithm		Dummy entry - not as
070	+	0002	001: Standard algorithm		Dummy entry - not as
071	+	0016	000: No interpretation		Dummy entry - not as
071	-	0006	001: Standard algorithm		Dummy entry - not as
151	+	0025	000: No interpretation		Dummy entry - not as
151	-	0023	000: No interpretation		Dummy entry - not as

Figure 5.25 Customizing of External Transaction Codes

In Figure 5.25, you can see transaction code 051, which is provided by the bank. The second column displays the plus/minus sign. It enables you to differentiate between incoming and outgoing payments. In this example, it is a cash receipt. These two columns show the criteria that are checked for every item on the bank statement. If the Customizing and file correspond, the following *logic* is used.

Posting rule

First of all, you can find the *posting rule* (see Figure 5.24). It provides all relevant information such as document type and posting key necessary to create a posting. In our example, the 0001 posting rule maps incoming payments via a clearing account. Here, you have to make posting to both the G/L and subsidiary ledger:

- General Ledger Accounting: bank to cash receipt account
- Accounts Receivable: cash receipt account to customer

The *cash receipt account* is simply a clearing account that enables you to ensure that all items on the bank statement were posted correctly. The account is always debited against the bank account; the credit is made against subledger accounting or, for bank charges or interest, against another G/L account.

Figure 5.26 illustrates the settings of posting rule 0001 for the posting to G/L accounting.

Posting Rule 0001
Posting area 1

Debit		Credit	
Posting Key	40	Posting Key	50
Sp.G/L Indicator		Sp.G/L Indicator	
Acct symbol	BANK	Acct symbol	INCOMINGPAYMENT
Compression		Compression	

Document Type SA
Posting Type 1
Posting on acct key
Reversal Reason

Figure 5.26 "Posting Rule 0001" in G/L

The POSTING AREA field indicates that this is a posting of the G/L. 1 stands for the general ledger; 2 for the subsidiary ledger.

Both for the debit item and credit item, the posting key and account symbol are defined; the latter is described in the following text.

In addition to the document type, the type of posting is also specified. It describes the posting transaction in detail, for example, a G/L account posting or a clearing entry in the subsidiary ledger.

Account symbol

With the *account symbol* (see Figure 5.24), the SAP system provides a lean and systematic account determination solution for all enterprises that have more than one bank account—which includes almost all enterprises.

The basic concept of the account symbol is that, on the one hand, the chart of accounts always contains one G/L account for each bank account and, on the other hand, that the clearing accounts for the possible business transactions are based on this account. Moreover, it is assumed that the G/L accounts always follow the same numbering logic. Figure 5.27 illustrates this procedure.

Assign Accounts to Account Symbol

Act Symbol	Acct Mod.	Currency	G/L acct	Acct Symb. Desc.
CHARGES ❶	+	+	479000	Bank fees account
DUES	+	+	479000	Charges
INCOMINGCHECK	+	+	+++++++++8	Incoming checks
INCOMINGPAYMENT	+	+	+++++++++9	Cash receipt account
OTHERS	+	+	+++++++++5	Other bank trans.
OUTGOINGCHECK	+	+	+++++++++1	Outgoing checks acct
OUTGOINGPAYMENT	+	+	+++++++++2	Cash disbursement

Figure 5.27 Account Determination via the Account Symbol

The first row contains the BANK account symbol (see ❶ in Figure 5.27). In the G/L ACCOUNT column, no account number is defined. The system determines this number through the Customizing of the house banks. The entry of plus signs is called masking. Plus signs can be replaced by any character. The SAP system thus works in the same way as search engines on the Internet.

For the CHARGES account symbol, an account number is defined. This means, regardless of which bank raises the charges, that they are always posted to account 479000.

Number logic of the bank accounts

The following rows contain the account symbols for the different payment methods: INCOMINGPAYMENT and OUTGOINGPAYMENT as well as INCOMINGCHECK and OUTGOINGCHECK. Here, the G/L ACCOUNT column contains entries that are only partially masked. In this case, the system uses the G/L account number of the respective house bank account and replaces the last number with 2, 9, 1, or 8. Consequently, you do not have to specify all accounts explicitly. Additionally, this facilitates the work with the chart of accounts for the user departments because this specification indicates, for example, that an account is a cash disbursement account in bank areas that end with a 2.

A numeric example can look as follows:

- G/L account for bank account 113100 112880
- Cash disbursement account 11310**2** 11288**2**
- Cash receipt account 11310**9** 11288**9**

The definition of the account symbols and G/L account numbers usually do not cause problems in the configuration of the electronic bank statement. Instead, the challenge is the unique identification of the external transaction codes and the interpretation of the existing information to obtain a high level of automation.

Efficiency of Electronic Bank Statements [+]

Even if you use the existing user exit, you normally cannot obtain a 100% automatic posting of electronic bank statements against open items in Accounts Receivable. There are various reasons for this. Frequently, you come across incorrect or insufficient references in the payment medium and, of course, unexpected payment differences.

Today, there are numerous add-ons that have been developed by third parties. Some of these solutions may achieve better clearing percentages than SAP system tools.

However, in case of poor payment practices or missing information in the payment medium, even the best add-ons cannot help.

Manual post-processing

Unfortunately, data quality still requires manual interaction. First, you have to determine the correct customer and then identify the open items to which the incoming payment refers. If you cannot identify the customer, you cannot clear the cash receipt account. At the end of the month at the latest, the bank clearing accounts should be cleared to a large extent.

Posting on accounts

If you know the customer, but cannot identify the open item, you can post on account. In this case, the incoming payment is posted as an open item to the customer account. One of the problems here is that clarifying open invoices and payments and clearing them against each other is often neglected over long periods of time. Sooner or later, this leads to confusing accounts and makes your daily work more difficult.

Payment differences

Finally, we will turn our attention to the payment differences. Incoming payments are usually payments that are too low. You then have to decide—according to defined rules and individually for each case—how to proceed with short payments or the residual items. Small differences should usually be cleared against a difference account. If the difference is too high and is not acceptable, it must remain as the remaining amount on the customer account, and you must clarify the payment with the customer.

Small Difference

Tolerance limits

You can manipulate the amount of allowed *small differences* via Customizing. There are two options for defining these tolerance limits:

- The first tolerance limit can be maintained depending on the customer master.
- The second tolerance limit is user-dependent.

In both cases, the allowed tolerance limits are defined in absolute values in the local currency as well as in percentages and combined in what are called *tolerance groups*. In this context, at least one entry [BLANK] is necessary for user-dependent tolerances. This entry always applies if no specific tolerance group is defined in the customer or user master.

Configuring tolerance groups

You define *tolerance groups* in the Implementation Guide under FINANCIAL ACCOUNTING (NEW) · ACCOUNTS RECEIVABLE AND ACCOUNTS PAYABLE • BUSINESS TRANSACTIONS • INCOMING PAYMENTS • MANUAL INCOMING PAYMENTS • DEFINE TOLERANCE GROUPS FOR EMPLOYEES OR DEFINE TOLERANCES (CUSTOMERS).

Assigning tolerance groups

You also assign tolerance groups to users in the Customizing for manual incoming payments under the ASSIGN USERS/TOLERANCE GROUPS item. For the customers, the tolerance group is assigned in the company code-specific data of the customer master on the PAYMENT TRANSACTIONS tab.

Defining the difference account

By performing these steps, you defined up to which amount you can clear small differences without further clarification. However, you do not have to transfer the difference account manually. You can define it in the Implementation Guide under FINANCIAL ACCOUNTING (NEW) • ACCOUNTS RECEIVABLE AND ACCOUNTS PAYABLE • BUSINESS TRANSACTIONS • INCOMING PAYMENTS • INCOMING PAYMENTS BASIC SETTINGS • DEFINE ACCOUNTS FOR OVERPAYMENTS/UNDERPAYMENTS.

Resulting posting

For marginal payment differences, the following posting is made:

C...	Itm	PK	S	Account	Description	Amount	Curr.	Tx	Order	Profit Center	Segment
M001	1	40		113190	Deutsche Bank - EUR	991,50	EUR				
	2	40		881000	Unallowed customer d	8,50	EUR		100300	M_5100	M_OH
	3	15		D0002	B. Rott	1.000,00-	EUR				

Figure 5.28 Incoming Payment with Accepted Difference

In Figure 5.28, you can see an incoming payment of EUR 991.50. The corresponding open item is EUR 1,000.00. The difference of EUR 8.50 was posted to account 881000 (Unallowed customer deductions) via account determination.

Mapping in Profitability Analysis

Frequently, this account is mapped together with sales deductions in Profitability Analysis. As a result, it is included in the EBIT calculations and should therefore also be transferred to Controlling. As usual, this is done by also defining account 881000 as a cost element. However, the posting data does not lead to a Controlling object that you could use for this purpose because the postings are only made to balance sheet items—bank posting and receivable. It is not useful to manually transfer a Controlling object for each posting. To avoid this, you have to link the cost element with a Controlling account assignment. In this example, Transaction OKB9 was used to assign internal order 100300 to cost element 881000.

Large Variances

Variances in incoming payments

Unfortunately, in addition to acceptable small differences, there are also variances in incoming payments that are unacceptable. In these cases, you can still clear your open item but you have to create a residual item. The disadvantage of this residual item is that it is posted with the document number of the incoming payment and not with the number of the partially cleared invoice.

Figure 5.29 shows an example of an open customer invoice of EUR 7,000.00, of which the customer has only paid EUR 4,000.00. This means you have to create a residual item of EUR 3,000.00. This looks as follows on the customer account:

Stat	DocumentNo	Doc. Type	Doc. Date	Net due date	Σ	Amount in local cur.	LCurr	Clrng doc.	Clearing date
	1400000002	DZ	28.03.2009	28.03.2009		3.000,00	EUR		
					▪	**3.000,00**	**EUR**		
	1400000002	DZ	28.03.2009	28.03.2009		7.000,00-	EUR	1400000002	28.03.2009
	1800000002	DR	25.03.2009	25.03.2009		7.000,00	EUR	1400000002	28.03.2009
					▪	**0,00**	**EUR**		
Account D0002					▪▪	**3.000,00**	**EUR**		
					▪▪▪	**3.000,00**	**EUR**		

Figure 5.29 Posting of Residual Items

The only partially cleared customer invoice (DR document type) is displayed as cleared in the same way as the incoming payment (DZ document type) with EUR 7,000.00. At the same time, along with payment document 1400000002, an open item is created, called a residual item, of EUR 3,000.00. In this example, it is due immediately.

Alternatives

As an alternative to clearing the original invoice and creating a residual item, you can also post a *partial payment*. In this case, the invoice is not cleared. The customer account displays the incoming payment as an additional open item. There are user departments that do not like this kind of mapping of both residual items and partial payments; not least because software solutions are available that can partially clear open items. As an alternative to the creation of residual items, a *payment on account* is selected so that the invoice and the incoming payment are both displayed as open items.

Let us now turn our attention from the financial statement area to the effects of the sales process in the profit and loss statement. Here, the focus is on sales revenues.

5.6 Mapping Sales Revenues

Before discussing the mapping of sales revenues in the SAP system, this section first briefly describes the underlying legal conditions.

5.6.1 Time of the Revenue Recognition

Effects of financial accounting scandals

Recently, several financial accounting scandals have led to more stringent accounting regulations for sales revenues. Prominent examples are Enron and Worldcom. In the case of Enron, the premature and thus no longer period-based mapping of revenues could only be interpreted as financial statement falsification. Even though this was done intentionally in this case, the time-related correct separation of sales revenues must be carefully considered to avoid unintended errors.

Time of service performance

Receivables and revenues are frequently posted when the invoice is issued. From the contractual perspective, however, the time of service performance is decisive for the creation of receivables and revenues. The invoice does not have any legal relevance. If the service is actually performed before or after the invoice is issued, a revenue recognition with invoicing is not period-based and must therefore be corrected.

Revenue recognition methods

For this case, the SAP system provides an automated procedure. The revenue recognition does not depend on the time of the billing. The following three methods are available:

- **Revenue recognition at the time of billing**
  This is the default setting. The revenue is posted when the billing document is created.
- **Time-related revenue recognition**
  Here, revenues are recognized proportionally over a defined period of time. This is useful, for example, for maintenance contracts. In these cases, the time is defined by a start date and an end date that are specified in the sales order item. The revenues are evenly distributed across the time periods.

- **Activity-based revenue recognition**
  This case is used if revenue recognition should depend on specific events such as a delivery or reaching a milestone. For example, if for a maintenance contract, the total value of the contract is immediately invoiced to a customer but the services are performed step-by-step, the total value of the revenues is initially delimited. Each sequentially completed service package or milestone releases the delimitation of the corresponding partial revenue so that it is recognized on a period basis.

Revenue recognition depending on the individual case

This means—depending on the individual requirements in the enterprise—that revenues can be recognized on a period basis in the profit and loss statement. As a result, manual corrections and error sources are avoided. Furthermore, the SAP system increases the transparency of the financial statements using two additional G/L accounts, which map recognized but not yet invoiced revenues and invoiced but not yet recognized revenues separately. This procedure corresponds to the procedure of the GR/IR account in the purchasing process. You can find the corresponding Customizing in the Implementation Guide under SALES AND DISTRIBUTION • BASIC FUNCTIONS · ACCOUNT ASSIGNMENT/COSTING • REVENUE RECOGNITION.

For all enterprises that deliver stocked goods to their customers, revenue recognition plays a minor role. Here, it is only critical that the goods issue and billing are triggered on the same day or at least in the same period. This means that you have to pay attention—particularly toward the end of a period—that all issued goods are also billed and transferred to Financial Accounting.

5.6.2 Presentation of Sales Revenues

Transferring sales revenues to Financial Accounting is necessary because the original document is created in the SD component.

Creating the Billing Document in Two Steps

From an accounting perspective, the billing document is created in two steps. First, you generate a billing document in SD. Then, you can transfer the billing document to Financial Accounting. This two-step processing is not visible to the user. However, one of the consequences is that a separate billing document exists in both SD and Accounts Payable; that is, in Financial Accounting.

The determination of the revenue account assignment is technically located in SD because it provides all information on the customer, material, and order or billing document.

Prerequisites for the Revenue Account Determination

First determination of the accounts in the sales order

The *revenue account determination* already begins in the sales order. When a sales order is saved, the price determination is activated for the first time. Here, customer-specific and/or material-related deductions and surcharges such as rebates, freight costs, or taxes are calculated for the sales price (see Section 5.3, Price Determination as the Basis of the Value Determination). At this point, the account determination is also implemented to determine to which revenue (deduction) accounts the individual parts of the price determination should be posted in the Financial Accounting component later on.

Accounting requirements

When you start with the restructuring or revision of the revenue account determination, you should ask yourself how the accountant and corporate group consolidation want to map the sales in the profit and loss statement. This may involve a request for more detailed segmentation. Table 5.4 shows the requirements of Lederwaren-Manufaktur Mannheim.

Sales/Transaction Type	Performance/Delivery To Third Parties		Performance/Delivery To Affiliated Companies	
	Domestic	Abroad	Domestic	Abroad
Product Sales	800 000	801 000	802 000	803 000
Sales of Trading Goods	800 002	801 002	802 002	803 002
Sales of Spare Parts	–	–	–	–
Freight Revenues	888 000	888 100	888 000	888 100
Sales Deductions	809 000	809 100	809 000	809 100
Other Services (for Shoe Sales Only)	800 001	801 001	802 001	803 001
Provisions for Volume-Based Rebates (for Key Accounts Only)	89 000	89 000	89 000	89 000

Table 5.4 Requirements for the Revenue Account Determination of Lederwaren-Manufaktur Mannheim

The accounting department wants to focus on the sales type, for example, the sale of products or trading goods. However, it is also essential whether it is a domestic customer or a customer abroad and whether the enterprise is from the Lederwaren-Manufaktur Mannheim group or an external enterprise. These are custom requirements that need to be implemented in the system.

When you take a look at the columns in Table 5.4, you can see that the required differentiation can be implemented best using the customer master. The customer master must already indicate whether it is a domestic or foreign customer and whether the enterprise belongs to the group.

Account Assignment Groups

Customer account assignment group

For this purpose, the SAP system provides the Customer ACCOUNT ASSIGNMENT GROUP FIELD in the customer master. You can define the value of the field in Customizing via SALES AND DISTRIBUTION • BASIC FUNCTIONS • ACCOUNT ASSIGNMENT/COSTING • REVENUE ACCOUNT DETERMINATION • CHECK MASTER DATA RELEVANT FOR ACCOUNT ASSIGNMENT. These custom requirements are then implemented as shown in Figure 5.30.

AcctAssgGr	Description
01	3rd party domestic
02	3rd party abroad
03	affiliates domestic
04	affiliates abroad

Figure 5.30 Lederwaren-Manufaktur Mannheim Customer Account Assignment Group

Table 5.4 indicates that the accounting department wants to differentiate whether finished products or trading goods are sold. Spare parts are currently not sold. If this is supposed to be done in the future, the accounting department wants to map these separately as well. However, the chart of accounts does not provide an account for this case yet. Performed services, such as repairs, are also supposed to be mapped as separate items in the profit and loss statement.

Material account assignment group

To establish a connection between the material master and revenue account determination, the SAP system provides the Material ACCOUNT ASSIGNMENT GROUP FIELD. You have to maintain the field in the master record of all marketable materials. Lederwaren-Manufaktur Mannheim created the material account assignment group, as shown in Figure 5.31.

Acct assignment grp	Description
M1	LWM - Trading goods
M2	LWM - Finished goods
M3	LWM - Spareparts
M4	LWM - Services

Figure 5.31 Lederwaren-Manufaktur Mannheim Material Account Assignment Group

Combining the account assignment groups

You can now determine the accounts for the sales of finished products, trading goods, and other services from the combination of the customer and material account assignment groups.

Other services can only be rendered for shoe sales. However, this is a restriction that must already apply when the sales order is entered and not just when the billing document is created. Therefore, they are not considered for the configuration of this account determination.

For the accounts for freight revenues and sales deductions, a differentiation should be made between domestic and foreign customers only. Here, you can find the account via the customer account assignment group; you do not have to consider the material.

For the provisions for volume-based rebates, you have to take neither the material nor the customer into account. The posting is always made to account 89 000.

Table 5.5 shows the technical revenue account determination.

Customer Account Assignment Group	Material Account Assignment Group	Account Key	Account
C1	M1	Sales revenue	800 000
C1	M2	Sales revenue	800 002
C1	M4	Sales revenue	800 001
C2	M1	Sales revenue	801 000
C2	M2	Sales revenue	801 002
C2	M4	Sales revenue	801 001
C3	M1	Sales revenue	802 000
C3	M2	Sales revenue	802 002

Table 5.5 Lederwaren-Manufaktur Mannheim Revenue Account Determination

Customer Account Assignment Group	Material Account Assignment Group	Account Key	Account
C3	M4	Sales revenue	802 001
C4	M1	Sales revenue	803 000
C4	M2	Sales revenue	803 002
C4	M4	Sales revenue	803 001
C1	–	Freight revenue	888 000
C2	–	Freight revenue	888 100
C3	–	Freight revenue	888 000
C4	–	Freight revenue	888 100
C1	–	Sales deduction	809 000
C2	–	Sales deduction	809 100
C3	–	Sales deduction	809 000
C4	–	Sales deduction	809 100
–	–	Provision for volume-based rebates	89 000

Table 5.5 Lederwaren-Manufaktur Mannheim Revenue Account Determination (Cont.)

You already know the two concepts of customer account assignment group and material account assignment group. Table 5.5 additionally uses the *account key* concept. It indicates which accounting-relevant content the billing document maps. Section 5.3, Price Determination as the Basis of the Value Determination, introduced the account key and described that any Financial Accounting-relevant line of the price determination is assigned to an account key.

In Table 5.5, you can see that there are three queries for Lederwaren-Manufaktur Mannheim. You can use them to determine the revenue accounts:

1. Query of the combination from "customer account assignment group" and "material account assignment group" for sales revenues
2. Query of the "customer account assignment group" for freight revenues
3. Determination of the account key for provisions for volume-based rebates

Condition Technique

Condition technique of the revenue account determination

Both for the revenue account determination and the price determination, SAP uses *condition technique* and therefore enables you to define these different queries in the system.

Condition tables in the standard system

Condition tables are the core of the condition technique. The standard SAP system contains some of these tables. However, you can also define your own tables. The tables differ in number and values of the characteristics whose specific combination is used to find the revenue account. You can check and, if necessary, enhance the fields that are available for the account determination using Transaction OV25.

The values of the condition tables that are available in the standard system are listed in Table 5.6. You can see that five standard tables were searched to find a revenue account in different ways. The *chart of accounts* and *sales organization* criteria are always checked by default. The relevance of the *account assignment group* from the customer and material master and of the *account key* varies.

Table	Chart of Accounts	Sales Organization	Customer Account Assignment Group	Material Account Assignment Group	Account Keys
001	X	X	X	X	X
002	X	X	X		X
003	X	X		X	X
004	X	X			
005	X	X			X

Table 5.6 Standard Condition Table of SD Account Determination

For Lederwaren-Manufaktur Mannheim, you can map the sales revenues with standard table 001. For freight revenues and sales deduction, you do not require the material account assignment group and can therefore use table 002. For provisions for volume-based rebates, the values in table 005 are sufficient.

Reducing the Tables by the Sales Organization

It is striking that the standard tables include the sales organization in addition to the chart of accounts. The reason for this kind of procedure is that the revenue account determination is located in SD. In many cases, however, the sales organization is not relevant for the mapping of revenues in the financial statement. If many sales organizations are set up in SD, you should consider creating your own condition tables without sales organizations. This may considerably reduce the number of account determination entries and minimize the risk of incorrect entries.

Using the Access Sequence

Standard access sequence

You define the sequence in which the tables are queried in the *access sequence*. The SAP standard uses access sequence KOFI. However, you can also configure your own access sequence.

Because condition tables 001 to 005 are not processed in ascending order and table 004 is the last table (see Figure 5.32), the KOFI standard access sequence usually causes confusion in real life.

Access sequence KOFI Account determination

Overview Accesses

No.	Tab	Description	Requiremnt
10	1	Cust.Grp/MaterialGrp/AcctKey	
20	2	Cust.Grp/Account Key	
30	3	Material Grp/Acct Key	
40	5	Acct Key	
50	4	General	

Figure 5.32 Access Sequence KOFI

Here, you can see that the first access addresses the table with the highest level of detail. The principle of going from general to specific applies; that is, the system is supposed to execute the condition table with the most detailed grid first and the less detailed grid last. When it determines an account in a table, the determination stops.

Account Determination Type

You must assign the access sequence in the next step of an account determination type, which is always also a part of the condition tables in which the revenue accounts are defined at a later stage.

	CTyp	Name	AS	Description
	KOFI	Account Determinat.	KOFI	Account determination
	KOFK	Acct Determ.with CO	KOFI	Account determination

Figure 5.33 Account Determination Type Maintenance

In this context, the field description in the SAP system is confusing because the setting refers to the account determination types and not to the condition types (see Figure 5.33). The standard system provides the two account determination types KOFI (account determination) and KOFK (account determination with Controlling). However, you do not specify whether Controlling account assignment is considered until you define the account determination procedures.

Decision about KOFI or KOFK

To understand whether the SAP system uses the KOFI or KOFK account determination type, the concept of the *account assignment category* in the requirements class needs to be explained.

Chapter 3, Section 3.4.4 already discussed the determination of the requirements class. The detail view of the requirements class provides the ACCOUNT ASSIGNMENT CATEGORY field in the ACCOUNT ASSIGNMENT field group. This indicator enables you to specify whether the potential posting is made to a Controlling-relevant account assignment object. You additionally define which object type is addressed.

Requirements class in the revenue account determination

In Figure 5.34, you can see that the account assignment category E ❶ is specified. This means that Controlling account assignment is expected and it has to be a sales order item.

For the revenue account determination, it is initially only relevant whether an account assignment category is defined in the detail view of the requirements class.

- **With account assignment category**
  If an account assignment category is specified, the system uses the KOFK account determination type. Consequently, the G/L accounts defined in the account determination must be created as cost elements.
- **Without account assignment category**
  If no account assignment category is entered, the SAP system will not provide an account assignment object when a billing document is posted. Thus, if the G/L account that is defined in the account determination was a cost element, the posting would lead to an error due to the missing Controlling account assignment.

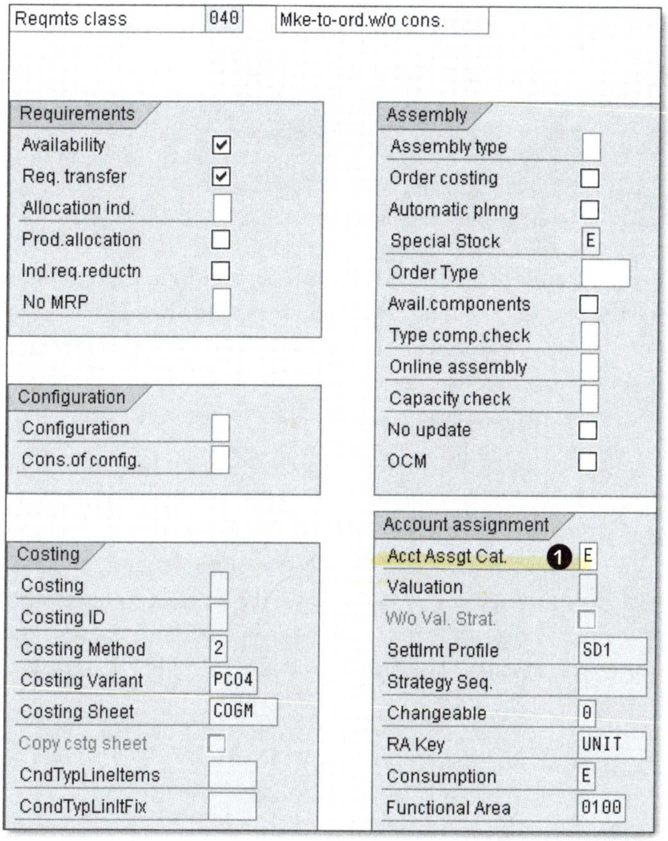

Reqmts class 040 Mke-to-ord.w/o cons.

Requirements
Availability ☑
Req. transfer ☑
Allocation ind.
Prod.allocation ☐
Ind.req.reductn ☐
No MRP

Configuration
Configuration
Cons.of config.

Costing
Costing
Costing ID
Costing Method 2
Costing Variant PC04
Costing Sheet COGM
Copy cstg sheet ☐
CndTypLineItems
CondTypLinItFix

Assembly
Assembly type
Order costing ☐
Automatic plnng ☐
Special Stock E
Order Type
Avail.components ☐
Type comp.check
Online assembly
Capacity check
No update ☐
OCM ☐

Account assignment
Acct Assgt Cat. ❶ E
Valuation
W/o Val. Strat. ☐
Settlmt Profile SD1
Strategy Seq.
Changeable 0
RA Key UNIT
Consumption E
Functional Area 0100

Figure 5.34 Specifying the Account Assignment Category in the Requirements Class

You can find the settings of the requirements class in the Implementation Guide under Sales and Distribution • Basic Functions • Account Assignment/Costing • Maintain Requirements Classes for Costing and Account Assignment.

Account Determination Procedure

Finally, you assign the account determination types to an *account determination procedure*. For each billing type that is used, you can define which account determination procedure should be deployed. The SAP standard already includes the KOFI00 procedure.

Procedure	KOFI00 Account Determination			
Reference Step Overview				
Step	Co...	CTyp	Description	Requiremnt
10	1	KOFI	Account Determinat.	3
10	2	KOFK	Acct Determ.with CO	2

Figure 5.35 Standard Account Determination Procedure KOFI00

The standard SAP system first tries to determine a neutral G/L account. Only then does the system search for a G/L account with Controlling account assignment. This is defined by the requirement. REQUIREMENT 3 indicates that no Controlling account assignment is available, REQUIREMENT 2 expects Controlling account assignment. The account assignment needs to be available when a billing document is created.

Pro forma invoice

Every billing type that contains items relevant for the financial statement must be assigned to an account determination procedure. A *pro forma invoice*, in turn, has a value of zero and therefore cannot generate a document in Financial Accounting; you also do not have to assign an account determination procedure to a pro forma invoice. You configure the settings under SALES AND DISTRIBUTION • BILLING • BILLING DOCUMENTS • DEFINE BILLING TYPES.

Account Keys

Standard account keys

The last element of the account determination is the *account key*. The standard SAP system provides numerous account keys but you can also define custom keys.

The account key should specify the business transaction in the billing documents such as revenues, discounts, or freight costs. The purpose is a detailed breakdown of the profit and loss statement for complete automation.

Link

You link the account keys with the billing document by assigning them to the condition types (see Figure 5.36).

Proc.	Step	Cntr	CTyp	Name	ActKy	Name	Accrls
ZM1000	110	3	RC00	Quantity Discount	ERS	Sales deductions	
	110	4	RB00	Discount (Value)	ERS	Sales deductions	
	302	0	NETP	Price	ERL	Sales revenues	
	310	0	PN00	Net Price	ERL	Sales revenues	
	320	0	PMIN	Minimum Price	ERL	Sales revenues	
	399	0	R100	100% discount	ERS	Sales deductions	
	810	1	HA00	Percentage Discount	ERS	Sales deductions	
	810	3	HD00	Freight	ERF	Freight revenue	
	815	0	KF00	Freight	ERF	Freight revenue	
	817	0	AMIW	Minimum SalesOrdrVal			
	818	0	AMIZ	Minimum ValueSurchrg	ERS	Sales deductions	
	820	0	HM00	Order Value	ERS	Sales deductions	
	895	0	PDIF	Diff.value (own)	ERS	Sales deductions	
	903	0	B003	Customer Rebate	ERB	Rebate sales deduct.	ERU

Figure 5.36 Assigning the Account Keys to the Condition Types of the Price Determination

You have now completed all preparatory work for the revenue account determination and can maintain the actual account determination.

Revenue Account Determination

Let us take a look at the necessary entries in table 001 for Lederwaren-Manufaktur Mannheim (see Figure 5.37) as an example.

Cust.Grp/MaterialGrp/AcctKey

App	CndTy.	ChAc	SOrg.	AAG	AAG	ActKy	G/L Account	Provision acc.
V	KOFI	M001	M001	D1	M1	ERL	800000	
V	KOFI	M001	M001	D1	M2	ERL	800002	
V	KOFI	M001	M001	D1	M4	ERL	800001	
V	KOFI	M001	M001	D2	M1	ERL	801000	
V	KOFI	M001	M001	D2	M2	ERL	001002	
V	KOFI	M001	M001	D2	M4	ERL	801001	
V	KOFI	M001	M001	D3	M1	ERL	802000	
V	KOFI	M001	M001	D3	M2	ERL	802002	
V	KOFI	M001	M001	D3	M4	ERL	802001	
V	KOFI	M001	M001	D4	M1	ERL	803000	
V	KOFI	M001	M001	D4	M2	ERL	803002	
V	KOFI	M001	M001	D4	M4	ERL	803001	

Figure 5.37 G/L Account Assignment in Table 001

Customizing of the revenue account determination

Depending on the chart of accounts in the CHARTS OF ACCOUNTS column, on the sales organization in the SALES ORGANIZATION column, on the account assignment groups for the customers (ACCOUNT ASSIGNMENT

GROUP column), on the material (Material ACCOUNT ASSIGNMENT GROUP column), and on the account key (ACCOUNT KEY column), one G/L account is entered for the posting in Financial Accounting in the G/L ACCOUNT column. The explanations provided so far already indicate that the Customizing of the account determination is not trivial. Therefore, Figure 5.38 additionally provides an overview of all necessary steps.

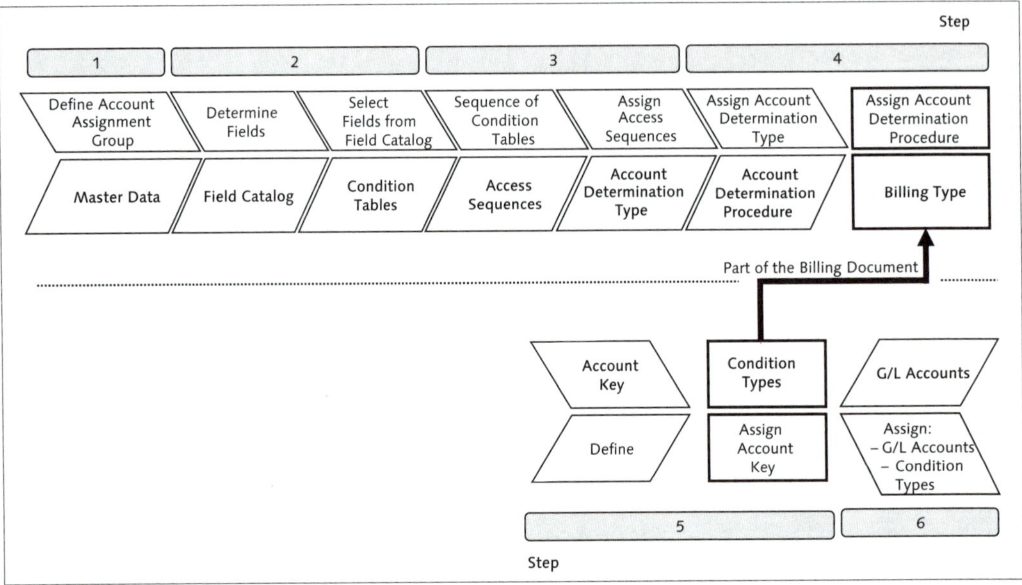

Figure 5.38 Overview of the Customizing Steps

As you already know from the discussion about the KOFI and KOFK account determination types, sales revenues can be transferred to Controlling. In this case, the integration is implemented with CO-PA but also with Overhead Cost Controlling.

5.6.3 Transfer to Overhead Cost Controlling

What is the degree of integration between SD and Overhead Cost Controlling? Overhead Cost Controlling consists of Cost Element Accounting and Cost Center Accounting as well as Order Management.

Account assignment to cost center/internal order

Cost centers can include revenues only statistically. Internal orders, in turn, can also update revenues in the actual. Therefore, it is the only account assignment object in Controlling that can include both costs and revenues. In real life, WBS elements are frequently used. These Controlling-relevant account assignment objects of the PS component can be structured better than internal orders and are therefore often the preferred choice.

In general, you can transfer revenues correctly to Controlling only if the cost element has been created with the correct cost element category, 11 (revenues). This specification in the master record of the cost element has the following effects:

- The values in Controlling are updated with a negative sign (exception: CO-PA).
- You can transfer values from SD to CO-PA.
- For cost centers, the values are updated only statistically. As a result, manual transfer postings in Controlling are possible but no distribution, assessment, or clearing.
- Values are not taken into account for the price calculation.

[+]

Distinction Between Revenues and Cost-Reducing Revenues

In addition to just revenues, cost accounting also refers to cost-reducing revenues. They are both primary cost elements; however, revenues are created with cost element category 11 and cost-reducing revenues with category 01.

Cost-reducing revenues are, for example, interest revenues or rent revenues. You can include these cost elements in the price calculation, which reduces the price of an activity type; for assessments, the costs to be assessed are reduced. You can only transfer cost-reducing revenues through secondary cost allocation in CO-PA. A direct integration as for "real" revenues is not possible.

True account assignment

However, the restriction that only one true account assignment object can be included for each document item still applies.

For example, two steps are necessary if you want to post sales revenues to orders or WBS elements and implement an evaluation in CO-PA. A posting is made to the order or WBS element when the billing document is created. Later—usually during month-end closing—the system transfers the values to CO-PA by settling the orders/WBS elements. When using CO-PA, you should therefore ask yourself which purpose the mapping of revenues in CO-OM or PS serves. Perhaps you can also meet the requirements in CO-PA.

Rebuilding the revenue account determination

Especially when you rebuild the revenue account determination, you do not know all sales processes at the beginning of the project. As a result, error messages may be output at regular intervals when you transfer billing documents to Financial Accounting. SAP provides useful tools to support you in analyzing these errors.

5.6.4 Troubleshooting for Revenue Account Determination

Troubleshooting lets you track the steps the system executes for the account determination. You are provided with detailed error descriptions, which enables you to adapt the account determination or the process.

Troubleshooting

You can access troubleshooting in different ways. If you already know the number of the faulty billing document, you should use the billing document display (Transaction VF03). From there, you can navigate to the logging via the Environment • Account Assignment Analysis • Revenue Accounts menu path.

List of blocked billing documents

If multiple billing documents contain errors or if you know neither the billing document nor the sales order, you can use the list display of blocked billing documents. You can find them in the user menu under Logistics • Sales and Distribution • Billing • Billing Document • Blocked Billing Docs (Transaction VFX3). A selection screen appears. Here, you can limit the search for faulty billing documents to sales organizations and other criteria. If problems occur during the transfer to Financial Accounting/Controlling, you have to select the two checkboxes Accounting Block and Error in AC Interface in the Incomplete due to field group. After the program has been started, the system displays a list of all billing documents that cannot be transferred to Financial Accounting/Controlling. Figure 5.39 shows an example.

Figure 5.39 List of the Blocked Billing Documents

Our example includes one billing document that cannot be transferred. The Incomplete due to column provides the corresponding explanation. The reason is an account assignment error. To analyze this error, you can navigate from here to the billing document and then go to the account assignment analysis. You can navigate there using the Environment • Account Assignment Analysis • Revenue Accounts menu path. Figure 5.40 shows an example of the screen the system then displays.

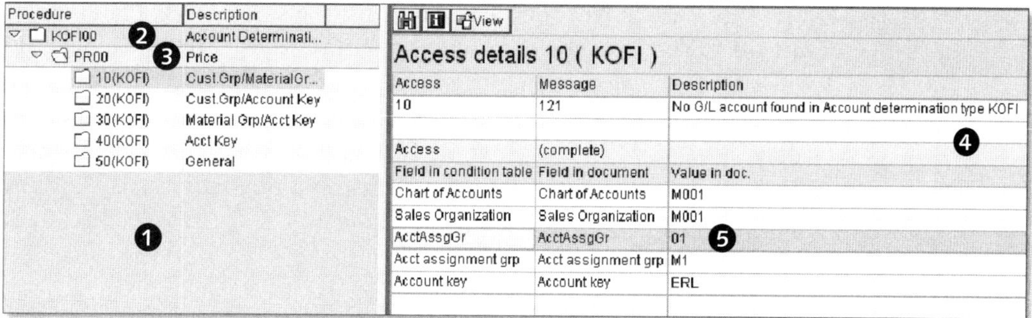

Figure 5.40 Analysis of Account Determination Errors

In the left area, you can view the structure of our Customizing for the revenue account determination ❶. In this example, you use the KOFI00 account determination procedure ❷ and must post the PR00 condition type ❸. For this purpose, the system browses the account determination tables in steps 10 to 50 until it finds an account.

The right area lists the checks that are performed in the steps and the corresponding result ❹. If you take a closer look, you can see that entry 01 is used as the CUSTOMER ACCOUNT ASSIGNMENT GROUP ❺. Because our account assignment groups begin with D, the customer master is probably not maintained correctly. When you have corrected this error, you can restart the transfer to Financial Accounting/Controlling. You can also use the icon to implement the transfer directly from the billing document.

Of course, you cannot solve every problem that easily. However, account assignment analysis is useful to identify problems. You can then solve them by changing master data (as in this case) or by adapting the Customizing of the account determination or costing.

This also requires close collaboration between all parties involved. User departments have to specify their requirements, and the Customizing experts of the SD, Financial Accounting, and Controlling components are responsible for finding a lean and clear solution.

5.7 Summary

In this chapter you learned that there is more than one value flow in the sales process that needs to be considered. The correct determination of the taxes incurred is often neglected. However, if you provide the prerequisites, you can implement the mapping in the system with the appropriate effort.

If you use sales order controlling, you must transfer incoming sales orders to CO-PA. The basis for populating the value fields is the price determination in SD. It also assumes a central role for the billing document and the determination of sales costs. Consequently, it is necessary that—in addition to taking into account the sales and distribution requirements—the price determination meets the cost accounting requirements. Many requirements can be mapped in the standard SAP system. If this is not possible, you can use user exits.

The first process that is relevant for accounting is the goods issue to the customer. The resulting change in stock is valuated with the current valuation price of the material. The account assignment results from the MM account determination. In Overhead Cost Controlling, this transaction can be mapped if the stock change account is defined as a cost element. The accounting-relevant CO-PA system also maps the goods issue because it is always populated according to Financial Accounting. Now, however, we no longer refer to changes in stock, but to sales costs. On a value basis, they are identical to changes in stock in Financial Accounting. Sales costs are not transferred to the costing-relevant CO-PA system until the billing document is created. Here, valuation takes place independently of the mapping in the financial statement.

Together with the billing document, the receivables and revenues are finally also posted in Financial Accounting. The following processes then take place solely in the Financial Accounting and Controlling components because now—hopefully—the only transaction that is left is the incoming customer payment. This transaction can—but does not have to—be transferred to Controlling.

Outstanding purchasing and brilliant sales and distribution are worth little if the products your company produces are not good. Put another way: a product based on a convincing idea with sound implementation can compensate for a lot of weaknesses.

6 Production Process

Previously, we considered the two major processes of procurement and sales and distribution. However, in all production companies, a large part of the value added is obtained from production—in other words, from creating products or providing services. This chapter covers with this important process. As usual, we will be using the example of Lederwaren-Manufaktur Mannheim and will thus be focusing on production companies.

High level of integration

No other area is categorized by such a high degree of integration as production. Here, we are dependent on the supply of materials from purchasing and stockholding; sales and distribution may provide detailed specifications as to what products should be manufactured, the number of units, and their configuration; and controlling supports production management by planning production costs and then analyzing them by reference to production. Production itself is responsible for the process and the value added. This strong degree of integration means that even a simple *production process* requires complex management in the affected areas.

Strategic decisions

Production processes are rarely simple, rather—to borrow once again from the language used in the SCOR model—they are characterized by a complex level of design. In addition, they have significant impact on strategic corporate decisions and at the same time, are guided by strategic decisions. Factors such as delivery dependability and cost savings are of great importance for corporate management and are key factors when making decisions on the product portfolio, the relocation of manufacturing plants, or deciding between in-house and external production.

[Ex]

Strategic Decisions at Lederwaren-Manufaktur Mannheim

Let us stay with the example of handbag production and look at the subproduct of a handbag handle.

It may be possible to outsource the production of handles in a cost-effective way through subcontractors. However, this would mean that we would have to incorporate the subcontractor into our internal production process. This would also make us dependent on the subcontractor's delivery reliability and quality, which can give rise to conflicts of goals. For resolution, results from quality management, controlling, and sales and distribution would be required and an unauthorized decision by the production area not made in consultation with all of the other areas affected could have fatal consequences.

Mapping possibilities in SAP ERP

This example illustrates how complex production decisions are. Yet, we have not even begun to analyze the effects that outsourcing has on operational business. Adjustments would be required in the SAP system in any event. The precise adjustments that would be required would depend on the individual circumstances because the SAP system also provides a range of solutions for mapping production. Generally, the PP (Production Planning and Control) or PP-PI (Production Planning for Process Industries) components provide the basis for this. These can be enhanced with additional components such as APO (SAP Advanced Planning & Optimization) for material requirements planning.

Although we also want to look at the logistical aspects of production in this chapter, we will concentrate on the value flows that arise in the course of a production cycle. The specification of the reference value for which we want to monitor and analyze the operational service performance has far-reaching consequences for the production cycle: should the company be managed based on the results of individual products, production orders, or even sales orders? The answer to this depends to a large extent on the production methods we apply. First off, the adapted SCOR model can give us a good overview. We will therefore look at this to start.

We will then turn to the topic of product cost planning. This is generally based on data provided by logistics: planned purchase prices for raw materials, production times, or bills of material from production.

Production cost planning with SAP

Product cost planning with SAP allows order-neutral cost planning and price formation for materials. Here, you can determine and analyze the cost composition (proportion of material, production, and overhead costs) and the value added of individual production steps, for example.

After planning, you continue with the current process and cover cost object controlling. This allows operational costs to be assigned to operational services. Here, the value flow from the origin of costs through to reporting in CO-PA is also shown.

Cost object controlling

However, let us first clarify what substeps the production process comprises by drawing on the SCOR model.

6.1 Production Process in the SCOR Model

We are now in the Production (Make) section of the SCOR model. This covers the manufacturing of intermediate and finished products (see Figure 6.1).

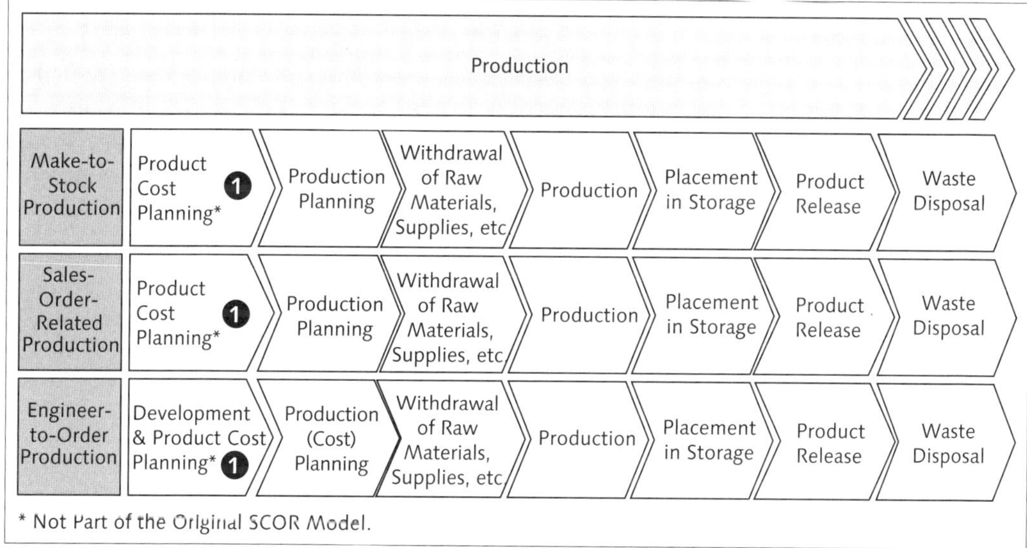

Figure 6.1 Production Process in the SCOR Model

In the SCOR model, the process begins directly with the logistical planning of the production activity. From our point of view, this again misses the point because you cannot usually map the production in the SAP system until a semi-finished or finished product has been cost. We therefore modify the original model again and add the product cost planning step at the beginning.

Manufacturing process

Production varies from company to company not only in its in- and output but in particular in the production cycle. Here, the SCOR model also distinguishes between the process types make-to-stock production, make-to-order production and engineer-to-order production. These have significant influence on the logistical processes of the material flow and the resulting value flow. Let us look at the process types' impact on the value flow.

Make-to-stock production

Make-to-stock production initially "only" aims to increase warehouse stocks of finished products. Customer requirements are then only covered from the warehouse. There is thus no direct connection between production and sales orders. Here, market-oriented production can only be obtained through sales-oriented planning.

Sales-order-related production

In the context of *make-to-order production* (Make-to-Order), the production process is triggered based on existing construction or production documents. Here, the sales order triggers the manufacturing of a product. In terms of controlling, in this configuration it is interesting to compare the cost of goods manufactured with the revenues from the sales order.

Engineer-to-order

Engineer-to-order production (Engineer-to-Order) describes a production process that begins with the product's design. The sales order thus does not trigger production but rather the initial planning and design of the product. Production commences later, after a corresponding delay. Accordingly, engineer-to-order is the most complex production type in terms of planning and preparation.

These different procedures require individual production process definitions from the IT department. SAP interprets these aspects in the areas of product cost planning, cost object controlling, and actual costing/material ledger.

Material ledger

Many companies baulk at the introduction of a material ledger, although they would all very much like to have an actual costing of material costs. They are fearful both of the expense of the implementation and ongoing supervision and the expected volume of data. The material ledger updates each document with a material reference in a separate database, allowing actual costs to be calculated at period-end. It has been estimated that around 3,000 to 4,000 companies have activated the material ledger. No-one can give an exact figure. However, it is clear that only a very small proportion of companies with SAP implementations uses the material ledger. We will therefore not look at this topic any further.

As a result, based on our example of Lederwaren-Manufaktur Mannheim, we will only cover product cost planning and cost object controlling throughout the remainder of the chapter.

6.2 Basic Product Cost Controlling Data

The topmost objectives for product cost controlling are, on the one hand, calculating the product price based on the available master data or manual inputs and, on the other hand, price updates in the material masters. As we mentioned earlier, product cost controlling in the SAP system is characterized by a high level of integration between logistics and controlling. In particular, in making our costing, we can access master data from materials management and production control. Combined with information that we collect from controlling, we get the product cost planning.

6.2.1 Logistical Master Data

The most important production control master data for us are the following:

- Bill of material
- Work center
- Routing

We will briefly look at these objects now.

Bill of Material

Bill of material and assembly

A *bill of material* is a complete listing of all components of a semi-finished or finished product. Depending on the industry, alternative terms such as material or ingredient list are used. When we combine several bills of material with another bill of material—effectively creating a hierarchy—we talk about an *assembly* or a single-level BOM.

Material reference

Bills of material are always created in reference to a material. As an example, let us look at the simplified bill of material for shoes (see Figure 6.2).

You can find Transaction CS01 for creating a material BOM in the application menu under LOGISTICS • PRODUCTION • MASTER DATA • BILLS OF MATERIAL • BILL OF MATERIAL • MATERIAL BOM. First, you define the header data for a bill of material. Here, you define for what material and in what plant the bill of material is valid. Within the system, the bill of material is automatically given a BOM number.

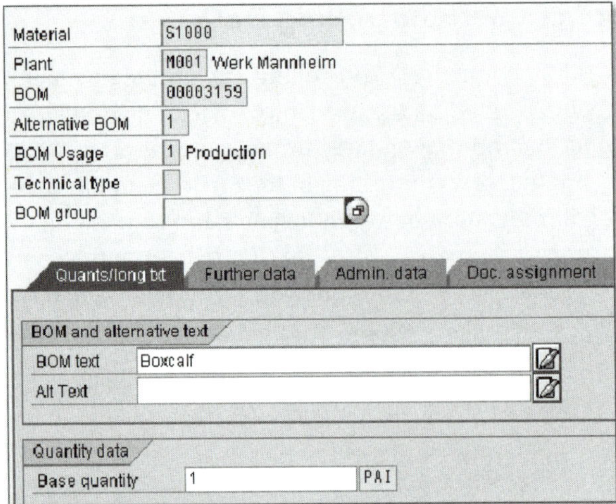

Figure 6.2 Header Data for a Bill of Material

The BOM USAGE field (see Figure 6.2) is not interesting for many companies because this involves working with universal bills of material. However, it would also be possible—for example, in costing and production—to work with various bills of material. With the ALTERNATIVE BOM field, you can maintain different bills of material for a product at the same time. This is important in the foodstuffs industry, for example, because here, the quality of the raw materials determines the precise composition (e.g., more/less liquid).

Figure 6.3 shows the bill of material for product S1000.

Material | Document | General

Item	ICt	Component	Quantity	Un		As	SIs	Valid From	Valid to
0010	L	S1010	1	PC		☑	☐	15.01.2009	31.12.9999
0020	L	S1020	1	PC		☑	☐	15.01.2009	31.12.9999
0030	L	S1050	1	PC		☑	☐	15.01.2009	31.12.9999
0040	L	S1060	1	PC		☑	☐	15.01.2009	31.12.9999
0050	L	S1098	5	M		☐	☐	15.01.2009	31.12.9999
0060	L	S1070	1	PAI		☐	☐	15.01.2009	31.12.9999

Figure 6.3 Bill of Material for Product S1000

The product consists of six components. Entry L in the column ITEM CATEGORY means stock item; in other words, all components are inventory-managed materials. In the column As you can see that a checkmark is set for the first four lines. This indicates that these are materials that in turn have a bill of material. With the *BOM explosion* (Transaction CS11), you can identify all components at a glance (see Figure 6.4).

Material S1000
Plant/Usage/Alt. M001 / 1 / 01
Description Oxford, Boxcalf
Base Qty (PAI) 1
Reqd Qty (PAI) 1

Lv	Item	Ob...	Component number	Object description	Ovfl	Comp. Qty (CUn)	Un	Asm
1	0010		S1010	Bootleg left		1	PC	☑
1	0020		S1020	Bootleg right		1	PC	☑
1	0030		S1050	Sole - left		1	PC	☑
1	0040		S1060	Sole - right		1	PC	☑
1	0050		S1098	Yarn		5	M	☐
1	0060		S1070	Bootlace		1	PAI	☐
1			S1010	Bootleg left				☐
2	0010		S1011	Outer boot leg front, left		1	PC	☑
2	0020		S1012	Outer boot leg back, left		1	PC	☑
2	0030		S1013	Strap, left		1	PC	☑
2	0040		S1014	Inner boot leg, left		1	PC	☑
2	0050		S1015	Cover left, left		1	PC	☑
2	0060		S1016	Cover right, left		1	PC	☑
2	0070		S1099	Thread		20	M	☐
2	0080		D1000 DCU 000 00	Cutting pattern with technical de		1	PC	☐
1			S1020	Bootleg right				☐
2	0010		S1021	Outer bootleg front, right		1	PC	☑

Figure 6.4 BOM Explosion for Material S1000

Whenever we can access a bill of material when calculating product costs, we will do so, to calculate the most realistic possible prices for our products. However, now production must also specify what machines and employees are required to create the product. The SAP system collects this information in *work centers*.

Work Center

A *work center* is a unit that performs steps in the production process. In process industries, we also find the description of the *resource*. Examples include machines (machine groups), entire production lines, or individual people or teams.

At Lederwaren-Manufaktur Mannheim, we opted to primarily map shoe production in Mannheim—with its large proportion of manual work—through work center M001-S (shoes work center) (see Figure 6.6). This corresponds to our conditions in production because a workshop is used in which all steps are performed.

Definition of the activities

The work center activities—in other words, the individual work that a work center can perform—are defined and stored in the *master record*. You can find the required Transaction CR01 in the application menu under Logistics • Production • Master Data • Work Centers • Work Center. The Standard Value Key is stored on the Basic Data tab. For example, if we use the key SAP1 from the standard system, the system proposes the activities setup time, machine time, and time and labor data. You can see this in Figure 6.5.

Standard value key: SAP1 — Normal production

Standard Values Overview

Key Word	Rule for Maint.	Ke	Description
Setup	no checking		
Machine	no checking		
Labor	no checking		

Figure 6.5 Defining the Standard Value Key

Link to Controlling

The link to the Controlling is provided on the Costing tab. Figure 6.6 shows the work center for creating shoes in our Mannheim subsidiary as an example.

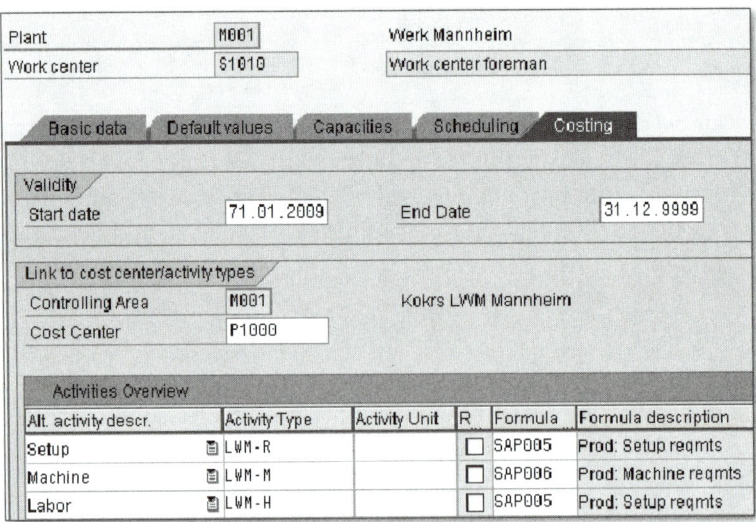

Figure 6.6 Work Center M001-S

"Costing tab"

Here, the work center is assigned to a *cost center*. Whether one assigns several work centers to a cost center is a philosophical question. A 1:1 ratio requires more cost centers than are actually required from a controlling perspective. If our cost center is assigned to multiple work centers, this may become confusing when it comes to cost center planning.

On the COSTING tab, we again find the activities that were defined using the standard value key. They are now joined to activity types. The activity types represent the connector between technical work specifications (production times) and the calculated valuation (costs/allocation records). We can therefore only store activity types for which an activity price has been stored in combination with the selected cost center.

Routing

The specification as to what work centers are involved in manufacturing a product is made based on *routings* (also referred to in process industries as *master recipe*). The workflow for manufacturing a semi-finished or finished product is therefore described. As you can see in Figure 6.7, a routing must always be created with reference to a material.

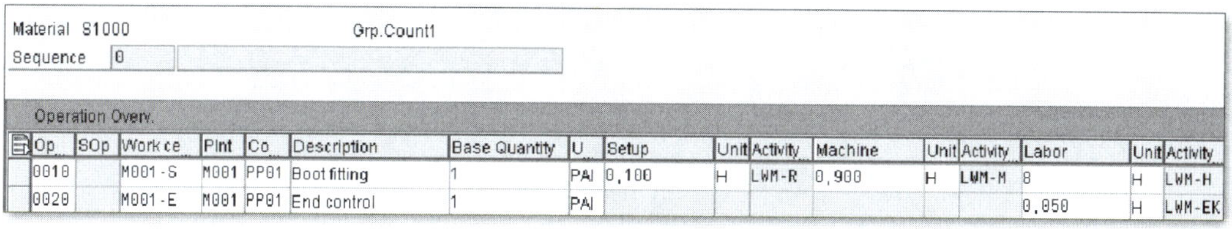

Material S1000 Grp.Count1
Sequence 0

Operation Overv.

Op	SOp	Work ce	Plnt	Co	Description	Base Quantity	U	Setup	Unit	Activity	Machine	Unit	Activity	Labor	Unit	Activity
0010		M001-S	M001	PP01	Boot fitting	1	PAI	0,100	H	LWM-R	0,900	H	LWM-M	8	H	LWM-H
0020		M001-E	M001	PP01	End control	1	PAI							0,050	H	LWM-EK

Figure 6.7 Routing for Material S1000

The work centers M001-S (shoe assembly) and M001-E (final check) are used to manufacture product S1000. In the individual rows, you can also see how long the individual activities should take. Routings are defined under LOGISTICS · PRODUCTION · MASTER DATA · ROUTINGS.

The bill of material, work centers, and routings are required in the system at the very latest when production of a product begins. However, from a controlling perspective, the data should already be available earlier so that it can be taken into account in planning the product costs. You can find more information on this in Section 6.3, Product Cost Planning.

Before we can begin to calculate materials, however, we must also address a number of prerequisites in Controlling.

6.2.2 Prerequisites in Controlling

Activity types

We have already used the term *activity type* for the definition of work centers. Activity types are used to determine the activities that are provided by a cost center. You define activity types under the menu path Accounting • Controlling • Cost Center Accounting • Master Data • Activity Type (see Figure 6.8).

Activity Type	LWM-H	manual time	
Controlling Area	M001	Kokrs LWM Mannheim	
Valid From	01.01.2009	to	31.12.9999

Basic data | Indicators | Output | History

Names

Name	manual time
Description	production time (manual)

Basic data

Activity Unit	H	Hour
CCtr categories	*	

Allocation default values

ATyp category	1	Manual entry, manual allocation
Allocation cost elem	619000	DAA Production
Price indicator		
☐ Actual qty set	☐ Average price	
☐ Plan quantity set	☐ PreDistribFixedCosts	

Variance Values for Actual Allocation

Actl Acty Type Cat.		As in planning
Act. price indicator		

Figure 6.8 Defining an Activity Type

Here, you can see the activity type LWM-H, which appears for Manual Time in production. Because this relates to the manual time activity, it makes most sense to enter the activity in the activity unit Hour. The allocation cost element entered is also important—here, it is 619000 (DAA Production, DAA = Direct Activity Allocation). It is used later for the posting. Cost element 619000 is a secondary cost element of type 43 (posting of activities/processes).

[+]

Showing Activity Types Through Cost Elements

It is important that you create all cost elements you want to use to show activity types with cost element type 43. Otherwise, you cannot enter them here.

However, we only have the activity type's master record and now also have to combine the cost center and the activity type. To do this, choose the menu path ACCOUNTING • CONTROLLING • COST CENTER ACCOUNTING • PLANNING • ACTIVITY OUTPUT/PRICES • CHANGE.

Maintaining activity prices

We can tell from this application path that we are now in the area of planning. We also come across the term *activity price*. An activity price refers to the price associated with an activity type. Figure 6.9 shows an example for maintaining activity prices.

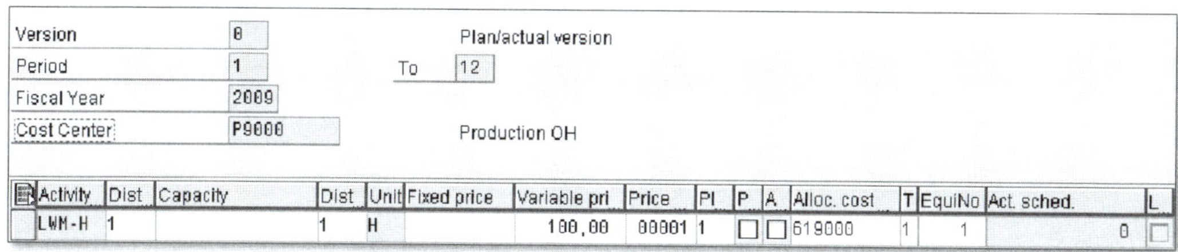

Figure 6.9 Planning the Activity Type LWM-H

An activity price is always defined for a combination of cost center and activity type. This means that depending on the cost center from which it is provided, an activity type can have different prices for the intra-enterprise allocation. It is possible to maintain both fixed and variable activity prices. Maintenance can be performed both manually, as shown in Figure 6.9, and automatically using cost center planning.

Once we have maintained activity prices for all activity types, we could begin to calculate our product costs. Nevertheless, Customizing is required for this as well. There are a number of basic settings that we need both for product cost planning and cost object controlling. We will describe these settings next.

6.2.3 Basic Product Cost Controlling Settings

Costing variant

The lynchpin of product cost controlling is the *costing variant*. This incorporates all of the most important settings.

In the Implementation Guide, you can find the costing variant under CONTROLLING • PRODUCT COST CONTROLLING • PRODUCT COST PLANNING • MATERIAL COST ESTIMATE WITH QUANTITY STRUCTURE • COSTING VARIANT: COMPONENTS. Figure 6.10 shows the most important components of the costing variant.

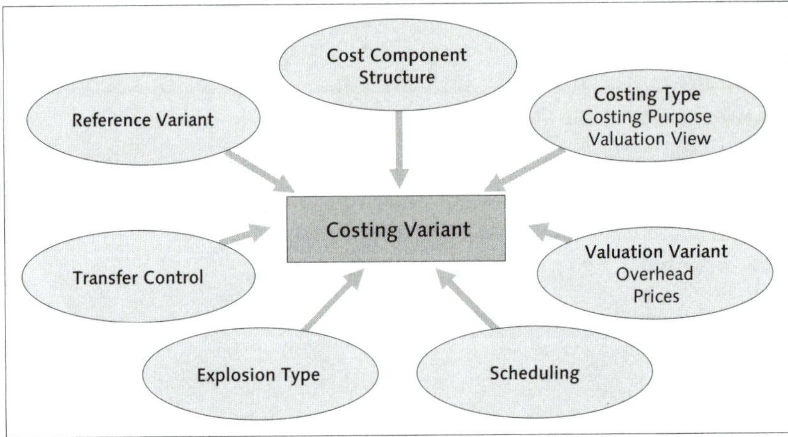

Figure 6.10 Costing Variant Components

We will now discuss the individual components of the costing variant in more detail.

Cost Component Structure

Cost component split

The *cost component structure* is a kind of template that is used to define a *cost component split*. The cost component split allows us to combine individual cost elements into groups and process them further. When you define the cost component structure, you must first consider what rows you later want to see in the reporting for the cost of goods manufactured. Figure 6.11 shows how a possible minimal specification can appear.

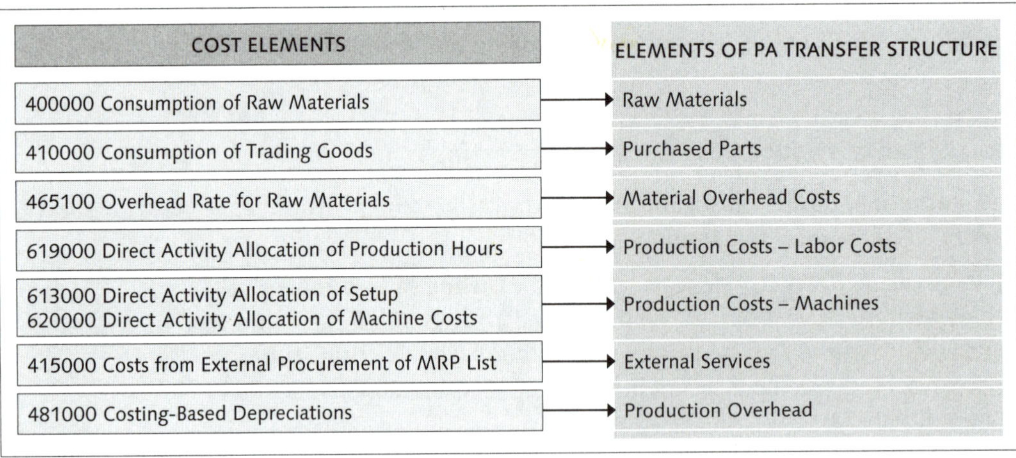

Figure 6.11 Cost Component Structure

If the production consists of several stages, we must consider throughout every stage what information should be passed on to the next stage.

[Ex]

Layering Information Across Various Stages

As an example, let us again look at shoe manufacturing by Lederwaren-Manufaktur Mannheim. A shoe consists of several semi-finished products such as the leg and sole. We must decide whether in the finished product, we want to see the cost of goods manufactured for these semi-finished products only as material usage or broken down by the individual items, the cost origin. As mentioned earlier, this transaction is known as *cost component split*.

Customizing the cost component structure

You can define what cost component structure is used in the cost component structure Customizing, which you will find in the Implementation Guide under CONTROLLING • PRODUCT COST CONTROLLING • PRODUCT COST PLANNING • BASIC SETTINGS FOR MATERIAL COSTING • DEFINE COST COMPONENT STRUCTURE.

Change View "Assignment: Organiz. Units - Cost Component Struct": Over

New Entries

Dialog Structure
- Cost Component Structure
  - Cost Components with Attributes
    - Assignment: Cost Compone
    - Update of Additive Costs
    - Transfer Structure
- Cost Component Views
- Assignment: Organiz. Units - Cost C
- Cost Component Groups

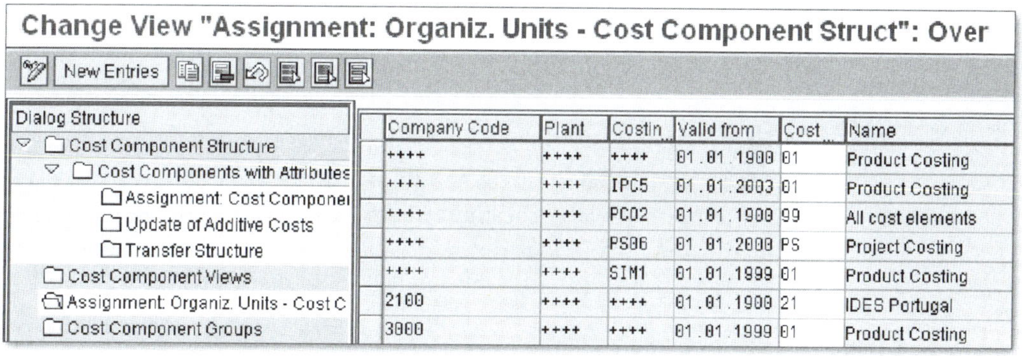

Company Code	Plant	Costin...	Valid from	Cost ...	Name
++++	++++	++++	01.01.1900	01	Product Costing
++++	++++	IPC5	01.01.2003	01	Product Costing
++++	++++	PC02	01.01.1900	99	All cost elements
++++	++++	PS06	01.01.2000	PS	Project Costing
++++	++++	SIM1	01.01.1999	01	Product Costing
2100	++++	++++	01.01.1900	21	IDES Portugal
3000	++++	++++	01.01.1999	01	Product Costing

Figure 6.12 Linking the Cost Component Structure and Costing Variant

Masking

As shown in Figure 6.12, the display is masked. With this technique, plus signs (which you will be familiar with from Internet search engines) are used as placeholders. The first entry therefore applies for all company codes, all plants, and all costing variants because the plus signs can be replaced by any character. The table should be read as follows:

- **Line 1**
  As long as there is no detailed entry, cost component structure 01 is always used because this applies for all company codes, plants, and costing variants.
- **Line 3**
  Costing variant PC02 always works with cost component structure 99.

This entry overrides the entry from the first line for the costing variant PC02.

- **Line 6**
  Company code 2100 always works with structure 21.

Views

In addition, you can also look at a cost component structure using different views:

- Cost of goods manufactured
- Cost of goods sold
- Sales and administration costs
- Physical inventory (based on commercial law)
- Physical inventory (based on tax law)
- Inventory valuation

Depending on how the individual elements are controlled, they are shown or not shown in the various views. However, the views are also responsible for the value update in other components. The components of the material valuation view are thus applied for calculating the standard price.

Costing Type

The *costing type* defines the usage category of the costing (e.g., base planning object or material cost estimate) and the permitted price update in the material master. Should we decide to update the price, this is done at the start of the period, either on the key date or without a date.

[Ex]

Updating the Price on the Key Date

If we calculate our prices for the following year at year-end, for example, we will choose 01/01 as the key date for the following year. The "old" price is therefore still used for goods movements during the current year. However, from 01/01 of the subsequent year, the system works with the newly-cost price.

We determine the usage category according to the price we update in the material master (see Figure 6.13).

As you can see here, we must distinguish between three important costing types: the standard cost estimate, inventory costing, and the current cost estimate or modified standard cost estimate.

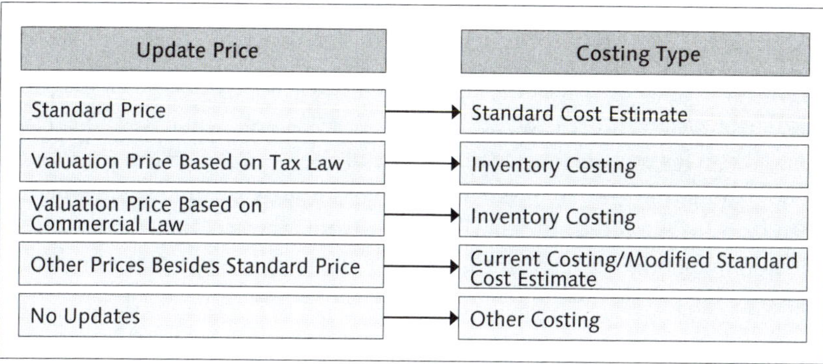

Figure 6.13 Price Update and Costing Type

Standard cost estimate

The *standard cost estimate* is usually started at the beginning of the fiscal year. The prices thus determined are entered as standard prices in the products' material masters and then usually apply for the entire year. However, when we perform a costing, we will first just make a note of the prices. They are then entered as future planned prices in the material master. The prices can then be used for further material valuations. For example, in calculating finished products, we can draw on the future planned prices for semi-finished products. When the prices are released, they are used as up-to-date standard prices. Thus, they are now reflected in Financial Accounting because each goods movement of standard price materials is valued with these prices.

Inventory costing

We talk about *inventory costings* when we do not update the standard price in the material but rather the valuation price based on tax law or commercial law. Needless to say, this form of costing is thus performed at year-end before the balance sheet is compiled. It is now important that the price fixing corresponds to the relevant accounting system. This can also mean that the newly determined price is not used, as a result of the lowest value principle. Unlike for the standard cost estimate, which leads to a revaluation of the warehouse stock when the standard price changes, an inventory costing does not generate any direct postings.

Creating an Additional Standard Cost Estimate [+]

If you want to subsequently calculate variances or work in process through cost object controlling, you will need a standard cost estimate for the product.

Current costing/ modified standard cost estimate

Both the current costing and the modified standard cost estimate are started during the fiscal year. Both forms draw on the current quantity structure. The difference is that the *modified standard cost estimate* performs the price calculation according to the standard cost estimate, whereas the *current costing* accesses the latest price information. Both costing forms are applied if the production parameters have changed and we want to analyze the effects on the material prices. The prices from both costing forms can be updated as planned prices in the material master. They can thus serve as the basis for further costings.

Valuation view

The costing type also determines the valuation view. We can choose between legal, group, and profit center valuation. Particularly when using the material ledger, which enables multiple valuation, it is also important to define the valuation view.

The costing type thus has far-reaching effects on the objective and usage of a costing.

Valuation Variant

Each costing variant also contains a *valuation variant*. The valuation variant defines how the prices of the materials, activity types, processes, and external services used are determined. As an example of this, you can see the price calculation for material components in Figure 6.14.

In our example, the SAP system first tries to find a price in a purchasing info record. The system then checks whether there is a planned price 1. If this is not the case, the system accesses the standard price or, in Step 4, the moving average price.

You can also choose from numerous different prices on the other tabs. In each case, you must put these in a sequence that should always begin with the most realistic price.

Pricing procedure

On the Overhead Costs tab, the system determines what overheads should be calculated based on a *pricing procedure* (see Figure 6.15).

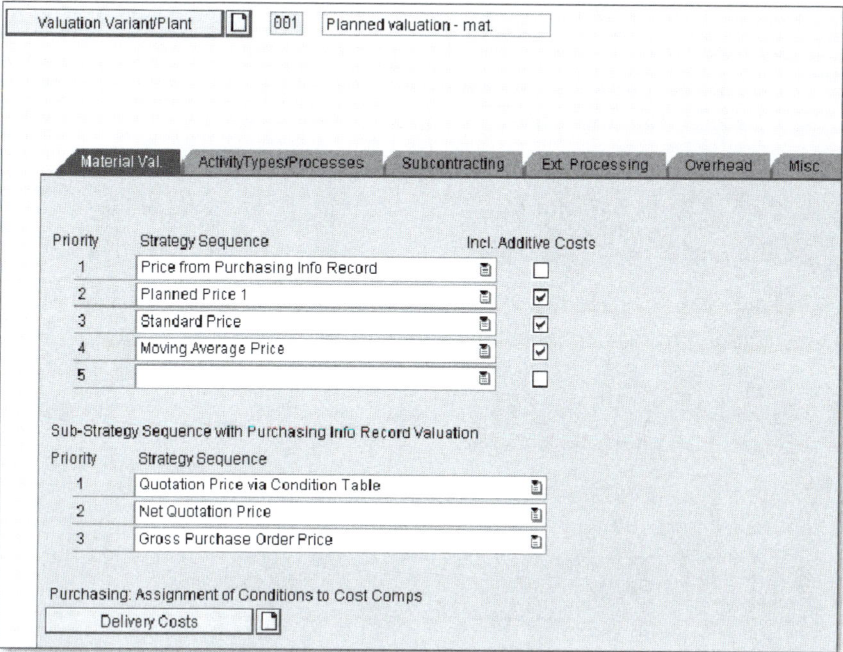

Figure 6.14 Valuation Variants

Procedure M001 Standard1/OH — Check

Costing sheet rows

Row	Base	Overhea...	Description	From	To Row	Credit
10	B000		Material			
20		C000	Material OH	10		E01
30			Material usage			
40	B001		Wages			
45	B002		Salaries			
50		C001	Manufacturing OH	40		E02
60			Cost of labour	40	50	
70			Cost of manufacture			
80		C002	Administration OH			E03
90		C003	Sales OH	70		E04
100			Cost of sales			

Figure 6.15 Pricing Procedure M001

The *pricing procedure* is confusing at first but actually has a simple mathematical structure. First, we must write all rows into the pricing procedure that we require for calculating our overheads. Because the values that are determined will later flow into contribution margin accounting, we must also keep their structure in mind. Three of the rows in Figure 6.15 serve as a basis for the calculation:

- Line 10 is the basis for the material overhead costs in Line 20.
- Line 40 is the basis for the material overhead costs in Line 50.
- Although Line 45 was defined as a baseline, it is not currently used.

Behind each of these rows are hidden cost elements whose balances are each added to form a base value when the overhead is calculated.

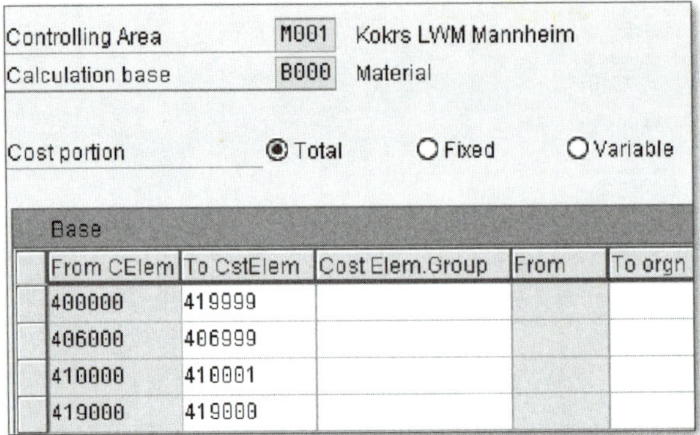

Figure 6.16 Determining the Calculation Base

Determine calculation base

In the individual calculation bases, only fixed or variable or total costs can be taken into account for a cost element. Figure 6.16 shows base B000 from line 10 (as shown in Figure 6.15). This relates to the direct material costs. The cost elements stored here are stored as consumption accounts in the MM account determination; that is, behind the following transactions, for example:

- GBB-VAX (WA for sales orders without account assignment)
- GBB-VBO (consumption from the stock of material provided to vendor)
- GBB-VBR (consumptions)
- GBB-VNG (scrapping, destruction)
- GBB-VQY (sampling with account assignment)

Percentage rate

We must calculate rows 20, 50, 80, and 90 from Figure 6.15 because they represent overheads. For each of these rows, first it is defined what other line in the schema serves as a basis for the costing (columns FROM/TO ROW, see Figure 6.15). We maintain the overhead itself time-dependently as a percentage key. To guarantee this time-dependency, there an overhead key exist only in the pricing procedure itself, behind which the additional Customizing is hidden (see Figure 6.17).

O/H Rate	C000	Material OH
Dependency	D000	Overhead Type

Overhead rate

Valid from	To	CO Area	Ovrhd type	Percentage	Unit
01.01.1992	31.12.9999	1000	1	20,000	%
01.01.1992	31.12.9999	1000	2	20,000	%
01.01.1992	31.12.9999	2000	1	20,000	%
01.01.1992	31.12.9999	2000	2	20,000	%
01.01.2009	31.12.9999	M001	1	3,000	%
01.01.2009	31.12.9999	M001	2	3,000	%

Figure 6.17 Defining the Percentage Rates

Parallel percentage rates can be maintained by supplying the overhead type (OVERHEAD TYPE) and overhead key (OVERHEAD KEY). The overhead type differentiates by actual, planned, and committed overhead application. The overhead key can be stored for a range of cost objects in the master record. It is possible, for example, to have a differing overhead application of material costs for finished products and research and development. In the case of Lederwaren-Manufaktur Mannheim, three percent material overhead costs are currently calculated.

Credit

Finally, we must also update the overheads that are calculated. We define what cost element and Controlling account assignment are used here in the credit (see Figure 6.18).

Controlling Area	M001	Kokrs LWM Mannheim
Credit	E01	Credit Material

Credit

Valid to	Cost Elem.	OrGp	Fxd %	Cost Center	Order	Business Pro
01.01.2009	655101		*	P9000		
31.12.9999	655101		*	P9000		

Figure 6.18 Defining the Credit

To update the overheads, a cost element and an account assignment object to be credited must be entered. The debit is then made on the cost object. The cost elements stored here must be of type 41 (overhead rates). In the case of Lederwaren-Manufaktur Mannheim, a separate cost center that is assigned to production is credited.

Scheduling

The validity period of the costing, and the explosion and valuation date are determined through *scheduling*. Here, the explosion date determines the reference date with which the quantity structure is built. The valuation date decides at what reference date the quantity structure is then valued; in other words, at which date the system finds valid prices. The values that are stored are default values and can be adjusted in the material cost estimate.

Explosion Type

The *explosion type* function defines how the system looks for valid BOM and routing alternatives.

Reference Variant

The *reference variant* defines how the system accesses other costings. When referencing other costings, a distinction must be made between the data transfer and the revaluation of individual items.

[Ex]

Distinguishing Between Data Transfer and Revaluation

Let us take a new handbag as an example, where we can draw on semi-finished products that have already been cost. When transferring data from other costings, we would not re-calculate the price of the semi-finished products; rather, we would use the existing price. For a revaluation, we calculate the price of the semi-finished products as well as the price of the handbag.

Transfer Control

Transfer control is part of the reference variant. It is what makes referencing other costings possible and defines how the system should look for existing costings to transfer existing costing data from another costing.

[+]

Menu Paths in the Implementation Guide

You can find all of the settings described in the Implementation Guide under CONTROLLING • PRODUCT COST CONTROLLING • PRODUCT COST PLANNING • MATERIAL COST ESTIMATE WITH QUANTITY STRUCTURE • DEFINE COSTING VARIANTS or COSTING VARIANT: COMPONENTS.

You will only find the cost component structure and the pricing procedure for the overhead calculation elsewhere, namely under CONTROLLING • PRODUCT COST CONTROLLING • PRODUCT COST PLANNING • BASIC SETTINGS FOR MATERIAL COSTING.

After the Customizing has been fully set up, we can finally begin to plan the product costs.

6.3 Product Cost Planning

Product cost planning is used for order-neutral cost planning and for material price costings. It allows a detailed analysis of the cost composition of a company's products.

Mapping in SAP ERP

The CO-PC-PCP (product cost planning) component is available in the SAP system for product cost planning. It is used for the following activities:

- To determine the cost of goods manufactured and sold for a product
- To identify a product's variable and fixed-cost portions
- To prepare the contribution margin accounting for a product
- To decide on in-house production or external processing
- To identify the most favorable lot size from a cost-accounting perspective

The results from the costing are transferred to the material master record through the *price update*.

6.3.1 Types of Product Cost Planning

Product's life cycle

Various methods for calculating product costs are available to us in the SAP system. The individual costing procedures can be distinguished in particular by the availability of technical specifications from production (especially bills of material and routings). Therefore, when choosing the instrument for planning, the current point in the lifecycle of the product to be cost plays an important role. Figure 6.19 illustrates this relationship.

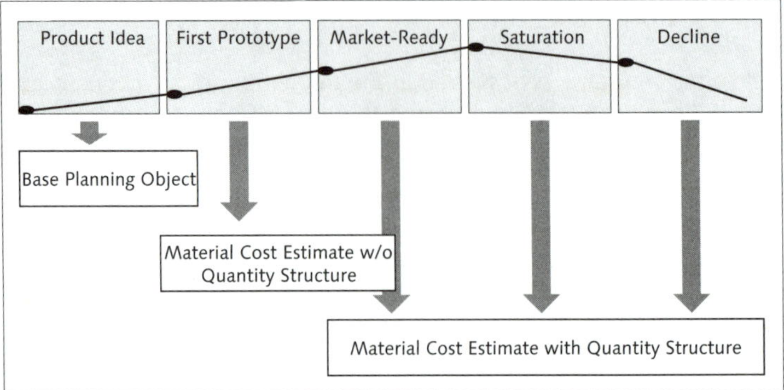

Figure 6.19 Types of Product Cost Planning in the Product Life Cycle

Four costing procedures

There are four costing procedures depending on the availability and completeness of the technical quantity structures:

- Base planning object and simulation costing
- Costing without quantity structure
- Costing with quantity structure
- Ad-hoc costing

Let us now look at these costing procedures in more detail.

Base Planning Object and Simulation Costing

Rough costing

Before we have an exact picture of our product, we can use *base planning object and simulation costing* to perform a rough costing. This allows us to answer the question "What if, ...?" Base planning object and simulation costing is characterized by the mostly manual specification of the cost components. It is therefore used when there is only a rough picture of the product but as of yet, there are no specifications from production.

Decision-makers

Base planning object and simulation costing supports management decisions on the further pursuit of new product ideas. Remembering the SCOR model, in Figure 6.1, base planning object and simulation costing supports the first phase of development and product cost planning in engineer-to-order production. However, we can also use it in sales and distribution when preparing a quotation.

[!]

Updating the Material Prices is not Possible

It should be noted that it is not possible to update material prices with a base planning object.

Costing Without Quantity Structure

Unit costing

Where base planning object and simulation costing helped us decide to continue to pursue a product idea, *costing without quantity structure* can support us in the next step. Here, we again do not yet access master data from production because it has not yet been started. As of yet, there are therefore no BOMs or routings available and all required data must be entered manually. We also call this form of costing *unit costing*.

Key tasks of costing without quantity structure are as follows:

- Assigning the overhead costs in the production and material area to the product.
- Assigning and storing the costs determined as cost elements.
- Displaying the material usage costs for semi-finished products broken down by cost elements

Using initial material master data

With the base planning object, there is no master data whereas with costing without quantity structure, there is manual planning of the cost of goods manufactured and sold with the aid of the initial material master data. In the SCOR model (see Figure 6.1), costing without quantity structure supports the development and product cost planning phase. During the next process step at the latest—production planning—we can then access a quantity structure.

Costing with Quantity Structure

Including bill of material and routing

When we begin with production, bills of material and routings must be created there. We can use these during *costing with quantity structure*, also called the cost estimate. The quantity structure in the costing is then built automatically. For *make-to-order production*, the quantity structure is created from the bill of material and the routing. For *repetitive manufacturing*, the relevant bill of material and the rate routing are taken. During *process manufacturing*, the quantity structure is built based on master recipes.

[+]

Order-Neutral Transaction

Here, costing with quantity structure is still an order-neutral transaction. Thus, we still do not need a manufacturing order. We can draw on the results of the costing for the material valuation by updating the value determined as the standard price.

Ad-hoc Costing

Ad-hoc costing manages without an object reference. It performs rapid cost simulation of frequently-planned projects. There is no price update option. Easy Cost Planning planning forms are the basis for the costing.

Easy Cost Planning

Easy Cost Planning calculates costs using the unit costing function (planning without quantity structure). Individual planning templates are created without reference to bills of material or routings. Easy Cost Planning does not just provide a template for ad-hoc costing; it also forms the basis for costing internal orders, projects, and investment measures.

By way of example, we will now look at a costing with quantity structure and a base planning object in detail. These two costing types are used very frequently. Here, the costing with quantity structure, through access to logistical master data, provides the best results for production companies. The base planning object is a good example for the costing of a product at a time when there is hardly any supporting information in production.

6.3.2 Material Cost Estimate with Quantity Structure

Mass processing with costing run

There are different starting points in the application menu to start a material cost estimate. A company will generally select mass processing through a *costing run*. You can reach the costing run in the application menu through Accounting • Controlling • Product Cost Controlling • Product Cost Planning • Material Costing • Costing Run • Edit Costing Run, or directly with Transaction CK40N.

Worklist

We can anticipate the selection of the materials being cost in a worklist. Transaction CKMATSEL allows us to select materials using many of the fields in the material master such as the material type, valuation class, or profit center.

Costing Run

Regardless of this, we must first create a new costing run (see Figure 6.20).

Create costing run

A number of important criteria are specified when the costing run is created. The costing run date is used as a default value for scheduling. You can change this default date on the Dates tab. You also define the costing variant with which the run is performed. From this, the SAP system determines the contents of the Valuation tab (see Figure 6.21).

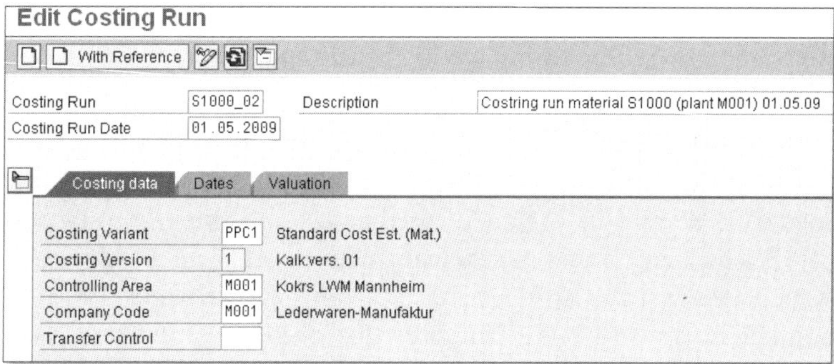

Figure 6.20 Creating a Costing Run

Costing data | Dates | Valuation

Legal Valuation

Valuation Variant	001	Planned valuation - mat.
Costing Sheet	COGS	
Costing Sheet - Material Components	COGS	

Figure 6.21 Costing Definition for the Run

When you store the costing run, the system gives you the required additional operations (see Figure 6.22):

Store costing run

1. Selection of the products to be cost
2. Structure explosion
3. Actual costing
4. Analysis of the results
5. Marking of the cost prices and therefore updating in the material master
6. Release, and thus activation, of the cost prices and revaluation of existing material stocks

Create Cost Estimate

Flow Step	Authorization	Parameter	Execute	Log	Status	Materials	Errs	Still Open
Selection	❶							
Struct. Explosion	❷							
Costing								
Analysis								
Marking								
Release								

Figure 6.22 Operations in the Costing Run

Define steps and parameters

You must first define the selection or processing parameters for each operation. The overview will be completed as processing continues, as shown in Figure 6.24.

We begin the processing in the first SELECTION line (see ❶ in Figure 6.22) by clicking on the icon in the PARAMETER column. There, we must define what materials should be included for the costing. After the selection parameters have been stored, a new icon is displayed in the EXECUTE column with which we can start the actual selection. We can check the result in a number of steps in a log. The presence of logs is indicated by an icon in the corresponding line in the LOG column. If errors occur or not all materials have been processed, this is shown in the ERRORS and STILL OPEN columns.

Finally, for each of the rows from SELECTION to ANALYSIS (see ❷ Figure 6.22), we must run through the steps for the parameter definition and execution. The provisional goal is a marked costing that can be seen in the material master as a future planned price (see ❶ in Figure 6.23).

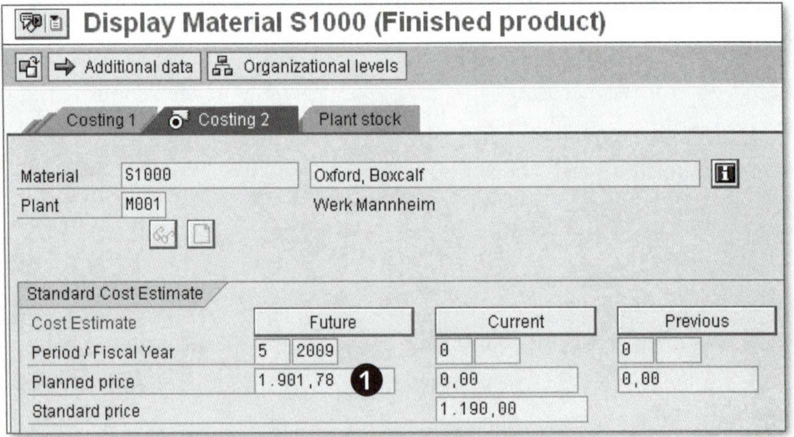

Figure 6.23 Future Planned Price from the Costing Run

To obtain this status, we must execute all costing run operations with at least a yellow traffic light and preferably with a green traffic light (see Figure 6.24).

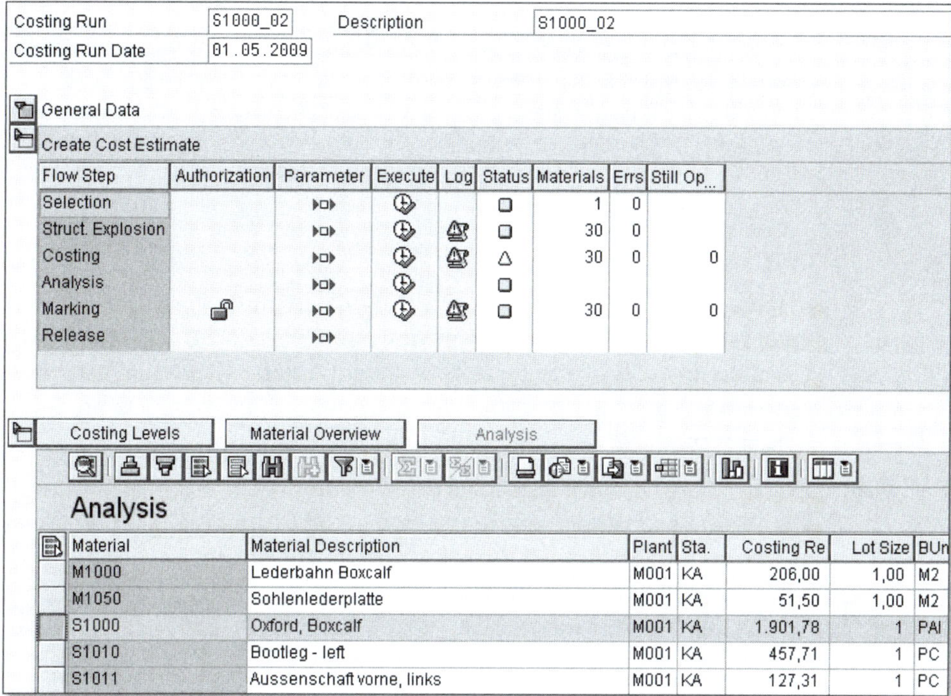

Figure 6.24 Status Development in the Costing Run

Selection

Typically, a costing run is started for all semi-finished and finished products;—that is, all standard price materials—at least once a year. Usually, this run takes place at year-end in preparation for the following year. At this time, the new activity prices from cost center accounting and any changed overhead rates should be available.

Structure Explosion

During the structure explosion, the system first determines—across all manufacturing levels—what material components and activities are required. All of these components must then be taken into account during the actual costing.

[+]

BOM Explosion

The BOM explosion function is unproblematic if all semi-finished and finished products have a standard price. If the company also has components with a moving average price, we must ensure in our costing that prices are not also updated for materials we do not want to calculate.

Costing

In the actual costing, the SAP system tries to determine a price for all of the input factors determined in the previous step. This means that prices must be entered or calculable for all purchased materials, external activities, subcontracting operations, and also for semi-finished products produced in-house and internally-provided services.

Valuation variant

Exactly how the procedure appears for costing valid prices is determined by the *valuation variant*, which is stored in the costing variant. The system proceeds chronologically for costing models.

[Ex]

Chronological Approach for Costing Models

Let us look at the costing for a shoe in Lederwaren-Manufaktur Mannheim: first, the individual parts of the sole are cost.

We must take the prices of the raw materials into account just as much as the internal machine, setup, and wage costs. Next, the finished sole can then be cost, which is composed of the individual components and of the machine, setup, and wage costs. At the end of the hierarchy is the finished shoe, which is cost last.

We have defined whether we will newly cost each component or will use existing costings with transfer control (part of the costing variant).

Date control

Especially with costing runs at year-end, *date control* is also important because it defines for which date the system tries to find valid prices. The effects become clear with internal activity allocations such as the machine hours: we usually create the activity prices, in other words the "prices" for the work centers, with a validity from 01/01 (if applicable, fiscal year = calendar year). Thus, if we start a costing run on12/28 to cost the material prices from 01/01, we must also take the activity prices into account that apply from 01/01 and not those from 12/28. Otherwise, we would be working with obsolete activity prices from cost center accounting.

Flow Step	Authorization	Parameter	Execute	Log	Status	Materials	Errs	Still Open
Selection						1	0	
Struct. Explosion						30	0	
Costing						30	0	0
Analysis								
Marking						30	0	0
Release								

Figure 6.25 Overview of the Operations and Results

In Figure 6.25, you can see that all flow steps (exception: release from costing) have been run. Logs were created in the steps SELECTION, STRUCTURE EXPLOSION, COSTING, and MARKING. These should be carefully checked before you release a run. The costing step was completed with "only" a yellow traffic light because no routings were found for individual components of product S1000. This should not bother us at this point; however, in real life, we would have to investigate why no price could be determined.

Analysis

Under the flow overview (see Figure 6.26), you can see the three buttons COSTING LEVELS, MATERIAL OVERVIEW, and ANALYSIS.

Costing Levels | Material Overview | Analysis

Analysis

Material	Material Description	Plant	Sta.	Costing Re	Lot Size	BUn
M1000	Leather panel	M001	KA	206,00	1,00	M2
M1050	Leather sole sheet	M001	KA	53,05	1,00	M2
S1000	Oxford, Boxcalf	M001	KA	1.541,18	1	PAI
S1010	Bootleg left	M001	KA	457,71	1	PC
S1011	Outer boot leg front, left	M001	KA	127,31	1	PC
S1012	Outer boot leg back, left	M001	KA	53,05	1	PC
S1013	Strap, left	M001	KA	53,05	1	PC
S1014	Inner boot leg, left	M001	KA	127,31	1	PC
S1015	Cover left, left	M001	KA	31,83	1	PC

Figure 6.26 Analysis of the Costing Results

Using these three options, you can check the result of your costing. The analysis view is shown in Figure 6.26. There, you can find the price of our cost product and all parts used. Here, you again discover the price of EUR 1,901.78 that you already saw in Figure 6.23 as the future price in the material master. After the analysis has finished with a positive result, we can mark the costing.

Marking and Release

Marking

To mark the costing, we must allow this function for the current period. This happens company-code-specifically.

To get to the view PRICE UPDATE: ORGANIZATIONAL MEASURE, you must click on the padlock in the MARKING line (PERMISSION column) in the flow overview of the costing run (see Figure 6.27).

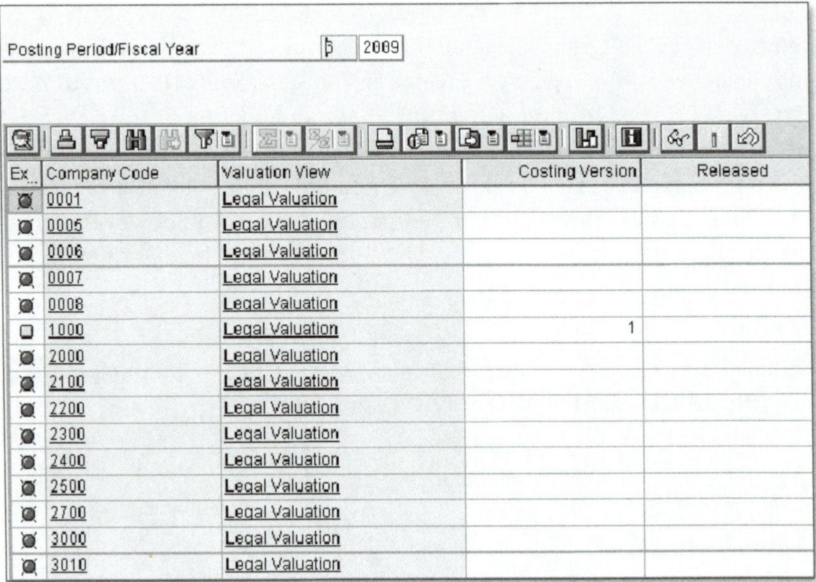

Posting Period/Fiscal Year 5 2009

Ex...	Company Code	Valuation View	Costing Version	Released
	0001	Legal Valuation		
	0005	Legal Valuation		
	0006	Legal Valuation		
	0007	Legal Valuation		
	0008	Legal Valuation		
	1000	Legal Valuation	1	
	2000	Legal Valuation		
	2100	Legal Valuation		
	2200	Legal Valuation		
	2300	Legal Valuation		
	2400	Legal Valuation		
	2500	Legal Valuation		
	2700	Legal Valuation		
	3000	Legal Valuation		
	3010	Legal Valuation		

Figure 6.27 Allowing the Price Update

Release

Marking the costing updates the cost prices in the material masters of the affected products as future planned prices. If we begin to release the costing as the final step, the previously planned price becomes the current price in the material master. Here, you must define in the costing type that the standard price should be updated.

Updating standard prices causes a revaluation of the existing material stocks. Therefore, the MM period closing program (see Chapter 7, Section 7.5.1, Period Closing for the Material Master) must have taken place for the current period at this point.

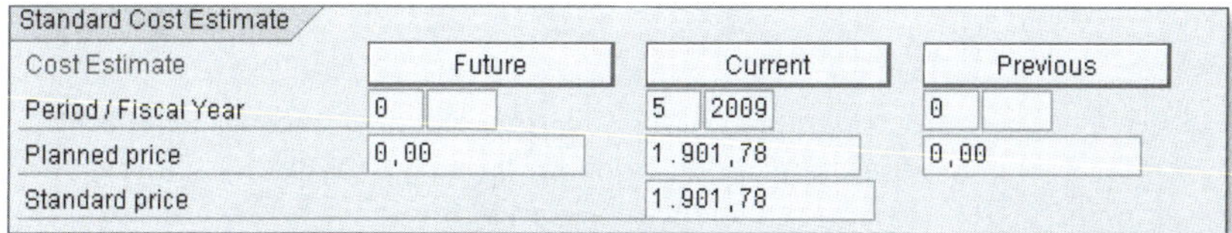

Figure 6.28 Current Price After Costing Release

[!]

Releasing a Costing

You must ensure that a costing is not released until it has been intensively checked and found to be correct. As long as the costing is only marked, you can still change it without any problems or even discard it altogether. This is no longer possible after the costing has been released. There is a delete function; however, it should only be used in individual cases. The SAP system only allows a costing to be released once for each period.

Unit Costing

As we have seen, the costing run is a simple tool to determine the current material prices. If we only want to calculate a single product, we can also create a unit costing as an alternative to the costing run.

In our example, we would use Transaction CK11N for this. You can find it in the application menu under ACCOUNTING • CONTROLLING • PRODUCT COST CONTROLLING • PRODUCT COST PLANNING • MATERIAL COSTING • COST ESTIMATE WITH QUANTITY STRUCTURE • CREATE. To update the price from this costing, we must then switch to Transaction CK24 (price update) to explicitly trigger it again.

In addition to looking at actual material costing with quantity structure, we will now take a look at the *simulation and base planning object* in more detail.

6.3.3 Simulation and Base Planning Object

Simulation and base planning object

The Controlling component and the PP component are entry points for the simulation and base planning object. In Controlling, you can reach them in the application menu via ACCOUNTING • CONTROLLING • PRODUCT COST CONTROLLING • PRODUCT COST PLANNING • REFERENCE AND SIMULATION COSTING • CREATE BASE PLANNING OBJECTS, or directly using Transaction KKE1.

[+]

Concept

Although the term *simulation and base planning object* is always used in the SAP system, in the literature and in everyday language the term is more commonly reduced to *base planning object*. From here on, we will therefore only talk about the base planning object.

To cost a product without master data, a base planning object must first be created (see Figure 6.29). The system queries the most important data for the product being cost. In addition to the company code and plant, the system also queries a profit center and the pricing procedure being used, which was already discussed in detail in Section 6.2.3, Basic Product Cost Controlling Settings.

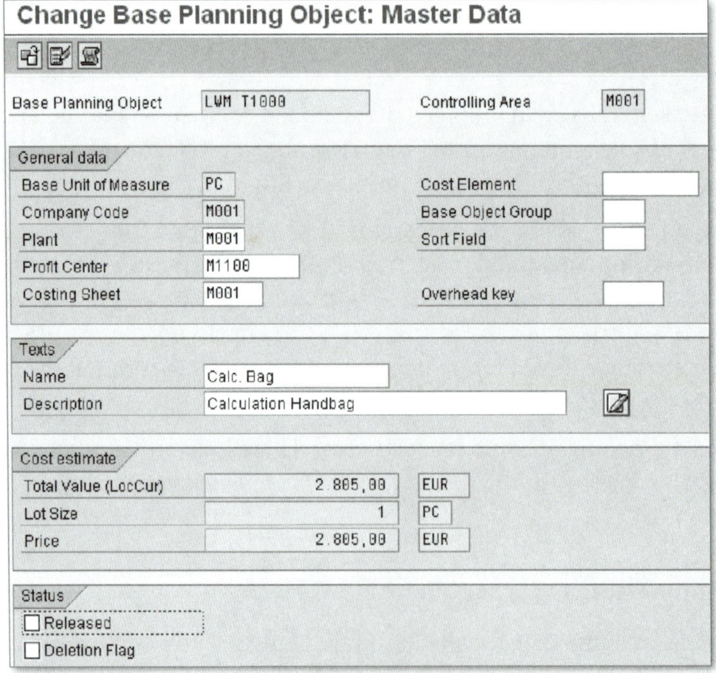

Figure 6.29 Creating a Base Planning Object

A costing variant must also be given for controlling the costing.

Costing variant

If we have created a base planning object as shown in Figure 6.29 and Figure 6.30, the system automatically creates a master record for the costing. Assignments, units of measure, and texts for this base planning object are stored here. The system determines the costing result based on the costing variant stored in the costing. In particular, the costing variant is used to define how the individual costing items that are manually entered for the costing should be valued.

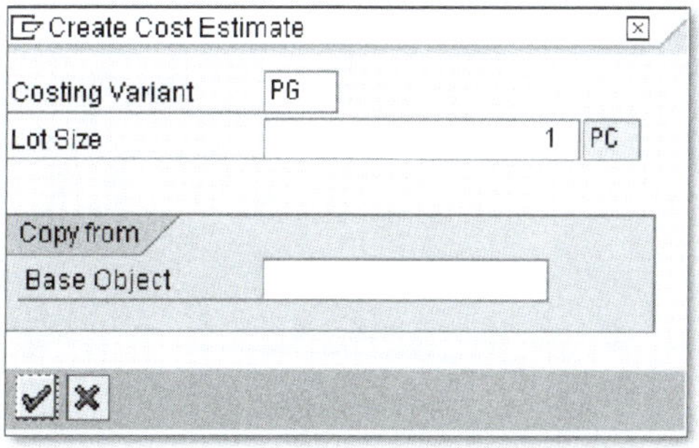

Create Cost Estimate
Costing Variant PG
Lot Size 1 PC
Copy from
Base Object

Figure 6.30 Choosing the Costing Variant

Lederwaren-Manufaktur Mannheim uses the costing variant PG for base planning objects.

List screen

For the base planning object, the components of the product being cost—and thus the individual costing items—must be entered in the *list screen*, which is similar to a spreadsheet. You can choose between three different views, which can be individually set:

- View/list screen-1: Resources
- View/list screen-2: Texts, variable items, and totals
- View/list screen-3: Simple formulas

The list screens only differ in their layout and thus in their data input logic. In list screen-1, the costing is created based on the material (resource); in list screen-2, it is created based on descriptive texts (assuming no material numbers are known). In list screen-3, the costing is determined or described using formulas.

We will continue with list screen-1. This produces the costing shown in Figure 6.31.

Item category

Each item in the list screen must be supplied with an *item category* (M = Material, I = In-house production, etc.). This serves as a default for the data entered for the costing or read by the system and how the cost calculation for the item takes place. Figure 6.32 shows an example for an item's detail view.

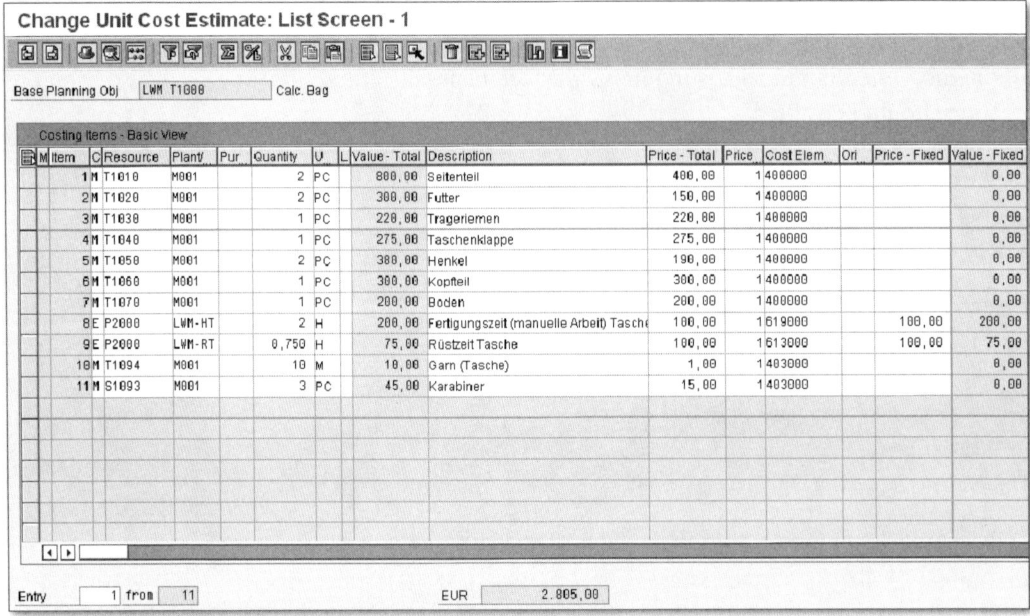

Change Unit Cost Estimate: List Screen - 1

Base Planning Obj LWM T1000 Calc. Bag

Costing Items - Basic View

Item	C	Resource	Plant/	Pur	Quantity	U	L	Value - Total	Description	Price - Total	Price	Cost Elem	Ori	Price - Fixed	Value - Fixed
1	M	T1010	M001		2	PC		800,00	Seitenteil	400,00	1	400000			0,00
2	M	T1020	M001		2	PC		300,00	Futter	150,00	1	400000			0,00
3	M	T1030	M001		1	PC		220,00	Trageriemen	220,00	1	400000			0,00
4	M	T1040	M001		1	PC		275,00	Taschenklappe	275,00	1	400000			0,00
5	M	T1050	M001		2	PC		380,00	Henkel	190,00	1	400000			0,00
6	M	T1060	M001		1	PC		300,00	Kopfteil	300,00	1	400000			0,00
7	M	T1070	M001		1	PC		200,00	Boden	200,00	1	400000			0,00
8	E	P2000	LWM-HT		2	H		200,00	Fertigungszeit (manuelle Arbeit) Tasch	100,00	1	619000		100,00	200,00
9	E	P2000	LWM-RT		0,750	H		75,00	Rüstzeit Tasche	100,00	1	613000		100,00	75,00
10	M	T1094	M001		10	M		10,00	Garn (Tasche)	1,00	1	403000			0,00
11	M	S1093	M001		3	PC		45,00	Karabiner	15,00	1	403000			0,00

Entry 1 from 11 EUR 2.805,00

Figure 6.31 List Screen-1 for the Base Planning Object

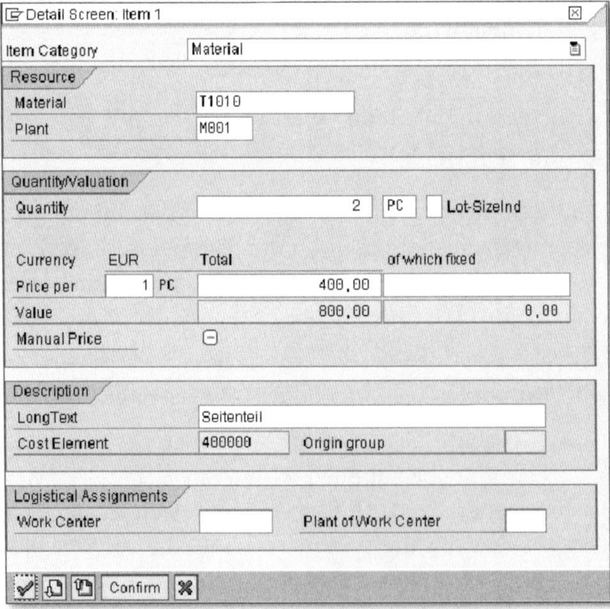

Figure 6.32 Detail Screen in the Base Planning Object

Header for the base planning object

Texts and additional information—in particular the price date—can be stored for the entire costing. This information is initially generated automatically when the base planning object is created but can also be adjusted if required. You can view and change this information in the header (see Figure 6.33).

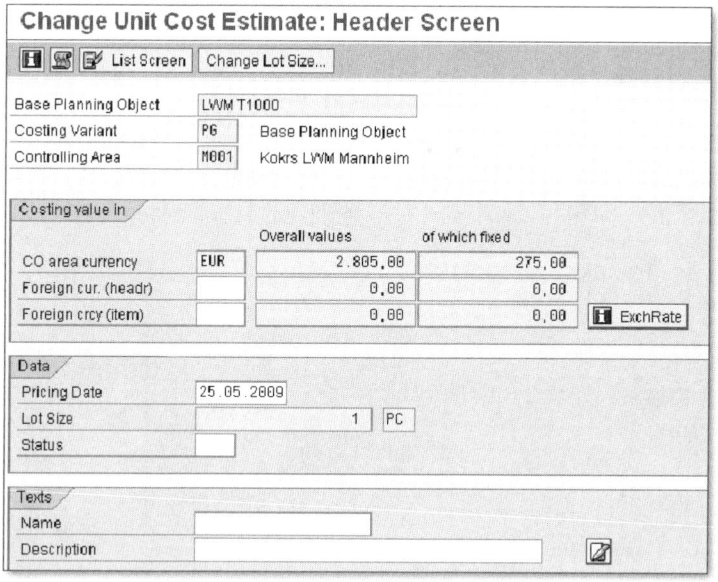

Figure 6.33 Header in the Base Planning Object

Temporary and final storage

To be able to complete the base planning object, the data entered must first be temporarily stored and then saved. This means that only temporary storage takes place when you first save in the list screen. The final storage of the costing takes place subsequently in the header. You automatically return to the header after the temporary storage.

[+]

Explode costing

Similar to single-level BOMs, costings can in turn be entered into a base planning object. This produces a hierarchically-arranged costing model.

To now be able to display the components of additional costings contained in a costing, you can dissolve the former (the additional items contained). To do this, access the costing items for the integrated costing, to show this by item.

Figure 6.34 shows a complete base planning object implemented Here, the RELEASED indicator shows in the base planning object. However, this status has no meaning for the system. Thus, this is a field we can use for our own purposes, for example, to note that a base planning object has reached its final status.

Revaluation of the base planning object

Because you cannot rule out that master data may have changed since the last basic object costing, you can use Transaction KKEB to *revaluate* the base planning object. This not only affects single-level costings but also works for multi-level interlaced costings. If the revaluation should be performed for a large number of costings, it should be performed in the background. This will avoid long runtimes. When the revaluation run is complete, all you have to do is save the changes.

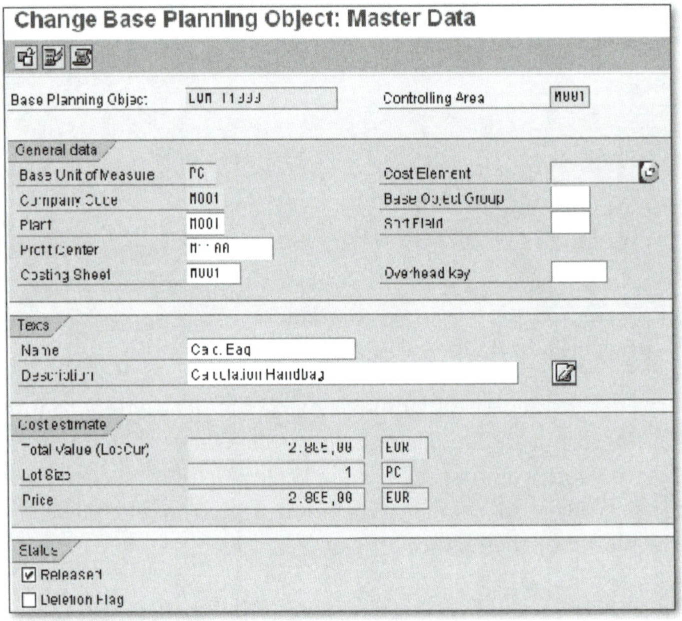

Figure 6.34 Completed Base Planning Object

Update in the material master not possible

As with ad-hoc costing, the price determined from the base planning object cannot be updated in a material master because it only involves the simulation of a costing. However, you can use the stored base planning object as a template for a base planning object without quantity structure, provided that material master data is available.

You have now been shown two detailed examples for the planning of product costs. The "vague" base planning object, which you can use for "What if?" scenarios, and costing with quantity structure, which is closely interlocked with production and which accesses production master data.

6.4 Cost Object Controlling

Cost object controlling (CO-PC-OBJ) is a prerequisite for assigning costs to different products, product groups, or sales orders. It allows current and continuous product controlling. A variance analysis is possible using a comparison of planned costs from product cost planning and costs actually incurred. This will ultimately increase the transparency of the cost of goods manufactured. There are different forms of cost object controlling, depending on the production type and objective. We will analyze the most important characteristics in this section. You will learn about the benefits and limits of the individual characteristics and consider the possible value flow in each case. Because period-end closing is an important element in Controlling at this point, we will also examine the steps arising here in more detail.

However, first you should familiarize yourself with cost object controlling terms in SAP.

6.4.1 Cost Object Controlling Functions in SAP ERP

In the last section, you learned that product cost planning is order-neutral. This means that it plans production costs irrespective of individual production orders. As a result, we can only work with planned prices, quantities, and times.

[Ex]

Order-Neutral Product Cost Planning

For example, we will assume that we will always produce 500 units of our Kelly Bag 1. However, variations may occur in operational business. For example, because we can currently sell more bags on the market and use free production capacity, we can produce another unplanned 300 units.

Calculate target costs

Because our cost of goods manufactured also includes fixed-costs, a smaller lot size automatically means higher production costs per unit. This is because each product is debited by a proportionally higher percentage of fixed-costs. The objective of cost object controlling is to calculate the production order's target costs—in other words, to convert the target costs to the actual production quantity. In the event of a variation, cost object controlling will support you with the analysis.

Controlling Types

However, it is not always possible or useful to analyze individual production orders, as is shown by the belts, for example, that Lederwaren-Manufaktur Mannheim produces en masse. The SAP system therefore distinguishes between three different types of controlling:

- Periodic cost object controlling/periodic product controlling
- Order-related cost object controlling/order-related product controlling
- Product cost by sales order

Use of the individual characteristics depends on the organization of production. For make-to-order production, order-related cost object controlling is useful, whereas periodic product controlling is ideal for the production of bulk goods.

Periodic cost object controlling

The basis for *periodic product controlling* is a longer-term consideration of capacity loading and crediting of cost objects. Generally, we look at the costs that arise during a period and are not just focused on individual manufacturing orders but rather the development throughout a period. To affect this, we use *product cost collectors* as the cost objects, which we will look at later in more detail. You should always opt for periodic product controlling if your product is being manufactured without any changes over a long period.

In the case of Lederwaren-Manufaktur Mannheim, this applies to the production of belts. Here, we have a small product portfolio that has been stable for several years. It is interesting to analyze how the production costs develop over the years.

Order-related cost object controlling

The goal of *order-related cost object controlling*, on the other hand, is to analyze the costs for a specific manufacturing order. The main emphasis is not the time aspect but the analysis of individual production lots. We use the manufacturing order as a cost object for this type of product controlling.

Product cost by sales order

With *product cost by sales order*, we are leaving the area of pure cost controlling. By making the items in a sales document the cost object, we can now also consider the revenues generated, along with the production costs that have arisen.

More Detailed Information on the Types of Controlling [+]

Following our discussion of the fundamental functions in cost object controlling and the explanation of the period-end closing, we will look more closely at these three important types of controlling.

You will find additional information on period-related product controlling in Section 6.4.3; order-related product controlling in Section 6.4.4; and product cost by sales order in Section 6.4.5.

Cost Objects

The following *cost objects* are available in an SAP system:

- **Manufacturing orders**
  There are two known characteristics for manufacturing orders:
  - Production order
  - Process order

  You define whether a manufacturing order is a cost object in the order type. If you are not using a PP or PP/PI, you can also use *production orders* in Controlling. This involves production orders without quantity structure with which production is mapped from a Controlling perspective.
- **Sales document items**
  Sales document items can also serve as cost objects. Although this also incorporates the items for queries and offers, in this context we are generally talking about *product cost by sales order*. This means that a sales order's items become cost objects.
- **Product cost collector**
  Product cost collectors are used in periodic product controlling to collect the actual costs for the period. You can use product cost collectors for anonymous warehouse production and for mass production in combination with valuated sales order stock. Product cost collectors are created with reference to a material, a production process, or a plant.
- **Cost object node/Cost object hierarchy**
  The cost object hierarchy and its nodes can be used like a product cost collector.

- **General cost objects**
  This type of cost object is used to analyze intangible products and services. The costs collected here can subsequently be charged either to a cost center or to CO-PA.
- **Classic account assignment objects**
  Additionally, classic account assignment objects such as projects and PSP elements, networks, and internal orders can also serve as cost objects.

As you can see, you can choose from many objects in the SAP system; which objects you use within your company is an individual decision.

[+]

Effects of Production Typologies on Cost Object Controlling at Lederwaren-Manufaktur Mannheim

Lederwaren-Manufaktur Mannheim's *shoes* are produced in make-to-order production as customers request them. Because the entire production process for a pair of shoes always starts in relation to a sales order, sales order controlling is ideal in this situation.

Handbags are produced both under the company's own label and as make-to-order production for customers. The costs and variances for the production lot are relevant for production. Accordingly, order-related product controlling is used for this.

Belts are produced in make-to-stock production, unchanged over a long period of time, and in high numbers. Analysis of costs for individual production orders is not control-relevant. It is much more interesting to know what costs or variations have been incurred during a period. Production of belts therefore requires periodic product controlling.

Cost Calculation in the Production Process

The basis for cost object controlling is the calculation of the costs at different times. A distinction is made between the following types:

- Preliminary costings
- Simultaneous costings
- Period-end closing

In the course of production over time, we get the scenario shown in Figure 6.35.

	No Production	Ongoing Production	Period End
Product Cost Planning	Product Cost Planning		
Cost Object Controlling	Preliminary Costing	Simultaneous Costing – Material Withdrawals – Transaction Confirmation	Final Costing/Closing – Work in Process – Overhead Application – Final Costing – Settlement

Figure 6.35 Time Schedule for Product Cost Controlling

Preliminary Costing

Time of creation

Preliminary costing generally takes place at the time a cost object is created. The planned costs are determined in relation to the planned quantities. These are drawn on in determining later production variances. However, one could also conceivably draw on preliminary costings for various production versions of a product when making the production decision. In sales order controlling, the costing is generally performed when the sales order is stored. The standard cost estimate on a cost object can be restarted if parameters such as the product's bill of material change.

Simultaneous costing

Before production is complete

As part of simultaneous costing, you can analyze the costs that have arisen to date, before a production process has been completed (within the period for periodic product controlling). The following transactions can trigger costs for the cost objects:

- Material withdrawals for material components
- Debiting the cost object through postings in Financial Accounting (e.g., incoming invoice)
- Confirmation of times
- Intra-enterprise activity allocations and repostings

The costs may already be coupled with credits from the cost object. The credit is usually obtained by issuing products to the warehouse. For standard price materials, the product is valued at the standard price. Any variances arising from the production are generally posted later during period-end closing.

Simultaneous costing is thus the product of the entry of actual costs and credits for the cost objects.

From the perspective of the SCOR model, the withdrawal of raw materials, supplies, and consumables, actual production and placement in storage fall under simultaneous costing.

[+]

Period-End Closing

Period-end closing, after preliminary costing and simultaneous costing, is the third and final costing to take place within the production process. Because this step is the most substantial and most important, we will devote a separate, extensive section to its discussion.

6.4.2 Period-End Closing

Period-end closing comprises several substeps. First, the cost objects are debited with costs through overheads. Then, final costing takes place, during which the work in process and the variances are determined. Finally, the cost objects are charged to other cost objects or to the profit and loss statement.

Overhead application

The Customizing of the pricing procedure is taken for the calculation and posting of *overheads*. This was already described in Section 6.2.3, Basic Product Cost Controlling Settings. Various transactions are available to perform the overhead application, depending on the cost object; however, they are all similar. For purposes of clarity, we are using Transaction KI12 for the individual processing of production orders.

Overhead cost controlling

The system presents the overhead application in detail. In Figure 6.36, you will find the calculation logic from the pricing procedure in Figure 6.15. The resulting postings in overhead cost controlling are also shown (see Figure 6.37).

Cost accounting

The update run for the overhead calculation directly creates a document in cost accounting. With this document, we can settle the cost object stored in the credit in the amount of the overhead rates against the production order (see Figure 6.38). From the credit specifications in Figure 6.18, we get cost center P9000 for the first line from Figure 6.37.

Display ORD 651994 5/2009: Item - Conditions

Item 1

Qty 0,000 Net 1.148.763,65 EUR

Tax 0,00

Pricing Elements

N	CnTy	Name	Amount	Crcy	per	U	Condition value	Curr.	Status	NumC
	B000	Material					1.004.778,84	EUR		0
	C000	Material OH	3,000	%			30.143,37	EUR		0
		Material usage	0,00	EUR	1		1.034.922,21	EUR		0
	B001	Wages					0,00	EUR		0
	B002	Salaries					0,00	EUR		0
	C001	Manufacturing OH	5,000	%			0,00	EUR		0
		Cost of labour	0,00	EUR	1		0,00	EUR		0
		Cost of manufacture	0,00	EUR	1		1.034.922,21	EUR		0
	C002	Administration OH	7,000	%			72.444,55	EUR		0
	C003	Sales OH	4,000	%			41.396,89	EUR		0
		Cost of sales	0,00	EUR	1		1.148.763,65	EUR		0

Figure 6.36 Overhead application for a Production Order

Actual Overhead Calculation: Product Cost Collector Debits

Debits

Senders	Receivers	Cost Elem.	Val/COArea Crcy
CTR P9000	ORD 702665	655101	212,82
CTR P9000		655300	511,48
CTR P9000		655400	292,27
			1.016,57

Figure 6.37 Information for Posting Overheads

DocumentNo Doc. Date Document Header Text RT RefDocNo User Name Rev RvD

700000005 29.05.2009 AHOELZLW

PRw	OTy	Object	CO object name	Cost Elem.	Cost element name	Val/COArea Crcy
1	ORD	651994	Kelly Bag 1	655101	OHS Raw Material	30.143,37
2	CTR	P9000	Production OH	655101	OHS Raw Material	30.143,37-
3	ORD	651994	Kelly Bag 1	655300	OHS Administration	72.444,55
4	CTR	P9000	Production OH	655300	OHS Administration	72.444,55-
5	ORD	651994	Kelly Bag 1	655400	OHS Sales & Distrib.	41.396,89
6	CTR	P9000	Production OH	655400	OHS Sales & Distrib.	41.396,89-

Figure 6.38 Controlling Document for the Actual Overhead Calculation

Financial Accounting

Because real-time integration is activated at Lederwaren-Manufaktur Mannheim, a document is also directly generated in Financial Accounting (see Figure 6.39). However, this document has no impact on the balance sheet.

CoCd	Itm	L.item	PK	S	Account	Description	Amount	Curr.	Tx	Profit Center	Segment
M001	1	000001	50		810500	RTI:int.rev.CC-inter	30.143,37-	EUR		M9999	MANF
	2	000002	50		810500	RTI:int.rev.CC-inter	72.444,55-	EUR		M9999	MANF
	3	000003	50		810500	RTI:int.rev.CC-inter	41.396,89-	EUR		M9999	MANF
	4	000004	40		850500	RTI:int.cost CC-int	30.143,37	EUR		M1100	M_BAGS
	5	000005	40		850500	RTI:int.cost CC-int	72.444,55	EUR		M1100	M_BAGS
	6	000006	40		850500	RTI:int.cost CC-int	41.396,89	EUR		M1100	M_BAGS

Figure 6.39 Accounting Document for the Actual Overhead Calculation

This concludes our discussion of the overhead application and we will turn to the next step in the closing process, final costing.

Final Costing

The overhead application is followed by final costing, where the work in process and the variations are determined.

Work in Process

Costs without a product

Work in process (WIP), shows costs in production that have not yet been set against a finished product (semi-finished or finished product). Thus, the value of the unfinished products is determined.

Products without posting

In order-related product controlling, the exact opposite situation can also arise: a semi-finished or finished product has already been delivered from production to the warehouse; however, not all corresponding material withdrawals and confirmations have been posted. In this case, provisions are formed for production costs that are still anticipated. This is also part of the WIP calculation in the SAP system. From here on, we will group both under the term WIP.

The goal of WIP calculation is the period-related assignment of revenues and costs as part of the period-end closing (see Chapter 7, Section 7.10, Manual Postings). A WIP calculation is possible for the following objects:

- Product cost collectors, but only at target costs
- Production order, generally at actual costs
- Sales-order-related production with valuated sales order stock

Valuation at target/actual costs

During a WIP calculation at *actual costs*, WIP per production order is calculated from the difference between the accrued and the settled actual costs; that is, on the one hand from the debits for material withdrawals, intra-enterprise activity allocations, external services, and overhead costs and on the other hand from the credits from deliveries to the warehouse.

Calculation at *target costs* valuates all consumptions and transactions reported for production orders or for repetitive manufacturing at target costs. Therefore, no relationship is formed with the actual values.

If the production order has been delivered in full or technically completed, the WIP stock is dissolved automatically during the next WIP calculation. For illustration, take a look at the sample figures in Table 6.1.

	Period 1	Period 2	Period 3
Material withdrawals	EUR 1,000.00	EUR 2,500.00	EUR 500.00
Material OC (3%)	EUR 30.00	EUR 75.00	EUR 15.00
Confirmation			
Machine hours	EUR 400.00	EUR 500.00	EUR 100.00
Direct labor costs	EUR 300.00	EUR 600.00	EUR 200.00
Setup times	EUR 100.00	EUR 100.00	–
Production OC (5%)	EUR 40.00	EUR 60.00	EUR 15.00
Accumulated costs	EUR *1,870.00*	EUR *3,835.00*	EUR *830.00*
Goods receipts	–	EUR 2,500.00	EUR 5,000.00
WIP at period-end	EUR 1,870.00	EUR 1,335.00	–
Current WIP	–	EUR 1,870.00	EUR 1,335.00
Required adjustment of WIP	*EUR +1,870.00*	*EUR –535.00*	*EUR 1,335.00*

Table 6.1 WIP Sample Figures

Example of "handbag production through three periods"

Here, you can see the cost accounting of a production order from bag production across three periods. In the first period, we withdrew material from the warehouse and reported setup, machine, and production times on the order. However, no finished bags have yet been handed over to the warehouse. At period-end, material withdrawals and confirmations have already debited the production order with EUR 1,800.00. As the first step in the period-end closing, we have also calculated overhead costs (OC) on these direct costs. Costs totaling EUR 1,870.00 have thereby accrued to the order. These costs are not coupled with any credit through a goods receipt of bags. We must therefore form a WIP of EUR 1,870.00.

Further costs were incurred in the second period so that the order—following application of overhead costs—bears costs of EUR 3,835.00 at period-end. These are now already set against a partial delivery of bags to the warehouse. As a result of this partial delivery, the order was credited in the amount of EUR 2,500.00 so that only costs of EUR 1,335.00 remain. We must therefore reduce the WIP of EUR 1,870.00 posted in Period 1 by EUR 535.00. Thus, we disclose a WIP of EUR 1,335.00 at the end of Period 2. From a technical point-of-view, the production order to date has had a status of FREE (released).

Additional costs of EUR 830.00 (including overhead application) are accrued in the third period. The production order was terminated during the period; that is, it now has the status DELD (delivery completed) or TCPL (technically completed). There was a delivery to the warehouse for a value of EUR 5,000.00. We must now fully dissolve the existing WIP of EUR 1,335.00.

Results analysis key

The cost object controls whether work in process is calculated. A *results analysis key* must be assigned to it. The key consists of a six-digit ID and a name and is created with Transaction OKG1. To avoid incorrect entries, we can define default values at the level of the order type and plant combination that take effect when the cost object is created.

Results analysis version

The central object for WIP calculation is the *results analysis version*, which primarily controls the behavior of the WIP calculation. We can understand the results analysis version as enhanced Customizing for the versions in cost accounting. Therefore, you must first also activate the WIP calculation for the desired version in general Controlling. You can find the function in the Implementation Guide under CONTROLLING • GENERAL CONTROLLING • MAINTAIN VERSIONS. The WIP/RESULTS DETERMINATION indicator must be set in the controlling-area-specific view.

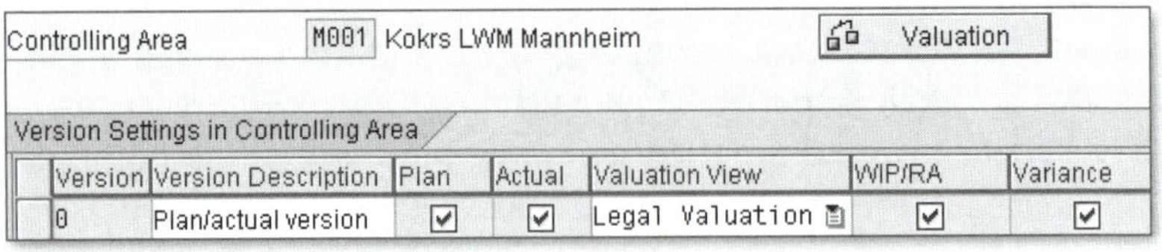

Controlling Area M001 Kokrs LWM Mannheim [Valuation]

Version Settings in Controlling Area

Version	Version Description	Plan	Actual	Valuation View	WIP/RA	Variance
0	Plan/actual version	☑	☑	Legal Valuation	☑	☑

Figure 6.40 Set WIP Relevance for Version

All versions with this indicator can be set up as a results analysis version. You can find the Customizing in the Implementation Guide under CONTROLLING • PRODUCT COST CONTROLLING • COST OBJECT CONTROLLING •

Product Cost by Order • Period-End Closing • Work in Process • Define Results Analysis Versions.

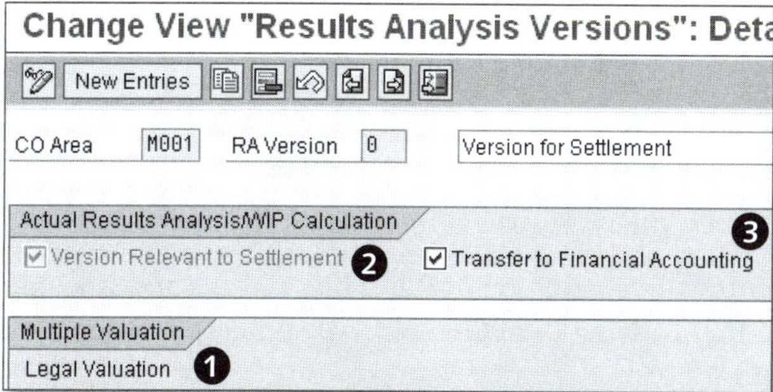

Figure 6.41 Creating a Results Analysis Version

Figure 6.41 shows the results analysis version for version 0 in the controlling area. From the version in the field group Multiple Valuation, we can see the reference Legal Valuation ❶, which has no further relevance for us at this point. The indicator Version Relevant to Settlement ❷ is also already preassigned and can no longer be changed.

Version 0 is—in principle—relevant to settlement; pure plan versions are not relevant to settlement.

Posting in the general ledger

The transition to general ledger accounting is activated with the indicator Transfer to Financial Accounting ❸. It is important that the required account determination has been set up before this indicator is set (see Figure 6.42). The account determination is defined using Transaction OKG8.

Change View "Posting Rules in WIP Calculation and Results Analysis": O

New Entries

CO Ar..	Comp..	RA Ver..	RA category	Bal./Cr.	Cost Elem..	Record..	P&L Acct	BalSheetAcct	Acc..
M001	M001	0	WIPR			0	893000	793000	
M001	M001	0	RUCR			0	239000	79000	
M001	M001	0	RUCO			0	239000	79000	
M001	M001	0	RIML			0	239100	79100	

Figure 6.42 Account Determination for Posting in the General Ledger

Maintaining the account determination

The account determination is maintained dependent on the company code and controlling area, the results analysis version, and the *results analysis category*. We must store both a balance sheet and income statement account. The income statement accounts may not be created as cost elements in Ccontrolling because Controlling is supplied with the values via a separate route.

Categories for WIP posting

The following categories are available for the posting of WIP:

- WIPA: Work in process, must be capitalized
- WIPW: Work in process, can be capitalized
- WIPN: Work in process, cannot be capitalized
- RFKA: Provisions for missing costs, must be capitalized
- RFKW: Provisions for missing costs, can be capitalized
- RFKN: Provisions for missing costs, cannot be capitalized

Automatic posting

If you opt for an automatic posting of WIP in Financial Accounting, you must have at least stored the accounts for work in process that must be capitalized and provisions for missing costs that must be capitalized. Following your own accounting policy, values that can be capitalized can also be transferred. WIP that cannot be capitalized may not be transferred; the corresponding provisions can be transferred.

Extended control

The SAP system uses default values for WIP calculation behavior. Should these be changed, extended control must be activated, which you can see in Figure 6.43.

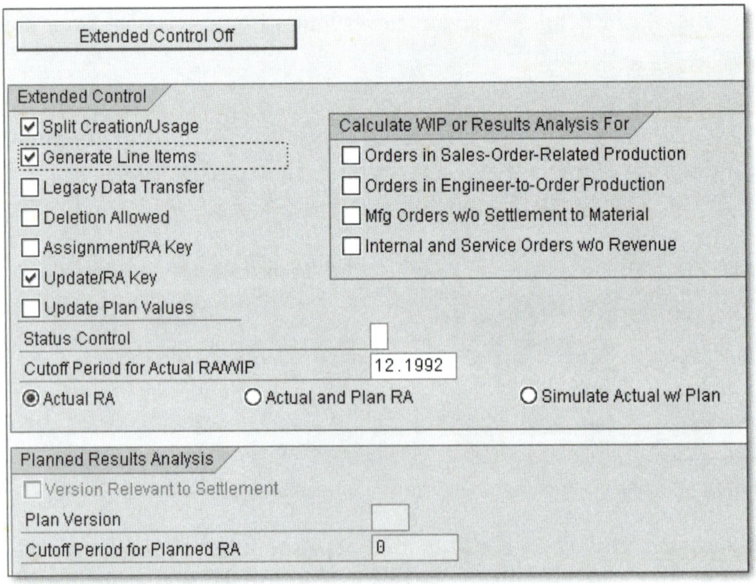

Figure 6.43 Extended Control for the Results Analysis Version

Extended control lets you use different accounts the SAP system offers for creation and dissolution.

Extended Control [Ex]

We activated extended control for Lederwaren-Manufaktur Mannheim because we want to disclose creation and consumption separately. This allows us to distinguish between these two transactions within a period. Alternatively, we could also view only the WIP summary change.

Writing line items

For a company smaller than Lederwaren-Manufaktur Mannheim, writing line items can also be activated. This makes detailed evaluations possible as to who has performed a results analysis when and with what values. Because keeping line items always has a negative effect on system performance, this function should not be activated for larger data volumes. Activating the indicator UPDATE/RESULTS ANALYSIS KEY gives you the option to take the results analysis key into account for finding the cost element.

However, a cost element is first required for technical reasons to display the results analysis key in Controlling. Here, we can only enter a single cost element in the TECHNICAL RESULTS ANALYSIS COST ELEMENT field (see Figure 6.44).

Cost Elements On	Technical RA Cost Element	1004200

Figure 6.44 Simple Account Assignment for WIP

Detailed maintenance of cost elements

However, you can also maintain cost elements with greater granularity. To do this, we must click on the button shown in Figure 6.44, COST ELEMENTS ON. This displays additional fields in which we can store cost elements. All cost elements we want to store here must be of type 31 (results analysis). In the case of Lederwaren-Manufaktur Mannheim, we have stored separate cost elements for valuated actual costs and calculated costs (see Figure 6.45). At this point, a detailed reporting system would thus be possible.

Cost Elements Off

Cost Elements: Results Analysis Data	
Valuated Actual Costs	675300
Calculated Costs	675200

Cost Elements: Down Payment Allocation		Cost Elements: Plan Values of Valuation	
Reduction in REB		Plan Costs of Valuation	
Down Payment Surplus		Plan Revenue of Valuation	

Figure 6.45 Extended Cost Element Finding for WIP

Updating of WIP

WIP updating takes place on other cost elements. You maintain the required cost element determination for this in the Implementation Guide under CONTROLLING • PRODUCT COST CONTROLLING • COST OBJECT CONTROLLING • PRODUCT COST BY ORDER • PERIOD-END CLOSING • WORK IN PROCESS • DEFINE UPDATE. After we defined in Figure 6.43 that we differentiate between WIP creation and consumption in the update, we get the result shown in Figure 6.46 for Lederwaren-Manufaktur Mannheim.

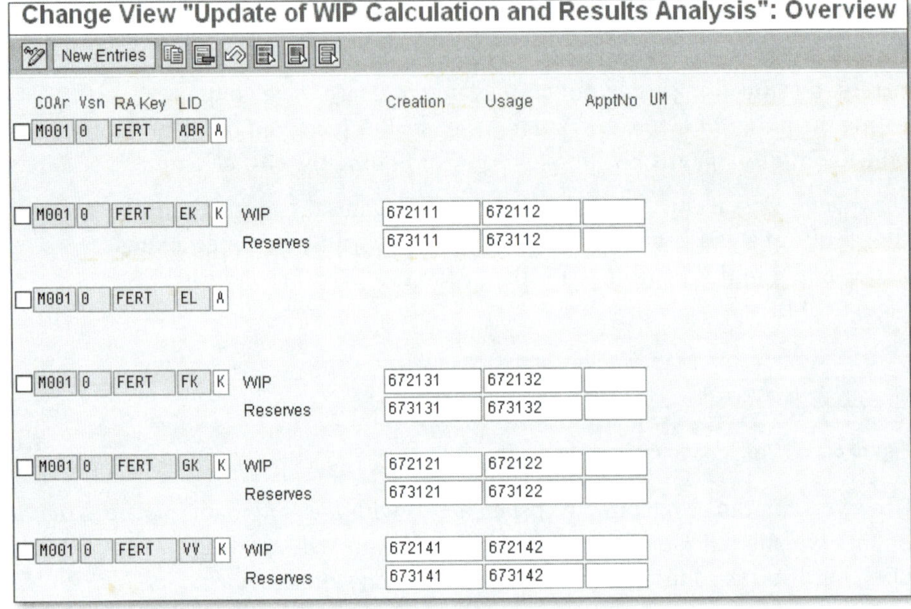

Change View "Update of WIP Calculation and Results Analysis": Overview

COAr	Vsn	RA Key	LID			Creation	Usage	ApptNo	UM
M001	0	FERT	ABR	A					
M001	0	FERT	EK	K	WIP	672111	672112		
					Reserves	673111	673112		
M001	0	FERT	EL	A					
M001	0	FERT	FK	K	WIP	672131	672132		
					Reserves	673131	673132		
M001	0	FERT	GK	K	WIP	672121	672122		
					Reserves	673121	673122		
M001	0	FERT	VV	K	WIP	672141	672142		
					Reserves	673141	673142		

Figure 6.46 Account Determination/WIP Determination

To determine a cost element, the controlling area, version, capitalization key, line identification, and category are used. In this combination, we store a cost element for both WIP formation and WIP consumption.

Definition of the line identification

You have already learned about the version and results analysis key. The *line identifications* (line IDs) determine the origin of the costs; in other words, they group the cost elements with which cost objects were debited and credited such as material or overhead costs, for example. You must define the line IDs in Customizing, following the structure of the contribution margin accounting. Figure 6.47 shows the line IDs for Lederwaren-Manufaktur Mannheim.

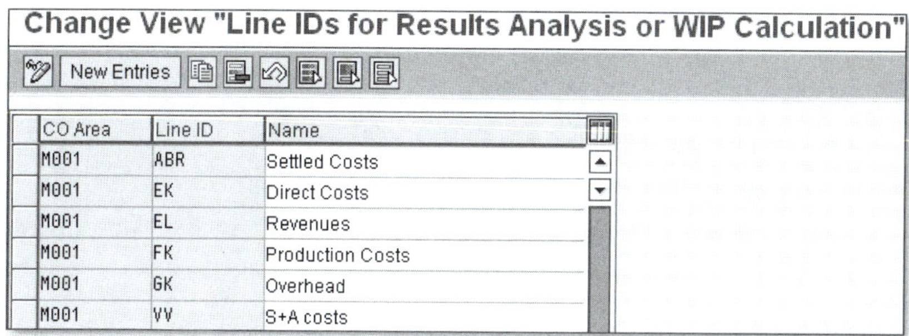

Change View "Line IDs for Results Analysis or WIP Calculation"

New Entries

CO Area	Line ID	Name
M001	ABR	Settled Costs
M001	EK	Direct Costs
M001	EL	Revenues
M001	FK	Production Costs
M001	GK	Overhead
M001	VV	S+A costs

Figure 6.47 Definition of the Line Identifications

The line IDs are defined using Transaction OKGB. Cost elements are then assigned to each line. This allows you to define what cost elements will later be displayed as settled costs, for example, as direct costs or revenues. Because the line IDs are also used for settlement into the result, lines such as revenues that are not relevant for WIP formation are also present here.

Assignment of line IDs and cost elements

The cost elements are not assigned in the form of cost element groups. Here, the SAP system again works with the masking method (see Figure 6.48), to which you have already been introduced (e.g., in the context of the cost component structure in Figure 6.12).

Change View "Assignment of Cost Elements for WIP and Results Analysis"

New Entries

CO A	RA V	RA Key	Masked Co	Ori	Masked Co	Maske	Business Proc.	D	V	Apportionment Reason	Accounting Indicat	Valid-Fro	ReqToC	OptToCap	CannotBeCap
M001	0		00004+++++	++++			++++++++++++	+	+	++	++	001.1993	EK		
M001	0		00006+++++	++++	++++++++++	++++++	++++++++++++	+	+	++	++	001.1993	FK		
M001	0		0000655+++	++++	++++++++++	++++++	++++++++++++	+	+	++	++	001.1993	VV		
M001	0		00006551++	++++	++++++++++	++++++	++++++++++++	+	+	++	++	001.1993	GK		
M001	0		00008+++++	++++			++++++++++++	+	+	++	++	001.1993	EK		
M001	0		000080++++	++++			++++++++++++	+	+	++	++	001.1993	EL		
M001	0		000081++++	++++			++++++++++++	+	+	++	++	001.1993	ABR		
M001	0		0000895+++	++++			++++++++++++	+	+	++	++	001.1993	ABR		

Figure 6.48 Assignment of Line Identification and Cost Elements

Cost element determination is specifically maintained for a controlling area, the version, and potentially a results analysis key. The (original) cost elements are displayed masked as much as possible.

Category

The last dimension to determine the posting is the *category*. Moreover, we again specify the type of costs incurred. The following characteristics are relevant for WIP:

- **A Settled costs**
  This includes all credits for manufacturing orders. This means that the cost elements for the goods receipt to warehouse in particular must be

assigned here. In the MM account determination these are the accounts for the GBB AUA and GBB AUF transaction.

- **K Costs**
  These include all costs that can be formed for WIP.
- **N Costs not to be taken into account**
  All cost elements for which no WIP is determined such as administrative overheads and sales overheads should be assigned here.

To help clarify, Figure 6.49 shows an overview again of the relationships in the Customizing for WIP calculation.

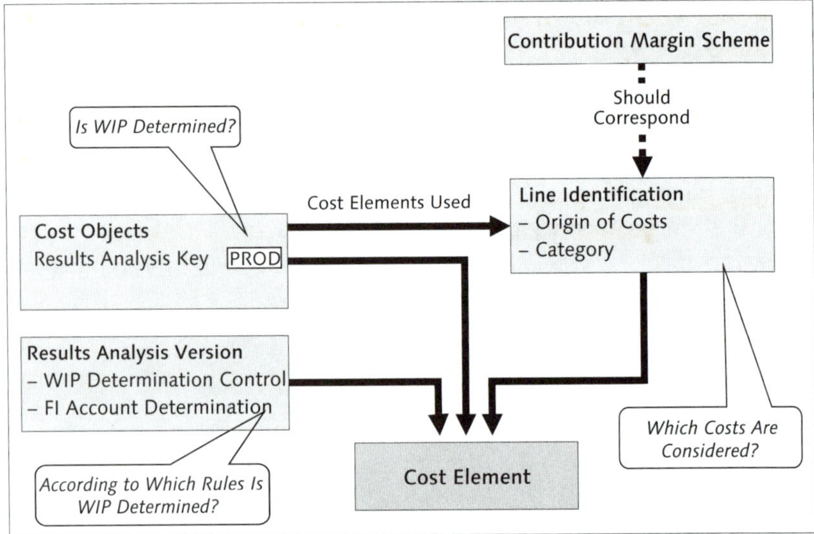

Figure 6.49 Schematic Display of WIP Customizing

WIP is calculated, for example, using Transaction KKAX (Determine work in process: individual processing). The determined values are shown here as well (see Figure 6.50).

Exception	Cost Object	Typ	Crcy	Σ	WIP (Cumul.)	Σ	WIP (per.chang)	Material
ooo	ORD 651994		EUR		1.245.373,15		1.245.373,15	T1000
ooo	**Order Type PP01**			▪	**1.245.373,15**	▪	**1.245.373,15**	
ooo	**Plant M001**			▪▪	**1.245.373,15**	▪▪	**1.245.373,15**	
ooo			**EUR**	▪▪▪	**1.245.373,15**	▪▪▪	**1.245.373,15**	

Figure 6.50 Result for the WIP Calculation

However, there is no WIP posting yet at this point. It is performed later as part of the settlement.

Variance

Variance calculation

The variances are also analyzed prior to the settlement. This happens as part of the *variance calculation*. The operation of this function is largely preassigned by the SAP system. Above all, you can decide which of the variance types offered in the standard system you want to use. Figure 6.51 shows an overview of the settings to be entered for this function.

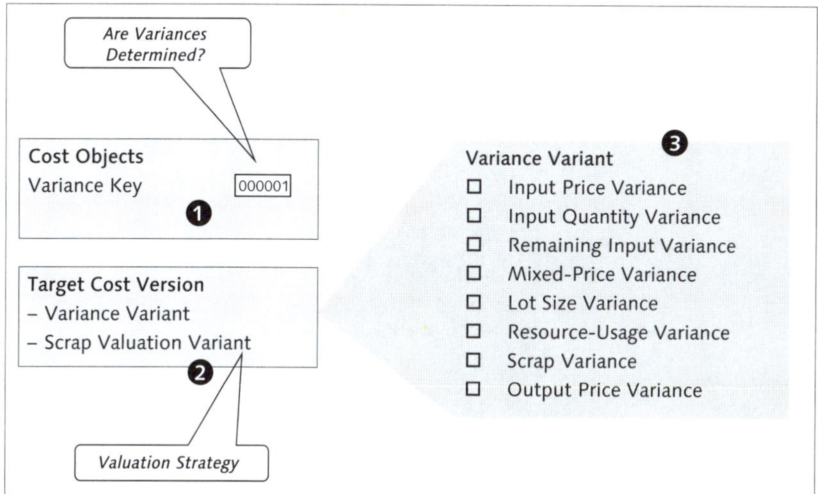

Figure 6.51 Schematic Display of the Customizing for the Variance calculation

Variance key

For variances to be determined on a cost object, it must bear a *variance key*. The key also determines whether scrap is calculated and whether line items are updated. The familiar principle applies here as well: no line item updating for mass processings! The variance key is maintained as a default value for each plant that is involved in the material maintenance. When you create a production order or product cost collector for the material, you get the proposal from the material master.

Target cost version

The version takes on a central role, just as for the WIP calculation. The valuation variant and the variance variant are assigned to it. The *valuation variant* defines at what price the scrap should be carried. You have the following options:

- Planned costs from preliminary calculation
- Value from an alternative material cost estimate to determine the target costs (the costing variant and version must be assigned)
- Price from the ongoing standard cost estimate

These three valuation methods can be given priorities, where not all prices are included.

Variance variant

The *variance variant* is the core of deviation recording—it defines the relevant variance categories. You can see all of the available categories in Table 6.2. You can divide them into two groups: variances on the input side and on the output side and you have the display options shown in the table.

Variance categories	
Input Side	
Input price variance	Differences from planned and actual prices of the resources used (e.g., price increase for moving average price raw materials).
Input quantity variance	Differences from planned and actual required quantities of the resources used (e.g., excess consumption of raw materials or longer production times).
Resource-usage variance	Arisen through a changed composition of resources (e.g., use of a different type of leather for bags).
Remaining input variance	All remaining variances on the input side (e.g., caused by higher overhead rates).
Output Side	
Output price variance	Difference from the credit for target and actual costs. Can only arise if the material is not delivered to the warehouse at the standard price (e.g., moving average price).
Mixed-price variance	Similar to the output price variance, however with a material managed at a mixed price.
Lot size variance	Variances that arise from the distribution of fixed costs with changed lot sizes.
Remaining variance	All variances that cannot be assigned to another category, such as rounding differences. Is also used if there are no target costs.
Scrap	
Scrap variance	Difference arising from the confirmation of the scrap.

Table 6.2 Overview of the Variance Categories

Calculating the variances

For the WIP calculation, however, first only the variances are calculated. This can be done using Transaction KKS2 (Variance Calculation – Individual Processing), for example. This function again offers us detailed logging of the results. As an example, in Figure 6.52, you can see the explanation for the value of a scrap variance. All components are shown with their corresponding value.

Explanation: Scrap

Valuation Date	22.10.2009
Valuation Basis	Plan Costs from Orders
Order	652202

OperRespon	OpAc	Cost Elem.	Name	Origin	Σ Scrap	Σ Scrap, Fxd	Input quantity	Unit
0010		655101	OHS Raw Material	P9000	113,22			
					▪ 113,22			
	0010	400000	Raw Materials 1	M001/T1099	1.000,00		10	PC
		400000	Raw Materials 1	M001/T1070	127,30		2	PC
		400000	Raw Materials 1	M001/T1060	127,32		4	PC
		400000	Raw Materials 1	M001/T1010	254,60		4	PC
		400000	Raw Materials 1	M001/T1020	1.293,68		2	PC
		400000	Raw Materials 1	M001/T1030	126,28		2	PC
		400000	Raw Materials 1	M001/T1040	127,30		2	PC
		400000	Raw Materials 1	M001/T1050	302,60		4	PC
		403000	Operating Supplies	M001/S1091	0,24		24	PC
		403000	Operating Supplies	M001/S1095	0,52		2	PC
		403000	Operating Supplies	M001/S1094	6,00		150	M
		403000	Operating Supplies	M001/S1092	348,00		12	PC
		403000	Operating Supplies	M001/S1093	60,00		4	PC
		613000	DAA Setup Auxilary	P2000	0,07	0,07	0,001	H
		619000	DAA Production	P2000	400,00	400,00	8	H
		620000	DAA Machine Costs	P2000	250,00	250,00	5	H
	0010				▪ 4.423,91	▪ 650,07		
0010					▪▪ 4.537,13	▪▪ 650,07		
					▪▪▪ 4.537,1	▪▪▪ 650,07		

Figure 6.52 Variance Calculation—Explanation for the Scrap Variance

MM account determination

The posting of the variances uses the MM account determination. For standard price materials, the variances are posted as price variances. For materials with a moving average price, there is a revaluation of the material affecting net income. If there is a material shortage—in other words, if there is less material in the warehouse than a production order delivered—this procedure can lead to unrealistic prices. At this point it is therefore again important that all produced materials are managed at the standard price as much as possible, as SAP suggests.

Posting does not take place until the next step, the *settlement* of the cost object.

Settlement

Settlement profile

The central object of settlement is the *settlement profile*. It determines whether a cost object is subject to settlement and forms a bracket around all of the settings for the settlement of cost objects. You can find the Customizing for this in the Implementation Guide under CONTROLLING • PRODUCT COST CONTROLLING • COST OBJECT CONTROLLING • PRODUCT COST BY ORDER • PERIOD-END CLOSING • SETTLEMENT.

As shown in Figure 6.53, in the settlement profile, you first define whether actual costs or sales costs may, can, or must be settled.

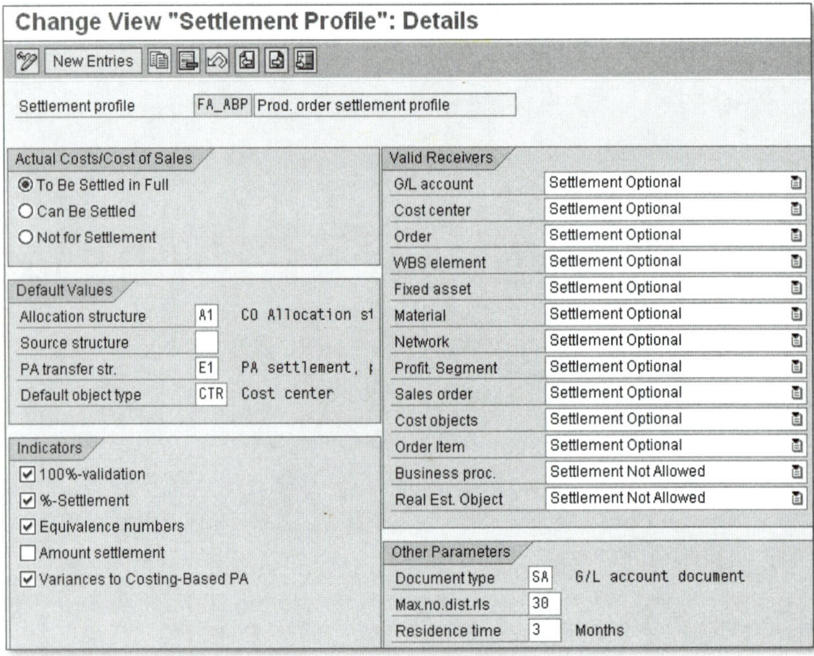

Figure 6.53 Settlement Profile

If you opted for TO BE SETTLED IN FULL (see Figure 6.53), a cost object settlement is not possible as long as it has not been fully settled. This strict check is no longer made when you choose the indicator CAN BE SETTLED. Finally, with the entry NOT FOR SETTLEMENT, it is not possible to settle costs or variances. In this case, only WIP can be calculated and posted.

In the first two cases, variances are also only transferred to CO-PA if the indicator VARIANCES TO COSTING-BASED PA is selected. In the settlement profile, you also define what recipients can be addressed for the settlement. Here, you can choose between SETTLEMENT NOT ALLOWED, SETTLEMENT OPTIONAL, and SETTLEMENT MANDATORY.

Definition of the allocation structure

A series of settings is made directly in the settlement profile. Furthermore, it also refers to additional important elements for the settlement. The first is the *allocation structure*.

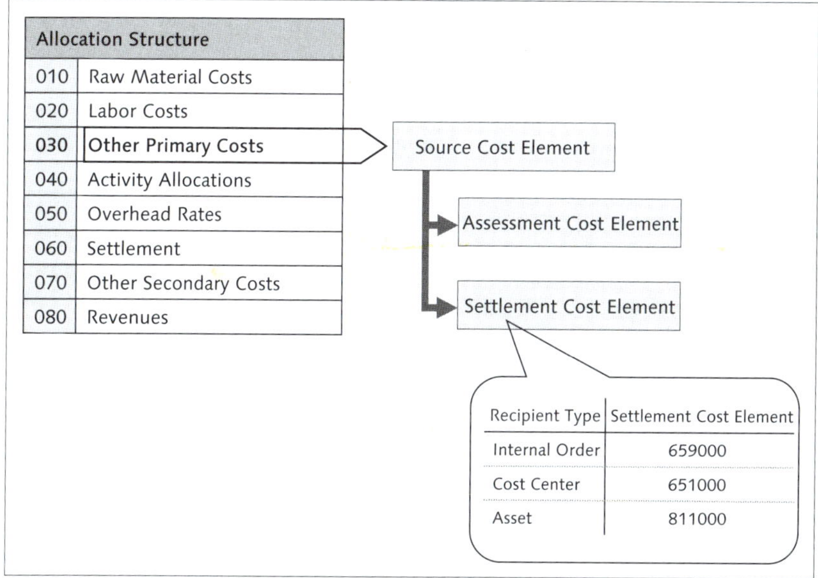

Figure 6.54 Allocation Structure

The allocation structure (see Figure 6.54) defines what cost elements are grouped and thereby passed on to the receiver object. The individual lines in the structure can be described as an assignment. In defining the assignment, you must follow the existing reporting requirements. For example, in Figure 6.54, there are separate lines for costs from activity allocations and settlements. If you do not require this differentiation, you can define a single "internal transactions" line. The relevant source cost elements, generally in the form of cost element groups, are stored for each line.

Group cost elements

Thus, you create a grouping of cost elements that are further processed together in the settlement. In defining the source cost elements, you must ensure that no cost element may be maintained in duplicate; in other words, in two assignments. This situation would result in an error during settlement because of the risk that values would be on-debited twice. For the onward charging you can—subject to the restrictions of individual cost objects—maintain an assessment cost element or settlement cost elements.

Cost element calculation for each recipient type

When settling the cost objects, you must maintain the settlement cost elements. You can do this depending on the recipient type. Figure 6.54 shows the recipient types internal order, cost center, and asset. In this arrangement, we need at least two cost elements for technical reasons:

- Settlement for the internal order and cost center must be made through a secondary cost element of type 21 (internal settlement).
- An accounting document must be generated for settlement to an asset. A primary cost element with type 22 (external settlement) is therefore required.

Alternatively to the cost element calculation for each recipient type, settlement under original cost elements can also be activated. In this case, the cost object is credited with the debit cost elements. The original cost element information is thus passed on to the recipient.

PA transfer structure

A *PA transfer structure* must be defined for the settlement of costs to CO-PA, which specifies in what value fields the source cost elements are updated. In its structure, the PA transfer structure is comparable with the allocation structure just described. The key difference is that no cost elements but rather value fields are stored as the objective. You will also find a detailed description of the PA transfer structure in Chapter 3, Section 3.5, CO-PA as a Central Reporting Tool.

Source structure

A *source structure* can also be maintained for the settlement of co-products—that is, by-products that arise during production such as whey during the production of cheese. In this structure, cost elements with which the production order is debited can be grouped so that they are treated as one unit in the settlement.

Figure 6.55 shows a schematic overview of the control functions for the settlement.

In defining settlement rules, the difficulty is not to maintain individual regulations. Rather, it is the interplay of settlements across several phases and cost objects. The challenge is to aggregate the values in such a way that simple and focused reporting is possible. At the same time, the granularity must be fine enough that all desired information is also available for all reporting-relevant cost objects.

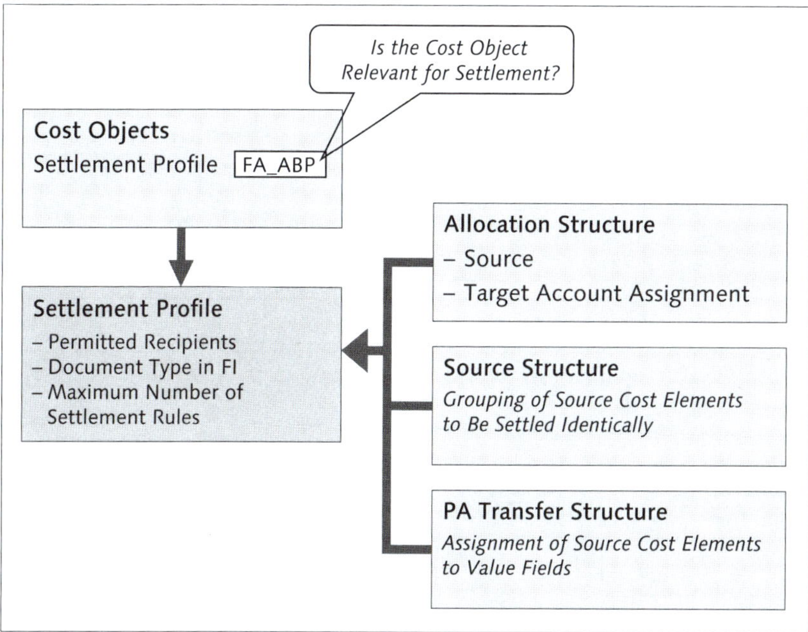

Figure 6.55 Schematic Overview of Settlement Control

The method and route of the settlement determine what analyses are later possible. For the (re)design of the value flow it is recommended that you use a graphic display. Figure 6.56 shows an example.

"Manufacturing of a new product" example

You see the same transaction with two different mappings in Controlling. In both cases, a new product is manufactured as part of research and development (R&D) work.

Let us assume that we are dealing here with the shoe production of Lederwaren-Manufaktur Mannheim. Because we always use sales orders as cost objects for ongoing production, we also chose this procedure for our handling of R&D. This is admittedly not necessary from a logistical point of view because there is no real sales order. However, from a settlement point of view, we do not have to differentiate this way between R&D production and ongoing production in Controlling.

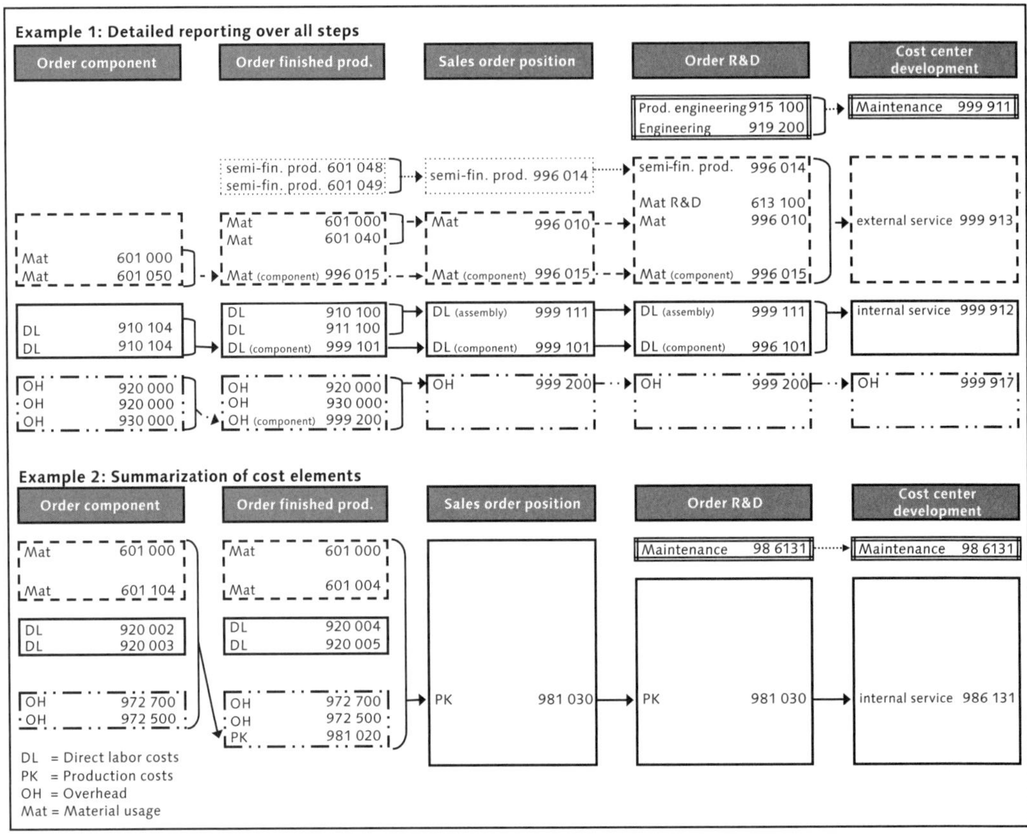

Figure 6.56 Value Flow for R&D Production Across Several Phases

First, a component such as the sole of the shoe is produced, for which there is a separate production order. This order is settled against the production order for the finished shoe. Additional costs are added here. This order is now settled against an item in the sales order. From there it goes—via detour through an internal order (order type R&D)—to our development cost center:

- In the first example, the settlement profiles are set up so that the origin is identifiable across broad sections of the value flow. For example, in the step before last (the R&D order), we can also see that a semi-finished product entered the product in the second stage.
- The second example does not include this detailed representation. Here, all costs with a single cost element (981 030) are already passed on as soon as the component's order is settled to that of the finished product.

The advantage of the first variant is the possibility of having a detailed display of the individual cost components. Variant two, on the other hand, is clearer in its disclosure of costs and is easier to set up. To decide which variant you prefer, you must ask yourself on what cost objects you want to observe the cost scheduling and how important the development of the individual cost elements is.

We have now reached the end of the process with the successful settlement of the cost object. However, so far we have only addressed the topic of cost object controlling in general terms. Next, we will therefore look at the particular characteristics of the individual production types.

6.4.3 Period-Related Product Controlling

As already mentioned in Section 6.4.1, Cost Object Controlling Functions in SAP ERP, we distinguish between three major types of controlling. We will now look at these in more depth.

"Leather belts" example

Let us look at the production of leather belts as an example for a period-related product controlling. The leather belts are not manufactured using sales-order-related production but are anonymously handed over from production to the warehouse. Given the volume of products and production orders for each period, the result of individual production orders or even of an individual product is not of interest to us. We only ever look at the period result.

Cost Objects

We use *product cost collectors* as cost objects for leather belt production. In Section 6.4.1, Cost Object Controlling Functions in SAP ERP, it was already mentioned that these are created in reference to a material, production process, or plant. The choice of controlling level has far-reaching effects because it determines the level of detail at which planned, target, and actual costs are updated. Thus, the level is specified at which variance analyses are possible. The behavior of the product cost collector changes with the plant reference value. It is therefore no longer possible to perform a preliminary costing.

If we go into production with a new belt model, we must ensure that the product cost collector is created before starting production. This is done manually. In Figure 6.57, you can see the product cost collector for material G1000.

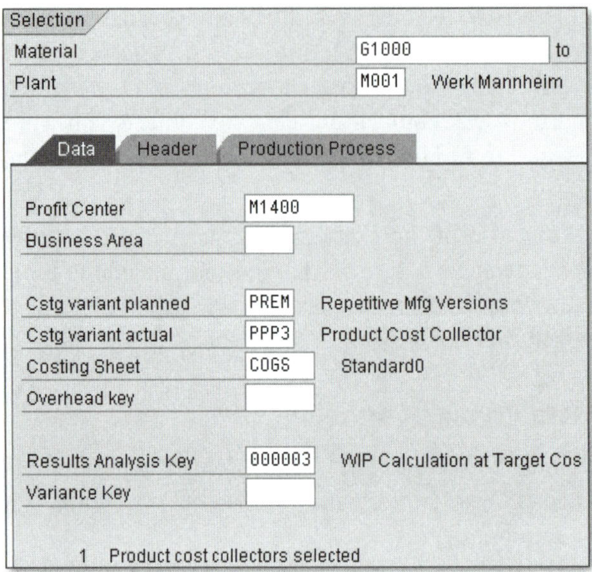

Figure 6.57 Product Cost Collector in Belt Production

Create product cost collector

The product cost collector is created using Transaction KKF6N. From a technical perspective, a product cost collector is an order of type 05—product cost collector. To avoid the risk of incorrect entries when they are created, you can enter default values for product cost collectors in Customizing. You do this in the Implementation Guide under CONTROLLING • PRODUCT COST CONTROLLING • COST OBJECT CONTROLLING • PRODUCT COST BY PERIOD • PRODUCT COST COLLECTORS • DEFINE COST-ACCOUNTING-RELEVANT DEFAULT VALUES FOR ORDER TYPES AND PLANTS.

The order type of the production order must also be adjusted. In the plant/order type combination, you must define that you are working with a product cost collector. You configure this setting in the production Customizing under the menu path PRODUCTION • SHOP FLOOR CONTROL • MASTER DATA • ORDER • DEFINE ORDER-TYPE-DEPENDENT PARAMETERS. There, the indicator must be set on the COST ACCOUNTING tab.

Product cost collector in the production order

If, for example, you use Transaction CO01 to create a production order, you will find a reference to the product cost collector in two places on the CONTROL tab (see Figure 6.58).

You can branch to the cost collector in Controlling using the PRODUCT COST COLLECTOR button. Furthermore, through production process 100091331, you can create the link to the cost collector because the production process is also stored there.

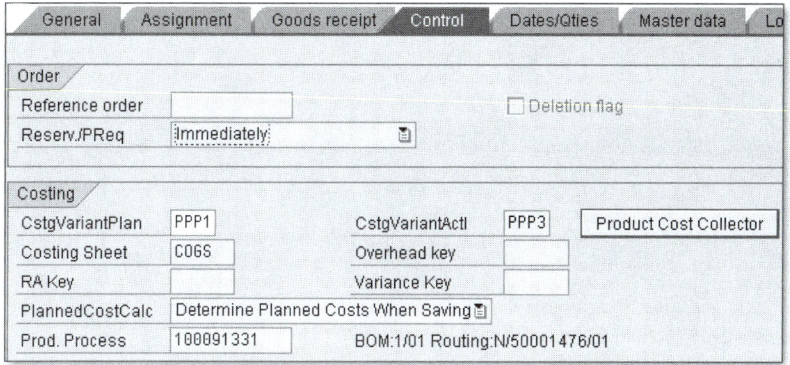

Figure 6.58 Control Data in the Production Order

The status of the production order also provides information on the cost object. If a product cost collector is assigned, the production order has the status PCCU (Product Cost Collector Used).

The production order is only used as an account assignment object for logistical transactions such as a goods withdrawal. The costs that arise are directly attributed to the product cost collector.

Preliminary Costing

Preliminary costing of the product cost collector

Because the product cost collector bears the costs, not the production order, we must also create the preliminary costing for the cost collector. The costing is started with Transaction MF30 (Creation of preliminary costings for product cost collectors). The transaction only creates an error log; it does not directly show the result of the costing.

If you now go back into Transaction KKF6N (Display Product Cost Collectors), you can see all available costings on the Header tab (see Figure 6.59).

Preliminary costing for product cost collector

Status	Costing Date (Key)	Valid from	Costing Variant	ProdCstgNo
KA	02.04.2009	02.04.2009	PREM	100091331
KA	20.05.2009	20.05.2009	PREM	100091331
KA	22.05.2009	22.05.2009	PREM	100091331
KA	23.05.2009	23.05.2009	PREM	100091331

Figure 6.59 Selecting the Preliminary Costing

Double-clicking takes you to the most up-to-date costing.

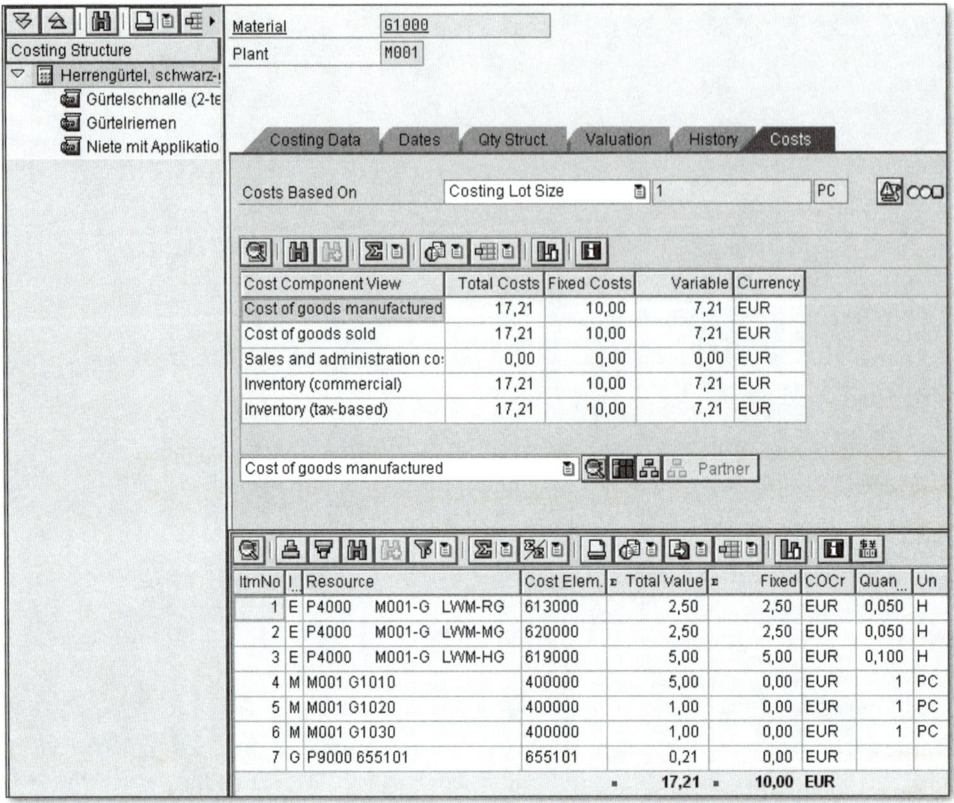

Figure 6.60 Preliminary Costing in the Product Cost Collector

Display according to the cost component structure

In Figure 6.60, you can see the preliminary costing for product G1000. The upper part of the screen shows the individual views according to the cost component structure. You already became familiar with these views in Section 6.2.3, Basic Product Cost Controlling Settings. You can control which view is displayed in the lower portion of the screen through the selection in the center of the screen. In Figure 6.60, you can also see the breakdown by element view for the cost of goods manufactured.

Simultaneous costings

During periodic product controlling, we concentrate on the results at the end of the period. Accordingly, the focus is not on simultaneous costing. If we nevertheless want to observe the cost scheduling in a period, we again do so in relation to the product cost collector, and not to the production order.

Using a product cost collector for period-end closing is more interesting.

Period-End Closing

From the controlling perspective, the overhead application, variance calculation, and settlement of the cost collectors could also take place within a period. The figures that have accrued up to that point would then always be processed. However, because here, you only ever get a partial view of what is going on in production, you should perform all activities together at the end of the period:

- Calculation of the overhead rates
- Valuation of the work in process
- Calculation of variances
- Settlement of the cost collectors

You can find all of these functions in the application menu under ACCOUNTING • CONTROLLING • PRODUCT COST CONTROLLING • COST OBJECT CONTROLLING • PRODUCT COST BY PERIOD • PERIOD-END CLOSING.

You should note that the WIP calculation in periodic product controlling is performed at target costs. To assess to what extent production orders are completely processed or still open, refer to the confirmations for production orders (for repetitive manufacturing: reporting point backflushes).

Value Flow

Shown schematically, in periodic cost object controlling, we get the value flow shown in Figure 6.61.

During the current standard cost estimate, accumulating transactions such as goods consumption and internal activity allocations (see Figure 6.61) are assigned to production orders. However, costs accrue in Controlling on the cost collector. A credit can be obtained from the delivery of finished goods to the warehouse. In period-end closing, the cost collector can receive additional costs through an overhead application. All costs now on the cost collector—less credits from deliveries to the warehouse—are passed on to CO-PA. Disclosure of variances is possible here (see Section 6.4.2, Period-End Closing). As a second branch in the value flow, the WIP and price variances are transferred to Financial Accounting.

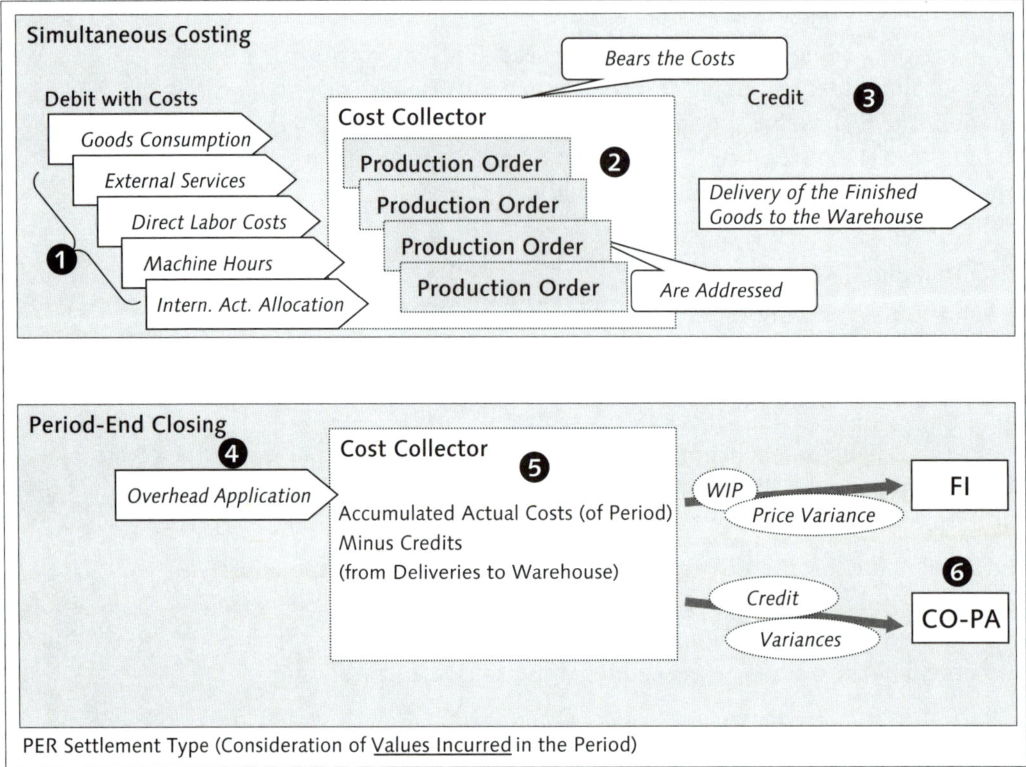

Figure 6.61 Value Flow in Periodic Cost Object Controlling

[+]

Settlement Types

The settlement type determines the system behavior for the settlement of orders.

For cost object controlling, the two types *periodic settlement* (PER) and *full settlement* (GES) are available. The most important difference arises when costs are taken into account while a settlement is being performed.

- **PER**
  With settlement type PER, only the costs of the settlement period are taken into account.
- **FUL**
  With settlement type FUL, on the other hand, all historical costs not yet settled—from the settlement period and prior periods—are included.

6.4.4 Order-Related Product Controlling

"Handbags" example

The example we used to illustrate order-related product controlling was handbag production at Lederwaren-Manufaktur Mannheim. Some of the handbags are manufactured according to special customer requirements; however, usually, they are produced in stock. We opted for order-related cost object controlling for this product line.

Cost Objects

Lederwaren-Manufaktur Mannheim uses production orders from the PP component as cost objects. Production orders are generally created with reference to a material, using, for example, Transaction CO01. Here, you must select the production plant and the order type as well as the material. The CONTROL tab is particularly important for cost accounting. The criteria for order settlement are defined here (see Figure 6.62).

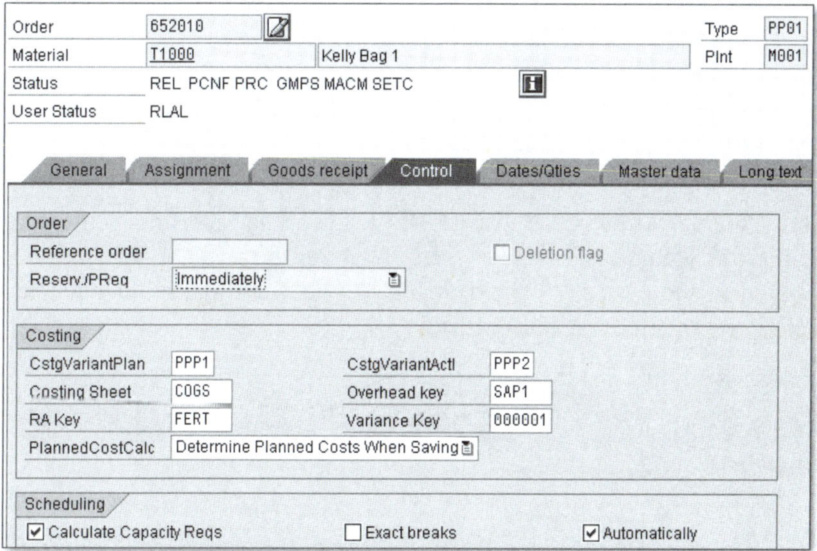

Figure 6.62 Cost-Accounting-Relevant Control of a Production Order

Typically, all required fields are filled with default values when the production order is created (see Figure 6.63). If these have been correctly stored, you do not have to intervene here. You maintain the default values in the Implementation Guide under PRODUCTION • SHOP FLOOR CONTROL • MASTER DATA • ORDER • DEFINE ORDER TYPE-DEPENDENT PARAMETERS.

Change View "Order Type-Dependent Parameters: Overview": Details

New Entries

Plant M001 Werk Mannheim

Order Type PP01 Standard Production Order (int. number)

Planning | Implementation | Controlling | Display profiles

Controlling

Cstg variant planned PPP1 Production Order - Plan ☐ Cost Collector

Cstg variant actual PPP2 Production Order - Actual

Results Analysis Key FERT WIP Calculation for Production Orders

Planned Cost Calcul. Determine Planned Costs When Saving ☐ Net Order Price

Distribution Rule

Default Rule PP1 Production Mat.Full settlement

Figure 6.63 Maintaining Default Values

You have already learned about the significance and control of costing variants and the capitalization key. In this example, you do not have to manually trigger the preliminary costing. The planned cost determination defines that this takes place automatically when the order is stored. The *default rule* is new. These are rules proposed by the SAP system governing how settlement rules are built. With anonymous make-to-stock production, the material is stored as the recipient of the settlement.

In Figure 6.64, you can see that FUL has been selected as the settlement type (this column is visible as SETT...). Here, the accrued costs are not settled in the period in which they arise but when the order has been delivered or is technically completed.

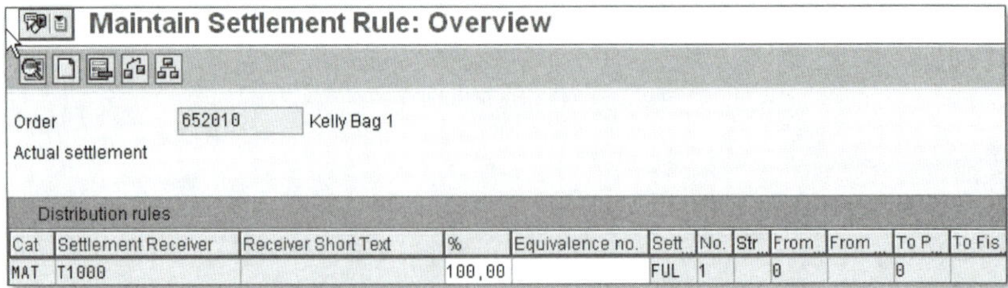

Figure 6.64 Settlement Rule for a Production Order

The settlement profile is maintained cross-plant in the order type of the production order (here, PP01).

Preliminary Costing

Generally, as in the example in Figure 6.62, the preliminary costing will take place automatically when the production order is stored. Alternatively, you can start the costing manually. To do so, use Transaction CO02 (Change production order) to go into the master record and select the icon. The order is then re-cost. You can see the result in the cost analysis, which you can reach via GoTo • Costs • Analyze. The material must have a released costing for this to work. If there is no released costing for the material at the time that production begins, you will later be unable to set target costs against actual costs.

Cost Elem.	Cost Element (Text)	Origin	Σ	Total plan costs	Σ Total actual costs	Currency
400000	Consumption, raw material 1			83.977,00	83.849,70	EUR
403000	Operating Supplies Consumed			10.369,00	10.369,40	EUR
895000	Factory output production orders			114.699,00-	0,00	EUR
613000	Dir. Int. Act. Alloc. Setup Auxilary	P2000/LWM-RT		10,00	10,00	EUR
619000	Dir. Int. Act. Alloc. Production	P2000/LWM-HT		10.000,00	6.000,00	EUR
620000	Dir. Int. Act. Alloc. Machine Costs	P2000/LWM-MT		6.250,00	3.750,00	EUR
655101	Overhead Surcharge - Raw Material	P9000		2.830,38	0,00	EUR
			•	**1.262,62-**	• **103.979,10**	**EUR**
			••	**1.262,62-**	•• **103.979,10**	**EUR**

Figure 6.65 Planned Costs for a Production Order

In Figure 6.65, the first actual costs have already been posted on the order. Nevertheless, there has not yet been a delivery of finished products to the warehouse. The credit for the order (line 3) is therefore only filled in the plan.

Simultaneous Costing

After the production order has been released, consumptions and activities can be entered on it. A production order is credited through delivery of the production product to the warehouse.

Period-End Closing

The period-end closing in order-related cost object controlling corresponds to the scope already described in Section 6.4.1, Cost Object Controlling Functions in SAP ERP. Overhead application, WIP calculation, variance calculation, and settlement of the production order are possible. With the exception of WIP, you could perform these activities following completion of the production order (status delivered or technically completed). However, collective processing at the end of the period is recommended. You can find all of the required steps for this in the application menu under Accounting • Controlling • Product Cost Controlling • Cost Object Controlling • Product Cost by Order • Period-End Closing.

Significance of the order status

In the standard system, processing of a production order is determined by the order status.

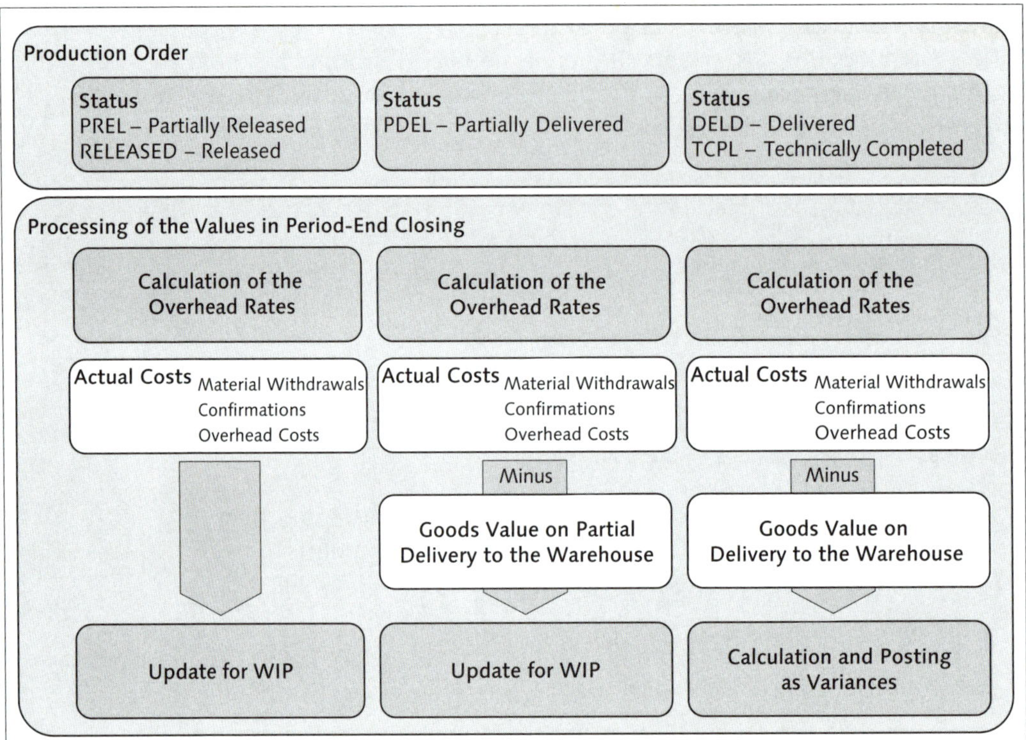

Figure 6.66 Relevance of the Order Status in the Period-End Closing

The first step in the settlement—if we are working with overhead rates—is the overhead application of direct costs. This takes place regardless of the status of the order. As long as the order is only debited with costs but no credit has taken place through a delivery of finished products to the warehouse, the order has the status PREL (partial release) or REL (released). The costs arising are fully posted as work in progress (WIP). If some of the products have already been delivered to the warehouse, the order status switches to PDEL (partially delivered). During WIP calculation, the accrued costs are reduced by the goods value on delivery to the warehouse. When the production order carries the status DELD (delivered) or TCPL (technically completed), the WIP stock for this order is fully dissolved. The actual costs from the order, less the credit from the delivery to the plant, produce the variances that have arisen (for details on this, see Section 6.4.2, Period-End Closing).

Value Flow

Shown schematically, in order-related cost object controlling, we get the value flow shown in Figure 6.67.

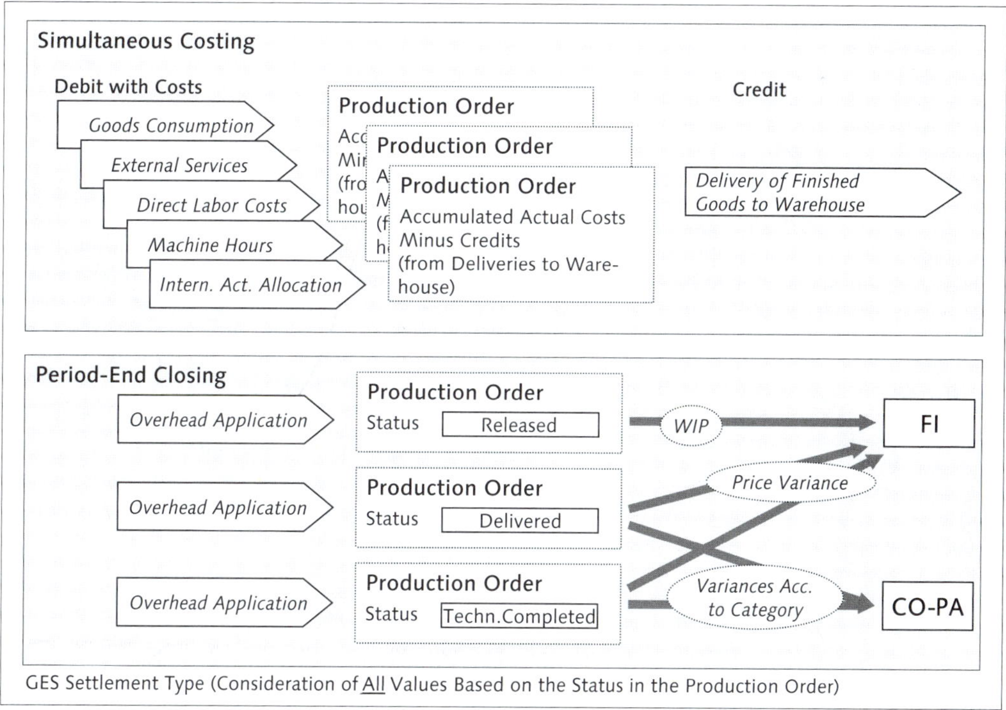

Figure 6.67 Value Flow of Order-Related Cost Object Controlling

Costs from goods consumption, external services, and internal service supplies are collected during simultaneous costing for individual production orders. A credit can take place within the period through the delivery of products to the warehouse.

At the period-end closing, the WIP and price variances are transferred to accounting. The variances are transferred to CO-PA. Together with the credits from deliveries to the warehouse, the production orders show a balance of zero at the end.

6.4.5 Product Cost by Sales Order

"Shoes" example

We will illustrate product cost by sales order using the production of leather shoes at Lederwaren-Manufaktur Mannheim.

With product cost by sales order, sales order items do not only carry revenues but also costs.

Cost Objects

Valuated vs. non-valuated sales order stock

SAP offers different characteristics for product cost by sales order. A key aspect here is whether you want to work with valuated or non-valuated sales order stock.

You can find arguments for both solutions in Table 6.3.

Mapping of valuated sales order stock	Mapping of non-valuated sales order stock
▸ Parallel display of quantity flow and value flow ▸ Production controlling takes place in the same manner as order-related cost object controlling (anonymous make-to-stock production). ▸ Complete disclosure of costs at each manufacturing level ▸ Ability to calculate production variances and scrap ▸ Ability to use in sales order controlling for complex make-to-order production	▸ Goods movements do not cause any postings in Financial Accounting. ▸ Disclosure of stock in Financial Accounting only after results analysis and settlement at the end of the period. ▸ Costs of semi-finished products are directly assigned to the sales order item on the calculation of results. ▸ Disclosure of costs on the production order only for manufacturing of the finished product. ▸ No variance calculation for production orders. (Not recommended.)

Table 6.3 Valuated vs. Non-Valuated Sales Order Stock

Usually, you will work with valuated sales order stock. First of all, this way, you generate a value flow that directly—and in particular, immediately—follows the quantity flow. Additionally, this procedure offers you more evaluation possibilities in Controlling. Lederwaren-Manufaktur Mannheim uses this type of cost object controlling for the manufacturing of shoes. Each shoe is specially manufactured for customers following an order. Therefore, we want to analyze for each sales order whether it will be—and has been—profitable for us. At the same time, we want to observe the cost scheduling already during production time.

Requirements class defines sales-order-related production

Production of a product in sales-order-related production is primarily determined by the requirements class. It must refer to account assignment type M (make-to-order production). Settings in the requirements class and the determination were already described in Chapter 3, Section 3.4.4.

As with cost collectors and the production order, the sales order also carries Controlling-relevant data, if it is a cost object. You can find the fields in the sales order item on the Account Assignment tab (see Figure 6.68).

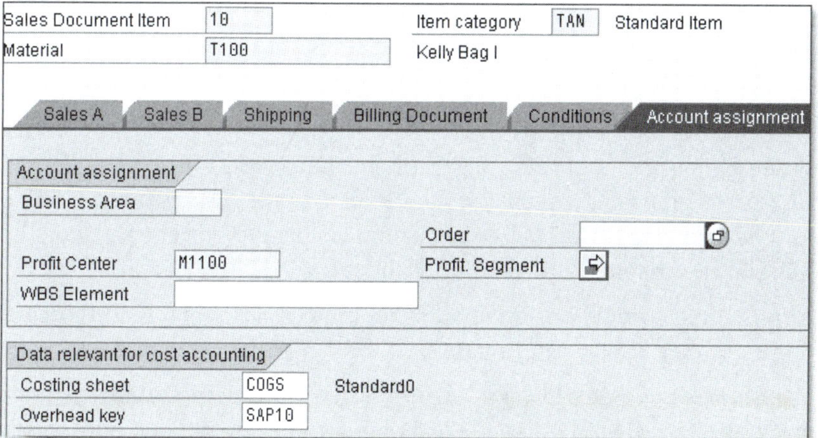

Figure 6.68 Account Assignment Information for a Sales Order Item

Derivation of the profitability segment

In the Account Assignment field group, you can see the Results Object field. Here, you can check the derivation of characteristics, value, and quantity fields for CO-PA. You can reach the detail view of the results object using the icon (see Figure 6.69).

All of the fields with a gray background in Figure 6.69 are automatically derived from the sales order. This is possible, for example, for customer, article and also for organizational units such as company code, plant, and sales organization.

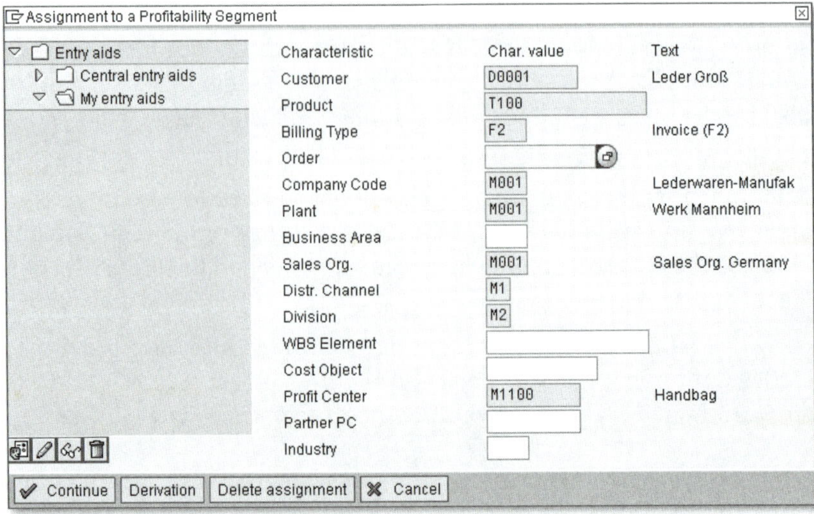

Figure 6.69 Account Assignment for the Results Object

Preliminary Costing

Revenue planning

Aside from a preliminary costing for the planned costs calculation, you can also perform *revenue planning* in sales order controlling. Revenue planning is used if *limitations* should be calculated for planned revenues. Here, the system uses the price calculation for the sales order in SD.

You can select from two variants for preliminary costing: sales order costing and order BOM cost estimate.

Performing a sales order costing

A *sales order costing* is always performed at the item level. You can create it not just in reference to sales orders but also for queries and quotations. The planning data can be determined through product costing or unit costing. You can update the result as condition values in the price determination schema and thus also copy it to CO-PA.

Standard Condition Types for the Transfer of Costing Values

The SAP system offers two condition types in the standard system for the transfer of costing results into the sales order price determination:

- EK01 for values that should flow into the price formation
- EK02 for the display of statistical values

Whereas sales order costing occurs directly on the sales order or its item, the *order BOM cost estimate* accesses *BOMs* that are not a component of the sales order. This form of preliminary costing is used with very complex BOMs that can also be developed further during a construction phase. Over time, it is possible to gradually cost individual components. This makes the final costing of the sales order item higher performing.

Order BOM cost estimate

Preliminary costing is controlled through the requirements class. Here, you determine whether and in what form a costing can or must be performed. Furthermore, the costing variant, pricing procedure, settlement profile, and capitalization key are stored in the requirements class.

Control through the requirements class

Simultaneous Costing

Let us remain with our example of sales order controlling with valuated sales order stock, and let us look at the value flow for simultaneous costing using a sales order for a pair of shoes.

Example "value flow for valuated sales order stock"

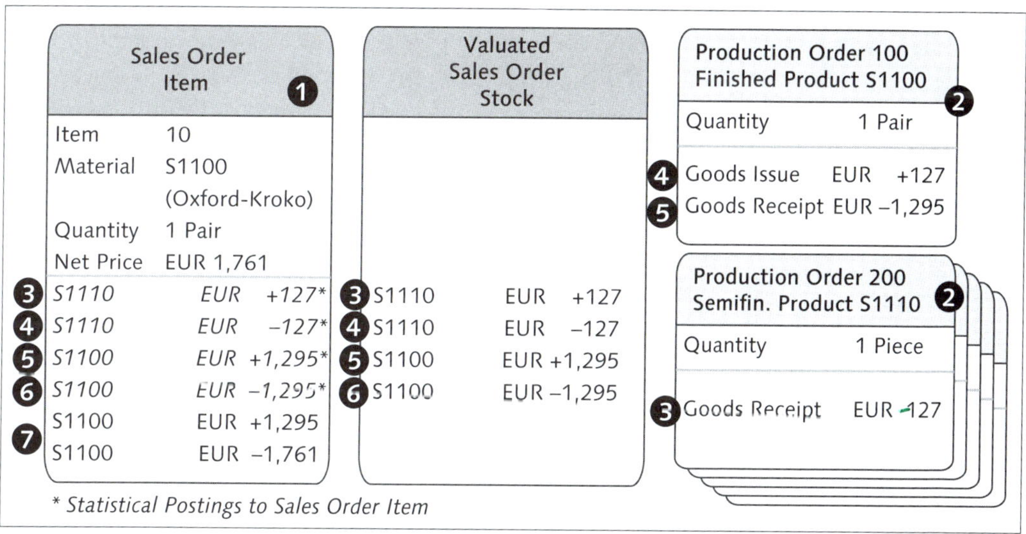

Figure 6.70 Value Flow—Sales Order Controlling with Valuated Sales Order Stock

Value Flow for Simultaneous Costing: Step by Step

❶ Enter a sales order for a pair of Oxford-Kroko shoes, net price EUR 1,761.00

❷ Creation of the production orders for the finished product and semi-finished products

❸ Delivery of the semi-finished product from production order 200 to the warehouse, value EUR 127.00

❹ Stock withdrawal of the semi-finished product S1110 for production order S1100, value EUR 127.00

❺ Delivery of finished product S1100 to the warehouse, value EUR 1,295.00

❻ Goods issue to the customer, value EUR 1,295.00

❼ Billing document to the customer, value EUR 1,761.00

First, a sales order is created for a pair of men's shoes ❶. The sales order results in several production orders being created: one per semi-finished product and one for the finished product ❷. Delivery of the semi-finished product S1110 ❸ from production to the warehouse leads to an increase in the valuated sales order stock, which is mapped in Financial Accounting. We can also construct a commitment on the sales order through this movement. However, to do so commitments management for sales orders must be active (see also Chapter 4, Section 4.4, Updating Commitments), and the affected balance sheet account must be created as a cost element of type 90. The withdrawal of the semi-finished product ❹ for the production order for the shoe reduces the stock again and credits the sales order again. Delivery of the finished shoe ❺ again leads to a stock build-up and a debiting of the sales order. What is important is that all previous postings on the sales order item are only statistical!

Following the goods issue ❻, the sales order finally shows real costs. Here, the account is used that is stored in the MM account determination for Transaction GBB (Offsetting entry to stock posting) combined with the account modification constant VAY. VAY is used because there is a Controlling account assignment: the sales order item. To this end, this account must be created as a cost element. The sales order stock is now zero again. The revenues are then assigned with billing document ❼ and the transfer into the accounting on the sales order item.

Further processing of the values on the sales order item occurs as part of period-end closing.

Period-End Closing

Period-end closing in sales order controlling is different from that in periodic and order-related cost object controlling. Although the process also begins with the overhead application (now through Transaction VA44), the *results analysis* then follows.

Results analysis

The results analysis is used to calculate the work in process. The goods in transport can also be calculated. This may be necessary if there has been no billing document yet for a goods issue to the customer. This procedure is not desired in many companies. Especially at the end of the period, companies therefore strictly enforce that all goods issues have been invoiced. The results analysis can unite the functions of WIP and variance calculation. Therefore, neither Customizing nor the execution differ significantly from what was explained in the previous sections.

Initially, the results analysis also does not result in postings. These do not take place until *settlement*.

Settlement to CO-PA

For the period-end closing in sales order controlling, you must pay particular attention to the paths through which the values reach CO-PA. You can transfer production variances directly from the production orders to CO-PA. However, alternatively, the value flow can also initially refer from the production orders to the sales orders. Therefore, the sales orders bear all costs—including variances—and can thus be settled to CO-PA. Regardless of the value flow chosen, documents of record type C (order and project settlement) are created in CO-PA.

6.5 Summary

Even if in this chapter, we were only able to show the basic principles of product cost controlling, it is clear that the SAP system offers a broad range of tools and mapping options. In product cost planning, we depend on the preparations by logistics. Only if there is meaningful master data in production, can we calculate realistic prices for our products. If logistics is not yet in a position to supply us with sufficient information, we must fall back on base planning objects or costings without quantity structure. Depending on the stage in the product lifecycle, we can therefore count on realistic results from product cost planning only to a limited extent.

Because the production type also has effects on the valuation possibilities in Controlling, the decision on the production type cannot be made by production alone. We must define in Controlling what dimensions are relevant for corporate management, for example:

- The accruing costs for a period
- The production run costs
- The sales order margin

Accordingly, we must then opt for periodic, order- or sales-order-related cost object controlling. What is difficult in the design for the value flows is not the design within a stage, but the display across multiple production phases, as was shown in Figure 6.56. In this case, the settlements must also be built across several stages. To generate optimal value flows, these must be consistently designed and subsequently adhered to. However, before defining the value flows, the structure of the profit and loss statement must be clear. This is the only way to know to what depth costs must be passed on across the production phases into the CO-PA component.

In closing and reporting, the following three processes always converge: procurement, sales, and production. If you have ignored value flows so far, you will now become painfully aware of their existence.

7 Closing and Reporting in SAP ERP

So far, we have focused on the value flows for procurement, sales, and production processes. However, we have yet to consolidate or prepare these three value flows. This is the task of period-end closing in Financial Accounting and Controlling. To prepare the data for reporting, the accumulated values are processed further (through reclassifications, distributions, transfer postings, or revaluations). Here, the goal is to display all relevant figures and key figures from the area of *financials*. Whether a (key) figure is relevant can only be decided on a case-by-case basis, that is, for each enterprise. This brings us directly to corporate management, which, as already mentioned in Chapter 2, The Concept of Integrated Values Flows, is also the task of Controlling.

In this chapter, we will use a sample closing procedure document to consider the main tasks and activities in Financial Accounting and Controlling. To this end, we will provide a detailed breakdown of each individual task.

The purpose of month-end closing activities is to equip decision-makers in enterprises with relevant information. Financial Accounting focuses on the *balance sheet* and *profit and loss statement* (P&L), whereas Controlling serves many different interest groups and delivers target group-specific information (for example, from Cost Center Accounting, Profit Center Accounting, or CO-PA).

Regardless of whether you are dealing with quarter-end closing or year-end closing, the general ledger version you use is extremely important; in other words, classic general ledger accounting or the SAP General Ledger in SAP ERP. We will first take a look at some important topics in conjunction with SAP General Ledger.

7.1 Innovations in SAP General Ledger

In Section 3.3, International Requirements, we discussed parallel ledgers in SAP General Ledger. We have not used parallel ledgers with Lederwaren-Manufaktur Mannheim because our user departments are familiar with the concept of parallel accounts and we do not want to incorporate a delta valuation area into Asset Accounting. Here, we are working solely with the standard ledger 0L.

7.1.1 Activating Different Scenarios

Ledger update scenarios

The scenarios activated in each case determine which fields are updated in the individual ledgers. The following *scenarios* are available in the standard SAP system:

- FIN_CCA Cost Center Update
- FIN_CONS Preparation for Consolidation
- FIN_GSBER Business Area
- FIN_PCA Profit Center Update
- FIN_SEGM Segmentation
- FIN_UKV Cost-of-Sales Accounting

Even though it is possible to reassign scenarios after postings have been made in SAP General Ledger, you cannot add your own scenarios to this list.

In addition, existing posting data is not supplemented with updated information from a new scenario. For example, if you activate segmentation retroactively, the segment information is not added to existing postings. For this reason, now may be a good time to carefully check which scenarios could be relevant for your enterprise, both now and in the future. If in doubt, we recommend that you add one more scenario than necessary.

Cost Center Update

The only exception to this rule is the Cost Center Update because it is technically possible to use the Cost Center Update to represent Cost Center Accounting in the general ledger. At present, this seems to only make sense for small applications because Cost Center Accounting in Controlling still provides more options in terms of allocations and evaluations.

Preparation for Consolidation

Any enterprise wishing to consolidate should activate the "Preparation for Consolidation" scenario, which makes sure that the trading partner and the consolidation transaction type are updated in SAP General Ledger. You need both pieces of information to process the posting data in consolidation.

Business Area

We have already discussed the importance of the "Business Area" account assignment object in Chapter 3, Section 3.2, Entity Model. If you decide to use the business area in SAP General Ledger, you must activate this scenario.

Profit Center Update

In real life, numerous discussions take place in relation to the "Profit Center Update" scenario in the general ledger. This scenario virtually replaces the conventional solution of Profit Center Accounting in the EC-PCA module. Such discussions are usually initiated by a controller who is concerned by the fact that the accounting department in his enterprise is to assume responsibility for Profit Center Accounting. The project management team must allay any fears the controller may have. Chapter 3, Section 3.2, Entity Model, already discussed at length the way in which an enterprise should map changes within an organizational structure.

Performance was an extremely important consideration for the first few projects migrated to SAP General Ledger. With increasing experience, however, the initial fears concerning unacceptable wait times (especially in reporting) as a result of large volumes of data soon lessened. If you are thinking about activating the Profit Center Update scenario, you should nevertheless keep the following in mind:

- Effects on the planning process
- Discontinuation of local postings to Profit Center Accounting (postings to the general ledger instead)
- General effects associated with reorganization
- No allocations to reconciliation accounts or to accounts managed on an open item basis

Segmentation

The new "segment" account assignment object has already been described in Chapter 3, Section 3.2, Entity Model. After you activate this scenario, a new *Segment* field is ready for input in the profit center master data, enabling each profit center to be assigned to a segment. When a posting is made, the segment is derived from the profit center with account assignment. It is then updated in the Financial Accounting document and in the totals table in SAP General Ledger.

Cost-of-Sales Accounting

One important functional enhancement associated with SAP General Ledger is the way in which cost-of-sales accounting is represented in the general ledger. The classic general ledger was unable to represent the account assignment object for cost-of-sales accounting (the functional area). Therefore, if you require cost-of-sales accounting, you must use the *cost-of-sales accounting ledger*, a special ledger provided by SAP. However, when you activate the cost-of-sales accounting scenario, this additional ledger is no longer required in SAP General Ledger. There are two advantages to this:

- Because there is only one dataset, differences can no longer arise between the general ledger and the cost-of-sales accounting ledger.
- You no longer have to transfer two datasets (general ledger and cost-of-sales accounting ledger) to BW.

Even if the basic recommendation is to activate all relevant scenarios, this should not be done without due consideration.

The SAP General Ledger offers another considerably less critical tool, *real-time integration*.

7.1.2 Effect of Real-Time Integration of Controlling with Financial Accounting

The *real-time integration* of Controlling with Financial Accounting is an important new feature you can activate when using SAP General Ledger. This function enables Controlling to initiate a document flow at the individual document level for the very first time.

The goal of real-time integration is to transfer all account assignment changes that occur in Controlling but are relevant for Financial Accounting from Controlling to Financial Accounting. One example would be changes to the functional areas for cost-of-sales accounting reporting as a result of cost center assessments.

Reconciliation ledger

Before real-time integration, the *reconciliation ledger* and Transaction KALC were used to transfer changes in account assignment from Controlling to Financial Accounting. This function has the disadvantage that you can only use it for summarized postings. In general, the following situations trigger a posting to Financial Accounting:

- A change in functional area
- A change in business area
- Cross-company-code postings

With the introduction of real-time integration to the standard system, this list has been extended to include the following triggers:

- A change in profit center
- A change in segment

Need for real-time integration

It is necessary to extend this list to include the profit center if, when implementing SAP General Ledger, you decide to represent Profit Center Accounting in the general ledger, and not in the classic EC-PCA module as was previously the case.

You are already familiar with using the *segment* as an additional account assignment object (Chapter 3, Section 3.2, Entity Model). Distributions or assessments in Controlling can also result in shifts between segments. Because the segment can only be fully evaluated in SAP General Ledger, these shifts must be transferred to Financial Accounting.

To activate real-time integration, you must set up a corresponding variant in Customizing (see Figure 7.1). You do this in the Implementation Guide under the menu path FINANCIAL ACCOUNTING (NEW) • FINANCIAL ACCOUNTING GLOBAL SETTINGS (NEW) • LEDGERS • REAL-TIME INTEGRATION OF CONTROLLING WITH FINANCIAL ACCOUNTING • DEFINE VARIANTS FOR REAL-TIME INTEGRATION.

Var. for R-T Integ. M001

Variants for Real-Time Integration CO->FI
[x] R.-Time Integ:Active Key Date:Active from 01.01.2008
[x] Acct Deter.: Active

Document Type CF
Ledger Group (FI) 0L
Text RTI CO --> FI LWM

Selection of Document Lines for Real-Time Integration CO->FI
( ) Use Checkboxes [x] Cross-Company-Code [x] Cross-Profit-Center
[ ] Cross-Business-Area [x] Cross-Segment
[x] Cross-Functionl-Area [ ] Cross-Fund [ ] Cross-Grant
( ) Use BAdI
( ) Use Rule Rule
(•) Update All CO LIs

Technical Settings
[ ] Trace Active
[ ] Do Not Summarize Documents

Figure 7.1 Customizing a Real-Time Integration Variant

Specifying a real-time integration variant

Here, you can see that the chosen VARIANT for real-time integration is active from 01/01/2008. The posting date used when entering a Controlling document is relevant here. If you want to migrate existing General Ledger Accounting to SAP General Ledger, you can use key date activation (KEY DATE: ACTIVE FROM field) to easily transport Customizing for the real-time integration variant to your production system before the migration key date.

Document type

The DOCUMENT TYPE for the Financial Accounting documents is also specified in the variant. To clearly distinguish this data from the other posting data in general ledger accounting, you should use an exclusive document type here. The document type specified requires an internal number assignment. It must post to G/L accounts only, but nevertheless allow for intercompany postings.

Scope of real-time integration

The most important thing is to specify the scope of real-time integration. You do this by determining which Controlling transactions will be transferred to Financial Accounting (SELECTION OF DOCUMENT LINES FOR REAL-TIME INTEGRATION CO→FI field group). SAP provides the following four options:

- Use of checkboxes
- Derivation via a BAdI
- Use of a rule
- Transfer of all line items from Overhead Cost Controlling

Use of checkboxes

The easiest thing to do is to use *checkboxes*. As you can see in Figure 7.1, up to seven fields are available. To correctly display company code balance sheets, you must, at the very least, set the CROSS-COMPANY-CODE indicator, which transfers all transactions that cause a change in company code to Financial Accounting.

BAdI "FAGL_COFI_LNITEM_SEL"

The most powerful and most individual option concerns the use of BAdI FAGL_COFI_LNITEM_SEL. With this BAdI, the SAP system enables you to make independent decisions concerning the transactions you want to transfer. If you have very detailed requirements in terms of real-time integration, you should always use a BAdI to satisfy your reporting requirements in the general ledger.

Using a BAdI for Derivation Purposes

For example, it is a good idea to use BAdI FAGL_COFI_LNITEM_SEL if you want to transfer all transactions (aside from settlement) to CO-PA. This is because you cannot clearly distinguish between an "order to order" settlement and an "order to profitability segment" settlement.

Use of a rule

As an alternative to using a BAdI, you can define a rule. In this case, you must make the following fundamental decision: Do you prefer a programmed solution (for example, a BAdI) in your system or a rule that can be created in Customizing? In the case of complex rule sets, it is preferable to use BAdIs, for greater clarity. A prerequisite for BAdI usage is their implementation by an experienced developer.

Transferring all line items

The last variant available is the option to transfer all line items from Overhead Cost Controlling. One weakness of this variant is that the standard system wants to transfer the settlement to CO-PA in Financial Accounting. Moreover, a critical aspect of this variant is the volume of documents expected in Financial Accounting because every single activity allocation, assessment, distribution, or order settlement is transferred to Financial Accounting.

Influencing the posting

These four variants only determine which transactions will be transferred to Financial Accounting. However, if you also want to influence the posting to Financial Accounting, for example, because you want to transfer your own account assignment object to Financial Accounting, you must also activate BAdI FAGL_COFI_ACCIT_MOD.

Document summarization

To reduce the volume of documents to be posted, you can activate *document summarization* (for Financial Accounting documents) in real-time integration. This process depends on whether SAP General Ledger is active.

- **SAP General Ledger is not active**
  If SAP General Ledger is not active, documents are summarized on the basis of the following reconciliation ledger characteristics: (partner) functional area, (partner) business area, (partner) company code, funds, and grants. All other account assignments (for example, the cost center and internal order) are eliminated from the transfer.
- **SAP General Ledger is active**
  If SAP General Ledger is active, the configuration of ledger Customizing is important. If, for example, the cost center is updated in the general ledger, this account assignment cannot be eliminated when summarizing the Financial Accounting document.

SAP recommends that you activate document summarization in a production system.

After you have decided which data you want to transfer from Controlling to Financial Accounting, you must give account determination some thought. The following two scenarios require account determination:

- Posting of transactions that occur for secondary cost elements
- Representation of cross-company-code transactions

You can configure the necessary settings in the Implementation Guide under the menu path Financial Accounting (New) • Financial Accounting Global Settings (New) • Ledgers • Real-Time Integration of Controlling with Financial Accounting • Account Determination for Real-Time Integration. Let us take a closer look at both scenarios:

Account determination for secondary cost elements

Even though you are now familiar with the Cost Elements field in the totals table FAGLFLEXT in SAP General Ledger, you still need a G/L account for postings in Financial Accounting. Consequently, for all transactions that occur in Controlling for secondary cost elements (e.g., assessments or internal activity allocations), you must use account determination to find a P&L account for the posting. There are two ways to represent account determination: simple account determination, which depends on the transaction in Controlling, or *extended account determination* (with substitution).

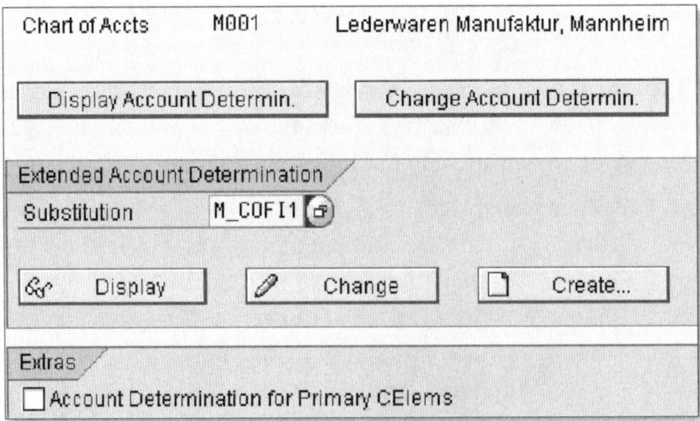

Figure 7.2 Account Determination for Real-Time Integration

Your decision to use simple or extended account determination depends on whether you enter a substitution in the Extended Account Determination section. As you can see in Figure 7.2, Lederwaren-Manufaktur

Mannheim uses the substitution M_COFI1, which was selected because we want to distinguish between the sender and receiver values. *Sender values* represent internal revenue, whereas *receiver values* represent internal expenditure.

Substitution in four steps

We also differentiate between intra-company-code transactions and cross-company-code transactions. For this reason, our substitution comprises four steps (see Figure 7.3).

Reconciliation ledger: Acct determ.	
FICO001	Sample substitution, incl. reversal
M_COFI1	AccDet RTI operating concern M001
Step 001	CCode internal, sender
Step 002	CCode internal, receiver
Step 003	Cross Ccode, sender
Step 004	Cross Ccode, receiver

Figure 7.3 Steps in Account Determination "M_COFI1"

As a sample allowed entry, Figure 7.4 shows step 001, which is used to assign a G/L account to the sender values in intra-company-code transactions. This substitution step is necessary if it concerns a Controlling transaction within a company code and if you are working with the sender item (see Figure 7.4).

Substitution M_COFI1 AccDet RTI operating concern M001
Step 001 CCode internal, sender

Prerequisite

```
RCL_ICCF-BEKNZ = 'H' AND
RCL_ICCF-RBUKRS = RCL_ICCF-SBUKRS
```

Substitutions (if prerequisite is met)

Field	is substituted by:	
G/L account	Constant value	810500

Figure 7.4 "Step 001" in Account Determination "M_COFI1"

Here, you can see that you initially query the debit indicator RCL_ICCF-BEKNZ under PREREQUISITE to identify whether you are working with the sender or receiver item. The debit indicator H for Credit means that the sender item is currently being processed here. We then query RCL_ICCF-RBUKRS = RCL_ICCF-SBUKRS to clarify whether the sender and receiver belong to the same company code.

If both prerequisites are fulfilled, G/L account 810500 (Real-time integration: internal revenue from intra-company-code transactions) is used to transfer the Controlling line item to Financial Accounting.

The other steps vary in terms of whether the sending and receiving company codes are identical or whether they concern the sending or receiving company code. In principle, however, the queries always follow the same pattern.

[+]

Creating Real-Time Integration Accounts as Neutral Accounts

Any account you determine in account determination for real-time integration must not be created as a cost element.

Because all postings to such accounts originate in Controlling, it would be incorrect to use a primary cost element for another balance carryforward to Controlling. Therefore, it is also important that only real-time integration is used for postings to the accounts specified in account determination.

"Account Determination for Primary CElems" indicator

In the SAP system, the ACCOUNT DETERMINATION FOR PRIMARY CELEMS indicator (see Figure 7.2) enables you to use account determination to represent all real-time integration postings. We will illustrate the effect by way of an example:

Our marketing cost center transfers EUR 1,000 (for the "Marketing costs" primary cost element) to Sales. Figure 7.5 shows the transfer posting document.

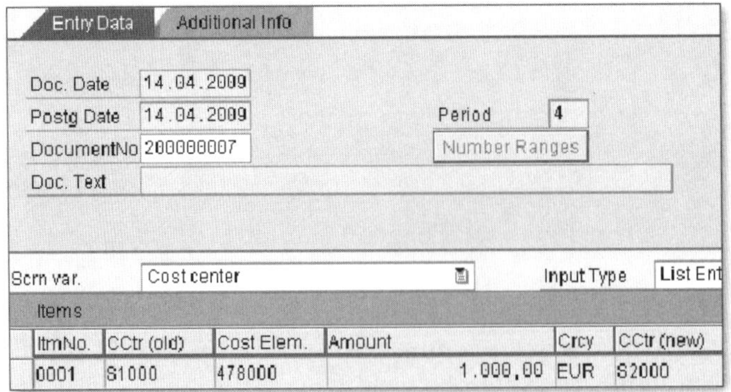

Figure 7.5 Manual Transfer Posting from Cost Center to Cost Center

If you do *not* activate account determination for primary cost elements, the transaction creates the posting to Financial Accounting shown in Figure 7.6.

Data Entry View

Document Number	100000002	Company Code	M001	Fiscal Year	2009
Document Date	14.04.2009	Posting Date	14.04.2009	Period	4
Reference		Cross-CC no.			
Currency	EUR	Texts exist	☐	Ledger Group	0L

C...	Itm	PK	S	Account	Description	Amount	Curr.	Tx	Cost Center
M001	1	50		478000	Marketing/Sales Rep.	1.000,00-	EUR		S1000
	2	40		478000	Marketing/Sales Rep.	1.000,00	EUR		S2000

Figure 7.6 Account Determination for Real-Time Integration: Secondary Cost Elements Only

Here, you can see that, in Financial Accounting, both the credit and debit entries are posted to the primary cost element that was used for the manual transfer posting in Controlling. One disadvantage of this procedure is that the P&L accounts become a little unclear if there are numerous primary cost distributions in Controlling. However, if you use a separate document type, the real-time integration documents are easy to identify and can be hidden, if necessary.

The posting also looks different if you use account determination for primary cost elements (see Figure 7.7).

Data Entry View

Document Number	100000004	Company Code	M001	Fiscal Year	2009
Document Date	14.04.2009	Posting Date	14.04.2009	Period	4
Reference		Cross-CC no.			
Currency	EUR	Texts exist	☐	Ledger Group	0L

C...	Itm	PK	S	Account	Description	Amount	Curr.	Tx	Cost Center
M001	1	50		810500	RTI:int.rev.CC-inter	1.000,00-	EUR		S1000
	2	40		850500	RTI:int.cost CC-int	1.000,00	EUR		S2000

Figure 7.7 Account Determination for Real-Time Integration: Primary Cost Elements

The system has now used the account determination shown in Figures 7.3 and 7.4. The amount credited to cost center S1000 is shown as internal revenue, whereas the amount debited to cost center S2000 is shown as internal expenditure.

For this variant, only special accounts are used to transfer all of the real-time integration postings to Financial Accounting, thus solving the potential problem of lack of clarity in primary accounts. However, this also reduces the information content for general ledger reporting because larger amounts accumulate on the accounts specified in account determination for real-time integration than on the accounts specified in account determination for secondary cost elements only (the first variant).

To prevent information loss, we decided not to use account determination for primary cost elements for Lederwaren-Manufaktur Mannheim (see Figure 7.2).

Cross-company-code transactions

The account determination just shown represents the income and expense items from real-time integration. With cross-company-code transactions, the receivable from or the payable to the other company code involved must also be represented in the balance sheet. As you can see in Figure 7.8, *intercompany clearing account determination* is always maintained in a relationship between two company codes. Both company codes (sending and receiving) must belong to the same controlling area so that allocations can occur between them.

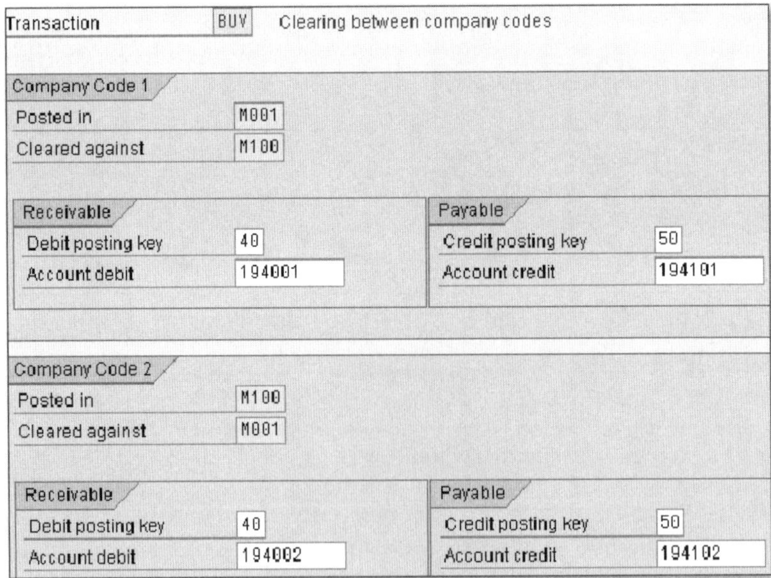

Figure 7.8 Intercompany Clearing Account Determination

Here, you can see that you can specify one receivables account and one payables account for each company code. There is nothing to prevent you from using one account to represent both receivables and payables. However, different accounts should be used for each company code relationship. Lederwaren-Manufaktur Mannheim has created the following clearing accounts for the branch offices in Mannheim and for the holding company:

- In company code M001 (Lederwaren-Manufaktur Mannheim)
  - 194001 (Receivables from company code M100)
  - 194101 (Payables to company code M100)
- In company code M001 (Lederwaren-Manufaktur Holding)
  - 194002 (Receivables from company code M001)
  - 194102 (Payables to company code M001)

In the balance sheet, this account determination enables you to clearly see the receivables from and payables to any particular company code. Furthermore, from a consolidation perspective, it is possible to clearly identify and eliminate such sales within a corporate group.

[+]

Account Determination Identical for Both Real-Time Integration and the Reconciliation Ledger

SAP has incorporated its existing reconciliation ledger functions into real-time integration. Consequently, account determination is identical for both functions. When migrating to SAP General Ledger and subsequently activating real-time integration, you should make sure, if necessary, that the existing account determination in the production system is not adjusted ahead of schedule. This would result in mid-year changes in account determination, which you should avoid for reasons of clarity.

You can thus see why it is necessary to establish real-time integration if you want to use Controlling transactions to represent changes in account assignment in General Ledger Accounting. Customizing is not very complicated because the account determination used here is identical to the account determination used in the reconciliation ledger. However, when compared with the reconciliation ledger, real-time integration has one major advantage: It not only reconciles Controlling and Financial Accounting at the end of the period but immediately posts each relevant Controlling document (in accordance with the specifications made in Customizing) to General Ledger Accounting. Consequently, the postings are easier to understand and, more important, General Ledger Accounting and Controlling can be reconciled at any time.

[+]

Excursus: Internal Invoicing or Intercompany Billing

There are two ways in which cross-company-code transactions can be represented:

- Via activity allocations in Controlling
- Via invoicing

Many enterprises do not permit cross-company-code allocations in Controlling because if allocations cross legal units (company codes), both the service provider and the recipient of the service have to produce an outgoing/incoming invoice. To ensure this, invoices are created and sent in the same way as they are for external customers. The recipient of the service then uses an invoice receipt to post this invoice (just as with third-party providers). In some enterprises, invoices are created for activity relationships between segments or business units within a company code.

This variant solves the formal problem of invoicing. However, there is a danger that a manual implementation of this process may contain incorrect entries that could later cause problems during consolidation.

However, such integration also means that it is necessary to reschedule the times for Controlling and Financial Accounting actions in period-end closing. With real-time integration, all of the actions within Overhead Cost Controlling can still result in changes in the general ledger, which brings us to the topic of planning period-end closing.

Integrative closing process

We may take it for granted but one of the greatest problems associated with the closing process is the need for close cooperation between Financial Accounting und Controlling. Even though logistics specialists frequently do not distinguish between these two areas, in practice, it is always surprising how little cooperation exists between both. One common *closing procedure document* is an important tool for close cooperation. The appendix contains a sample closing procedure document. In the next section, we will describe key closing activities.

7.2 HR Data Transfer

Special HR system

Because HR data requires the highest level of confidentiality, *Human Resources* (HR) is usually not mapped in an SAP ERP system in which Logistics and Accounting are used actively. In addition, wage and salary payments, social insurance contributions, and all other salary-related payments are not made from the ERP system, ensuring that nobody analyzes the figures and obtains information about salaries. However, because we want to create a complete balance sheet in Financial Accounting, and because

Cost Accounting also requires wage and salary expenses, it is necessary to transfer these values to the ERP system on a monthly basis. Ideally, we must connect an SAP ERP HCM system (HCM = Human Capital Management). We can do this in the standard SAP system.

HCM and SAP ERP

The data transfer from HCM to Accounting forms part of payroll in the HCM system. Because most enterprises make wage and salary payments before the last day of the month and because this requires a certain degree of internal preprocessing, payroll is updated, for example, ten days before the end of the month.

A significant part of the required Customizing is implemented in the HCM system. However, the G/L accounts are determined in the ERP system. All relevant settings are made in the Implementation Guide under the menu path PAYROLL • PAYROLL: [COUNTRY] • POSTING TO ACCOUNTING • ACTIVITIES FOR AC SYSTEM • ASSIGNING ACCOUNTS.

Figure 7.9 shows a schematic diagram of account determination.

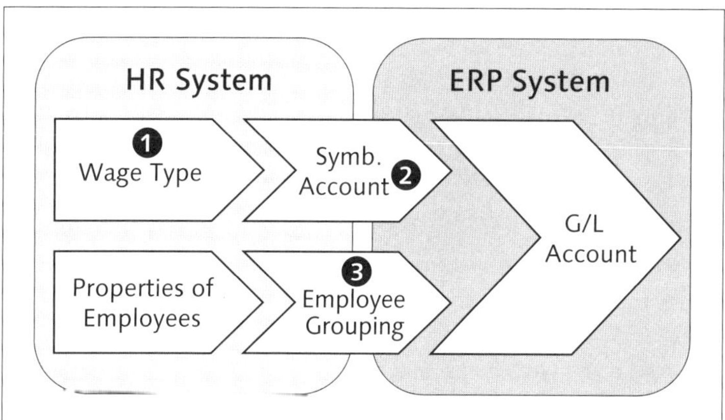

Figure 7.9 Schematic Diagram of Account Determination for the HR Interface

Symbolic account

The *wage type* (see Figure 7.9) and *employee* are the starting points for account determination. Each wage type in the HR system references a *symbolic account*. For example, there could be two wage types, fixed salary and variable salary. From a Financial Accounting perspective, this distinction is irrelevant. Consequently, both wage types can point to the symbolic account "Salary."

Employee grouping

The employee grouping (for example, the customer account assignment group for revenue account determination) is not contained in the employee master record. Instead, it is defined in the HR system and determined using rules that are based on employee characteristics. Workers paid on an hourly basis and salaried employees would be a classic example of a grouping.

[+]

Number of Employees per Cost Center

At least three employees must be assigned to any cost center associated with wage and salary costs. This is the only way to prevent an employee in a cost center from comparing the total personnel costs of the cost center against his or her own salary and inferring the salary of his or her colleague. However, to ensure greater data security, numerous enterprises assign at least five employees to each cost center. The more employees are assigned to a cost center, the less transparent is each individual salary.

Transfer from HR to Financial Accounting

In the standard system, *Application Link Enabling* (ALE) is used to connect the HR system to Accounting. System administrators must configure the necessary Customizing settings. In particular, symbolic accounts, employee groupings, Controlling account assignments, and amounts are transferred from the HR system interface. Information concerning employees or wage types is not transferred.

Effects of using SAP General Ledger

To automatically and, in particular, correctly update all business transactions when using SAP General Ledger and activating the "Document split" function, it is necessary to make some adjustments to the HR system.

Frequently, HR systems are outsourced or centralized in larger corporate groups. Consequently, an HR system serves more companies than an ERP system. In turn, this means that the HR team cannot fulfill all requirements by introducing SAP General Ledger because some customers do not use SAP General Ledger. However, there is a workaround for this situation.

Workaround

In HR, documents are generally created for each company code; in other words, one very large document is created that comprises all posting data. If the number of lines in the document exceeds 999, the document is "split" and a new document is created. However, when you use the "document split" function, this procedure produces technically incorrect documents because the system cannot recognize existing 1:1 relationships between P&L accounts and balance sheet accounts. For this reason, it is necessary to create a posting variant for payroll in the HR system. In this variant, the document split can be based on the account assignment object (see ❶ in Figure 7.10). Consequently, a separate document is created for each cost center. Therefore, when posting to Financial Accounting, there is no need to split the document, thus avoiding splits that are technically incorrect.

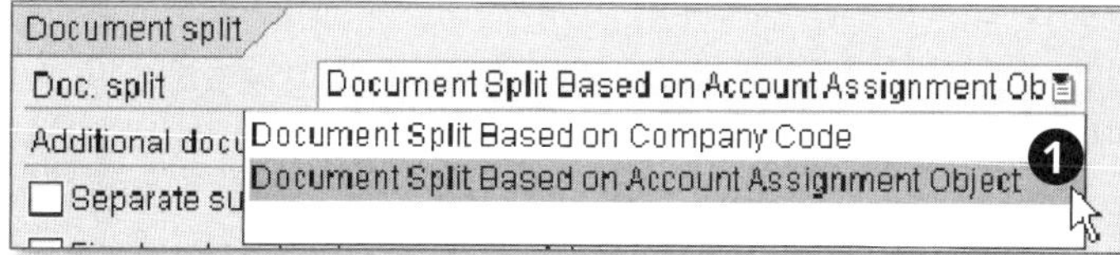

Figure 7.10 Document Split Control

The setting described here and shown in Figure 7.10 is available in the Implementation Guide under the menu path PAYROLL • PAYROLL [COUNTRY] • POSTING TO ACCOUNTING • ACTIVITIES IN THE HR SYSTEM • CREATE POSTING VARIANTS and must be made in the HR system.

As a result of this "document split" workaround, considerably more documents are created in Financial Accounting and Controlling. However, they require very little adaptation by HR.

7.3 Inventory

Inventory methods

The term *inventory* usually means the initial receipt of warehouse stock. On the one hand, you want to know whether the stock (in accordance with SAP Inventory Management) corresponds with the physical stock in the warehouses. On the other hand, however, you are legally required to conduct an annual physical inventory of the warehouse stock. Legally, there are four ways in which you can organize inventory:

- **Periodic inventory**
  Stocktaking takes place on the balance sheet key date or up to ten days before or after.
- **Deferred inventory**
  Stocktaking takes place a maximum of three months before, or two months after, the balance sheet key date.
- **Continuous inventory**
  All warehouse stock is counted but the period spans the entire year.
- **Sample-based physical inventory**
  Only the most valuable materials are counted and the results are extrapolated to the total stock.

Standard method

Periodic inventory is the standard method required by law, whereby stocktaking takes place on the balance sheet key date or up to ten days before or after. Because this is extremely difficult—if not impossible—in large enterprises, other procedures exist (subject to permission).

Procedures subject to permission

Deferred inventory allows you to extend the stocktaking period to up to three months before or two months after the balance sheet key date. With seasonal businesses (such as mulled wine producers), in particular, this enables you to wait until such time when stocks are as low as possible. Alternatively, you can implement a *continuous inventory* whereby all warehouse stock is counted but the period spans the entire fiscal year. If this is not possible, due to the quantities stored or the goods movements, the last remaining option is *sample-based physical inventory* whereby the most valuable goods are counted so that you have recorded the lion's share of the goods on a value basis. Samples are then drawn from the remaining goods so that an overall result can be calculated.

[+]

Mandatory Reference to Balance Sheet Key Date

When you choose a method other than periodic inventory, you must provide evidence of proper inventory management that permits, without any question, the pre-calculation or back-calculation of stock to the balance sheet key date.

The SAP system supports you by enabling you to initially determine the scope of the inventory and then print out the inventory documents for stocktaking purposes. After you have verified the actual stock, you can record and post it in the SAP system. This posting triggers a document in MM and Financial Accounting, thus changing the value of the balance sheet account in Financial Accounting. For the offsetting entry, the system accesses MM account determination. The account for income/expenditure from inventory differences is determined using Transaction GBB (Offsetting Entry to Inventory Posting) and the general grouping code INV (for more information, see Chapter 4, Section 4.5.3, Determining Transactions).

In the application, all required transactions are available under the menu path LOGISTICS • MATERIALS MANAGEMENT • PHYSICAL INVENTORY.

From a Financial Accounting and Controlling perspective, the physical inventory is an activity that is part of year-end closing. However, because this is usually the responsibility of warehouse management, accounting does not have to devote too much time to this activity.

So far, we have only discussed inventory in terms of warehouse stock. However, we also want to know about the fixed assets within an enterprise and, in particular, their location, which brings us to our next topic, namely Asset Accounting.

7.4 Activities in Asset Accounting

Functions in Asset Accounting

Next to Accounts Receivable Accounting and Accounts Payable Accounting, Asset Accounting is the most frequently used form of subledger accounting in SAP. As its name suggests, it is responsible for the management of fixed assets. Both material and non-material objects, "real assets," and assets under construction can be mapped here. One possible function, which is neither elegant nor user-friendly, involves mapping leasing in combination with parallel accounting. However, this is a special topic that we will not discuss in further detail here. Nevertheless, the *Lease Accounting Engine* (LAE) provides additional functions if leasing plays a significant role within an enterprise that wants to represent parallel accounting.

At this point, we will consider the most important closing activities in Asset Accounting. Prior to the actual period-end closing, all capitalizable assets under construction should be settled as real assets so that this step is already finished for the actual closing.

7.4.1 Settlement of Assets Under Construction

AuC – managed on a line item or balance basis

Assets under construction (AuCs) gather costs that are accrued for assets. If an asset is not yet ready for use, it must not be shown as a capitalized asset. Moreover, it must not be depreciated. Any costs accrued before an asset is capitalized (ready for use) are assigned to an AuC. AuCs are always created in a special asset class.

The SAP system has two types of AuCs, which differ in how their values are posted:

As a single asset type, an AuC can be managed on a line item basis.

However, because this is not absolutely necessary, you can also manage AuCs on a summary basis; that is, the values assigned to an AuC are cumulated for each receipt. In general, however, AuCs are managed on a line item basis, thus enabling you to see each line item during settlement and therefore delicately control which values will be posted to which capitalizable assets.

Capitalization or return to P&L

When capitalizing AuCs, it may become apparent that not all of the costs accrued can be capitalized. A good example is a project for implementing SAP software. The following costs are accrued over a period of several months: consulting, hardware, licenses, use of an enterprise's own employees, and so on. Even if there are legal requirements concerning the ability to capitalize values, the individual interpretation always determines which costs are ultimately capitalized. We call this an "active balance sheet policy." If the project makes poor progress, it may be canceled. In this case, all of the values accumulated to date must be posted directly to the costs, thus resulting in a 100% reduced revenue in the current fiscal year. By specifying a cost center as a target object, the AuC capitalization function can also fulfill this requirement.

Time spent

The amount of time spent capitalizing AUCs depends on which costs are posted to AuCs: only those costs that really affect AuCs or perhaps all target assets if, for example, we allow the purchasing department to create AuCs in purchase orders. Even though an individual AuC is quickly settled, the time involved may be significant as a result of the large number of transactions.

Distribution rule

To settle an AuC, you must first maintain a *distribution rule* for each asset. You access the relevant function in the application menu under the menu path ACCOUNTING • FINANCIAL ACCOUNTING • FIXED ASSETS • POSTING • CAPITALIZE ASSET UNDER CONSTRUCTION • DISTRIBUTE.

You must use the distribution rule to define the target objects to which you want to transfer post AuC values. An example is provided in Figure 7.11. Here, 83 % of the costs are allocated to a capitalized asset and 17 % are allocated to a cost center, that is, directly to Overhead Cost Controlling.

Fixed asset 40000004 0 Laser
Actual settlement

Distribution rule group 1

Cat	Settlement Receiver	Receiver Short Text	%
FXA	20000007-0	Laser	83,00
CTR	P9000		17,00

Figure 7.11 Entering a Distribution Rule

Maintaining the settlement profile

You define all permitted receiver categories (asset, cost center, WBS, and so on) in the *settlement profile*, which is assigned to the company code and valid for all AuCs. The AI profile (settlement of assets under construction) is used in the standard system and you can make changes in Transaction OKO7.

All of the AuC items that have been assigned a distribution rule are now shown in the overview with a green traffic light status.

Figure 7.12 shows that, so far, a distribution rule has been entered for only two of the three line items in asset 40000004. However, you can already start to settle the values. The system will process only items whose status is green. Figure 7.13 shows the document created for settlement purposes.

Company code M001
Asset 40000004 Laser
Sub-number 0

Status	DRG	DocumentNo	Doc. Date	TType	Ast.val.dt	Amount
	1	1700000000	04.03.2009	100	01.04.2009	10.997,48
	2	1900000000	01.03.2009	100		2.602,52
		5000000014	01.04.2009	120		25.000,00
						▪ **38.600,00**

Figure 7.12 Overview of Line Items in an AuC

The first two posting lines show that the AuC has been credited with EUR 13,600.00 in total, of which EUR 1,869.57 was a transfer posted to cost center P9000. Account 214000 in line 3 was automatically determined using the account determination for Asset Accounting. The remaining amount (EUR 11,730.43) was posted to a capitalized asset. This also explains the distribution of retirements from the AuC: They do not correspond to the acquired line items shown in Figure 7.12. Instead, they are grouped according to the receiver (in our case, the capitalized assets and the cost center).

C...	Itm	PK	Account	Description	Amount	Curr.	Cost Center	Profit Center	Segment
M001	1	75	32000	000040000004 0000	1.869,57-	EUR		M1400	M_BELT
	2	75	32000	000040000004 0000	11.730,43-	EUR		M1400	M_BELT
	3	40	214000	AuC settle to CO	1.869,57	EUR	P9000	M9999	MANF
	4	70	11000	000020000006 0000	2.602,52	EUR		M1400	M_BELT
	5	70	11000	000020000007 0000	9.127,91	EUR		M1400	M_BELT

Figure 7.13 Document for AuC Settlement

You should ensure that the AuC settlement process is finished before the depreciation posting run starts because the settlement process may cause the values associated with capitalized assets to change.

[+]

Excursus: Account Determination for Asset Accounting

It goes without saying that the connection between Asset Accounting and General Ledger Accounting involves a great deal of integration and automation. It is therefore necessary to establish an account determination that determines a G/L account for each transaction in Asset Accounting. Several transactions are available for configuring account determination. The main one is Transaction AO90, which you can use to configure all required settings.

Account determination depends on three items: the chart of depreciation, the chart of accounts, and the valuation area. Furthermore, it is assigned to the relevant asset classes.

In addition to the accounts for *acquisition and production costs* (APCs), accounts must be specified for the depreciation of an asset as well as for gains and losses resulting from the sale of an asset.

7.4.2 Depreciation Posting Run

Toward the end of settlement, postings must also be stopped in Accounts Payable Accounting, which means that, from the perspective of Asset Accounting, there are no further changes to the *acquisition and production costs* (APCs) of an asset. The only way to produce additional APCs is to confirm working times or material consumptions for assets produced in-house. However, internal expenses should be confirmed and posted before an AuC is fully settled.

Depreciation key

The periodic *depreciation posting run* is used to facilitate the legally required deduction of *depreciation* from APCs. We generally start the depreciation posting run on a monthly basis and it is fully automated in SAP systems. This requires some degree of Customizing and concerns rules that are used to calculate depreciation. These rules are summarized in a *depreciation key*, and each capitalized asset obtains a depreciation key for each valuation area.

Function of the depreciation posting run

In the depreciation posting run, the system calculates the depreciation amount that needs to be posted and the amounts that have already been posted. The depreciation posting run then posts the difference to the general ledger.

Integration with Controlling

Integration with Controlling is a key consideration when developing the concept of Asset Accounting. Essentially, it is possible to transfer the values of each valuation area to Controlling. However, you should ask yourself why you need all of these values. In some enterprises, you would think that we were still living in the Stone Age times of hunters and gatherers; in other words, absolutely everything is transferred to Controlling. However, if you take the example of transferring depreciation in accordance with local law and International Financial Reporting Standards (IFRS) to Controlling, you must later remember (in Overhead Cost Controlling reports) not to consider some of the cost elements; in other words, those in accordance with local law or IFRS. Otherwise, the depreciation amounts you take into account would be too high.

If you use parallel ledgers to represent parallel accounting in SAP General Ledger, you can only transfer the master depreciation area to Controlling because the other ledgers in the general ledger are not integrated with Controlling.

Master area = international accounting

It has become widely accepted in the SAP world that international law, not local law anymore, is used in the master depreciation area because most large enterprises conduct their day-to-day business in accordance with international law. Local law is only relevant for legal or taxable year-end closings. Therefore, in the master area, we usually adopt the valuation approach that is also relevant for Controlling. This approach suffices if you transfer only those values to Controlling.

Permitted Controlling objects

After you have decided which type of accounting you want to transfer to Controlling, you must ask yourself the following question: For which Controlling objects do you want to enter an account assignment for depreciation? Much is possible but not everything makes sense. You would think that account assignments to cost centers or internal orders should be identical. However, this is completely untrue. The rules here are considerably tighter, especially as a result of implementing SAP General Ledger and activating the "document split" function. The main reason for this is the procedure used to derive profit centers in the standard SAP system. Even though SAP can explain the logic here, this does not mean that the logic is very good. Consider the following, at the latest when implementing SAP General Ledger:

- Avoid maintaining more than one Controlling account assignment within a capitalized asset.
- If you have created APC accounts and/or accumulated depreciation accounts as cost elements (category 90), test not only the transactions but also the account assignment derivations for depreciation. This is the deciding factor.
- Make sure that all of the Controlling objects (cost centers, orders, WBS elements, etc.) specified in assets also have a good profit center assignment.

Example: Multiple Controlling account assignments in asset master

Example: We have always specified a cost center in our assets. In asset 20000005, we have also specified an internal order for depreciation purposes. The depreciation posting run recognizes both account assignments, as shown in Figure 7.14.

Cost Ctr	Int. order	Description	Σ	Plan.Amt	Σ	Amt Posted	Σ	Amount TBP
P4000	100301	Ord.depreciation		2.415,68-		260,68-		8,00-
		Ord.depreciation	▪	**2.415,68-**	▪	**260,68-**	▪	**8,00-**
Depreciation area 20			▪▪	**2.415,68-**	▪▪	**260,68-**	▪▪	**8,00-**

Figure 7.14 Depreciation Posting Run with Cost Center and Internal Order

Two behaviors in the standard SAP system now come into play:

- If both a cost center and internal order are specified, the actual posting is made to the order (value type 4).
- Only a statistical posting is made to the cost center (value type 11).

Accordingly, the profit center and segment are also derived from the master record for the internal order. This behavior applies to the depreciation posting run. However, the SAP system never accesses the internal order for an asset acquisition. Therefore, in our example, the profit center and segment are derived from the cost center.

	Cost Center	Internal Order	Company Code
Controlling account assignment	P4000	100301	M001
Profit center	M1400	M5100	–
Segment	M_BELT	M_OH	–
Asset acquisition	EUR 12,078.40	–	EUR 12,078.40
Book value before depreciation posting run	EUR 12,078.40	EUR -260.68	EUR 11,817.72
Depreciation posting		EUR -8.00	EUR -8.00
Book value after depreciation posting run	EUR 12,078.40	EUR -268.68	EUR 11,809.72

Table 7.1 Value Chart of an Asset with a Profit Center and Segment

Table 7.1 shows an asset in which cost center P4000 and internal order 100301 have been specified. We also see which profit centers and segments are associated with the Controlling account assignments.

An asset acquisition amounting to EUR 12,078.40 is posted to the account assignments for the cost center. The depreciation posting, on the other hand, is assigned to the internal order. The last column shows that the book value fell to EUR 11,809.72 after the depreciation posting run. However, if we consider the book values for each profit center or segment, the situation looks very different.

The profit center and segment for the cost center still show a book value of EUR 12,078.40, whereas the profit center and segment for the internal order show a negative APC of EUR –268.68.

Consequently, you can see that multiple Controlling account assignments in the asset master may produce incorrect balance sheet displays at the profit center and segment level.

However, this is a master data maintenance and posting logic problem in Controlling rather than a problem with the depreciation posting run. We will therefore skip to the next periodic task in Asset Accounting, periodic APC values posting.

7.4.3 Periodic APC Values Posting

In earlier SAP releases, only the master depreciation area could immediately trigger postings in the general ledger (due to asset transactions such as acquisitions, retirements or transfer postings). For all other valuation areas, it was necessary to start *periodic APC values posting* in Transaction ASKB or in the application menu under the menu path ACCOUNTING • FINANCIAL ACCOUNTING • FIXED ASSETS • PERIODIC PROCESSING • APC VALUES POSTING. This function analyzes which asset transactions took place since the last update run for this transaction. These changes are then transferred to General Ledger Accounting. The account determination for Asset Accounting is used here.

Even if non-master depreciation areas could trigger postings when there were asset transactions, this would be unnecessary. Thus, many enterprises still use periodic APC values posting today. However, online posting has a great advantage in that BAdI `ACC_DOCUMENT` can be used to access the posting.

[+] **Periodic APC Values Posting at Fiscal Year End**

It is important to restart periodic APC values posting at the end of the fiscal year, after all of the transactions have been posted in Asset Accounting. This is the only way the SAP system can allow complete year-end closing in Asset Accounting.

7.4.4 Asset Accounting Inventory

In Section 7.3, Inventory, you learned about the various inventory options in Materials Management. Unfortunately, there is considerably less system support for fixed assets. Even though SAP provides asset master fields in which we can specify the inventory relevance as well as the date of the last inventory, there are no standard tools for automatically filling these fields. We therefore have to rely on customer developments or Microsoft Excel.

7.4.5 Technical Processing

Reconciling Asset Accounting and General Ledger Accounting

To enable you to check whether all APC values postings have been transferred correctly to the general ledger, SAP provides a report that *reconciles* Asset Accounting with the general ledger. Unfortunately, this activity not only gets a raw deal in many user departments, it may not even be known.

We can use Transaction ABST2 for reconciliation purposes. In the application, this function is available under the menu path ACCOUNTING • FINANCIAL ACCOUNTING • FIXED ASSETS • PERIODIC PROCESSING • YEAR-END CLOSING • ACCOUNT RECONCILIATION.

This function is used to reconcile the totals for each balance sheet account and accumulated depreciation account in Asset Accounting (table ANLC) with the account balances in the general ledger. This comparison is possible at the company code, G/L account, and business area level. Here, it is important that there are no manual postings to the accounts for asset account determination, in particular, the APC accounts and the accumulated depreciation accounts. If there are technical reasons for adjusting the asset values in the general ledger, you should use adjustment accounts for this purpose.

SAP recommends that you start this report before each year-end closing. Furthermore, SAP recommends that this reconciliation report should form part of every month-end closing. Then, if any differences come to light, you only have to check the posting data for a period of one month. However, if you only run the reconciliation report once a year, you have to check a much larger volume of data if a difference is detected. In addition, note that many enterprises have to report quarterly or bi-annual (every six months) figures to interested parties outside the enterprise (banks, for example). Problems would then arise if, for example, you had to adjust February's figures in December because you detected a difference. This would result in you changing figures that have already been reported.

[+]

Checking whether a Job Has Ended Properly

You can use Transaction ARAL (Application Log) to check that all of the jobs started as part of periodic activities have ended properly.

Fiscal year change

The *fiscal year change* in Asset Accounting is purely a technical necessity. We can regard Transaction AJRW (Fiscal Year Change) as a balance carryforward for Asset Accounting: The accumulated values are transferred (carried forward) to the new fiscal year. The fiscal year change has another function: asset transactions cannot be posted to the new year until the relevant transaction has started. Consequently, the fiscal year change should already start at the end of the previous year. Technically, this is only possible in the last period.

This function is available under the menu path ACCOUNTING • FINANCIAL ACCOUNTING • FIXED ASSETS • PERIODIC PROCESSING • FISCAL YEAR CHANGE.

Year-end closing

At the end of the fiscal year, you must perform the following action in Asset Accounting: *year-end closing* in Transaction AJAB, which locks the old fiscal year against asset transactions. To make sure that closing is executed correctly, the SAP system runs year-end closing to check that all depreciation amounts have been calculated and posted correctly.

This function is available in the application menu under the menu path ACCOUNTING • FINANCIAL ACCOUNTING • FIXED ASSETS • PERIODIC PROCESSING • YEAR-END CLOSING • EXECUTE.

After you have completely closed the old fiscal year, you can create final reporting in Asset Accounting. Here, the asset history sheet is, without doubt, the most important report.

7.4.6 Creating the Asset History Sheet

You can call the *asset history sheet* under the menu path ACCOUNTING • FINANCIAL ACCOUNTING • FIXED ASSETS • INFORMATION SYSTEM • REPORTS ON ASSET ACCOUNTING • NOTES TO FINANCIAL STATEMENTS • INTERNATIONAL • ASSET HISTORY SHEET.

An asset history sheet shows the development of a fixed asset over a defined period of time (usually a fiscal year). The layout of the asset history sheet is mainly determined by the *asset history sheet version* because its columns are defined there. The standard SAP system contains multiple versions of asset history sheets. However, you can also create your own versions. To do this, you must first define an *asset history sheet group* in the Implementation Guide under the menu path FINANCIAL ACCOUNTING (NEW) • ASSET ACCOUNTING • INFORMATION SYSTEM • ASSET HISTORY SHEET. This group must comprise an ID and name only. In the asset master, an asset history sheet group is defined for all transaction types in Asset Accounting. Therefore, when creating a new asset history sheet, you only have to enter the required asset history sheet group in the column headers— not all transaction types you want to show there.

The asset history sheet in the standard SAP system does not contain a special display for AuC settlements. This has been frequently requested in recent times. At present, however, this user department requirement can only be satisfied by creating a new asset history sheet.

7.5 Period Control

The fiscal year change is used to determine the fiscal year in which postings to Asset Accounting are possible (see also Section 7.4.5, Technical Processing). For Financial Accounting and Controlling purposes, it is also important to determine, even within a fiscal year, the periods in which postings can be made as well as the periods locked against postings.

[Ex]

Period Locked Against Postings

Invoices or goods movements, for example, can no longer be entered in a period for which closing operations have been performed. A period must be fully locked against postings before its data can be extracted and transferred to SAP NetWeaver BW.

We can summarize this complex topic under the term *period control.*

In the SAP system, there are many places where you can control whether postings can be made to a particular period. The important issue of period control is not a feature of the Financial Accounting or Controlling modules. However, it is regularly reported to Financial Accounting/Controlling module administrators if problems occur. Period control concerns period closing for the material master.

7.5.1 Period Closing for the Material Master

You can use *period closing* for material masters (Transaction MMPV) to define the periods in which material movements can be posted. The *period closing program* must run at night, between the end of one period and the start of another, so that, when work commences, goods movements can also be posted to the new period. It is best to schedule this job in the background.

Settings for period closing program

The settings for the period closing program and the way in which they affect the ability to post materials is much more interesting than the period closing program run itself. The relevant settings are made in the Implementation Guide under the menu path Logistics • General • Material Master • Basic Settings • Maintain Company Codes for Materials Management. You then access the following transaction (see Figure 7.15).

Co	Company Name	Year	Pe	FYr	M	FYr	LM	ABp	DBp
M001	Lederwaren-Manufaktur	2009	4	2009	3	2008	12	☑	☐
M100	LWM Belgium	2009	4	2009	3	2008	12	☑	☐

Figure 7.15 Settings for MM Period Closing Program

The DBp indicator (Disallow backposting after a change of period) is of particular interest here. In our case, it defines whether we can still generate material postings in period 3-2009 even though the current period is 4-2009. Because we have not set the DBp indicator for Lederwaren-Manufaktur Mannheim, we can still enter material movements in the previous period. This makes it easier to plan tasks as part of month-end and year-end closing. However, we must not overlook the fact that a backposting to a previous period may cause the system to automatically create adjustment postings to adjust the moving average price.

It goes without saying that backposting is only possible if the period is also still open in Financial Accounting.

7.5.2 Opening and Closing Posting Periods

Posting periods in Financial Accounting

In Financial Accounting, you open and close *posting periods* in Transaction OB52, which is available in the application menu under the menu path Accounting • Financial Accounting • General Ledger Accounting • Environment • Current Settings • Open and Close Posting Periods. An example is shown in Figure 7.16.

Var.	A	From acct	To account	From per.1	Year	To period	Year	From per.2	Year	To period	Year	AuGr
M001	+			3	2009	4	2009	13	2009	16	2009	
M001	A	1	9999999999	4	2009	4	2009	13	2009	16	2009	
M001	D	1	ZZZZZZZZZZ	4	2009	4	2009	13	2009	16	2009	
M001	K	1	ZZZZZZZZZZ	4	2009	4	2009	13	2009	16	2009	
M001	M	1	9999999999	4	2009	4	2009	13	2009	16	2009	
M001	S	1	9999999999	3	2009	4	2009	13	2009	16	2009	

Figure 7.16 Opening and Closing Posting Periods in Financial Accounting

Variants

The posting periods are not controlled for each company code. Instead, they are variant-dependent. In turn, these variants are defined in the company code parameters. All of Lederwaren-Manufaktur Mannheim works with variant M001, that is, the periods are opened and closed together for all company codes. We can specify the account types in the maintenance transaction, for example, S for G/L accounts or D for accounts receivable. However, there is always one entry that is masked with a plus sign in column A (Account type). This is shown at the very top of Figure 7.16. This entry decides which periods are still open (in our case, March and April 2009, and the special periods 13 to 16 for the year 2009). However, the restriction to period 4 for the account types A, D, K, and M means that only period 4 is open for these account types. Therefore, the detailed entry, not the masked entry, counts here.

Authorization group

At the very end of the table, you see the column AuGr (authorization group). You can use this column to restrict access to accounts and periods to certain employees or employee groups. Here, the Authorization Group field corresponds to the authorization object F_BKPF_BUP, which must be considered accordingly in authorization management. However, this authorization check can only be used for the first time interval, not for the second, which usually contains the special periods.

Posting periods in Controlling

Controlling also has its own posting periods. These are maintained in Transaction OKP1 or in the application menu under Accounting • Controlling • Cost Element Accounting • Environment • Period Lock • Change. Here, Controlling transactions, and not cost elements, are used to control period locks. An example is shown in Figure 7.17.

Here, period 4 (Figure 7.17), for example, is locked against down payments but we can still make settlements and continue to permit through-postings from Financial Accounting.

Period locks						
Transaction	01	02	03	04	05	06
ABC Actual process assessment	☑	☑	☑	☐	☑	☑
Actual Overhead Assessment	☑	☑	☑	☐	☑	☑
Actual Overhead Distribution	☑	☑	☑	☐	☑	☑
Actual Periodic Repostings	☑	☑	☑	☐	☑	☑
Actual activity allocation	☑	☑	☑	☐	☑	☑
Actual cost center accrual	☑	☑	☑	☐	☑	☑
Actual cost center split	☑	☑	☑	☑	☑	☑

Figure 7.17 Period Lock in Controlling

7.6 Foreign Currency Valuation

Today, very few enterprises post absolutely no documents in foreign currencies. In reporting, however, it is generally more useful to show all values in one currency so that the amounts are comparable. This is particularly true for the balance sheet, which we show in the local currency, that is, in the currency defined in the company code parameters. In principle, the SAP system facilitates this form of reporting by the very fact that any document amounts posted in a foreign currency are also updated in the local currency. Here, the currencies are converted using the exchange rate defined in each individual document. At the end of a period, however, we generally want items and balances in a foreign currency to be shown in accordance with the current exchange rate or the relevant accounting principles. A tool known as *foreign currency valuation* (Transaction FAGL_FC_VAL) is available for this.

Function of foreign currency valuation

You can use this program to valuate open items and G/L account balances. First of all, you determine the valuation differences to be considered. The system then outputs a list you can check. You can then work directly with the program to generate the required postings. A sample posting is provided in Figure 7.18.

In this example, we have an open receivable that had an original posting value of EUR 2,000.00 (local currency). On the balance sheet key date (December 31, 2009), however, the receivable only has a value of EUR 1,960.00. We therefore need to make an adjustment of EUR 40.00. Figure 7.18 shows both the devaluation of EUR 40.00 and the reversal of this foreign currency valuation (key date: January 01, 2010).

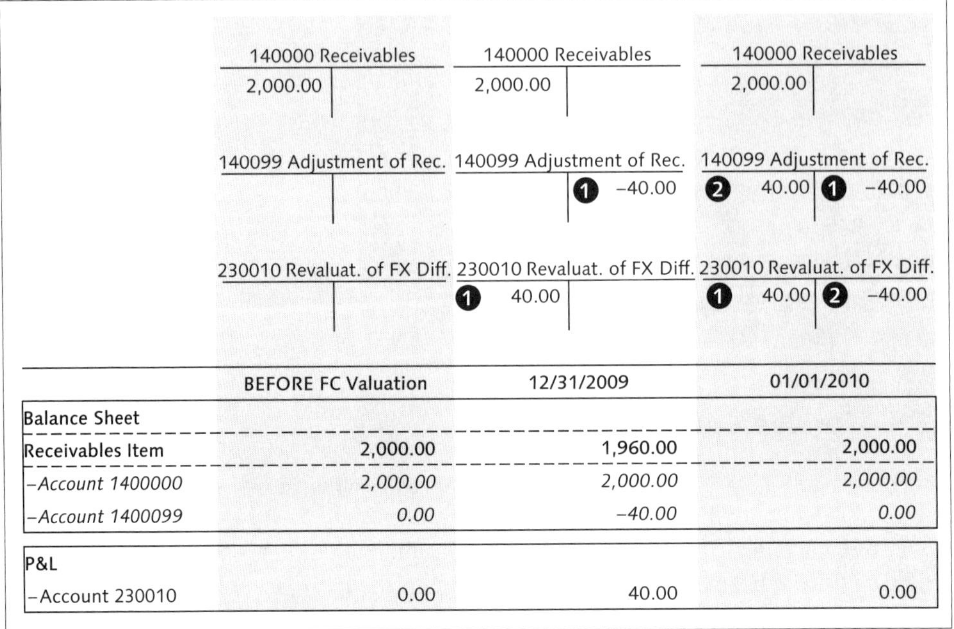

Figure 7.18 Example of Foreign Currency Valuation

Using an adjustment account

However, this adjustment is not made in the customer account or reconciliation account. Instead, it is made in an adjustment account, which is displayed together with the reconciliation account in the balance sheet; in other words, as one item. As a result, the balance sheet still shows a receivable of EUR 1,960.00 although we have not touched account 1400000.

Reversing an adjustment posting

Because foreign currency valuation involves a key date valuation, we will immediately reverse the adjustment posting in the subsequent period (in our example, January 01, 2010). Consequently, the balances in receivable adjustment account 1400099 and expense account 230010 are reset to zero, and the receivables balance sheet item once again has a balance of EUR 2,000.00.

[+]

Valuation for Balance Sheet Preparation

In the past, you could use the "valuation for balance sheet preparation" function, which saved valuation differences in a document. The reclassification run for receivables and payables (see Section 7.7, Reclassification of Receivables and Payables) then accessed these entries in the documents and posted the amounts. For this reason, reclassification should also take place after foreign currency valuation (which was not reversed in the subsequent period). However, this procedure is no longer possible when you use the "document split" function.

Acccount determination for the adjustment account

Both the adjustment account and the P&L account are determined using a defined account determination. You configure the necessary settings in the Implementation Guide under the menu path FINANCIAL ACCOUNTING (NEW) • GENERAL LEDGER ACCOUNTING (NEW) • PERIODIC PROCESSING • VALUATE • FOREIGN CURRENCY VALUATION.

With the introduction of SAP General Ledger, it is important that account determination is configured in the context of a particular valuation area, which, in turn, is used to assign accounting itself to the ledgers in the general ledger. You also configure these settings in the Implementation Guide under the menu path FINANCIAL ACCOUNTING (NEW) • GENERAL LEDGER ACCOUNTING (NEW) • PERIODIC PROCESSING • VALUATE.

Configuring valuation-area-specific account determination

To configure valuation-area-specific account determination, you need to know one simple trick. Without it, you will need good luck or simply a lot of time to find the correct button.

Figure 7.19 shows the following: When you select a chart of accounts, you can click on an inconspicuous button (bottom right) called CHANGE VALUATION AREA. If you click on this button, you can select the valuation area in the next dialog box. The maintenance table for account determination now shows the valuation area, together with the chart of accounts, as a classification criterion.

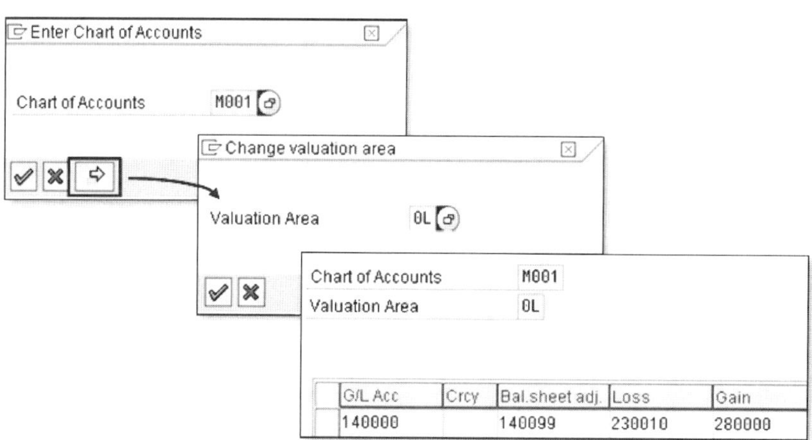

Figure 7.19 Valuation-Area-Specific Account Determination

This enables you to specify accounts that are not only specific to a chart of accounts, but also to a valuation area. You can link the valuation area with an accounting principle. These settings can be configured in the Implementation Guide under the menu path FINANCIAL ACCOUNTING (NEW) •

General Ledger Accounting (New) • Periodic Processing • Valuate • Assign Valuation Areas and Accounting Principles (see Figure 7.20).

Assignment of Valuation Area to Accounting Pri

Valuation Area	Acc.Princ.
0L	01
IA	IAS
LO	LOGA
US	GAAP

Figure 7.20 Assigning a Valuation Area and Accounting Principle

Assigning a ledger to an accounting principle

By assigning the accounting principles to the ledgers in SAP General Ledger, you can specifically post foreign currency valuation postings to individual ledgers. You can configure this assignment in the Implementation Guide under the menu path Financial Accounting (New) • Financial Accounting Global Settings (New) • Ledgers • Parallel Accounting • Assign Accounting Principle to Ledger Groups. An example is shown in Figure 7.21.

Importance of the target ledger group

To be more exact, the accounting principle is not assigned directly to a ledger but rather to a target ledger group. A target ledger group is a group of ledgers that can be processed together. For example, the second row in Figure 7.21 contains the accounting principle GAAP, which is assigned to target ledger group L7. L7 comprises the following two ledgers: one for US GAAP and one for IAS. As the first entry in the figure shows, we must also create a principle for individual ledgers such as master ledger 0L so that we can access it, for example, in account determination for foreign currency valuation.

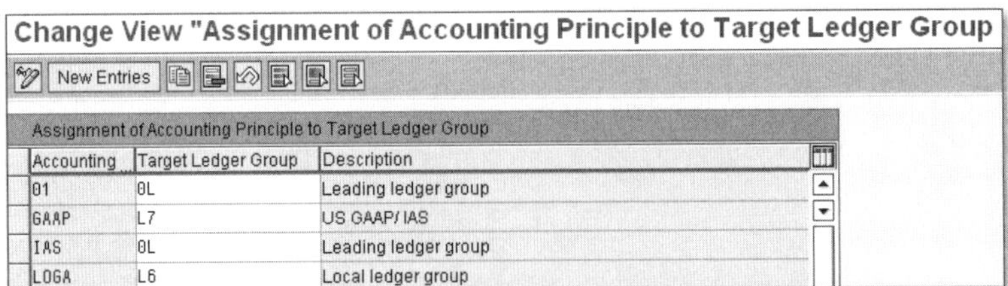

Change View "Assignment of Accounting Principle to Target Ledger Group

New Entries

Assignment of Accounting Principle to Target Ledger Group

Accounting	Target Ledger Group	Description
01	0L	Leading ledger group
GAAP	L7	US GAAP/ IAS
IAS	0L	Leading ledger group
LOGA	L6	Local ledger group

Figure 7.21 Assigning the Accounting Principle to the Target Ledger Group

This simple and effective tool, which facilitates the foreign currency valuation of G/L account balances and open items from general ledger accounting, accounts payable accounting, and accounts receivable accounting, ensures that balance sheet items are displayed correctly. The function described next serves the same purpose.

7.7 Reclassification of Receivables and Payables

Principles that govern the way in which receivables and payables are displayed in the balance sheet exist both in accordance with local and international accounting. This brings us to an additional step you should perform at least once at year-end closing—the *reclassification of receivables and payables*. This step, which you can implement using just one report in the SAP system, contains the following subtasks:

1. Transfer posting of open items when changing the reconciliation account in accounts receivable or accounts payable
2. Transfer posting of open items when changing the trading partner in accounts receivable or accounts payable
3. Transfer posting if vendors have debit balances or customers have credit balances
4. Reclassification according to duration

We will now take a closer look at each of these points.

Changed reconciliation accounts

Once again, your accounting philosophy determines whether or not you can change the *reconciliation account* in accounts receivable or accounts payable. One reason for changing this account could be significant financial involvement in a vendor company. Prior to the transfer, the "Payables for Goods and Services - External" reconciliation account was stored in its vendor master. We would now have to change this account to "Payables for Goods and Services - Affiliated Companies." As an alternative to making a change in the vendor master, we must create a new vendor master with the correct reconciliation account, transfer post any open items, and lock the old vendor master against postings.

We cannot avert a situation where a vendor issues a considerably large credit memo, thus resulting in an overall receivable against this vendor, or where we have to issue a credit memo to a customer, thus resulting in an overall payable towards this customer. Here, we use the terms "vendor with a debit balance" and "customer with a credit balance."

Vendors with debit balances/ customers with credit balances

In the balance sheet, you can no longer show a *vendor with a debit balance* among the payables under liabilities. Instead, the balance must be shown among the receivables under assets. The reverse is true for *customers with credit balances*. Consequently, adjustment postings are necessary for period-end closing. The SAP system uses automated processing to support you when determining the posting data affected and when making the relevant postings.

Reclassification according to duration

Finally, we still have to classify the receivables and payables according to duration. Usually, they are classified according to the following durations:

- Receivables and payables with a duration of 1 year or less
- Receivables and payables with a duration of 1 to 5 years
- Receivables and payables with a duration of over 5 years

For these postings, we use General Ledger Accounting only. Subledger accounting is not affected. However, because the reconciliation accounts are posted from subledger accounting only, you create adjustment accounts for all reconciliation accounts. In the balance sheet, the reconciliation account and adjustment account are shown as one balance sheet item, which means that the total balance for the balance sheet item is reduced or increased accordingly. Because these postings only concern adjustment postings for creating a balance sheet, all of the postings are performed on the balance sheet key date (for example, December 31, XXXX) and reversed again at the start of the subsequent period (for example, January 01, XXXX). The reclassification program performs both postings (the adjustment and the reversal) immediately.

Customizing for these functions is available in the Implementation Guide under the menu path Financial Accounting (New) • General Ledger Accounting (New) • Periodic Processing • Reclassify • Transfer and Sort Receivables and Payables.

In the application, you can access the function directly in Transaction FAGLF101 or in the application menu under the menu path Accounting • Financial Accounting • Accounts Receivable/Accounts Payable • Periodic Processing • Closing • Reclassify • Sorting/Reclassification (New).

In accounts receivable accounting, we need to discuss one final topic, value adjustment to receivables.

7.8 Value Adjustment to Receivables

In Chapter 5, Sales and Distribution Process, you learned that, unfortunately, there will always be customers who will not fulfill their payment obligations. Therefore, we have to anticipate that we will not receive payment for a certain percentage of our receivables. A *flat-rate value adjustment* is used for this purpose.

Flat-rate value adjustment

The flat-rate value adjustment can be posted manually or with the support of the system, in other words, automated. For the automated variant, you must maintain account determination in the Implementation Guide under the menu path FINANCIAL ACCOUNTING (NEW) • ACCOUNTS RECEIVABLE AND ACCOUNTS PAYABLE • BUSINESS TRANSACTIONS • CLOSING • VALUATE • VALUATIONS. Because postings are frequently manual, we will not discuss the automatic procedure in any further detail.

Individual value adjustment

However, you also have the option of *individual value adjustment*, which can only be posted manually and is always due when, in an individual case, you learn that you should expect to receive a reduced payment or no payment at all for a receivable. In everyday language, we describe this as *writing off a receivable*.

7.9 Balance Carryforward

At the end of the year, you must *carry forward the balance* in the general ledger and each subledger. For balance sheet accounts, the closing balances for the old fiscal year are transferred to period 0 in the subsequent year as the starting balances. No manual postings can be made to period 0. This period only contains the balance carryforward, while the balances of P&L accounts are transferred to the retained earnings accounts.

Balance carryforward in the general ledger

In the general ledger, you use Transaction FAGLGVTR for the balance carryforward. This transaction is also available in the application menu under the menu path ACCOUNTING • FINANCIAL ACCOUNTING • GENERAL LEDGER ACCOUNTING • PERIODIC PROCESSING • CLOSING • CARRY FORWARD • BALANCE CARRYFORWARD (NEW).

Balance sheet accounts and P&L accounts

Customizing is not required for the balance carryforward in balance sheet accounts. However, you have to configure a small account determination for P&L accounts. We configure this setting in the Implementation Guide under the menu path FINANCIAL ACCOUNTING (NEW) • GENERAL LEDGER ACCOUNTING (NEW) • MASTER DATA • G/L ACCOUNTS • PREPARATIONS • DEFINE RETAINED EARNINGS ACCOUNT. Here, you have to define a single-character ID and create a *retained earnings account* for this ID. Retained earnings accounts are balance sheet accounts that show the annual net income/loss. However, the SAP system does not generate a real posting for the balance carryforward. Instead, it generates a technical balance carryforward. Accordingly, the retained earnings accounts contain only the "appropriation of retained earnings" posting and perhaps manual postings resulting from a migration. The balance carryforward function cannot generate any postings.

[+]

Retained Earnings Accounts when Using Parallel Accounts for Parallel Accounting

If you use parallel accounts for parallel accounting, you must create at least three retained earnings accounts:

One for each type of accounting and one for shared accounts such as telecommunication costs or energy consumption costs (for more information, see the Mickey Mouse model in Chapter 3, Section 3.3, International Requirements).

Balance carryforward in subledger accounting

A balance carryforward is also required in open item accounting. For this purpose, you use Transaction F.07, which is available in the application menu under the menu path ACCOUNTING • FINANCIAL ACCOUNTING • ACCOUNTS RECEIVABLE / ACCOUNTS PAYABLE • PERIODIC PROCESSING • CLOSING • CARRY FORWARDS • BALANCE CARRYFORWARD.

Restarts

You usually start the balance carryforward function during the last posting period or when you want to make postings in a new fiscal year. In fact, after you start the balance carryforward function for the first time, every change made in the old fiscal year should be automatically included in the balance carryforward so that it is always up to date. However, experience has shown that individual postings are not retroactively included in the balance carryforward. For this reason, you should also restart the balance carryforward function at the start of the new fiscal year. Afterward, differences no longer occur.

7.10 Manual Postings

Manual postings are necessary in General Ledger Accounting, particularly during closing operations. Here, you have to make a wide variety of postings, for example, provision postings, the appropriation of retained earnings (subsequent to year-end closing), and accruals/deferrals.

Importance of accrual/deferral postings

You use *accrual/deferral postings* to move the effectiveness of postings to the posting period or fiscal year to which they technically belong. Table 7.2

provides an overview of business transactions that require accrual/deferral postings.

All four business transactions have one thing in common: a payment in a scenario that spans more than one fiscal year. If the payment is made in the subsequent year, we must post another receivable or payable. If the payment is made in the current fiscal year, we must defer the income or expense. Table 7.2 gives rise to the accruals/deferrals shown in Table 7.3.

Scenario	Amount	Payment	Duration	Distribution across Fiscal Years	
				2009	2010
Rental income 1	EUR 12,000.00	Dec. 01, 2009	12/2009 – 11/2010	EUR 1,000.00	EUR 11,000.00
Rental income 2	EUR 9,000.00	Jan 31, 2010	12/2009 – 02/2010	EUR 3,000.00	EUR 6,000.00
Rental expenditure	EUR 24,000.00	Feb. 01, 2009	02/2009 – 01/2010	EUR 22,000.00	EUR 2,000.00
Insurance contribution	EUR 15,000.00	Jan. 31, 2010	10/2009 – 09/2010	EUR 3,750.00	EUR 11,500.00

Table 7.2 Business Transactions for Accrual/Deferral Postings

Distribution across Fiscal Years		Required Accrual/Deferral	Accrual/Deferral Amount
2009	2010		
Income	Revenue	Deferred income	EUR 11,000.00
Revenue	Income	Other receivable	EUR 3,000.00
Expenditure	Loss	Deferred expense	EUR 2,000.00
Loss	Expenditure	Other payable	EUR 3,750.00

Table 7.3 Sample Accrual/Deferral Amounts

At year-end closing 2009, there is a deferred rental income of EUR 11,000.00 (see Table 7.2). The payment is made in 2009 but the rent for eleven months must be assigned to fiscal year 2010. With rental income 2, the payment will not be made until 2010 even though it concerns fiscal year 2009 (accrued income). Here, it is necessary to post another receivable of EUR 3,000.00. Rent of EUR 24,000.00 (see Table 7.2) is paid in advance for an entire year. After taking the duration into account, there is a deferred expense of EUR 2,000.00 on December 31, 2009. The insurance contribution is paid in arrears. We therefore need to post another payable of EUR 3,750.00.

Accrual Engine vs. manual posting

SAP provides the *Accrual Engine* for accrual/deferral postings. Here, you can define rules that will automate accrual/deferral postings. In practice, however, these postings are frequently manual postings and the necessary calculations and tracking usually take place in Microsoft Excel. Because only the posting method changes, not the value flow itself, we will not discuss this in any further detail.

7.11 Assessments and Distributions

Assessments and *distributions* are two *allocation* types that represent standard period-end closing activities in Overhead Cost Controlling. As a result of integrating Profit Center Accounting into SAP General Ledger and introducing segment reporting, the general ledger has been incorporated into the application area for allocations.

Explanation of terms: "assessment" and "distribution"

First, we need to explain the difference between distributions and assessments. With a *distribution*, you take all of the costs that have accumulated in a cost center, for example, and pass them on to a receiver object. The accounts or cost elements originally used to post the values to the cost center are used here.

Assessments, on the other hand, take all relevant cost center costs and post them to one or more receivers. However, a new cost element is used for this purpose. Therefore, the receiver object does not obtain any information about the original cost elements. For the assessment, a secondary cost element must be created in Controlling and a special G/L account in Financial Accounting. For clarity, both allocation types are shown in Figure 7.22.

Differentiation

As you can see in Figure 7.22, the difference between a distribution and an assessment lies in the display options at the receiver end. With a distribution, you see the individual accounts or cost elements already accrued for the sender. With an assessment, the receiver only knows that he has been debited with costs. In our example, the sender costs have been passed on to the receiver as a marketing expense. In Overhead Cost Controlling, an allocation structure enables you to use more than one assessment cost element within an assessment. The assessment cost element used to transfer post individual or grouped source cost elements is defined in the allocation structure.

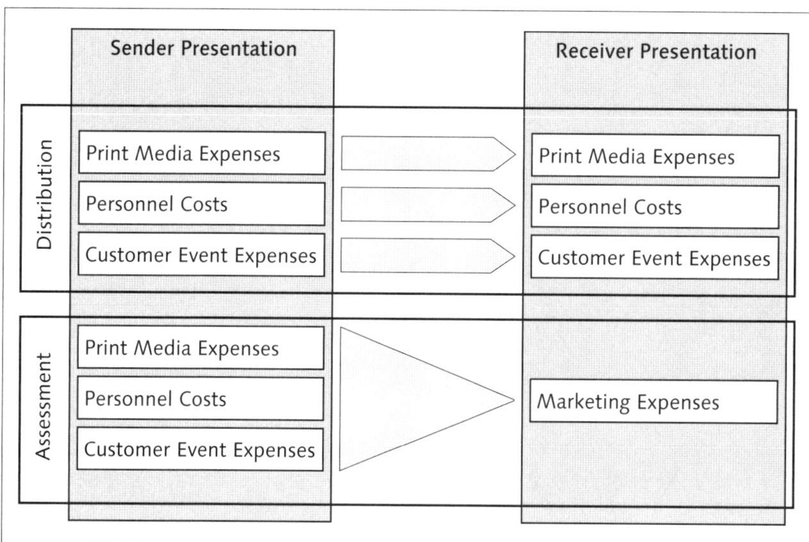

Figure 7.22 Distribution vs. Assessment

Distributions and assessments only differ slightly in terms of their preparation and execution, that is, an assessment cost element or assessment account must be specified for assessments.

Cycle definition

To perform an allocation, you must first create a *cycle* that will determine the basic properties of the allocation. The general ledger determines the ledger group in which the allocation is performed. At this point, it is important to decide whether you require iterative processing. It may be necessary if a receiver object is simultaneously the sender because the object may have already been credited but now obtains costs again as a result of another round of allocations. Consequently, our object would have to be credited again. However, too many iterative relationships cause problems such as increasingly poor performance and significantly longer processing times. You should therefore make sure that iterative processing steps are kept to a minimum.

Segment definition

However, a cycle does not define the sender and receiver in detail. These are first defined in *segments*. Note that a cycle can comprise several segments.

Figure 7.23 shows you that we want to distribute segment M_ZZZ (a dummy segment) to a set that contains all of the segments we use in company code M001. All accounts are considered here.

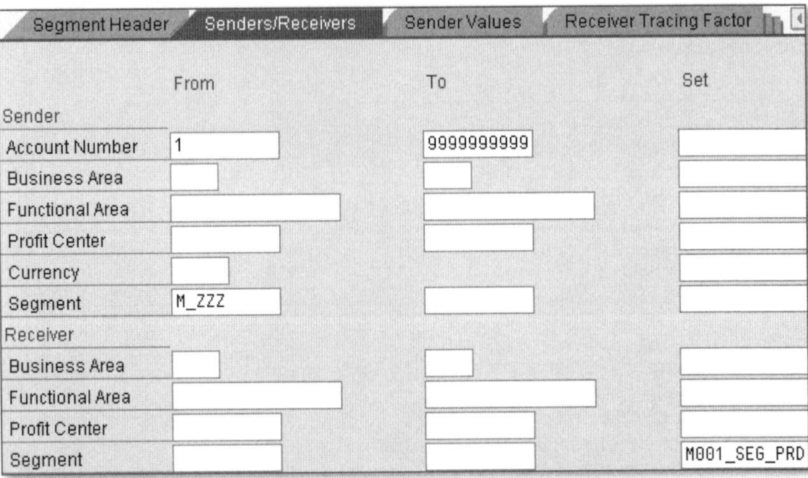

Figure 7.23 Definition of a Distribution Cycle – Segment Definition

Receivers

Segment	Factor per 100
M_BAGS	22
M_BELT	22
M_OH	34
M_SHOES	22

Figure 7.24 Specifying Distribution on a Percentage Basis

In a segment, you specify the way in which you want to distribute sender values to the receivers (see Figure 7.24). In our case, we have opted for distribution on a percentage basis. All product-related segments are debited with 22 percent of the values on the dummy segment, whereas the overhead segment is debited with 34 percent.

Maintaining and starting allocations

The application area determines the way in which you maintain and execute cycles. For example, you access a distribution cycle in SAP General Ledger in the application menu under the menu path ACCOUNTING • FINANCIAL ACCOUNTING • GENERAL LEDGER • PERIODIC PROCESSING • CLOSING • ALLOCATION • ACTUAL DISTRIBUTION. Here, you will find transactions for all important activities such as creating, changing, and executing cycles.

Inheriting information

You can use the inheritance function to control which information is provided for allocation postings. You must activate this function for each field (for example, the functional area) to be transferred from the sender to the receiver. With SAP General Ledger, you configure these settings in the Implementation Guide under FINANCIAL ACCOUNTING (NEW) • GENERAL LEDGER ACCOUNTING (NEW) • PERIODIC PROCESSING • ALLOCATION • DEFINE FIELD USAGE FOR DISTRIBUTION/ASSESSMENT.

Allocations as final closing steps

However, note that as a rule, all other postings must be made before you start allocations so that all sender objects have already been assigned all of their costs. Consequently, current postings in an old period and closing postings in Financial Accounting must be finalized, cost objects must be settled, and, in general, internal activity allocations must be concluded.

Special case: Assessment to CO-PA

Cost center assessment to CO-PA is a little different in terms of its Customizing or execution. Here, value fields are specified as receivers, and the corresponding allocation structures and PA transfer structures must be maintained. Generally, you settle all of the costs accumulated in cost centers to CO-PA. Only then can you fully calculate a contribution margin or EBIT in CO-PA. As an alternative to cost center assessment to CO-PA, you can proceed as follows: First, settle all cost centers to internal orders and then, settle the internal orders to CO-PA. The motto "many roads lead to Rome" applies here.

7.12 Reconciliation

This brings us to reconciliation or, more specifically, accounting reconciliation, intercompany reconciliation, reconciliation between Financial Accounting and inventory management, and reconciliation between Financial Accounting and Controlling.

7.12.1 Accounting Reconciliation

Accounting reconciliation helps you check that your SAP system is working correctly. It also helps you detect application errors.

This function (Transaction F.03 [Reconciliation]) is available in the application menu for accounts receivable accounting and accounts payable accounting under the menu path ACCOUNTING • FINANCIAL ACCOUNTING • ACCOUNTS RECEIVABLE • PERIODIC PROCESSING • CLOSING • CHECK/COUNT • RECONCILIATION (NEW).

The report compares the posted documents against the transaction figures and indexes. All of this data must concur. Deviations arise here for a number of reasons, the worst being a system malfunction. Frequently, however, deviations occur when activating or deactivating open item (OI) control for G/L accounts. Generally, you can resolve these deviations by restarting the relevant reports for activating or deactivating open item (OI) management. Often, such deviations occur because a balance carryforward is missing.

In each case, the relevant reporting procedures will not be correct unless all documents, transaction figures, and indexes correspond. Even though accounting reconciliation produces long runtimes, you should still run it as part of each period-end closing.

7.12.2 Intercompany Reconciliation

Today, consolidation no longer takes place in the ERP system even if an enterprise still actively uses the consolidation module EC-CS, which SAP continues to support.

Reconciling receivables and payables

Nonetheless, individual companies must conduct some preparatory work, known as *preparation for consolidation*, in the ERP system. An important aspect here is *intercompany reconciliation*, which involves reconciling data so that the internal business relationships, from a corporate group perspective, can be eliminated from the consolidation system later. In the consolidation process, this is much easier if the individual companies provide compatible figures.

Let us take the example of Lederwaren-Manufaktur Mannheim again: Our Belgian branch office uses, for example, the services of the German HR department. Consequently, Mannheim regularly passes on costs to Brussels, thus resulting in a receivable for the branch office Mannheim and a corresponding payable on the Belgian side. It is important that both companies post the receivable and payable for the same amount. To ensure this, SAP provides various tools such as intercompany reconciliation, which can work across various different ERP systems.

Customizing for this function is available in the Implementation Guide under the menu path Financial Accounting (New) • General Ledger Accounting (New) • Periodic Processing • Check/Count • Cross-System Intercompany Reconciliation. You then start the reconciliation process in the application menu under Accounting • Financial Accounting • General Ledger • Periodic Processing • Closing • Check/Count • Intercompany Reconciliation: Open Items/Accounts.

Organizational measures

If you send invoices on an intracompany basis and then manually post them again in the receiver company, it is important (when preparing for intercompany reconciliation) that the same "state" is represented in both forms of Financial Accounting at the end of the period; that is, you must ensure that an invoice created in an old period is also posted by the receiver in the same period. Here, some organizational rules are essential.

If the sending and receiving company codes are in the same controlling area, you can also use the activity allocations in Controlling to represent internal allocations (such as HR services for Lederwaren-Manufaktur Mannheim), which then lead you (via real-time integration) to documents in Financial Accounting. Technically, this ensures that the receivable and payable for the individual companies in question are always identical.

However, reconciliation within a company code is also a major topic. In terms of proper bookkeeping, you must ensure that, if document flows are automated, all of the Financial Accounting-relevant transactions are also transferred, for example, from Materials Management to Financial Accounting. You can check this using the many tools provided by SAP. We will discuss the most important ones next.

7.12.3 Reconciliation Between Financial Accounting and Inventory Management

List of stock values

Balance sheet accounts posted using MM account determination should only be posted automatically from the MM module. You can use the *list of stock values* to check whether the stock values in accordance with inventory management correspond with the account balances in Financial Accounting. This list is available in the application menu under the menu path LOGISTICS • MATERIALS MANAGEMENT • INVENTORY MANAGEMENT • PERIODIC PROCESSING • LIST OF STOCK VALUES, or you can access it directly in Transaction MB5L.

This report compares the warehouse stock value with the balance sheet account balance in accordance with MM account determination.

Execution on a Regular Basis [+]

You should execute this function on a regular basis, at the very latest as part of year-end closing.

7.12.4 Reconciliation Between Financial Accounting and Controlling

Generally, financial figures are reported from the Financial Accounting and Controlling modules. For this reason, Financial Accounting and Controlling must concur. There are many ways to reconcile data.

Reconciliation: Financial Accounting – Controlling – CO-PA

For example, you can use Transactions KEAT (check value flow from invoicing) and KEAW (check value flow from order/project settlement) for a *reconciliation* or variance analysis between Financial Accounting and CO-PA.

Reconciliation: Financial Accounting – Controlling

The reports for reconciling Overhead Cost Controlling with Financial Accounting are available in the application menu under the menu path ACCOUNTING • CONTROLLING • COST ELEMENT ACCOUNTING • INFORMATION SYSTEM • REPORTS FOR COST AND REVENUE ELEMENT ACCOUNTING • RECONCILIATION.

Reconciliation: Financial Accounting – EC-PCA

A very good instrument is also available for *reconciling* the general ledger and classic Profit Center Accounting (EC-PCA). This instrument is known as *ledger comparison*, which you access by calling Transaction GCAC. In technical terms, you use it to compare the relevant totals tables.

Comparison of Comp. code currency

Record Type	0	
Base Ledger	0L	Leading Ledger
Base Ledger Version	001	
Comparison Ledger	00	G/L Accnt Transaction Figures
Comparison Ldgr Vers	001	FI planning version 0 ledger 0
Fiscal Year	2009	
From Period	0	
To Period	16	

CoCd	Account	Crcy	Year	Base ledger	CompLedger	Difference
M001	11000	EUR	2009	188.932,11	188.932,11	0,00
M001	11010	EUR	2009	1.217,68-	1.217,68-	0,00
M001	32000	EUR	2009	110.000,00	110.000,00	0,00
M001	100000	EUR	2009	2.000,00-	2.000,00-	0,00
M001	112600	EUR	2009	2.000,00	2.000,00	0,00
M001	112605	EUR	2009	35.000,00-	35.000,00-	0,00
M001	113109	EUR	2009	20.000,00	20.000,00	0,00
M001	113190	EUR	2009	5.991,50	5.991,50	0,00

Figure 7.25 Ledger Comparison Between Financial Accounting and EC-PCA

In Figure 7.25, the posted values were compared at the account level. Additional criteria such as the functional area and profit center can also be specified here. In this context, you must only note that the queried characteristic exists in both ledgers. For example, a query (that includes a functional area) between a classic general ledger and a cost-of-sales accounting ledger is not useful because this area is not updated in the classic general ledger.

After all of the closing activities and the most important reconciliation work have been completed, you can start to evaluate the data. You can usually create part of the necessary reporting in the SAP ERP system. For example, you can also create a balance sheet in a business intelligence system such as SAP NetWeaver BW. However, to obtain a quick look at the balance sheet (for example, to check the effects of a manual closing posting), you call the balance sheet in the ERP system. To evaluate the data in SAP NetWeaver BW, you would have to transfer the posting to SAP NetWeaver BW first. However, there are a range of reports that are easier to map in SAP NetWeaver BW. For example, you should always choose an SAP NetWeaver BW implementation if you require data from different tables or complex calculations. Here, we will look at reporting in SAP ERP first. All of the SAP NetWeaver BW options are described in detail in Chapter 8, Reporting with SAP NetWeaver BW.

7.13 Reporting

The standard SAP system already contains several reports. In Financial Accounting, in particular, these standard reports can be used to fulfill the lion's share of the reporting requirements in user departments. The following sections will provide an overview of the standard reports available.

7.13.1 Reporting in General Ledger Accounting

The SAP General Ledger in the standard system contains various reports that record data for all key areas. These reports include:

- **Master data reports**
  These include a G/L account list and the change history for G/L accounts.
- **Document/journal entry reports**
  SAP provides the option of creating a document journal, that is, a complete list of all posted documents. This is a legal requirement in some countries. This report also shows any gaps in the document number assignment. This is very practical if a government tax audit or external audit needs to be performed.

- **Account balances**
  This report contains totals lists and account balances for each general ledger account.
- **Balance sheet and P&L statement/cashflow**
  SAP provides elaborate drilldown reports for cashflow calculations. Because most enterprises apply a different calculation logic, you generally have to create these reports yourself.

However, the most important report is the balance sheet and P&L statement, which we will discuss in more detail next.

Balance sheet and P&L statement

The *balance sheet* and *profit and loss statement* (P&L) are created, at the very latest, at the end of the fiscal year (but usually at the end of a quarter or period). The type of accounting applied within an enterprise determines the structure of the balance sheet and P&L statement. The profit and loss statement, in particular, has two different display types: one in accordance with *period accounting* and one in accordance with *cost-of-sales accounting*.

Period accounting vs. cost-of-sales accounting

Period accounting shows expenses in accordance with G/L items such as personnel or material expenses and deducts these from sales revenues and balance sheet changes for (un)finished products, whereas cost-of-sales accounting itemizes expenses in accordance with functional areas instead of expense types. For this reason, IFRS prefers this method and US-GAAP explicitly prescribes it.

Another important difference between period accounting and cost-of-sales accounting is the periodic assignment of expenses. In accordance with cost-of-sales accounting, only the expenses accrued for the sales revenues realized in the period are set against these sales revenues. Consequently, in accordance with cost-of-sales accounting, the balance sheet changes are not explicitly shown in the profit and loss statement, thus making it possible to show a product's performance within a period. In period accounting, all of the expenses within a period are shown. If, for example, a product is finished but not yet sold, the costs in the current period are shown as balance sheet changes.

We will now use a numerical example to illustrate the differences between period accounting and cost-of-sales accounting.

[Ex]

Period Accounting and Cost-of-Sales Accounting for Lederwaren-Manufaktur Mannheim

In the past period, the branch in Brussels delivered ten pairs of leather shoes and therefore achieved sales of EUR 14,000.00. Eight pairs were also produced in this period. Three additional pairs were produced but not yet delivered, and two pairs of shoes were produced in the previous period but only collected by the customer now. The warehouse stock therefore increased by one pair of shoes costing EUR 1,400.00. When you deduct the expenses accrued for materials, personnel, and depreciation, you are left with an operating profit (in accordance with period accounting) of EUR 5,600.00.

We will now transfer these figures to cost-of-sales accounting. To do this, the material expenses, personnel expenses, and depreciated amounts (according to the source) are transferred to the following functional areas: manufacturing, sales and marketing, and administration. The increase in stock from period accounting is assigned to the manufacturing functional area because the period has accrued manufacturing costs for the additional pair of shoes (see Figure 7.26).

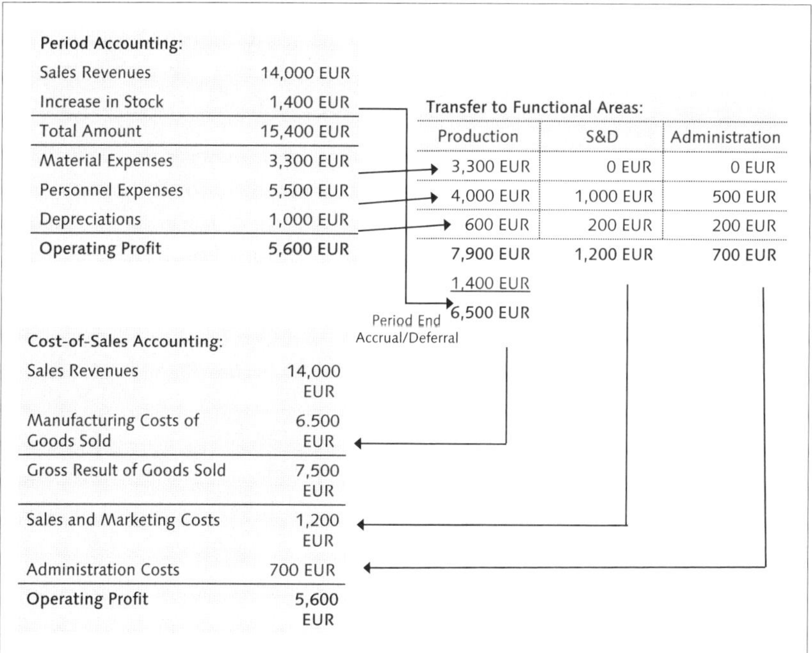

Figure 7.26 Transfer from Period Accounting to Cost-of-Sales Accounting

The most important finding is that the operating profit cannot change if the figures are transferred from period accounting to cost-of-sales accounting. However, the classification of the profitability analysis changes.

Different classification

In accordance with the overhead cost procedure, the accruing expenses are classified according to type, thus providing an answer to the following question: Which expenses have been accrued? In accordance with cost-of-sales accounting, the classification is according to function, thus making it possible to identify where or for which function expenses have been accrued.

Eliminating balance sheet changes

The balance sheet changes shown in accordance with period accounting correspond to the manufacturing costs of goods sold, which are calculated in accordance with cost-of-sales accounting. These costs concern production costs that must also be considered (reduction in stock) or deducted (increase in stock) because they are not accompanied by sales but rather by an increase in stock.

Material expenses, personnel expenses, and depreciated amounts are explicitly shown in accordance with period accounting. When transferred to cost-of-sales accounting, these items are allocated to the manufacturing costs of goods sold, sales and marketing costs, and administration costs. Here, only proportional values can be used for the manufacturing costs of goods sold. All period costs are transferred to the items for sales and marketing costs and administration costs.

SAP General Ledger and classic general ledger

SAP General Ledger allows the representation of both of these profit and loss statements in the general ledger for the very first time. When using the classic general ledger to display our figures in accordance with cost-of-sales accounting, you had to access the cost-of-sales accounting ledger, Profit Center Accounting or CO-PA, because the classic general ledger could not map the functional area. You have already learned about the functional area as an account assignment element for cost-of-sales accounting in Chapter 2, The Concept of Integrated Values Flows.

Creating a balance sheet structure

Here, the profit and loss statement in accordance with period accounting can be created together with the balance sheet. This requires you to create a balance sheet structure in Transaction OB58. A balance sheet structure always depends on the chart of accounts. Any number of balance sheet structures can be mapped for each chart of accounts. Unfortunately, if you use the report RFBILA00 to call a balance sheet structure in the general ledger, this structure cannot map any functional areas once SAP General Ledger has been activated. Consequently, if you want to show a profit and loss statement in accordance with cost-of-sales accounting, you must define your own reports. Drilldown reports, for example, are available for such purposes.

Reports according to profit center/segment

In general, you also have to define your own reports if you want to display your figures according to a profit center or segment. Even though SAP provides standard reports for this, you will generally want to incorporate the special features of your own corporate reporting into SAP reporting.

7.13.2 Reporting in Open Item Accounting

In the standard system, SAP also provides a range of useful reports for accounts receivable accounting and accounts payable accounting. These range from master data reports to sales lists and account balances as well as lists of open items. The option to classify open items according to due dates is particularly interesting here.

7.13.3 Reporting in Controlling

In Controlling, reporting can be divided into two areas: operative controlling and management reporting.

Operative controlling

Operative controlling is predominantly used at the cost center or order level, or, when using PS, at the project level. As the name implies, the purpose of operative controlling is to control business operations. Cost center managers can analyze the structure and scheduling of costs and compare them with planned figures (budgets). If the planned figures differ from the actual figures, some degree of regulatory intervention is necessary. The task of Controlling is to provide the necessary information. The standard SAP system includes a range of useful reports, which are available in the application menu under the menu path ACCOUNTING • CONTROLLING • COST CENTER ACCOUNTING • INFORMATION SYSTEM • REPORTS FOR COST CENTER ACCOUNTING. Here, you will find reports for actual figures, planned/actual comparisons, master data, and tariffs. Figure 7.27 shows an example of quarterly cost scheduling.

Cost centers: quarterly comparison		Date: 22.10.2009			Page: 2 / 2
Cost Center/Group	P9000 Production OH				
Person responsible	Heinrich Schuster				
Fiscal Year	2009				

Cost elements	1st qtr	2nd qtr	3rd qtr	4th qtr	Total year
214000 0000214000		1.869,57			1.869,57
* Debit		1.869,57			1.869,57
655101 OHS Raw Material		128.223,47-		16.852,68-	145.076,15-
655300 OHS Administration		308.163,72-		40.502,60-	348.666,32-
655400 Sales overhead rate		176.093,56-		23.144,34-	199.237,90-
* Credit		612.480,75-		80.499,62-	692.980,37-
** Over/underabsorption		610.611,18-		80.499,62-	691.110,80-

Figure 7.27 Quarterly Comparison of Actual Figures in Cost Center

Similar reporting options are available for internal orders.

Profit Center Accounting

In practice, Profit Center Accounting is also used for reporting in operative controlling. However, since the integration of Profit Center Accounting into SAP General Ledger, this approach has become increasingly difficult, particularly as a result of displaying secondary cost elements. Although you can map both the account number and cost element in SAP General Ledger, you usually do not transfer all transactions from Controlling to Financial Accounting. In the general ledger, internal business volumes are shown at the profit center level because cross-profit-center transactions must be transferred to Financial Accounting if you assign Profit Center Accounting there.

On the other hand, you cannot display sales between Controlling objects (cost centers, orders, and so on) if a real-time integration document has not been created in Financial Accounting. Consequently, profit center reports in the general ledger are not suitable for reflecting lower levels even if, at first glance, all of the information you need is available. Therefore, with the introduction of SAP General Ledger and its integrated Profit Center Accounting, it is important to ask yourself which level you currently want to analyze. You must then select the reports in Overhead Cost Controlling or in the general ledger accordingly.

Management Reporting

CO-PA can be helpful both in operative controlling and in management reporting. Within the business operations, profitability analyses for individual products, customers, or sales orders are of particular interest.

Displaying contribution margins

From a management perspective, CO-PA can be used, in particular, to show contribution margins at an aggregated level. In more and more enterprises, the main task of CO-PA is to supply a business warehouse with data. For more information, see Chapter 8, Reporting with SAP NetWeaver BW.

Profit centers and segments

Reports according to profit center or segment are particularly important elements of management reporting. It is possible to handle both areas in SAP General Ledger. Although SAP also offers a range of standard reports here, typically, you will have to create your own reports. The standard reports are available in the application menu under ACCOUNTING • FINANCIAL ACCOUNTING • GENERAL LEDGER • INFORMATION SYSTEM. Once again, however, a business warehouse provides the greatest flexibility in this context.

7.14 Summary

You can see that a standard SAP ERP system provides numerous reporting options. However, if these are insufficient, you can make use of standard tools such as drilldown reports or the Report Painter. If these do not give you the desired results, you can develop your own programs. Alternatively, you can switch to a BI/BW system. At the very least, however, you must be able to extract the required raw data from the ERP system.

A data warehouse cannot be filled until all closing activities have been completed. Financial Accounting and Controlling must work together to ensure that period-end closing runs smoothly. This has become even more important with the introduction of SAP General Ledger and real-time integration because the transactions in Controlling are posted directly back to Financial Accounting.

The sample closing procedure document at the end of this book (see Appendix A) shows approximately 50 substeps; however, these are just suggestions. Some enterprises have a considerably leaner structure and some organizations use more complex closing procedure documents. It is therefore important that you do not overlook your own reporting but instead understand it as the goal of period-end closing. In other words, anyone who does not have to show receivables or payables classified according to duration must not execute the corresponding step in closing. However, you should not economize when it comes to reconciliation tasks and account maintenance (GR/IR account). The longer differences and irregularities go unnoticed, the more difficult the task of researching the cause(s) and correcting the problem(s). Even if operative reports such as the balance sheet or cost center reports are available, which you are never permitted to fully transfer to BI/BW, you should not try to force SAP ERP to fulfill your last reporting requirement. SAP NetWeaver BW is much faster, easier, and consequently more cost-effective.

The previous chapter introduced you to reporting with SAP ERP. This chapter discusses reporting in SAP NetWeaver BW. It, of course, also focuses on the value flows in your enterprise.

8 Reporting with SAP NetWeaver BW

An SAP ERP system provides numerous reporting and analysis options. First of all, there are many standard reports delivered with the system. In addition, you can use various SAP tools if these standards are not sufficient: *queries, QuickViews, Report Painter*, or drilldown reports as well as custom LIS or SIS structures (LIS = *Logistics Information System;* SIS = *Sales Information System*). If this does not cover the reporting requirements of your enterprise, you can work with customer developments within the SAP ERP system. However, the flat table structure places clear limitations on reporting within the SAP ERP system and consequently, some reporting requirements cannot be met or only with a great deal of implementation effort for customer developments.

The easiest way to overcome these limitations is to use a data warehouse or business intelligence solution such as SAP NetWeaver Business Warehouse.

BW and BI in the SAP Environment [+]

Up to R/3, release 3.5, SAP's data warehousing product was called SAP BW; in ERP Release 7.0, it was renamed SAP NetWeaver BI. At the end of 2008, as a part of the acquisition of Business Objects, SAP NetWeaver BI was renamed SAP NetWeaver BW.

This chapter discusses these business intelligence solutions by SAP in more detail. How can your enterprise benefit from the use of SAP NetWeaver BW regarding the integrated value flow?

8.1 Basic Principles of Business Intelligence

Information systems in enterprises

The first management information systems were introduced in enterprises in the 1990s to provide IT support to decision makers. Then, as now, the goal has been to provide relevant enterprise information in such a way that it can be used by management.

Today more than ever, due to continuously intensifying competitive conditions, enterprises require a holistic approach that aims at the integration of strategy, processes, and technologies from usually distributed and inhomogeneous information sources. This holistic approach should provide success-critical knowledge about status, potentials, and perspectives in such a way that it is useful.

With SAP NetWeaver BW, SAP provides a data warehouse solution that contains all components required for comprehensive reporting, from data extraction from the source system, to various options for the storage, aggregation, transformation, and linking of datasets, to comprehensive reporting functions.

Business intelligence

Many definitions exist for *business intelligence* and *data warehousing*. In the SAP world, it is understood as the transformation of data, the generation of information from this data, and finally the building of action-oriented knowledge—which is the actual benefit for the enterprise.

Figure 8.1 illustrates the process of the derivation of action-oriented knowledge from mere datasets of IT systems: From the large amount of document data—which can amount to millions of documents—the first step is to derive relevant information for the description of the business situation ("knowing the business") using appropriate aggregation mechanisms or filtering. The term "business intelligence" also refers to the generation of recommendations for future actions from this information ("improving the business").

[+]

Terminology Definition

Let us briefly summarize the terms used in the context of SAP NetWeaver BW:

- **Business Intelligence (BI)**
  This is an integrated overall approach meant to ensure the integration of strategy, processes, and technologies; generate success-critical knowledge about status, potentials, and perspectives from distributed and inhomogeneous enterprise, market and competitor data; and provide the knowledge in such a way that it can be used by decision makers.
- **SAP NetWeaver BW**
  This is the data warehouse solution provided by SAP.

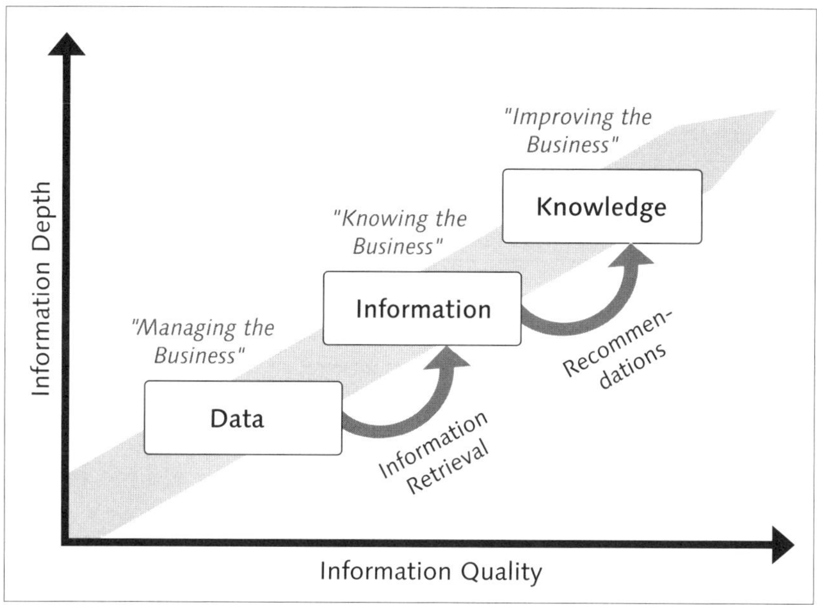

Figure 8.1 Information Gathering with Business Intelligence

Many enterprises face the problem of having a very heterogeneous system landscape. The relevant data is stored in various applications and even in different systems. This makes it complicated and time-consuming to gather and evaluate information.

Reporting in SAP ERP

The previous chapters already introduced different processes within an SAP ERP system. The formatting of this data for comprehensive evaluation would place a high workload on the SAP ERP system. This, in turn, would have a negative effect on the live system processes and the posting performance. If you are also interested in subsequent archiving of obsolete data, this situation gets worse because historical data then also needs to be included in the reports.

Integrating SAP NetWeaver BW with the information landscape

The data that is generated in operational systems such as SAP ERP, is necessary to execute and control business processes. Enterprises that deploy a business intelligence solution also pursue another goal: the analytical formatting of raw data to gain control-relevant information. For this purpose, you have to cleanse, enrich, and standardize the generated data because can you make decisions that result in correct synchronization with the operational processes (see Figure 8.2) only on the basis of profound and formatted data. Then, by learning from this data, can the enterprise take action and be competitive.

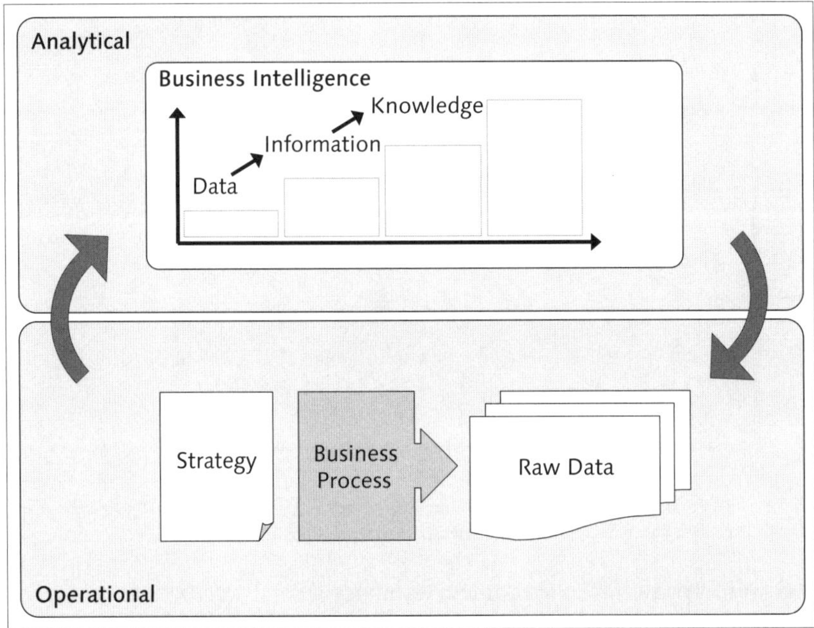

Figure 8.2 Integration of SAP NetWeaver BW with the Information Landscape

[Ex]

Drawing Conclusions from Enterprise Data

For our example company, Lederwaren Manufaktur Mannheim, the data gathered from SAP ERP lets the enterprise identify in SAP NetWeaver BW which handbag leather variations sell the most. As a result, the product portfolio can be adapted accordingly, to increase sales.

In the literature, this approach is also called a *closed loop process*. It illustrates that business intelligence is more than the modeling of data. The decisive criterion is that decisions are made and measures are taken because of gathered information.

SAP NetWeaver BW

With SAP NetWeaver BW, SAP provides an integrated data warehouse solution that covers all functions of the necessary data warehouse processes. These are the following:

- **Data acquisition**
  In addition to the extraction of data from SAP source systems, numer-

ous other feeder systems such as (relational) data bases, additional SAP ERP systems, or flat files can be used as information sources for reporting processes.

- **Data retention and modeling**
  SAP NetWeaver BW provides the *Data Warehousing Workbench*, a central administration tool for all functions such as setup, maintenance, and operation of the data warehouse.
- **Data retrieval layer**
  Aside from the *BEx Analyzer*, which is based on Microsoft Excel, *SAP Business Explorer* (BEx) supports browser-based web reporting.

Data acquisition

In SAP NetWeaver BW, master data and transaction data is acquired via *extractors*, also referred to as *DataSources*, which allow for the connection of different data sources. The following types of data sources are available:

- Files with flat structures
- Multidimensional and relational databases
- SAP ERP systems

Because many enterprises have a heterogeneous IT landscape, you usually have to use different sources to fill your SAP NetWeaver BW system. Because of their structures, the corresponding sources often require different extraction mechanisms. SAP NetWeaver BW allows for the connection of all of the data sources mentioned. For the extraction from SAP ERP source systems, it provides predefined extractors—these are explained in detail in Section 8.1.2, Business Content. If necessary, you can enhance existing extractors or define and use custom extractors.

Data retention and modeling

Data that has been extracted from the source system is then stored in *data targets* in SAP NetWeaver BW, which are also called *data providers* or *InfoProviders*. For this purpose, SAP NetWeaver BW provides various types of data targets, which differ in their data evaluation behavior.

InfoProviders in SAP NetWeaver BW

Reporting-enabled objects are divided into two groups:

- **Objects that contain physical data**
  Objects that contain physical data store their data in the data tables of the InfoProvider. This group includes *InfoCubes* (multidimensional *data structures*), *DataStore objects* (plain, relational data tables), as well as master-data-containing *InfoObjects* with texts and attributes.

- **Logical views**
  Logical views do not contain data. The data is stored either directly in the source system InfoProviders or in other BI InfoProviders. Examples of this are *MultiProviders, RemoteCubes, InfoSets*, and *virtual InfoCubes* with services.

Transformations

In the binding process, data-containing InfoProviders are connected with each other via what are called *transformations*. These are rules that define how data should be formatted within SAP NetWeaver BW. Key figures can be determined, or the data can be enriched with additional information. Thanks to the integration option for custom ABAP programs, there are virtually no limits for the enrichment and transformation of data.

Figure 8.3 shows a sample binding and provides an overview of the relationships between the individual SAP NetWeaver BW objects.

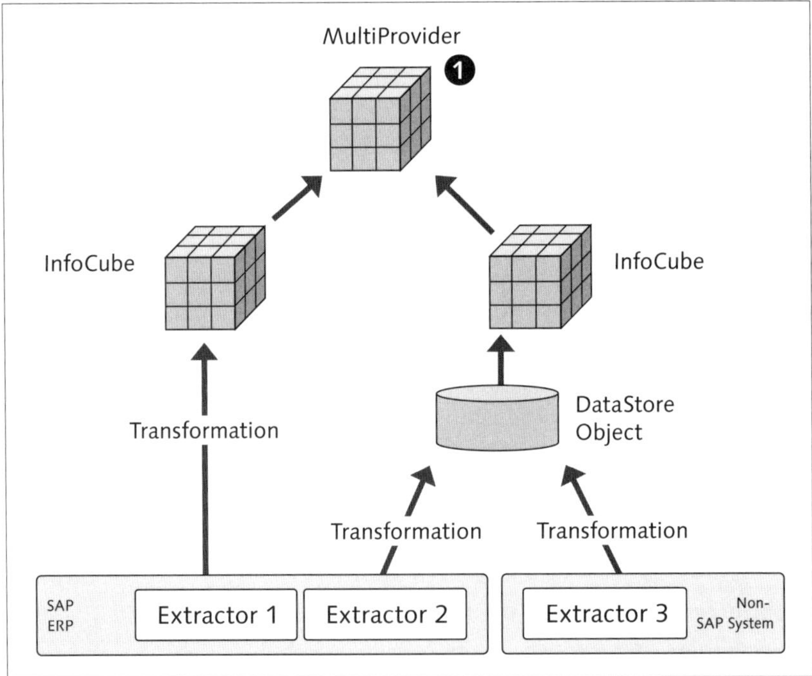

Figure 8.3 Sample Binding in SAP NetWeaver BW

To be able to process data from three different information sources in one report, as described before, you must store and transform or aggregate the data streams up to the detail view of the end user (here: MultiProvider) in different ways. The SAP NetWeaver BW system provides various options for this.

[Ex]

Sample Binding in SAP NetWeaver BW

To better understand the process illustrated in Figure 8.3, the following sample scenario is used: Reporting is set up for a group with enterprises that map their complete processes in SAP, as well as with enterprises that map their data only partially in SAP. In this case, two extractors are required, for example, for the data from CO-PA: one for enterprises that map all of their figures there and one for organizations whose data is not complete in CO-PA and must thus be enriched.

The enrichment takes place in the DataStore object that is—in addition to receiving CO-PA data—filled by a third extractor via a flat file, for example. The data is transformed with each of these three extractions.

Data retrieval

The data is retrieved via *queries*. Queries are made to the dataset within the data providers in the SAP NetWeaver BW system that display data for the user.

In addition to the selection of the appropriate reporting display format (which is further discussed in Section 8.1.1, Business Explorer Suite—Reporting with SAP NetWeaver BW), the reports' user groups assume a central role in an enterprise. The need for information of individual employees, departments, or hierarchy levels must be considered when you create reports.

SAP NetWeaver BW provides a consistent data basis that can be used to create different reports across the enterprise. At the same time, you can access this consistent dataset via a flexible authorization concept that considers target groups and tasks. This means you do not have to limit the data retention in the system to a user group. This limitation can also be implemented for the data representation in the actual reporting.

Figure 8.4 shows a three-layer user group model that purposefully implements clusters according to strategic, tactical, and operational reporting requirements.

Let us take a closer look at the pyramid:

- **Strategic reporting**
  At the top, you can see the strategic reporting, which addresses top management. It can be summarized as follows:
  - Five to ten Key Performance Indicators (KPIs)
  - High aggregation

  - No navigation/ease of use
  - Infrequent updates (updated monthly)
- **Tactical reporting**
  One level below, you will find tactical reporting, whose user group is middle management. It can be summarized as follows:
  - 10–35 KPIs
  - Medium aggregation and medium navigation
  - Infrequent updates (updated weekly or monthly)
- **Operational reporting**
  Operational reporting makes up the lowest level. It addresses business analysts of the respective enterprise and can be summarized as follows:
  - 25–75 KPIs
  - Hardly any aggregation, with a lot of navigation
  - Frequent updates (updated daily)

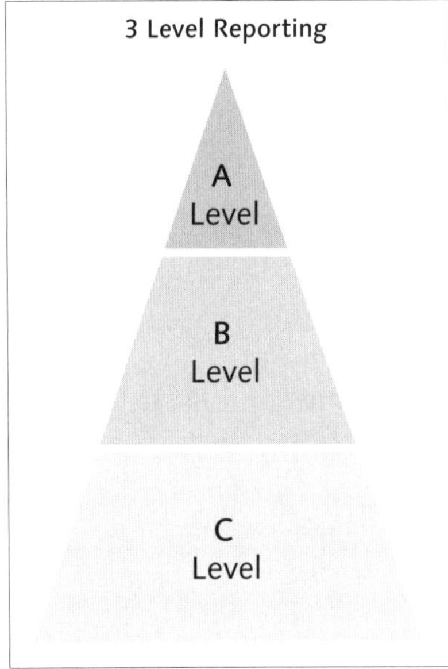

Figure 8.4 User Groups in SAP NetWeaver BW

Before you implement concrete reporting requirements in queries, you should cluster target groups according to user groups.

8.1.1 Business Explorer Suite—Reporting with SAP NetWeaver BW

The *Business Explorer Suite* (BEx Suite) provided by SAP is a flexible platform that allows for evaluation of business data. As a collection of programs and plug-ins, the suite provides comprehensive reporting and analysis functions.

BEx Query Designer

Regardless of whether you want to make your reports available in Microsoft Excel or via the web, selecting the data that should be retrieved via a query is the basis for any report. The query is created with reference to an InfoProvider. A graphical user interface, the *BEx Query Designer*, enables you to select the key figures and characteristics you want to provide in your report without programming knowledge.

The query designer allows for numerous modeling options:

- **Key figures**
  Key figures can be determined via formulas (such as contribution margins in the profit and loss statement).
- **Characteristics**
  You can preselect and restrict individual characteristics for the respective report recipient in the query definition already. Because the system immediately uses the desired filtering, you might save a lot of time during the call.
- **Variables**
  The use of variables enables users of the report to filter characteristic values when they execute the query. For example, when calling the financial statement, you can specify only individual accounts or account intervals, or you can set a filter for individual customers in the reporting of Profitability Analysis
- **Authorization concept**
  The authorization concept automatically prevents unauthorized users from accessing sensitive datasets. This enables business unit analysts, for example, to analyze the cost centers of their organizational unit only.
- **Expanding, navigating, and aggregating**
  Within the query and the dataset that corresponds to the authorization, you can expand, navigate between, and aggregate elements during use. You can define these options already when creating the query.

This means the query provides high flexibility both for creation and for use. After having defined the query, you can make it available to the report recipients in different ways.

BEx Analyzer

Especially popular with business analysts is the presentation of reports in Microsoft Excel. One of the oldest Business Explorer components is the *BEx Analyzer*, a tool that is fully integrated with Microsoft Excel. Especially if you want to continue to flexibly use the results after the report has been executed and carry out your own calculations and analyses, the BEx Analyzer is the appropriate tool.

As a plug-in for Microsoft Excel, the BEx Analyzer provides an additional toolbar you can use to access queries and SAP NetWeaver BW data (see Figure 8.5).

Executing queries

If variables are defined in the query, the system automatically opens a variable window when the query is started. Here, you can enter the desired values (see Figure 8.5).

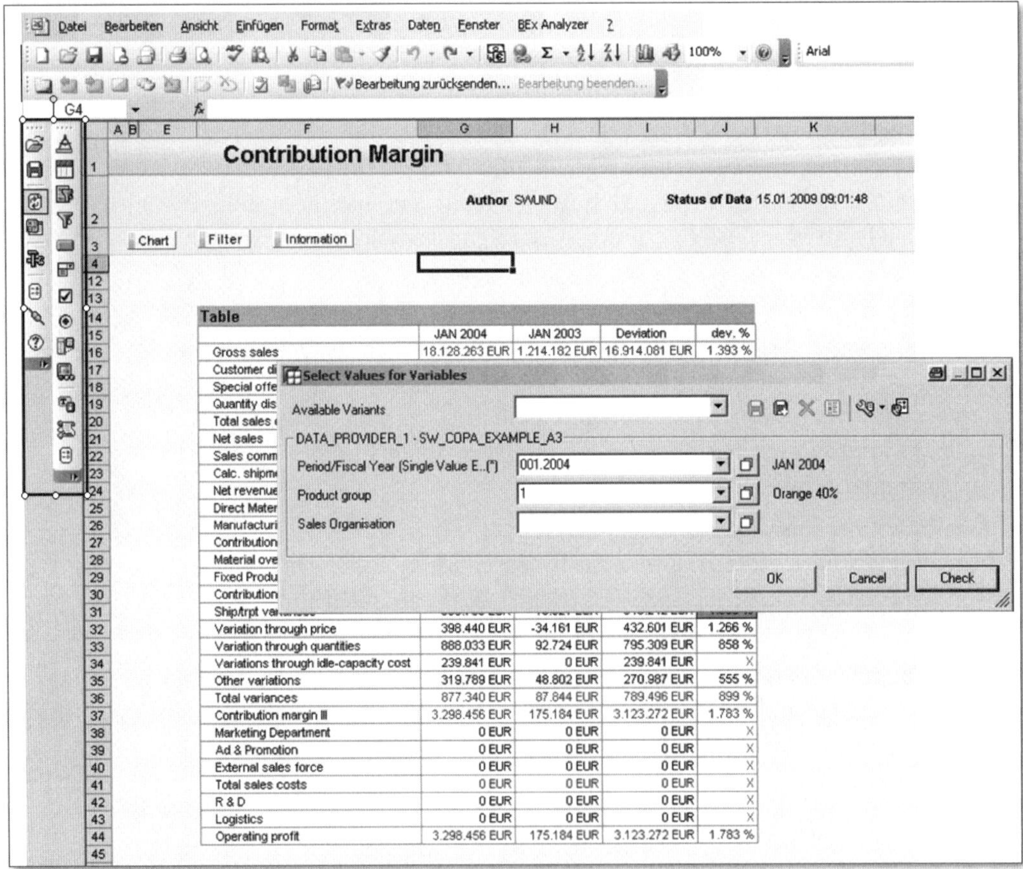

Figure 8.5 Report in the BEx Analyzer

In an open report, you can expand the elements as required and filter them for individual characteristics. Furthermore, all Microsoft Excel functions are available for additional processing of report results.

Web application

If you prefer a representative presentation of the information, you should output the reports via a *web browser*. Here, you also use the existing queries and provide them online via a portal across the entire enterprise. Figure 8.6 shows an example for the presentation via a portal. To provide you with a graphical overview, a curve chart was integrated into a bar chart.

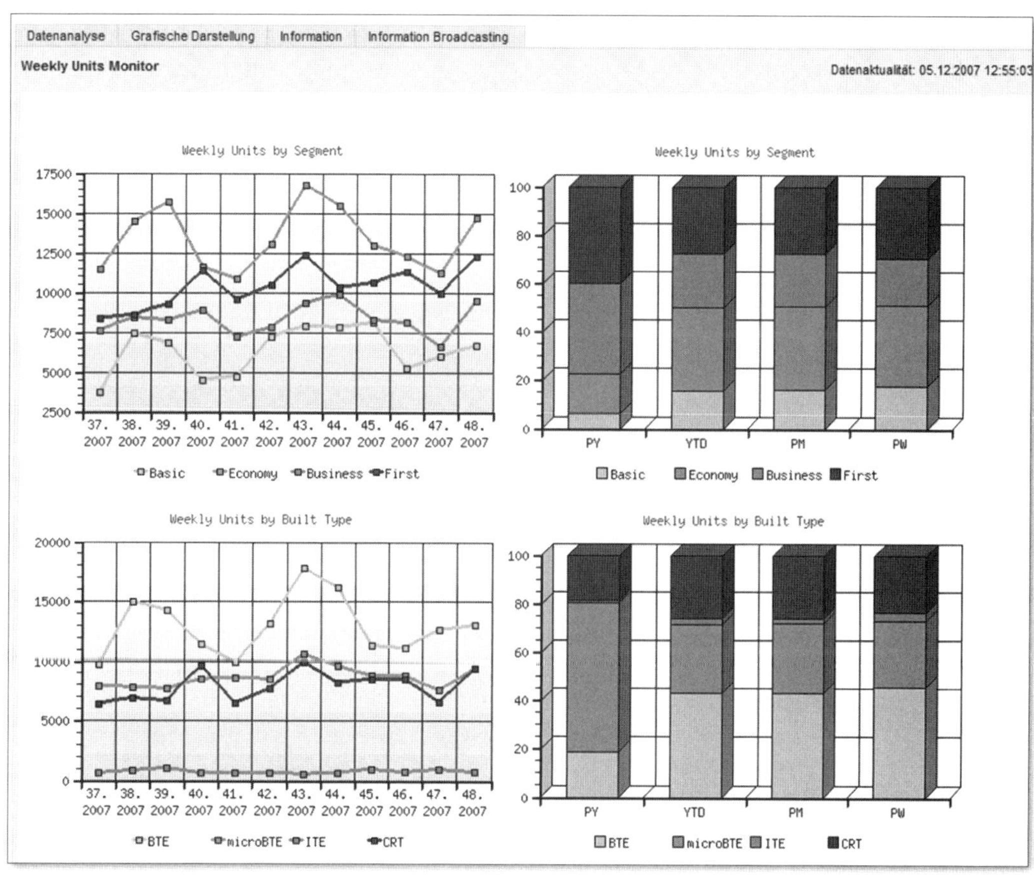

Figure 8.6 Mapping of Reports in a Web Browser

Design options

Whereas the BEx Analyzer places clear limitations on the graphical formatting of reports, the *BEx Web Application Designer* provides comprehensive design options. For example, the Web Application Designer enables you to map existing queries with graphics and components for selection and navigation on an HTML page. This ensures flexible and user-friendly navigation within the report after the query has been executed via drag-and-drop. If required, you can further enhance these standard functions through custom programming.

SAP Management Cockpit

When setting up highly aggregated management reporting, the presentation via a web browser assumes a central role as well because you can also use the Web Application Designer for setting up what are called *management dashboards* or *cockpits*. Owing to the acquisition of Business Objects in 2008, SAP also delivers comprehensive options for using frontend tools by SAP based on SAP NetWeaver BW, to design graphically appealing reporting environments and, for example, implement formatted reporting using Crystal Reports. Crystal Reports, from the portfolio of SAP BusinessObjects, allows for pixel-exact mapping and thus respective default print outputs of forms and so on. Alternatively, you can use third-party tools that support reporting on an SAP NetWeaver BW data basis.

Information broadcasting

To provide information for a wide range of users, you should distribute the reports via *information broadcasting*. In this case, information is formatted and sent—for example, via email—to the required recipient group.

Thus, SAP NetWeaver BW provides numerous ways to fulfill the information requirements in your enterprise. However, the challenge in an implementation project is also to initially only implement the truly important requirements. You can then define additional requirements of the individual target groups that are based on real-life experiences and thus ensure an efficient implementation with minimum strain on the project budget.

8.1.2 Business Content

You can considerably reduce the SAP NetWeaver BW-related implementation effort by using what is called *Business Content*. It contains predefined data extractors, storage structures, and evaluation scenarios for various business processes. SAP delivers these already fully configured.

Business Content is available for the SAP ERP source system and SAP NetWeaver BW area. The following sections further explain the two areas and introduce the necessary activation steps.

Business Content—SAP ERP

With Business Content for source systems, in the standard version, SAP already provides numerous DataSources for the retrieval of data from SAP ERP. The essential characteristic of many of these standard extractors is the *delta compatibility*. Here, the DataSource is capable of logging the source data that has been modified, deleted, and added since the last data extraction and providing only this new data to the SAP NetWeaver BW system. This restricts the data volume of the extraction to the required minimum and reduces extraction runtimes drastically, which are often critical for the overall operation and the operating costs in a complex group of systems.

An evaluation-ready document volume in the SAP NetWeaver BW system that, for example, includes documents for the last two years, uses only a fraction of the data volume for the daily extraction. If the DataSource does not provide for delta compatibility, the system has to load—on a daily basis—all of the documents of the last two years that can still change, to ensure a consistent dataset.

Before the DataSources can be used, you must activate them in the SAP ERP system and then explicitly copy them from Business Content (see Figure 8.7). This is done via the Implementation Guide (IMG) of the extractors in the source system, to which you can also navigate via Transaction SBIW.

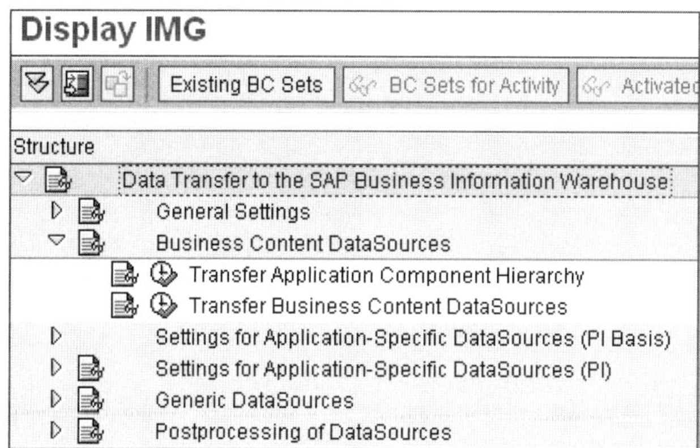

Figure 8.7 Implementation Guide—"Copy Business Content DataSources"

Application component hierarchy

Before you actually enable the required extractors, you have to copy the complete application component hierarchy from Business Content. This has to be done only once. This hierarchy organizes the various extractors in a hierarchical tree according to their dependency, for example, their different application areas such as Financial Accounting, Controlling, and Logistics (see Figure 8.8). In complex environments, the use of extractors from different areas permanently improves the business' structure.

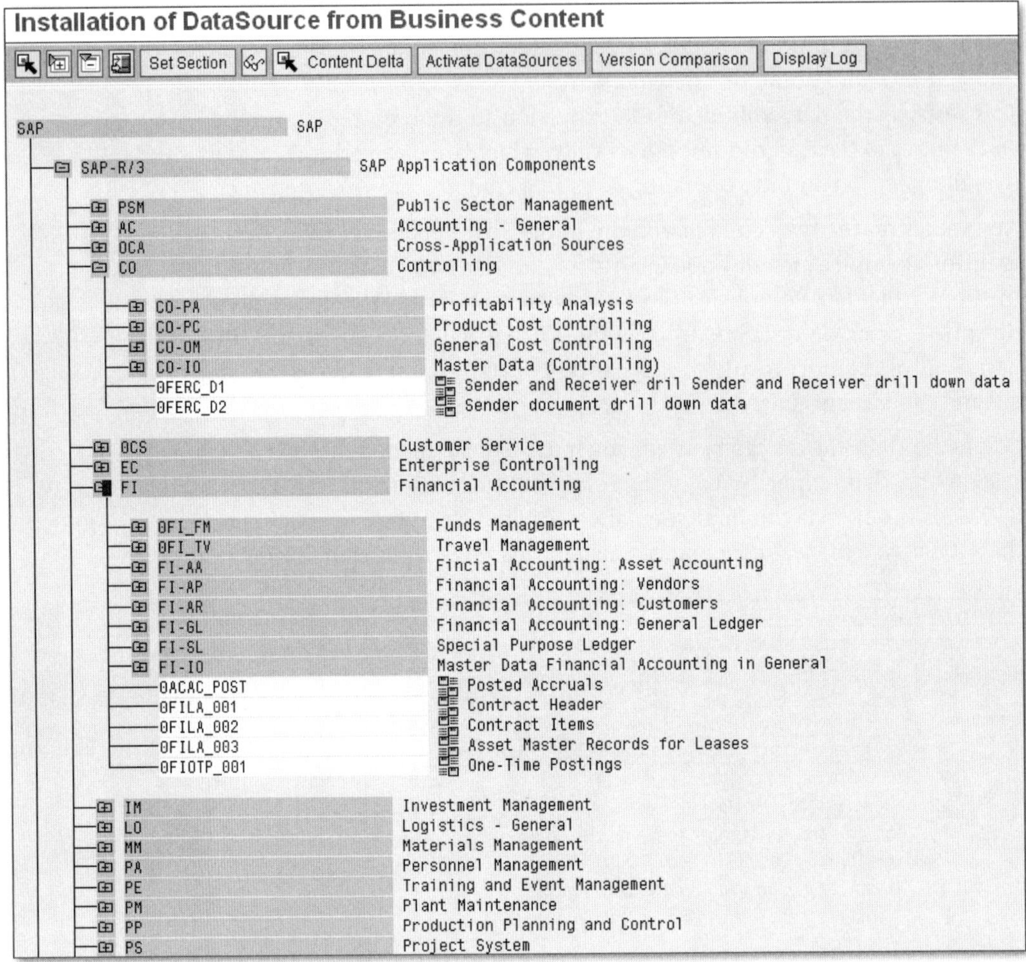

Figure 8.8 Application Component Hierarchy in SAP ERP

After you have activated the application component hierarchy in the SAP ERP system, you have to copy (replicate) it. This way, all activated extractors are assigned to the different hierarchy levels and SAP NetWeaver BW and can therefore be found easily. You also have to assign a hierarchy level (for example, the corresponding application component) to custom extractors when they are being created.

Afterward, you can select, copy, and activate the required extractors from Business Content. When you replicate the metadata to SAP NetWeaver BW, it is available in SAP NetWeaver BW for further usage.

[+]

Metadata

Metadata is descriptive data, for example, the quantity of the fields that were transferred to SAP NetWeaver BW, the definition of the usage of a delta method, or the specification of the application component.

Business Content—SAP NetWeaver BW

In the SAP NetWeaver BW system, the SAP system also provides Business Content for various application areas. This includes numerous preconfigured, analytical solutions that contain all binding aspects—from the receipt of the data that has been extracted in the source system to the query definition. Especially in highly standardized areas such as Financial Accounting, Business Content allows for fast and cost-efficient SAP NetWeaver BW implementation. You can copy the preconfigured objects without changes, adapt them, or use them as a template for your own objects.

Business Content by SAP NetWeaver BW

The collective term *Business Content* refers to an add-on to SAP NetWeaver BW that delivers various preconfigured objects.

This includes InfoProviders, queries, key figures, characteristics, transformations, update rules, workbooks, roles, and web templates.

Data Warehousing Workbench

You copy the Business Content objects in SAP NetWeaver BW using the *Data Warehousing Workbench* (DWB) (see Figure 8.9), which is the central working environment in SAP NetWeaver BW.

The Data Warehousing Workbench was renamed in SAP NetWeaver BW 7.0; in earlier releases, it had been called *Administrator Workbench*. You can access it from the menu via BUSINESS INFORMATION WAREHOUSE · MODELING · DATA WAREHOUSING WORKBENCH: MODELING or using Transaction RSA1.

Figure 8.9 shows an example of the tree structure presentation within the Data Warehousing Workbench. The left-hand side of the screen provides the different SAP NetWeaver BW objects, sorted by object categories such as queries or InfoCubes. You can copy them via drag-and-drop to the right screen area and collect them there for activation. The collected objects are then activated together and available for further use in SAP NetWeaver BW.

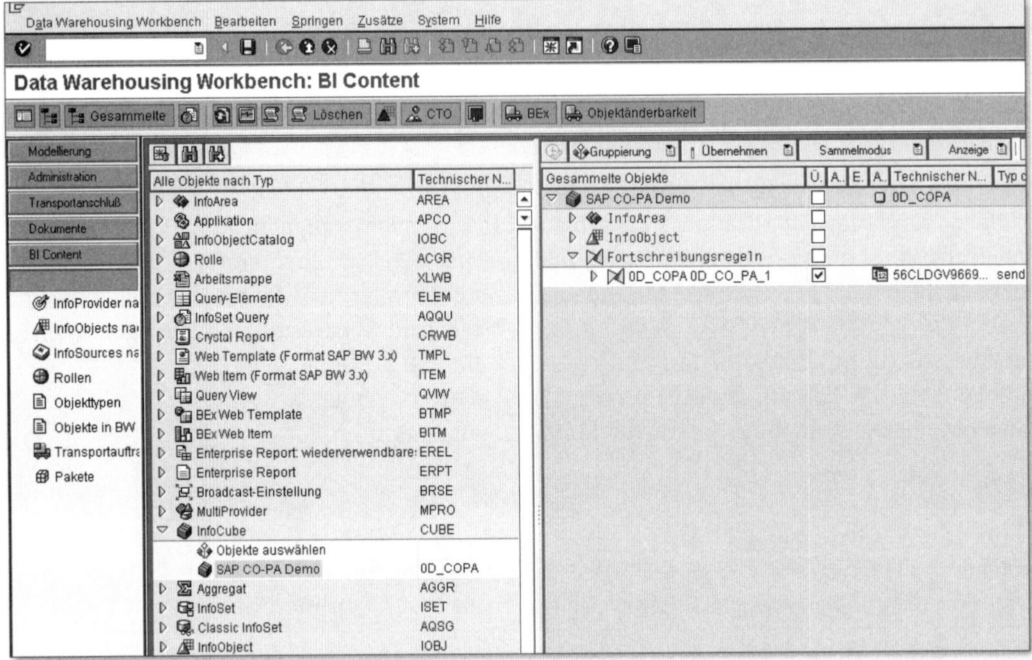

Figure 8.9 Data Warehousing Workbench

[+]

Adapting Business Content Objects

If you adapted or enhanced objects you copied from Business Content, you need to check which properties of the adapted object should be kept or overridden by a new activation when identical objects should be newly activated.

Critical reflection of using Business Content

SAP's Business Content is a good starting point for custom modeling in SAP NetWeaver BW; however, you should not deploy it without due consideration. Aside from the concrete reporting requirements of an enterprise, the design of the business processes also assumes a critical role in the underlying SAP ERP system.

To avoid additional project costs or unsatisfied users, it is important to check the requirements for the system prior to activation and carefully consider the use of Business Content for individual areas. Particularly for the formatting of data in queries, Business Content can reach its limits because of enterprise specifications. However, for binding and data modeling, you can use it as a valuable template and thus as an appropriate starting point for individual adaptations. This procedure often considerably reduces the project effort; thus, it makes sense to use an SAP NetWeaver BW system instead of third-party solutions that do not have this template character.

8.2 Data Acquisition Examples

Having discussed the basic principles theoretically, we will now turn to the practical design of two scenarios in an SAP NetWeaver BW system: the creation of a financial statement and a profit and loss statement at the profit center level from the SAP General Ledger and Profitability Analysis (CO-PA). In this context, this section focuses on a sample data acquisition of transaction data. Both scenarios can also be easily implemented in an BW system if you use Business Content.

Although the data sources and binding for the financial statement and profit and loss statement are standardized to a large extent, the design of the profitability analysis depends on the characteristic and value fields that are available in CO-PA.

8.2.1 Financial Reporting

The previous chapters already described SAP General Ledger accounting in the SAP ERP system in greater detail. Here, it also represents the data basis for the binding for the creation of a financial statement and a profit and loss statement in the business intelligence system.

General ledger: balances, leading ledger

To retrieve the transaction figure data from SAP General Ledger, SAP provides various DataSources. In the example, the GENERAL LEDGER: BALANCES, LEADING LEDGER (0FI_GL_10) extractor in the SAP ERP source system is used. The selected DataSource is delta-compatible and only extracts from the totals table of the leading ledger; in our case, from the FAGLFLEXT table.

Balances from any Ledgers [+]

You can also extract the totals tables of additional ledgers from SAP General Ledger accounting in SAP NetWeaver BW. For every additional ledger, you have to generate a specific DataSource in SAP ERP via Transaction FAGLBW03.

Naming the DataSource [+]

The naming of the DataSource follows this naming convention: The name of the generated DataSource is 3FI_GL_xx_TT, where xx stands for the ledger ID and TT indicates that it is a totals table.

Activating the DataSource

As described in Section 8.1.2, Business Content, you activate the GENERAL LEDGER: BALANCES, LEADING LEDGER DataSource (0FI_GL_10) from the application component hierarchy and then replicate it to SAP NetWeaver BW (see Figure 8.10).

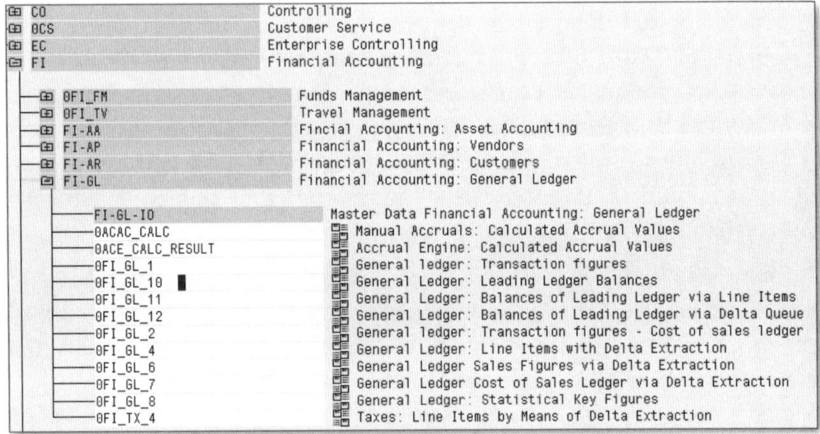

Figure 8.10 Activating the DataSource "0FI_GL_10"

Building the binding in SAP NetWeaver BW

In the next step, you build your binding in SAP NetWeaver BW. Here, you also use SAP NetWeaver BW's Business Content. In addition to the InfoObjects and data targets, it contains carryforward and update rules as well as query definitions. You can use the latter either without any changes or as a template for your own reports and evaluations. Figure 8.11 displays the individual objects in the binding of our sample scenario.

The activation of SAP NetWeaver BW's Business Content takes place in the Data Warehousing Workbench, as already explained in Section 8.1.2, Business Content. Here, you can activate and copy the objects—which are listed in Figure 8.11—individually or completely (that is, the entire binding) from Business Content.

A detailed description of the individual objects and their properties would go beyond the scope of this chapter. It therefore only focuses on some of the critical aspects.

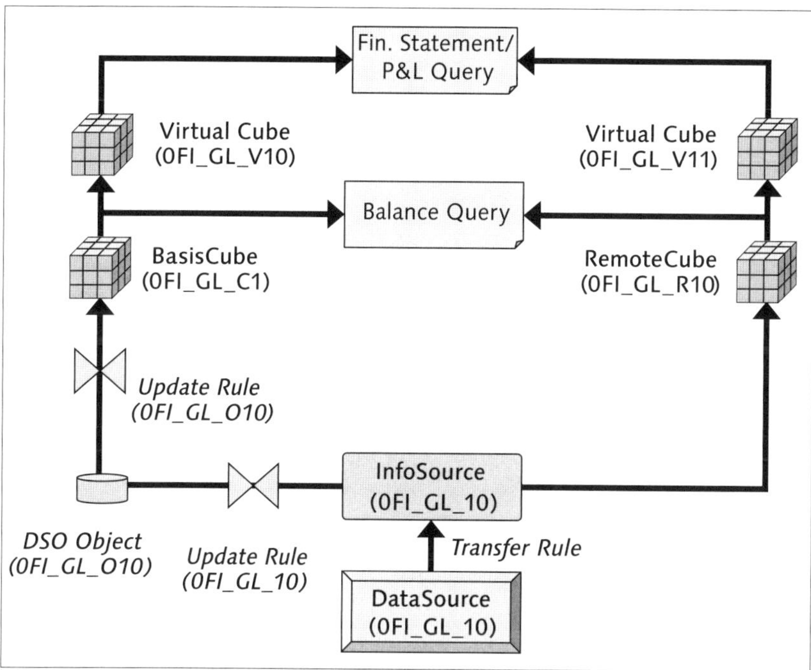

Figure 8.11 Binding in SAP General Ledger Accounting

After-image delta method

The GENERAL LEDGER (NEW): TRANSACTION FIGURES *DataStore object* (DSO) (0FI_GL_10) is required because of the delta method of our DataSource. This enables you to only retrieve the changes from the SAP ERP system that have been made or that have been added since the last modification. For this purpose, the delta of the sum of the previously extracted data records is determined in the DataStore object and updated to the GENERAL LEDGER (NEW): TRANSACTION FIGURES (0FI_GL_10) InfoCube.

Virtual cube with service

A *virtual cube* with the GENERAL LEDGER (NEW): FINANCIAL AND PROFIT AND LOSS STATEMENTS SERVICE (0FIGL_V10) FORMS THE BASIS FOR REPORTING THAT IS USED TO PRESENT THE financial statement OR PROFIT AND LOSS STATEMENT AS WELL AS PROFIT CENTER ACCOUNTING. As described in Section 8.1, Basic Principles of Business Intelligence, this kind of data provider merely provides a logical view of the data and is not often used in bindings—however, for a correct presentation of the financial statement, a virtual cube is indispensable. *Services* (individual function modules with ABAP code) are used to calculate the result for the presentation of a financial statement and profit and loss statement structure and to map accounts that were assigned correctly in the balance sheet structure based on the balance (contra items).

Remote scenario

Specifically for financial reporting, the SAP system also allows the use of a *RemoteCube* (right side of the binding in Figure 8.11). As a result, you do not have to load transaction data into SAP NetWeaver BW and store it there because the necessary data is directly read from the source system and consequently available for the reporting in real time. However, reporting via RemoteCubes also has disadvantages. Depending on your selection, particularly the reading of large data volumes can place a significant load on the source system, which also affccts the performance in the source system when operational processes are executed.

By activating all objects that are involved in the binding, you have created the prerequisites for loading data from the SAP ERP source system to SAP NetWeaver BW and thus use it to create queries.

G/L account balances

Various reports are feasible for the individual data basis levels. Queries that should display the account balance provide an overview of the transaction figures of the individual accounts. You can expand and filter this kind of report according to different characteristics such as profit center, functional area, G/L account, or periods.

Financial statement and profit and loss statement

The system also uses the G/L account balances as the basis for the financial statement and profit and loss statement reports and assigns and provides them via a virtual cube according to their position in the financial statement/profit and loss statement structure.

Financial Statement/Profit and Loss Statement Structure

The structures for the presentation of a financial statement and profit or loss statement do not have to be specifically created in SAP NetWeaver BW. You can extract balance sheet structures that have already been created in the SAP ERP system to SAP NetWeaver BW and thus make them available in the reports.

When creating financial statements across several characteristics, you can also create financial statements for individual profit centers, for example. The design of the report columns is also flexible; you can, for example, provide a good overview by mapping multiple reporting periods next to each other (see Figure 8.12). The determination of the variance as an absolute value or in percentages also allows for a good overview of the current situation.

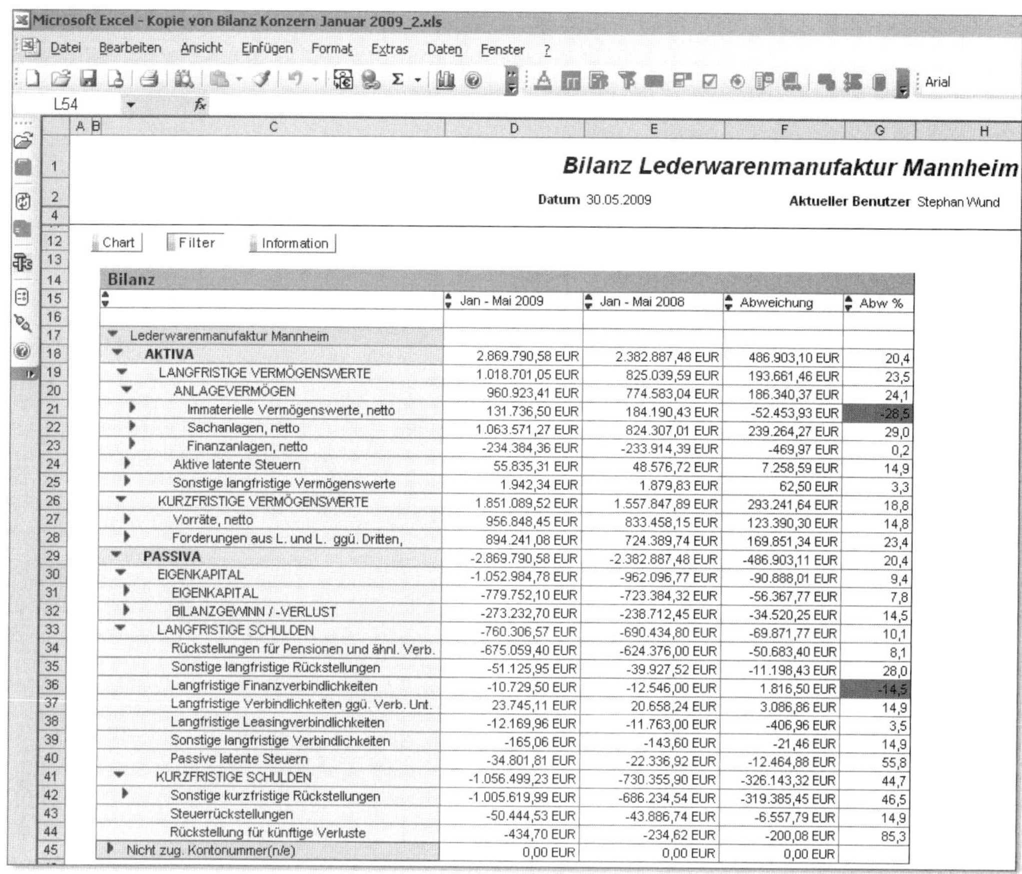

Bilanz

	Jan - Mai 2009	Jan - Mai 2008	Abweichung	Abw %
Lederwarenmanufaktur Mannheim				
AKTIVA	2.869.790,58 EUR	2.382.887,48 EUR	486.903,10 EUR	20,4
LANGFRISTIGE VERMÖGENSWERTE	1.018.701,05 EUR	825.039,59 EUR	193.661,46 EUR	23,5
ANLAGEVERMÖGEN	960.923,41 EUR	774.583,04 EUR	186.340,37 EUR	24,1
Immaterielle Vermögenswerte, netto	131.736,50 EUR	184.190,43 EUR	-52.453,93 EUR	-28,5
Sachanlagen, netto	1.063.571,27 EUR	824.307,01 EUR	239.264,27 EUR	29,0
Finanzanlagen, netto	-234.384,36 EUR	-233.914,39 EUR	-469,97 EUR	0,2
Aktive latente Steuern	55.835,31 EUR	48.576,72 EUR	7.258,59 EUR	14,9
Sonstige langfristige Vermögenswerte	1.942,34 EUR	1.879,83 EUR	62,50 EUR	3,3
KURZFRISTIGE VERMÖGENSWERTE	1.851.089,52 EUR	1.557.847,89 EUR	293.241,64 EUR	18,8
Vorräte, netto	956.848,45 EUR	833.458,15 EUR	123.390,30 EUR	14,8
Forderungen aus L. und L. ggü. Dritten,	894.241,08 EUR	724.389,74 EUR	169.851,34 EUR	23,4
PASSIVA	-2.869.790,58 EUR	-2.382.887,48 EUR	-486.903,11 EUR	20,4
EIGENKAPITAL	-1.052.984,78 EUR	-962.096,77 EUR	-90.888,01 EUR	9,4
EIGENKAPITAL	-779.752,10 EUR	-723.384,32 EUR	-56.367,77 EUR	7,8
BILANZGEWINN / -VERLUST	-273.232,70 EUR	-238.712,45 EUR	-34.520,25 EUR	14,5
LANGFRISTIGE SCHULDEN	-760.306,57 EUR	-690.434,80 EUR	-69.871,77 EUR	10,1
Rückstellungen für Pensionen und ähnl. Verb.	-675.059,40 EUR	-624.376,00 EUR	-50.683,40 EUR	8,1
Sonstige langfristige Rückstellungen	-51.125,95 EUR	-39.927,52 EUR	-11.198,43 EUR	28,0
Langfristige Finanzverbindlichkeiten	-10.729,50 EUR	-12.546,00 EUR	1.816,50 EUR	-14,5
Langfristige Verbindlichkeiten ggü. Verb. Unt.	23.745,11 EUR	20.658,24 EUR	3.086,86 EUR	14,9
Langfristige Leasingverbindlichkeiten	-12.169,96 EUR	-11.763,00 EUR	-406,96 EUR	3,5
Sonstige langfristige Verbindlichkeiten	-165,06 EUR	-143,60 EUR	-21,46 EUR	14,9
Passive latente Steuern	-34.801,81 EUR	-22.336,92 EUR	-12.464,88 EUR	55,8
KURZFRISTIGE SCHULDEN	-1.056.499,23 EUR	-730.355,90 EUR	-326.143,32 EUR	44,7
Sonstige kurzfristige Rückstellungen	-1.005.619,99 EUR	-686.234,54 EUR	-319.385,45 EUR	46,5
Steuerrückstellungen	-50.444,53 EUR	-43.886,74 EUR	-6.557,79 EUR	14,9
Rückstellung für künftige Verluste	-434,70 EUR	-234,62 EUR	-200,08 EUR	85,3
Nicht zug. Kontonummer(n/e)	0,00 EUR	0,00 EUR	0,00 EUR	

Figure 8.12 Financial Statement in Microsoft Excel Using the BEx Analyzer

8.2.2 Profitability Analysis

Profitability analysis represents another critical part of cost accounting in modern enterprises. You can use reports in SAP NetWeaver BW with its optimized multidimensional data structures to assess how the various products, customers, or profit centers affect the enterprise results.

Custom DataSources

As already discussed in Section 3.5, CO-PA as a Central Reporting Tool, the structures in CO-PA are customer-specific. This means that you also have to generate a custom, application-specific DataSource to extract the CO-PA transaction data in SAP NetWeaver BW.

In the Implementation Guide (Transaction SBIW) in the SAP ERP system, use the PROFITABILITY ANALYSIS menu item to navigate to the GENERATE TRANSACTION DATA DATASOURCE function (see ❶ in Figure 8.13).

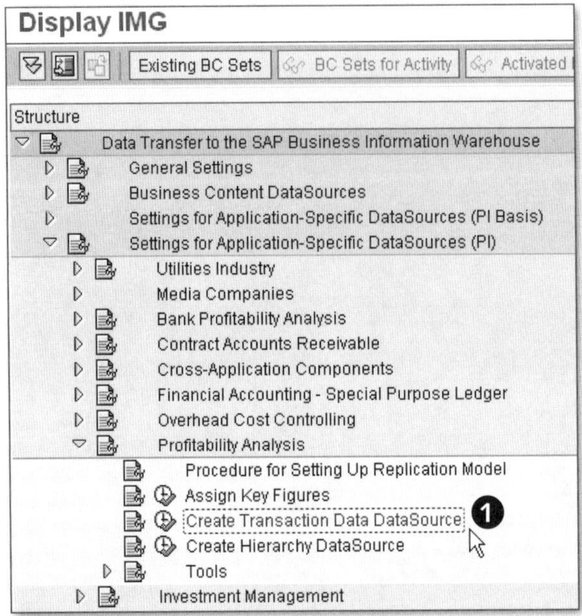

Figure 8.13 Implementation Guide—"Generate Transaction Data DataSource"

The next selection screen enables you to implement the basic settings for the DataSource that should be created. The name of the CO-PA DataSource is generated by the system and should not be changed. It consists of the client of the SAP ERP system (%CL, here 800) and the name of the *operating concern* (%ERK, here LWAG)—as a result, after the generation, the DataSource has the name 1_CO_PA800LWAG (see Figure 8.15).

Select the CREATE function and then the LWAG operating concern. The COST-ACCOUNTING-RELEVANT or ACCOUNTING-RELEVANT setting with reference to the operating concern depends on the CO-PA attribute in the SAP ERP system—in our case, it is a cost-accounting-relevant operating concern (see Figure 8.14).

In the next step, you select the fields in your DataSource in the CO-PA/SAP BW: DATASOURCE FOR TRANSACTION DATA dialog box. Here, you can select the characteristics and value fields that should be copied and then transferred to SAP NetWeaver BW via the extractor.

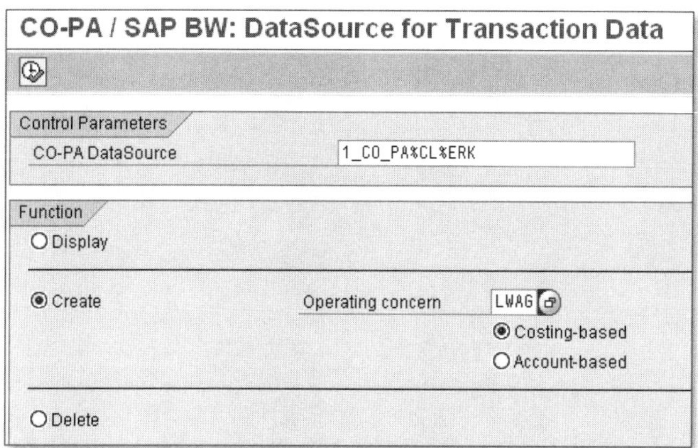

Figure 8.14 Selection Screen for the Creation of a CO-PA DataSource

Selection of Characteristics and Value Fields [+]

When creating the DataSource, you can freely select which characteristics from the object table or the line items should be extracted. Characteristics that are mandatory for correct extraction are already selected by the system and cannot be deleted.

When they are copied, you do not have to use determined key figures from the key figure scheme. The value fields already contain their values.

To allow for reporting in SAP NetWeaver BW that is as highly detailed and meaningful as possible, you must select all available characteristic values because all value fields are relevant for the key figures (see Figure 8.15).

When you click on the InfoCatalog button in the upper screen area, the system continues with the creation of the DataSource.

The last dialog box enables you to configure selection fields and hide fields for the generated DataSource if required. By clicking on the Save button, you conclude the creation of the DataSource. It is now available in the SAP ERP system as an active version and can be replicated in SAP NetWeaver BW.

Due to the already mentioned customer-specific design of Profitability Analysis in the SAP ERP system, no predefined binding is available in SAP NetWeaver BW's Business Content, as you learned in Section 8.2.1, Financial Reporting. You can use the corresponding default objects in SAP NetWeaver BW for individual characteristics such as customer, order, or cost element. The structure of the data targets and the bindings between them needs to be designed individually.

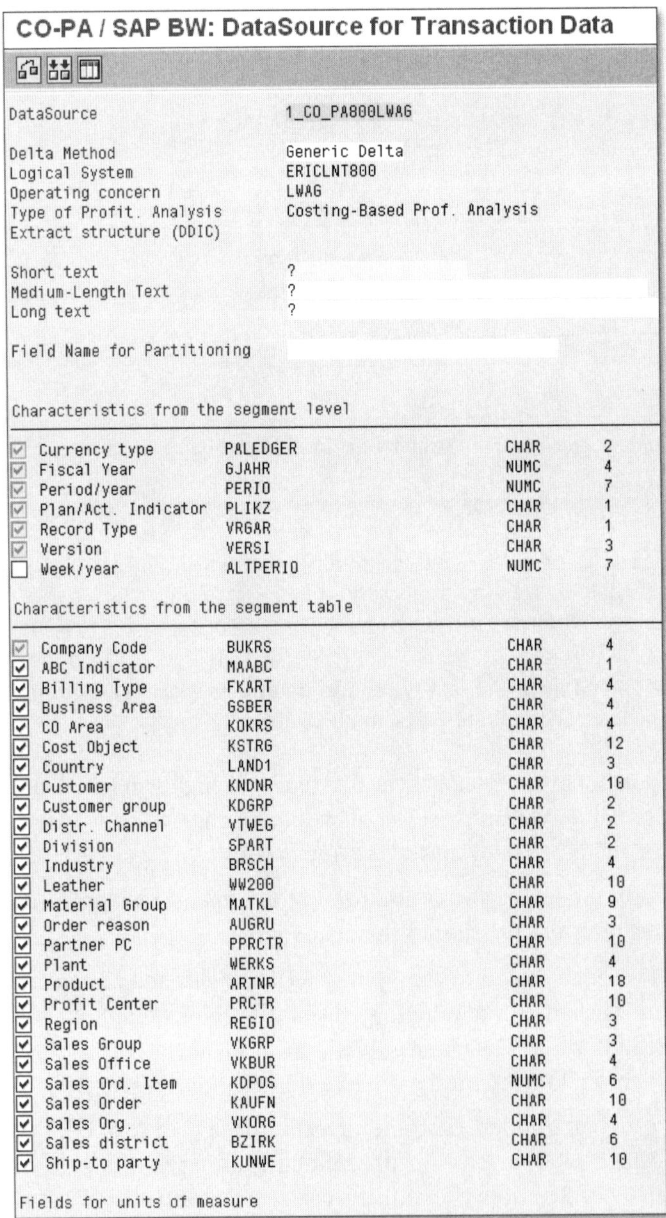

Figure 8.15 Selection of the Characteristic and Value Fields

Figure 8.16 provides an overview of a possible binding in SAP NetWeaver BW, starting with the data extraction from SAP ERP.

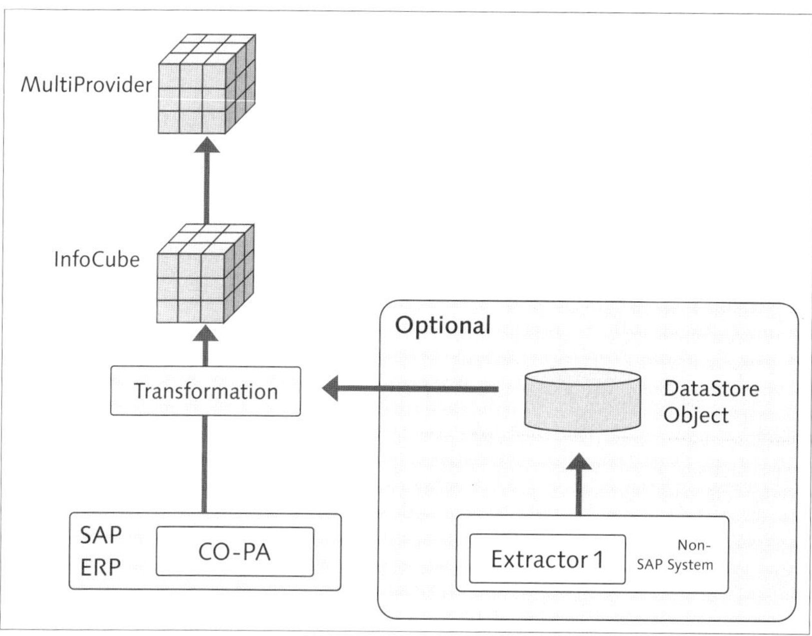

Figure 8.16 Sample Binding in Profitability Analysis

Additional information in SAP NetWeaver BW

Depending on the CO-PA design in the SAP ERP system, it may be necessary to load additional information into SAP NetWeaver BW—such as a group costing—and use it to enrich the CO-PA data. You can transfer this additional information to the SAP NetWeaver BW system, for example, by using flat files or other source systems.

Contribution margin scheme

The Profitability Analysis data basis in particular provides versatile design options for reports. To map the contribution margin scheme, you can carry out any calculation in the query definition to determine the individual contribution margins. The calculation can also include additional information (marked as optional in Figure 8.16) that is not available in the SAP ERP system.

Task-specific reports

Furthermore, Profitability Analyses supports many tasks in sales and distribution controlling. You can address the business issues of individual decision makers such as sales managers, product managers, and key account managers with task-specific tasks. Thanks to the independent definition of the reporting interface, SAP NetWeaver BW proves its superiority here over reporting in an SAP ERP system.

8.3 Summary and Outlook

An SAP ERP implementation that remains close to the standard system can also provide all evaluations necessary for reporting and which an enterprise needs for its daily business. However, due to the individual aspects of most successful enterprises, it can also be useful to enhance the reporting and make it more flexible with a business intelligence solution. Today more than ever, increasing dynamic modification of the markets and competition makes it necessary to be able to react quickly to changes in the business environment and derive recommendations for the future. Because it considerably improves the evaluation options and transparency of information in an enterprise, SAP NetWeaver BW is a sensible investment for enhancing the SAP ERP reporting basis.

As already indicated, in 2008, SAP took a significant step toward enhancement and flexibility of the available tools—particularly in the SAP NetWeaver BW environment. The acquisition of Business Objects ensured that various frontend tools for formatting and presentation of data in reporting were included in the SAP portfolio. Aside from the formatted reporting with Crystal Reports, web frontends such as Xcelsius should also be mentioned here.

In the planning application area, another acquisition resulted in an SAP-internal competitor for the SAP NetWeaver BW Integrated Planning component: OutlookSoft is a tool for strategic and tactical financial planning, which should replace the already existing planning applications in the medium to long term.

At the same time, it is SAP's declared strategy to keep today's BI/BW components with regard to data extraction, data modeling, data retention, binding, and master data integration as the enterprise data warehouse platforms for the future. The integration of the already mentioned new products still requires some development effort to ensure full integration with the BI platform.

The existing architecture and ability to use the existing tools as integrative parts are therefore still somewhat limited. As a result, market acceptance did not meet SAP's initial high expectations. Furthermore, using the newly acquired tools incurs additional license costs. Nevertheless, the versatile options the new software products provide will surely be used to an ever increasing extent and contribute to the higher transparency of information in enterprises.

The first step in a new direction is always the hardest. Using the implementation of the SAP General Ledger as an example, this chapter lets you observe and replicate the main steps in the value flow optimization process.

9 Optimizing Value Flows by Implementing the SAP General Ledger — A Real-Life Example

The introduction to this book described why value flows are interrupted in existing SAP systems. When systems are rolled out, the persons responsible generally decide against a big-bang approach; additional modules are added at a later stage; processes are modified in the course of time; and the system is adapted to these changes only patchily and at the last minute. This situation is concisely summed up by the terms "legacy system" and "historically evolved." Migrating a system to the SAP General Ledger accounting system offers an opportunity to revise and restructure the value flows in that system.

This chapter presents a project that has the initial goal of "only" migrating the system to SAP General Ledger. However, it is established at the start of the project that this is not possible without redesigning the value flows as well. This realization greatly expands the scope of the project.

Let us now take a look at the most important steps and decisions in the project, from the project charter right through to the project review.

9.1 Project Charter

Initial situation

The customer in our project is a large, international IT service provider. The company's business is twofold: it purchases and sells hardware and also provides consulting solutions and outsourcing services in the IT area. The main focus of its business is Europe.

Preparations: technical upgrade

For many years, the customer has mapped its internal processes in an SAP system. Recently, the company upgraded from SAP R/3 4.6C to SAP ERP. In doing so, the customer opted for what is known as a *technical upgrade*. This means that the focus is on transferring existing processing and their mappings to the new release while making as few changes as possible. No new functions were implemented. This approach is often taken to minimize project costs.

Because EU law dictates that comprehensive segment reporting—for both the balance sheet and the profit and loss statement—has to be carried out for business years that start on or after 01/01/2009, the goal was to upgrade to SAP General Ledger on this date. The parallel accounting principle—local law and IAS—was already implemented some years ago using what is known as the *account solution* (see Section 3.3, International Requirements). The standard cost of sales ledger 0F was also active. Profit Center Accounting was used both to represent the divisions and the organizational structure. Therefore, contrary to the advice from SAP, a matrix organization was used. The use of the account assignment object *segment* was intended to resolve this situation. The organizational structure, for its part, was to be transferred to segment reporting and Profit Center Accounting would from then on represent divisions only. The divisions are closely linked to products and customers.

9.1.1 Preliminary Considerations

Profit Center Accounting

One of the first decisions that had to be made in the project was whether Profit Center Accounting would continue to be mapped in the EC-PCA module or should be transferred to SAP General Ledger. This decision would have a significant influence on the project charter. Table 9.1 shows the pros and cons of this decision.

We already discussed the problems of reorganizations and the SAP General Ledger in Chapter 3, Section 3.2, Entity Model. This is a serious problem in many companies, especially large ones.

However, in our sample project, the benefits of a shared database for Financial Accounting and Controlling were judged to outweigh the disadvantages outlined in Table 9.1.

	Pro	Con
Profit Center Accounting EC-PCA	▸ Comprehensive reporting on secondary cost elements at the profit center level ▸ Local postings to EC-PCA ▸ Easier to map reorganizations	▸ No document splitting ▸ Separate document storage and therefore risk of deviating from EC-PCA and Financial Accounting
Profit Center Accounting in SAP General Ledger	▸ Balance sheet at the profit center level due to document splitting ▸ No differences due to shared dataset	▸ No reporting on secondary cost elements at the profit center level ▸ Profit center-only postings have to be made in G/L

Table 9.1 Pros and Cons of Integrating Profit Center Accounting With SAP General Ledger

This benefit was particularly important because the company's reporting concept was previously based on three data sources:

1. Accounting for legal reporting
2. Profit Center Accounting for internal reporting
3. CO-PA for internal reporting

The integration of Profit Center Accounting into SAP General Ledger made it possible to reduce these sources to two: SAP General Ledger and CO-PA. Because the company had approximately 5,000 active profit centers at the start of the project, the final hurdle was that of the expected data volume.

Calculating the data volume

Only limited practical data is available on SAP General Ledger so far Thus, even SAP cannot provide any reliable information on what data volumes can be used with SAP General Ledger without jeopardizing performance. The only certainty is that the two main influencing factors when it comes to performance are the number of individual documents and the rows created in the totals table of SAP General Ledger (FAGLFLEXT in the standard).

Totals table

The role of the totals table becomes clear if you examine the table structure of a new general ledger in a sample update.

Figure 9.1 shows an extract from the tables that are updated when a document is posted to Financial Accounting. A vendor invoice is posted; this posting is made to two expense accounts with different profit center and segment account assignments. The vendor line item in this case has neither a profit center nor a segment because the payable is a balance sheet item; therefore, there is no Controlling account assignment from which a profit center or segment could be derived.

Let us assume that document splitting has been activated for profit centers. This means that the vendor item is split in the general ledger view. The result is two payable items (see Figure 9.1). Splitting and account assignment are carried out in accordance with the expense item.

Table FAGLFLEXA

As in classic general ledger accounting, the data from the document is saved in tables BKPF (Document Header for Accounting) and BSEG (Document Segment for Accounting). The entry view for the document shows the data saved here. Thus, in this case, no profit center or segment is updated for the vendor items.

Also, the SAP General Ledger tables are now updated. In the standard, the general ledger view of the document items is entered in table FAGLFLEXA (General Ledger: Actual Line Items). As you can see in the figure, two payable items are shown that were already processed in the document splitting process. We are now deliberately using the term *payable item* rather than *vendor item* because vendor information is not saved at this point.

Table FAGLFLEXT

For performance reasons, reporting is usually based on another table called FAGLFLEXT (General Ledger: Totals). All data required for representing the activated scenarios is updated to this table (see Chapter 7, Section 7.1.1, Activating Different Scenarios). This means that non-essential information such as the posting key is not contained in the totals table. If you decide not to update the profit center in SAP General Ledger, the profit center will not be filled here either. A special row is updated for each combination of required fields. If a document contains a characteristics combination that is already present in table FAGLFLEXT, the values are added to the existing totals. Therefore, the more characteristics combinations—and therefore, rows—there are, the more entries are in table FAGLFLEXT.

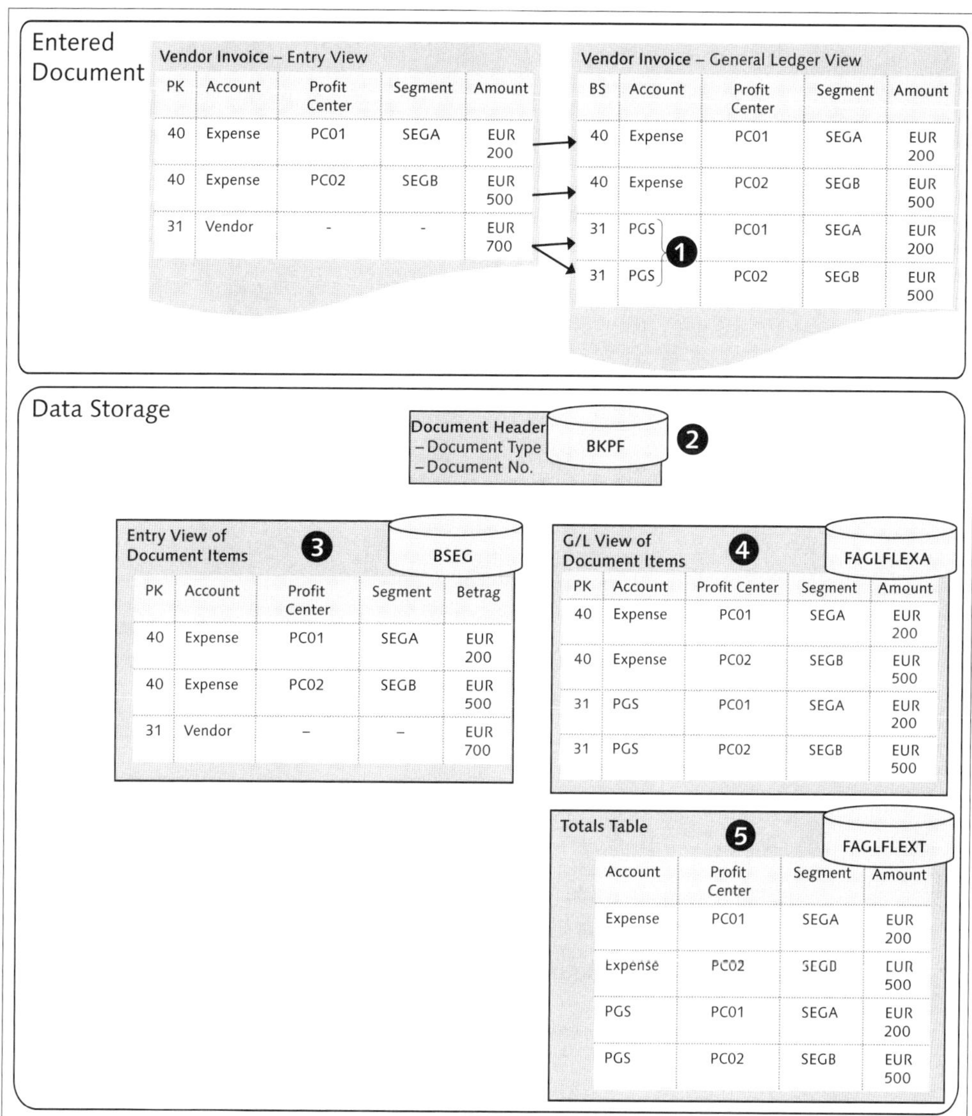

Figure 9.1 Save Document in SAP General Ledger

There are two ways to reduce the number of characteristics items:

Characteristics items

- **Represent as few characteristics as possible**
  You can reduce the number of characteristics that are represented by mapping Profit Center Accounting to the classic Profit Center Accounting (EC-PCA) rather than to the general ledger, for example. Note that

after you do so, you will no longer be able to activate document splitting for the profit center.

Therefore, the only correct way to represent payables at the profit center level at the time of posting is to update the profit center in Financial Accounting.

- **Reduce the number of characteristics instances**
  One way to reduce the number of instances of characteristics is to reduce the number of profit centers.

  The project implemented this by relocating the functional view to the SEGMENT field.

Calculating the expected data volume

SAP provides report RGUIST01 to enable you to simulate the number of entries that can be expected in the totals table in individual cases. This report is accessible via Transaction SA38. You can determine the basis of the calculation yourself. For the purposes of our example, we have decided to use the Profit Center Accounting tables. The results show that the number of profit centers has to be reduced.

Rules for deriving profit centers

Relocating the functional view to the SEGMENT field enabled us to reduce the number of profit centers by a factor of ten. However, this was possible only by deriving the segments separately, using rules created specifically for this purpose, rather than deriving them from the profit center in the SAP standard.

9.1.2 Actual Project Scope

The way was now clear for representing profit centers in SAP General Ledger, and the project scope was as follows:

- Implement SAP General Ledger for approximately ten company codes in three countries
- Transfer the functional view out of profit centers and functional areas
- Integrate the representation of cost of sales accounting into SAP General Ledger and close down the cost of sales accounting ledger
- Transfer Profit Center Accounting from EC-PCA to SAP General Ledger
- Implement document splitting for profit center and segment account assignments
- Develop segment derivation in-house

As you can see, the project was wide in scope; therefore, detailed planning and adherence to the project phases were very important.

9.2 Project Plan

Duration and final deadline

SAP General Ledger can be activated at the start of a business year only. This means that the final deadline of a project for migrating to SAP General Ledger is usually set in a hurry, and the project planning is done in the form of backward scheduling. In our customer's case, the business year is the same as the calendar year. Therefore, the system can go live on January 1 only. The project started in the second half of the previous year and ran for approximately 15 months.

After migration to SAP General Ledger, postings can no longer be made in previous business years. Before migration to the live system starts, there has to be an auditor's certificate for all affected company codes in the relevant previous year.

Migration and activation date

Migration date and activation date are two different things in migrations to the SAP General Ledger.

As you can see in Figure 9.2, the migration date is defined as 01/01/2009. In other words, the process of migrating the system from classic general ledger to SAP General Ledger takes place on this key date. The auditing company guaranteed that all of the certificates for all company codes would be available on 02/04/2009. The migration process therefore started on 02/06/2009, and the SAP General Ledger was activated two days later (on 02/08/2009). During this period, the live system was reserved exclusively for the migration process and all users except consultants, IT staff, and key users were locked.

Significance of the migration date

The migration date initially influences the behavior of the system in all postings to Financial Accounting and Controlling. Up until the migration date, all postings are still made to the classic G/L. A validation function in the SAP system enables you to check as early as in the posting process whether documents conform to the document splitting regulations in SAP General Ledger. In our case, it always has to be possible to derive a segment. SAP's *Migration Cockpit is used to activate the validation function.* In our project, a log was updated with information on all non-regulation documents whose posting date fell before 01/01/2009. An error message was created for documents with a posting date after 01/01/2009. In other words, even though SAP General Ledger was not yet active, no new documents were accepted that could no longer be updated in SAP General Ledger. This approach ensured high data quality and as smooth a migration process as possible.

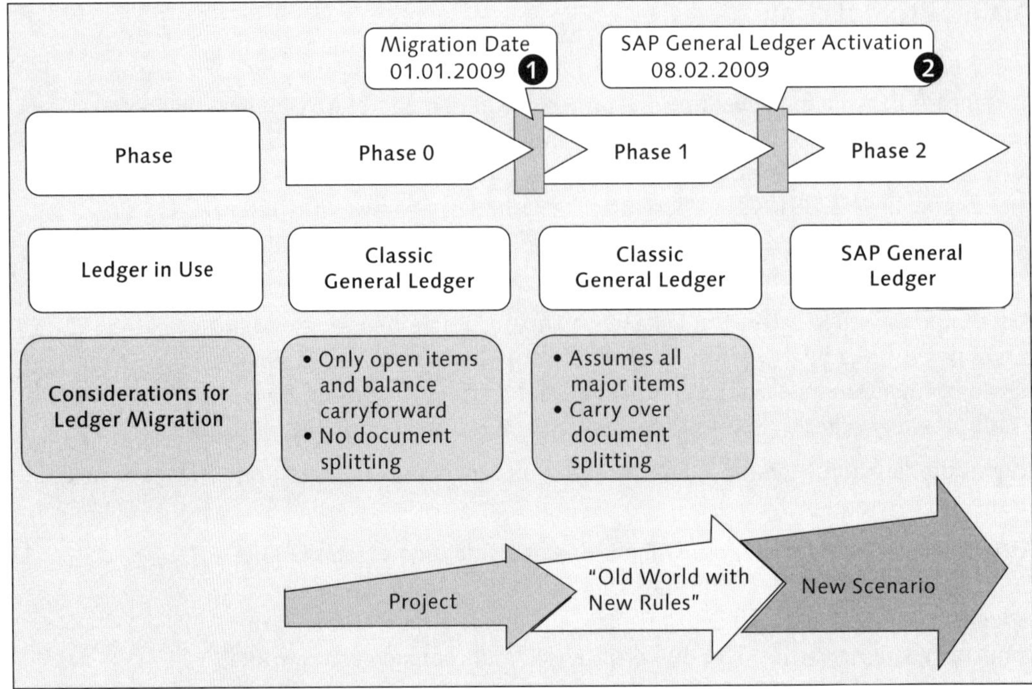

Figure 9.2 Effects of Migration Date and Activation Date

Migration scope

Another thing that the migration date influences is how the posting data is processed in the migration process. In the case of accounts managed on an open item basis, only items that are open on 12/31/2008 are transferred from the posting data in what is known as *phase 0* (period before migration date). For all accounts that are not managed on an open item basis, only the balance carryover is transferred, which means that only balance sheet values are transferred. The profit and loss statement is not transferred to SAP General Ledger. Because the system is not upgraded in a migration, the old documents can still be accessed afterward.

However, there is only restricted access to reports on business data from phase 0 in general ledger accounting. Thus, for example, after SAP General Ledger is activated, the standard balance sheet report (report RFBILA00) reads data from the SAP General Ledger tables only. Thus, in our project, it was no longer possible from this point on to call up the 2009 balance sheet with 2008 (before the migration date) as a comparison period.

Therefore, it is not possible initially to juxtapose comparison values from 2008 in a balance sheet and profit and loss statement that is created in SAP

General Ledger on 03/31/2009, for example. Only the posting data from phase 1 (after migration but before activation) is transferred in full. This means that unrestricted reporting on the 2009 business year is available to the customer in SAP General Ledger. Given that long runtimes can be expected for the technical transfer of individual documents for the current business year, phase 1 should be as short as possible.

9.2.1 Project Plan

The project plan shown in Figure 9.3 was agreed with the customer:

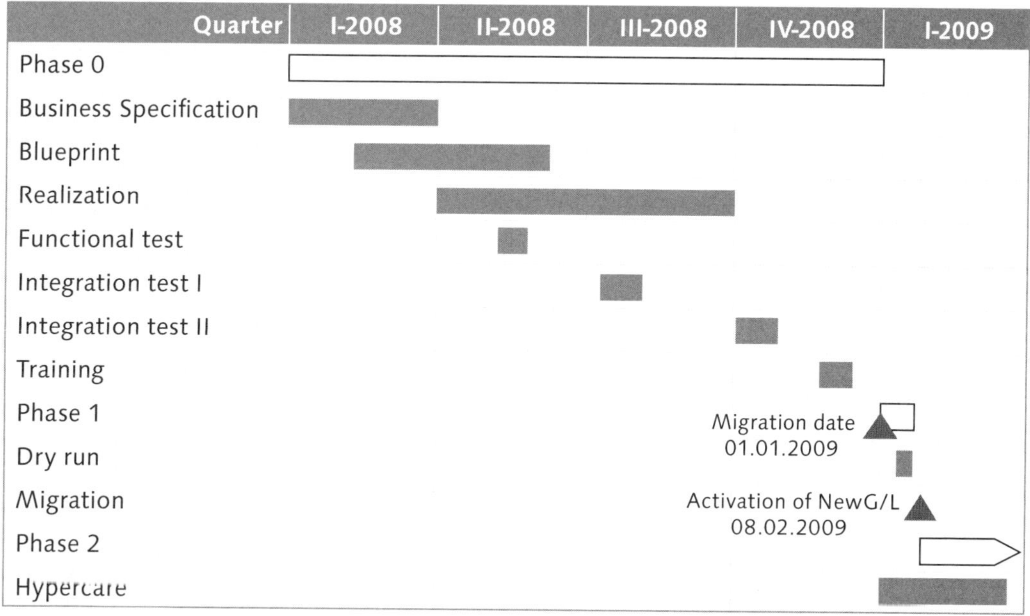

Figure 9.3 Project Plan

Overlap between the phases

If you look at this project plan, you will notice the overlap between the individual phases. The process of creating the technical concept in the blueprint phase, and the implementation, started before the blueprint was completed. The reason for this is the complex subject matter; interdisciplinary workshops involving the controlling, accounting and IT departments and consultants had to be held to clarify many of the issues.

Long hypercare phase

The hypercare phase is also known as *after-go-live support* and refers to the intensive support provided by the IT department directly after the system goes live. For the migration to SAP General Ledger, this phase is quite long and starts on the migration date, not on the date on which SAP General Ledger is activated. This is necessary because the document splitting regulations have to be used for postings from as early as phase 1 onward. Most of the problems that arise in this phase have to do with updates. The posting logic does not change after migration. The support focus from this point on is to explain the figures on which the migration was based.

In particular, some users find it difficult to tell the difference between the entry view and the general ledger view, and this topic generates a large number of queries.

9.2.2 Test Phases

Organizing the test phases

The test phases are sub-divided into three sub-phases:

- Phase 1 test (period from migration date to actual migration)
- Technical migration test
- Phase 2 test (after migration, with active SAP General Ledger)

Phase 1 test

The focus of the phase 1 test is on checking that all required processes can still be posted. Segment derivation was not an issue in this phase because SAP General Ledger was not yet active at this point. This test phase was scheduled to last one week.

Technical migration test

The technical migration test was then carried out over a period of five work days after the phase 1 test. This test checked the Migration Cockpit and the account assignment derivation during the migration process. Because we used different derivations here than those used in daily operations, the figures had to be agreed in detail at the profit center and segment level. Initially, however, all that was necessary was to carry out a reconciliation at the company code level by comparing the old and the new general ledger. This was done using Transaction GCAC (Compare Ledgers) (see Chapter 7, Section 7.12.4, Reconciliation Between Financial Accounting and Controlling). This reconciliation was undertaken by the consultants and the IT department. This way, everyone could be sure that all of the relevant data was migrated in full. The next step was to conduct a detailed reconciliation to check whether the account assignments were correctly derived and, for example, whether the totals at the profit center level in SAP General Ledger matched those in the EC-PCA module.

Detailed reconciliation by departments

The detailed reconciliation was significantly more difficult and, above all, more time-consuming than the purely technical check done in Transaction GCAC—the process took two weeks. This reconciliation was made more difficult because the functional area, profit center, and segment had to be re-derived for documents in the current business year. This cannot be done in the standard Migration Cockpit. If a document already contains one of the named account assignments, this account assignment is transferred from the entry view to the general ledger view.

A modification can be used to overwrite previously derived account assignments. For example, the currently valid assignments for cost center and order master data were used instead of the historic assignments, which meant that assignment changes could be deleted at the start of the business year. The disadvantage of this approach is that the entry view and the general ledger view of documents from phase 1 have different account assignments, as shown in Figure 9.4.

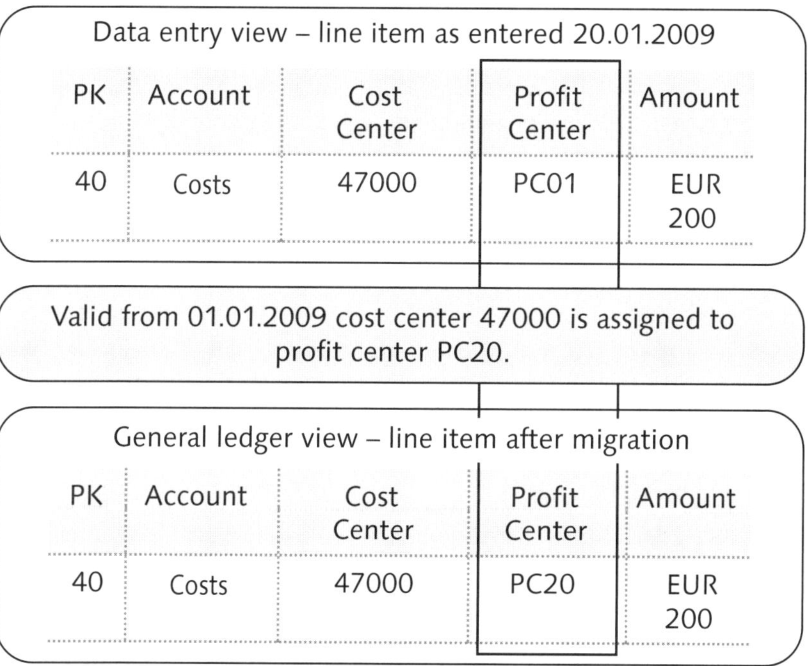

Figure 9.4 Manipulating Account Assignment in the Migration Process

Here, you can see that a document item was posted on 01/20/2009; that is, in phase 1. Profit center PC01 was derived in the posting process by means of the account assignment to cost center 47000. All documents in phase 1 were migrated in full; thus, this item is also processed by the Migration Cockpit. Let us assume that cost center 47000 was assigned to profit center PC20 after 01/20—that is, after the item was updated but before migration. The Migration Cockpit does not re-derive the profit center in the standard but the code can be modified to activate re-derivation. Now, in the re-derivation process, if we do not ask which profit center was stored for the cost center during document updating on 01/20/2009 and instead simply derive the currently assigned profit center, we are creating an inconsistency between the entry view and the general ledger view. The reason for this is that only the general ledger view is created in the migration process; the entry view remains unchanged. Because significant elements of reporting, especially the balance sheet, show the general ledger view, our inconsistent profit center derivation in the migration process has initiated a reorganization at the profit center level—a function that, for the moment, is not available in the SAP standard. The disadvantage of this procedure is that you have to take into account the profit center switch from PC01 to PC20 when reconciling the migration at the profit center level. If these kinds of switches are carried out on a large scale, it becomes very difficult to reconcile the migration at the profit center level.

In this project, this meant that it was not possible to carry out a reconciliation with classic Profit Center Accounting directly; instead, this had to be done using transitions, some of which were very complex. The same applied to the functional area and, therefore, to reconciling the cost of sales accounting ledger.

Phase 2 test

The last phase of the test checked how the system behaved when SAP General Ledger was activated. The two focus points of this test were the inbound interfaces (incoming and outgoing invoices from non-SAP systems and HR, and activity allocations from feeder systems to Controlling) and the month-end closing.

No modifications had to be made to approximately 50% of the interfaces. There were undesired effects in document updating in the case of approximately 30% of the interfaces; however, these effects were eliminated using custom document types and the associated Customizing in document splitting. For the remaining interfaces, modifications had to be made in the interfaces themselves and, in some cases, even in the feeder systems.

The activity plan for the month-end closing had to be modified for the following three reasons:

- Real-time integration was activated. This meant that there was no further need for the monthly reconciliation ledger run.

- Profit Center Accounting is now integrated into G/L. In other words, it was no longer possible to make local modification postings that did not involve G/L to Profit Center Accounting.
- In G/L, segment-level assessment was introduced. However, this could only be implemented after all Controlling transactions were completed because real-time integration could sometimes post new documents to Financial Accounting.

Two years ago, the customer established a fast-close process to facilitate the fact that the figures have to be sent to company headquarters on the second work day after the end of the month. Therefore, it was essential that after SAP General Ledger went live, the month-end closing process would run smoothly and, most important, without delays right from the start. To this end, the last integration test intensively checked all closing activities, from manual limitations to Asset Accounting and Controlling to automatic notification of figures to company headquarters.

9.3 Redesigning Value Flows

Due to the implementation of segment account assignment and the reduction in the number of profit centers, the account assignment derivations had to be checked from within several processes. Similarly, the separation of profit centers and segment meant that the segment derivation had to be determined for all processes. Although this lead to an enormous increase in the work required by everyone involved in the project, it did make it possible to significantly reduce the number of profit centers. Even though this was not an explicit part of the project charter, this situation highlighted the need to redesign several of the value flows.

9.3.1 Concept for Segment Derivation

Segment-specific field

In the SAP standard, the segment is derived from the profit center master records. SAP provides the SEGMENT field for this purpose. In our project, a decision was made not to use this field. Instead, a new, custom field in which the segment could be entered was added to all sales orders, internal orders, cost centers, and PSP elements to use the segment to functionally analyze the company. With the help of the BAdIs provided by the SAP system, the segment is read from these account assignment objects. Other solutions had to be developed for transactions that cannot access a

Controlling object such as the transaction for posting electronic account statements (Post Bank Account to Bank Clearing Account).

Customer-specific table

For this reason, customer-specific tables for storing fixed segments were defined. To find the correct segment, the user is asked for the company code, the document type, and the G/L account. The tables are then searched in a defined order; special cases are processed first, then general transactions. This procedure may remind you of the condition technique for revenue recognition that we discussed in Chapter 7, Section 5.7.3, Representing Sales Revenues. As examples, the following assignments were set:

- *Technical clearing accounts*, which by definition always have a zero balance (for example, split accounts for documents from the HR interface with more than 999 rows) have a dummy segment assigned to them. This segment is regularly checked to ensure that it maintains its zero balance.
- A range of *document types* to which a segment can be assigned due to a business transaction are assigned a segment directly using a Z table. These business transactions include asset sales that are initially posted to a clearing account. The correct segment account assignment is then made when the asset is posted to a clearing account.
- All *equity capital accounts* and *bank accounts* are by definition assigned to the overhead area. This is done using a direct connection between a G/L account and a segment in a Z table.

Unfortunately, in the first step, the document splitting process cannot divide incoming payments in a cause-specific manner. The reason for this is the document flow.

First, the system contains a billing document to a customer. The receivable—in other words, the open item in the customer account—can have a cause-specific segment assigned to it by the document splitting process in accordance with the counter-assignments.

Default segmenting for incoming payments

The Bank to Bank Clearing Account document is created in the process of updating the electronic bank statement. At this point, a link to the open item has not been set up, with the result that only a default segment can be used. Only after the open items have been reconciled in the bank clearing account and the customer account can the segment assignment from the billing document to the customer account be transferred to the bank clearing account. Reconciling the two open items in the bank clearing account causes a change of segment, which is updated to a segment clearing account (see Figure 9.5). The starting point in this case is an open customer invoice in the amount of €2,000. In the figure, you can see—on the one hand—an incoming payment on the electronic bank statement (€2,000). On the other hand, you can see the reconciliation of the open item in the customer account (€2,000).

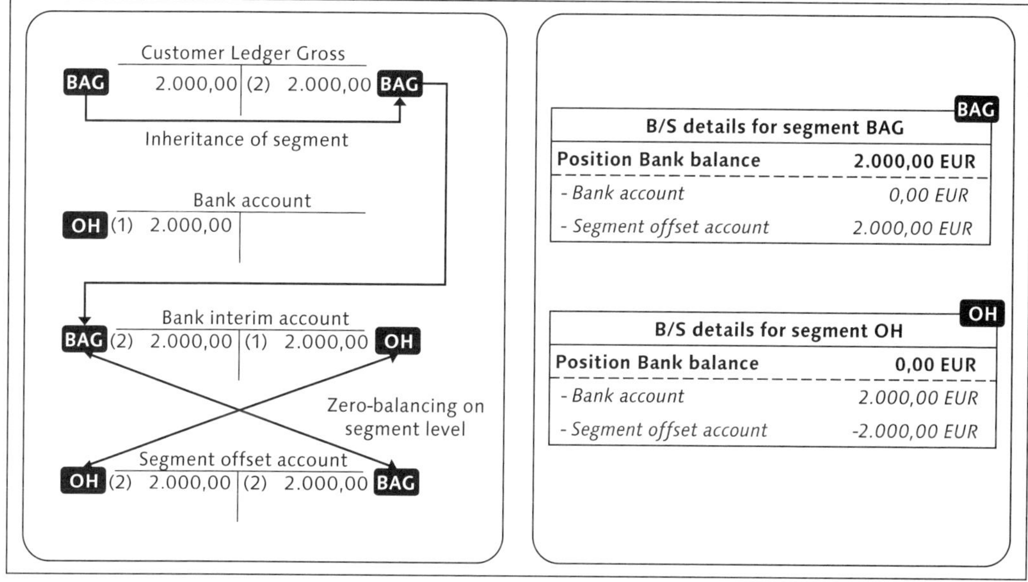

Figure 9.5 Correct Segment Representation for an Incoming Payment

The bank account is unaffected by these transactions. However, if we use a special segment clearing account to carry out the reconciliation in the bank clearing account and display this in the balance sheet structure in the bank accounts, we have at least managed to correctly display the segments for the balance sheet item.

Derivation procedure

A derivation procedure arose during the project that was complex but enabled balance sheet-quality segment reporting. To facilitate this, however, all enterprise processes had to be examined to establish what account assignments, if any, could be used to derive the segment.

9.3.2 Value Flows in the Procurement Process

Checking document types

The customer's procurement process is already very reliable; therefore, we do not need to concern ourselves with orders, goods receipt, and invoice verification. Accounts payable accounting is the only area where the use of the existing document types has to be checked and modified significantly. This is because, due to the document splitting process, it was no longer possible to always use the same document types for invoice and credit memo receipts, payment transactions, and account maintenance.

An overview was created to determine and document the uses of the various document types—see Figure 9.6 for an extract from the overview.

Document types (version per 30.04.2008)

Doc type	Acc Type	Rev DTyp	Trading Partner	Intercomp posting	Negative Posting	Account types A	D	K	M	S	Description	Comment	Business Transaction
AA	ADKMS	AA				X	X	X	X	X	Asset posting		0000
AB	ADKMS			X		X	X	X	X	X	Accounting document		1010
AN	AKMS	AN				X		X	X	X	Net asset posting		0000
AP	AS					X				X	AA periodic posting		0000
AS	AKS					X		X		X	statistical depreciation	Block!	
CF	ADKS					X	X	X		X	Reconciliation FI-CO	KALC	0000
CO	AS				X	X				X	Settlement	???	0000
D3	DS			X			X			X	Offsetting debits side	KBR3	1000
DZ	DS			X			X			X	Inc. payment (automati	Debit advice	1000
DÜ	DS	DÜ					X			X	Migration: Customer	CC migration customer	0000
KA	ADKMS	KA				X	X	X	X	X	Vendor document	Vendor / Vendor	0300
KF	ADKMS	KA				X	X	X	X	X	Down payment request	Noted item	0300
KZ	ADKMS		X	X		X	X	X	X	X	Outgoing payments	Payment	1000
KÜ	KS	KÜ						X		X	Migration: Vendor	Migration: Vendor	0000
PR	MS								X	X	Price change	Revaluation	0000
PS	MS								X	X	Price reduction		
RA	AKMS	RA				X		X	X	X	Sub.cred.memo stlmt		
RB	DKS						X	X		X	Travel expenses	Block!	0300

Figure 9.6 Assigning Document Types to Document Splitting Transactions

In the figure, you can see that every document type has a note attached, specifying both the account types that can be posted with that document type and the document splitting transaction with which it is associated.

Systems that have been in production use for more than ten years also have a range of document types that can be locked (such as AS and RB in our case) or document types for which the intended business transactions are unknown (such as Controlling in our case).

9.3.3 Value Flows in the Sales Process

The implementation of SAP General Ledger and the associated segment derivation had much wider-reaching effects in the sales process. In particular, stricter rules had to be applied for account assignment. For our project, several profit centers in existing sales orders had to be changed. The goal of these changes was to change the sales order assignment on a company-wide basis.

[Ex]

Causes of Incorrect Assignments

One example of incorrect assignments would be an order that was assigned to key account management instead of to the local sales and distribution organization, as it had been up to that point. Another example would be a sales order for which the correct profit center was not known when it was created, and a dummy profit center was therefore used.

In both cases, open value flows were interrupted and, ultimately, incorrectly displayed.

Problems with dummy account assignment

Before SAP General Ledger was implemented, incorrect assignments were undesirable from the Controlling viewpoint. Dummy account assignments, in particular, caused recurring problems in financial statements. Billing and assessment cycles created errors or returned incorrect results, and had to be canceled or repeated. In times of the fast close approach and hour-based closing procedure documents, this situation—at best—led to long work days for Controlling staff at best and—at worst—to delays reporting the figures.

Dummy account assignments were banned with the introduction of segment-based account balancing. It is also not possible anymore to make retroactive changes to profit centers and segments in sales orders. This was the only way to ensure high-quality segment balances. It was also recognized that the SD transactions had to be redesigned. Therefore, to avoid dummy account assignments, the cost elements that were previously posted to the sales and distribution transaction in goods issue postings were deleted. As described in Chapter 5, Section 5.4, Goods Issue, there is currently no Controlling object, although profit centers and segments can be derived from the sales order.

More than one segment per sales order?

In this project, a question reemerged that was touched on in Chapter 5, *Sales and Distribution Process*: can a sales order contain more than one segment? This question did not receive the same response in all of the countries involved. The country with the highest sales volume answered "No" because sales and distribution is sub-divided into teams in accordance with the functional reporting view. In the other countries, the organizations are so small that they could not work exclusively with segment-free sales orders. Because the cost objects were the internal orders associated with the sales orders rather than the sales orders themselves, the internal orders in this case had to be assigned at the item level. The internal orders were then used to derive one segment only.

Change management

The tests showed that using a BAdI to derive segments in the sales process was difficult. In production operations, the stricter account assignment rules again proved to be a challenge for change management in the project. To counteract these difficulties, additional information events and other measures were planned to spread the word about the methodology and benefits of the project.

9.3.4 Value Flows in Financial Accounting and Controlling

Account assignment manual

Little or nothing has changed in the value flows for Financial Accounting and Controlling. Nonetheless, as in other areas, the posting rules in these areas were extended and made stricter. A comprehensive *account assignment manual* was created to support staff in the affected areas. This manual was particularly useful for explaining the document splitting logic and the resulting rules. It also illustrated the document type management process, as shown in Figure 9.6.

Real-time integration

Real-time integration (RTI) was used to transfer all Controlling transactions—except transfers to CO-PA—to general ledger accounting. Although assessments and distributions at the profit center level are possible in SAP General Ledger (see Chapter 7, Section 7.11, Assessments and Distributions), in this case differences between general ledger and overhead cost controlling were not permitted. Therefore, all the more emphasis was put on ensuring that all account assignment objects in overhead cost controlling (cost centers, internal orders, and PSP elements) were transferred in full to CO-PA at month's end. This was the only way to guarantee that general ledger accounting and CO-PA had exactly the same EBIT.

Task list

The task list had to be revised, not least due to RTI. This meant that no general ledger figures could be reported as long as allocations and activity allocations were still being carried out in Controlling because these could affect the segment balance sheet. The direct updating made possible by RTI also had the effect that the posting periods in Financial Accounting had to be significantly longer (see Chapter 7, Section 7.5.2, Opening and Closing Posting Periods). Therefore, the first month-end closing after migration to the production system was an important milestone in the project. This closing ran smoothly, to the relief of all concerned.

9.4 Project Review

Ambitious schedule

In retrospect, given the extensive nature of the project charter, the project duration of 13 months to production migration was quite ambitious. Each of the intensive test phases created a greater understanding of the functioning of SAP General Ledger in general and document splitting in particular. Correspondingly, changes were made in all tests to document splitting and segment derivation.

Dry run

The dry run was carried out at the end of January 2009 in an up-to-date copy of the production system. This dry run involved implementing the migration with individual documents from phase 1 only. These documents already conformed to the rules of SAP General Ledger. This was therefore the first full, reliable test, and it was completely successful.

In the production system, most errors occurred when the fiscal year changed, as expected, because the new, stricter rules of SAP General Ledger had to be used for posting after the new business year began. These errors included incorrect document types and invalid combinations of document type and account. By the time of the migration in February, the organization had become used to the new posting and account assignment rules and only isolated error reports were received at this point. After that, there was a temporary resurgence in errors at the time of the month-end closing only.

The process of redefining the account assignment derivations for profit centers and segments was difficult to design and implement but created a better understanding of the processes and the system. Even though this particular benefit cannot be expressed in monetary terms, it is nonetheless a significant achievement of the project.

9.5 Summary

At the start of the project, the customer's value flows were like those in many companies that use SAP: historically evolved, inadequately documented and, first and foremost, unreliable. The frequent reorganizations at the profit center level were a telling sign that automatic profit center derivations (which in many areas, including in almost the entire sales process, were based on user exits) were not comprehensive enough. The quality of reporting was just as bad, with the figures in general ledger, profit center accounting, and CO-PA regularly deviating from each other. The implementation of SAP General Ledger was used as an opportunity to critically examine the existing value flows and to get rid of unreliable solutions in a systematic manner. This way, new value flows were created with the goal of significantly enhancing the quality of the reporting concept. What is more, the volume of work required to clarify inconsistencies at the end of periods was considerably reduced.

Appendices

A Sample Closing Procedure Document

At the end of Chapter 7, Section 7.1.2, Effect of Real-Time Integration of Controlling to Financial Accounting, we mentioned that the interaction between accounting and controlling in the closing process does not always work entirely smoothly. A shared *closing procedure document* is an important tool for close interaction between enterprise areas. The table below shows an example of this kind of document.

Closing Procedure Document for Printing [+]

To make it easier for you to use this sample flow, you can download the relevant files from *www.sap-press.com*.

No.	Day / Close of Month (U)	Activity	Responsible SAP Department	Chapter / Section in This Book
010	U-10	Transfer HR data	SAP General Ledger	7.2
020	U-10	FI-AA: fiscal year change	AA	7.4.5
030	U-2	Message about required provisions (such as imminent losses)	Controlling	
040	U-1	Physical inventory	MM	7.3
050	U	Book in most recent goods receipts	MM	4.6
060	U	Last credit-side payment run	BL	4.9.2
070	U	If required, adaptation of assessments and activity allocations	Controlling	
080	U	Settlement of assets under construction	AA	7.4.1
090	U	Last billing document run in sales and distribution	SD	5.7
100	U	Balance carryforward in general ledger and subledgers	SAP General Ledger, AR, AP	7.9

No.	Day / Close of Month (U)	Activity	Responsible SAP Department	Chapter / Section in This Book
110	U	Open new accounting period	SAP General Ledger	7.5.2
120	U+1m	Period closing program in MM	IT	7.5.1
130	U+1m	Book in most recent invoice receipts	AP	4.7
140	U+1m	Check transfer of invoices to Financial Accounting/Controlling	SD	
150	U+1m	Close accounts payable accounting	SAP General Ledger	7.5.2
160	U+1m	Close accounts receivable accounting	SAP General Ledger	7.5.2
170	U+1a	Foreign currency valuation	SAP General Ledger	7.6
180	U+1a	Reclassify receivables or payables	SAP General Ledger	7.7
190	U+1a	Interest calculation for balances and open items	SAP General Ledger	
200	U+1a	Book in and process most recent electronic account statements	BL	
210	U+1a	Reconcile inventory management and balance sheet accounts	SAP General Ledger	7.12.3
220	U+1a	Depreciation run in asset accounting	AA	7.4.2
230	U+1a	Periodic inventory posting for non-standard valuation area	AA	7.4.3
240	U+1a	Reconciliation asset accounting / general ledger accounting	AA	7.4.5
250	U+1a	Value adjustments to receivables	SAP General Ledger	7.8
260	U+2m	Update all provisions	SAP General Ledger	7.10
270	U+2m	Manual accruals/deferrals	SAP General Ledger	7.10

No.	Day / Close of Month (U)	Activity	Responsible SAP Department	Chapter / Section in This Book
280	U+2m	GR/IR account maintenance	SAP General Ledger	4.8
290	U+2m	GR/IR reclassification	SAP General Ledger	4.8
300	U+2a	Intercompany reconciliation	SAP General Ledger	7.12.2
310	U+2a	Large sales check	SAP General Ledger	7.12.1
320	U+2	Start recurring entries	SAP General Ledger	4.9.1
330	U+2	Start activity allocations and assessments in Controlling	Controlling	7.11
340	U+2	Application of overhead to orders	Controlling	6.4.2
350	U+2	WIP determination for orders	Controlling	6.4.2
360	U+2	Order settlement	Controlling	6.4.2
370	U+3	FI-AA: year-end closing	AA	7.4.5
380	U+3m	Settle overhead cost controlling in accordance with CO-PA	Controlling	3.5.2
390	U+3m	Assessment/distribution in SAP General Ledger	SAP General Ledger	7.11
400	U+3m	Close posting periods in Controlling	Controlling	7.5.2
410	U+3m	Close posting periods in Financial Accounting	SAP General Ledger	7.5.2
420	U+3a	Financial Accounting – Controlling reconciliation	SAP General Ledger/ Controlling	7.12.4
430	U+3a	Financial Accounting – CO-PA reconciliation	SAP General Ledger/ Controlling	7.12.4
440	U+3a	Create asset history sheet	AA	7.4.6

No.	Day / Close of Month (U)	Activity	Responsible SAP Department	Chapter / Section in This Book
450	U+3a	Reporting: financial statements and P/L in accordance with period accounting	SAP General Ledger	7.13.1
460	U+3a	Reporting: P/L in accordance with cost-of-sales accounting	SAP General Ledger	7.13.1
470	U+3a	Reporting in overhead cost controlling	Controlling	7.13.3
480	U+3a	Reporting in accordance with profit centers and segments	SAP General Ledger/ Controlling	7.13.1
490	U+3a	Advance return for tax on sales/ purchases and post tax payable	SAP General Ledger	
500	U+3a	Data snapshot in accordance with SAP NetWeaver BW	IT	8
510	U+4a	Summary EU message	SAP General Ledger	
520	U+4a	Message on foreign trade regulation	SAP General Ledger	

"Day/Close of Month (U)" Column

Problem with calendar-based planning

Several people and teams are usually involved in the month-end closing process. Therefore, it is not sufficient to determine tasks and responsibilities only; you also have to define when each individual task should be performed. If the periods correspond to calendar months, you can use calendar days for scheduling purposes. In our example, the period closing program in MM would have to be started on the first day of the month (row 120), and the summary message would have to be created on the fourth day of the month (row 510).

However, this approach becomes problematic if the closing days fall on weekends or public holidays. In any case, if the posting periods are separated from the calendar months (for example, the 4-4-5 variant), it does not make sense for scheduling to be based on calendar days.

Close of month approach enables separation

Therefore, closing procedure documents are usually based on what is known as the "close of period" (such as close of month). The close of period—abbreviated here as "U" for the German word "Ultimo"—refers to the last work day of a period. Using this day as the orientation point, the closing activities are planned into the new or old period on the basis of work days and not calendar days. Thus, in our example, we schedule the period closing program in MM on the basis of U+1, not on the first day of the month, and the summary message on day U+4.

Detailed planning

However, day-based planning is not usually adequate or detailed enough; units of half-days, at least, should be used. In this period closing document, we use the suffixes "m" for mornings and "a" for afternoons.

Some companies, especially large enterprises, plan on an hourly basis.

Explanation of the SAP Components

AA
Asset Accounting

SD
Sales and Distribution

AR
Accounts Receivable

AP
Accounts Payable

BL
Bank Ledger

B Transactions and Menu Paths

Transaction codes and menu paths are specified at several points throughout this book. This appendix contains a summary of these functions. The transactions and menu paths are grouped thematically and sub-divided by application and Customizing. All of the Customizing settings except those in the SAP NetWeaver BW area are made using the Implementation Guide, which you can access via Tools • Customizing • IMG • Edit Project (Transaction SPRO) in the application menu.

B.1 Controlling

B.1.1 Application

Overhead Cost Controlling

Create Primary Cost Element / Create Secondary Cost Element / Change Cost Element / Display Cost Element (KA01/KA06/KA02/KA03)
Accounting • Controlling • Cost Element Accounting · Master Data • Cost Element • Individual Processing • Create Primary / Create Secondary / Change / Display

Create / Change / Display Cost Element Group (KAH1/KAH2/KAH3)
Accounting • Controlling • Cost Element Accounting • Master Data • Cost Element Group • Create / Change / Display

Create / Change / Display Cost Center (KS01/KS02/KS03)
Accounting • Controlling • Cost Center Accounting • Master Data • Cost Center • Individual Processing · Create / Change / Display

Create / Change / Display Activity Type (KL01/KL02/KL03)
Accounting · Controlling • Cost Center Accounting • Master Data • Activity Type • Individual Processing • Create / Change / Display

Change/Display Activity Output/Prices (KP26/KP27)
Accounting • Controlling • Cost Center Accounting • Planning • Activity Output/Prices • Change/Display

Execute Actual Distribution (KSV5)
Accounting • Controlling • Cost Center Accounting • Period-End Closing • Single Functions • Allocations • Distribution

Execute Actual Assessment (KSV5)
Accounting • Controlling • Cost Center Accounting • Period-End Closing • Single Functions • Allocations • Assessment

Create / Change / Display Internal Order (KO04)
Accounting • Controlling • Internal Orders • Master Data • Order Manager

Run Reconciliation Ledger (KALC)
Accounting • Controlling • Cost Element Accounting • Actual Postings • Reconciliation with Financial Accounting

Open / Close Period (OKP1)
Accounting • Controlling • Cost Element Accounting • Environment • Period Lock • Change

Access to Cost Center Accounting Reports
Accounting • Controlling • Cost Center Accounting • Information System • Reports for Cost Center Accounting

Product Cost Controlling

Create / Edit Worklist for Costing Run (CKMATSEL/CKMATCON)
Accounting • Controlling • Product Cost Controlling • Product Cost Planning • Material Costing • Costing Run • Selection List • Create/Edit

Execute Costing Run (CK40N)
Accounting • Controlling • Product Cost Controlling • Product Cost Planning • Material Costing • Costing Run • Edit Costing Run

Create / Display Unit Costing with Quantity Structure (CK11N/CK13N)
Accounting • Controlling • Product Cost Controlling • Product Cost Planning • Material Costing • Cost Estimate with Quantity Structure • Create/Display

Price Update with Cost Estimate (CK24)
Accounting • Controlling • Product Cost Controlling • Product Cost Planning • Material Costing • Price Update

Create / Change / Display / Revaluate Base Planning Objects and Simulation Costing (KKE1/KKE2/KKE3/KKEB)
Accounting • Controlling • Product Cost Controlling • Product Cost Planning • Reference and Simulation Costing

Preliminary Cost Estimate – Product Cost Collector (MF30)
Accounting • Controlling • Product Cost Controlling • Cost Object Controlling • Product Cost by Period • Planning • Preliminary Costing for Product Cost Collector

Edit Product Cost Collector (KKF6N)
Financials • Controlling • Product Cost Controlling • Cost Object Controlling • Product Cost by Period • Master Data • Product Cost Collector • Edit

Period-End Closing for Product Cost Collector
Accounting • Controlling • Product Cost Controlling • Cost Object Controlling • Product Cost by Period • Period-End Closing

Actual Overhead Calculation: Production Orders (KGI2)
Accounting • Controlling • Product Cost Controlling • Cost Object Controlling • Product Cost by Order • Period-End Closing • Single Functions • Overhead • Individual Processing

Actual Overhead calculation: Sales Orders (VA44)
Logistics • Sales and Distribution • Sales • Product Cost by Sales Order • Period-End Closing • Single Functions • Overhead

WIP Calculation/Display for Order (KKAX/KKAY)
Accounting • Controlling • Product Cost Controlling • Cost Object Controlling • Product Cost by Order • Period-End Closing • Single Functions • Work in Process • Individual Processing • Calculate/Display

Variance Calculation (KKS2)
Accounting • Controlling • Product Cost Controlling • Cost Object Controlling • Product Cost by Order • Period-End Closing • Single Functions • **Variances** • Individual Processing

Actual Settlement: Order (KO88)
Accounting • Controlling • Product Cost Controlling • Cost Object Controlling • Product Cost by Order • Period-End Closing • Single Functions • Settlement • Individual Processing

CO-PA

Check Value Flow from Invoicing (KEAT)
Accounting • Controlling • Profitability Analysis • Tools • Analyze Value Flows • Check Value Flow in Billing Document Transfer

Check Value Flow from Order/Project Settlement (KEAW)
Accountings • Controlling • Profitability Analysis • Tools • Analyze Value Flows • KEAW - Check Value Flow from Order/Project Settlement

B.1.2 Customizing

Organizational Structure and Master Data

Maintain Controlling Area (OKKP)
Controlling • General Controlling • Organization • Maintain Controlling Area

Maintain Order Types (KOT2_OPA)
Controlling • Internal Orders • Order Master Data • Define Order Types

Internal Orders: Availability Control (KOAO) OKOB
Controlling • Internal Orders • Budgeting and Availability Control

Define Cost Center Categories OKA2
Controlling • Cost Center Accounting • Master Data • Cost Centers • Define Cost Center Categories

Account Derivations

Change Automatic Account Assignment / Set Default Account Assignment (OKB9)
Controlling • Cost Center Accounting • Actual Postings • Manual Actual Postings • Edit Automatic Account Assignment

Change Cost Center Determination (from SD) (OVF3)
Sales and Distribution • Basic Functions • Account Assignment/Costing • Assign Cost Centers

Profit Center Derivation of Characteristics in Sales Orders (0KEM)
Financial Accounting (New) • General Ledger Accounting (New) • Tools • Validation/Substitution • Substitution of Profit Centers in Customer Orders

Product Cost Controlling

Basic Settings for Product Cost Controlling
Controlling • Product Cost Controlling • Product Cost Planning • Material Cost Estimate with Quantity Structure • Define Costing Variants / Costing Variant: Components

Maintain Version in Controlling OKEQ
Controlling • General Controlling • Organization • Maintain Versions

Define Results Analysis Version (OKG9)
Controlling • Product Cost Controlling • Cost Object Controlling • Product Cost by Order • Period-End Closing • Work in Process • Define Results Analysis Versions

Define Results Analysis Key (OKG1)
Controlling • Product Cost Controlling • Cost Object Controlling • Product Cost by Order • Period-End Closing • Work in Process • Define Results Analysis Keys

Line IDs for Results Analysis or WIP Calculation
Controlling • Product Cost Controlling • Cost Object Controlling • Product Cost by Order • Period-End Closing • Work in Process • Define Line IDs

Assignment of Cost Elements for WIP and Results Analysis (OKGB)
Controlling • Product Cost Controlling • Cost Object Controlling • Product Cost by Order • Period-End Closing • Work in Process • Define Assignment

Update of WIP Calculation and Results Analysis (OKGA)
Controlling • Product Cost Controlling • Cost Object Controlling • Product Cost by Order • Period-End Closing • Work in Process • Define Update

Maintain Posting Rules in WIP Calculation and Results Analysis (OKG8)
Controlling • Product Cost Controlling • Cost Object Controlling • Product Cost by Order • Period-End Closing • Work in Process • Define Posting Rules for Settling Work in Process

Change Settlement Profile (OKO7)
Controlling • Internal Orders • Actual Postings • Settlement • Maintain Settlement Profiles

Maintain Default Value for Product Cost Collector
Controlling • Product Cost Controlling • Cost Object Controlling • Product Cost by Period • Product Cost Collectors • Define Cost-Accounting-Relevant Default Values for Order Types and Plants

Define Order Type dependent Parameters (Prepare Production Orders for Product Cost Collectors) (OPL8)
Production • Shop Floor Control • Master Data • Order • Define Order Type-Dependent Parameters

Define Cost Component Structure (OKTZ)
Controlling • Product Cost Controlling • Product Cost Planning • Basic Settings for Material Costing • Define Cost Component Structure

CO-PA

Edit Operating Concern (KEA0)
Controlling • Profitability Analysis • Structures • Define Operating Concern • Maintain Operating Concern

Edit Characteristics (KEA5)
Controlling • Profitability Analysis • Structures • Define Operating Concern • Maintain Characteristics

Edit Value Fields (KEA6)
Controlling • Profitability Analysis • Structures • Define Operating Concern • Maintain Value Fields

Define Characteristic Derivation (KEDR)
Controlling • Profitability Analysis • Master Data • Define Characteristic Derivation

Transfer Incoming Sales Orders and Invoices – Assign Value Fields (KE4I)
Controlling • Profitability Analysis • Flows of Actual Values • Transfer of Incoming Sales Orders / Transfer of Billing Documents • Assign Value Fields

Define PA Transfer Structure for Settlement (KEI1)
Controlling • Profitability Analysis • Flows of Actual Values • Order and Project Settlement • Define PA Transfer Structure for Settlement

Settle Production Variances (KEI1)
Controlling • Profitability Analysis • Flows of Actual Values • Settlement of Production Variances • Define PA Transfer Structure for Variance Settlement

B.2 Financial Accounting

B.2.1 Application

Master Data

Create/Change/Display G/L Account (FS00)
Accounting • Financial Accounting • General Ledger • Master Records • G/L Accounts • Individual Processing • Centrally

Postings

Create G/L Account Document (FB50)
Accounting • Financial Accounting • General Ledger • Posting • Enter G/L Account Document

Create Vendor Invoice (FB60)
Accounting • Financial Accounting • Accounts Payable • Document Entry • Invoice

Change/Display Posting Document (Entry View) (FB02/FB03)
Accounting • Financial Accounting • General Ledger • Doc ument • Change/Display

Clear Accounts (F.13)
Accounting • Financial Accounting • General Ledger • Periodic Processing • Automatic Clearing • Without Specification of Clearing Currency

Periodic Processing

Payment Run (F110)
Accounting • Financial Accounting • Accounts Payable • Periodic Processing • Payments

Create Posting Documents from Recurring Entry (F.14)
Accounting • Financial Accounting • General Ledger • Periodic Processing • Recurring Entries • Execute

Period-End Closing

Maintain GR/IR Clearing Account (MR11)
Logistics • Materials Management • Logistics Invoice Verification • GR/IR Account Maintenance • Maintain GR/IR Clearing Account

SAP General Ledger: GR/IR Clearing (F.19)
Accounting • Financial Accounting • General Ledger • Periodic Processing • Closing • Reclassify • GR/IR Clearing

Open/Close Posting Periods (OB52)
Accounting • Financial Accounting • General Ledger Accounting • Environment • Current Settings • Open and Close Posting Periods

Foreign Currency Valuation (FAGL_FC_VAL)
Accounting • Financial Accounting • General Ledger • Periodic Processing • Closing • Valuate • Foreign Currency Valuation (new)

Reclassify Receivables/Payables (FAGLF101)
Accounting • Financial Accounting • Accounts Receivable / Accounts Payable • Periodic Processing • Closing • Reclassify • Sorting/Reclassification (new)

Execute Balance Carryforward (SAP General Ledger) (FAGLGVTR)
Accounting • Financial Accounting • General Ledger Accounting • Periodic Processing • Closing • Carry Forward • Balance Carryforward (new)

Execute Balance Carryforward (Receivables/Payables) (F.07)
Accounting • Financial Accounting • Accounts Receivable / Accounts Payable • Periodic Processing • Closing • Carry Forward • Balance Carryforward

Maintain and Execute Actual Distribution in SAP General Ledger
Accounting • Financial Accounting • General Ledger • Periodic Processing • Closing • Allocation • Actual Distribution

Comparison: Documents / Transaction Figures (FAGLF03)
Accounting • Financial Accounting • General Ledger • Periodic Processing • Closing • Check/Count • Reconciliation (new)

Intercompany Reconciliation: Open Items/Accounts
Accounting • Financial Accounting • General Ledger • Periodic Processing • Closing • Check/Count • Intercompany Reconciliation: Open Items/ Accounts

Financial Accounting — MM Reconciliation (MB5L)
Logistics • Materials Management • Inventory Management • Periodic Processing • List of Stock Values

Financial Accounting – Controlling Reconciliation
Accounting • Controlling • Cost Element Accounting • Information System • Reports for Cost and Revenue Element Accounting • Reconciliation

Maintain Financial Statement Versions / P/L Structure (OB58)

Ledger Comparison (GCAC)

Access to SAP General Ledger Reporting
Accounting • Financial Accounting • General Ledger • Information System

Asset Accounting

Create / Change / Display Asset (AS01/AS02/AS03)
Accounting • Financial Accounting • Fixed Assets • Asset • Create / Change / Display

Distribute / Settle Asset Under Construction (AIAB/AIBU)
Accounting • Financial Accounting • Fixed Assets • Posting • Capitalize Asset Under Construction • Distribute

Execute Depreciation Run (AFAB)
Accounting • Financial Accounting • Fixed Assets • Periodic Processing • Depreciation Run • Execute

Execute Periodic Asset Posting (ASKB)
Accounting • Financial Accounting • Fixed Assets • Periodic Processing • APC Values Posting

Display Application Log (ARAL)
Accounting • Financial Accounting • Fixed Assets • Information System • Tools • Application Log

FI-AA / SAP General Ledger Reconciliation (ABST2)
Accounting • Financial Accounting • Fixed Assets • Periodic Processing • Year-End Closing • Account Reconciliation

Execute FI-AA Fiscal Year Change (AJRW)
Accounting • Financial Accounting • Fixed Assets • Periodic Processing • Fiscal Year Change

Execute FI-AA Year-End Closing (AJAB)
Accounting • Financial Accounting • Fixed Assets • Periodic Processing • Year-End Closing • Execute

Create Asset History Sheet (S_ALR_87011990)
Accounting • Financial Accounting • Fixed Assets • Information System • Reports on Asset Accounting • Notes to Financial Statements • International • Asset History Sheet

B.2.2 Customizing

Business Transactions

Change Automatic Account Assignment / Set Default Account Assignment (OKB9)
Controlling • Cost Center Accounting • Actual Postings • Manual Actual Postings • Edit Automatic Account Assignment

Substitution of Profit Centers in Customer Orders (0KEM)
Financial Accounting (New) · General Ledger Accounting (New) • Tools • Validation/Substitution • Substitution of Profit Centers in Customer Orders • Define Substitution Rules

Display MM Document Number in Financial Accounting Line Item Display
Financial Accounting (New) • Accounts Receivable and Accounts Payable • Vendor Accounts • Line Items • Display Line Items • Define Additional Fields for Line Item Display

Account Determination for GR/IR Clearing (OBYP)
Financial Accounting (New) • General Ledger Accounting (New) • Periodic Processing • Reclassify • Define Adjustment Accounts for GR/IR Clearing

Define Rules for Account Clearing
Financial Accounting (New) • General Ledger Accounting (New) • Business Transactions • Open Item Clearing • Prepare Automatic Clearing

Customize Tax on Sales/Purchases
Financial Accounting (New) • Financial Accounting Global Settings (New) • Tax on Sales/Purchases

Define Tax Codes for Sales and Purchases (FTXP)
Financial Accounting (New) • Financial Accounting Global Settings (New) • Tax on Sales/Purchases • Calculation • Define Tax Codes for Sales and Purchases

Select Tax Code per Transactions (OBZT)
Financial Accounting (New) • Accounts Receivable and Accounts Payable •

Business Transactions • Incoming Invoices/Credit Memos • Incoming Invoices/Credit Memos - Enjoy • Define Tax Code per Transaction

Define Variants for Real-Time Integration
Financial Accounting (New) • Financial Accounting Global Settings (New) • Ledgers • Real-Time Integration of Controlling with Financial Accounting • Define Variants for Real-Time Integration

Define Account Determination for Real-Time Integration
Financial Accounting (New) • Financial Accounting Global Settings (New) • Ledgers • Real-Time Integration of Controlling with Financial Accounting • Account Determination for Real-Time Integration

Periodic Processing

Payment Program Customizing
Financial Accounting (New) • Accounts Receivable and Accounts Payable • Business Transactions · Outgoing Payments

Define Tolerances for Customers and Employees
Financial Accounting (New) • Accounts Receivable and Accounts Payable • Business Transactions • Incoming Payments • Manual Incoming Payments • Define Tolerance Groups for Employees / Define Tolerances (Customers)

Assign Tolerance Groups to Users
Financial Accounting (New) • Accounts Receivable and Accounts Payable • Business Transactions • Incoming Payments • Manual Incoming Payments • Assign Users/Tolerance Groups

Set Accounts for Overpayment/Underpayment (OBXL)
Financial Accounting (New) • Accounts Receivable and Accounts Payable • Business Transactions • Incoming Payments • Incoming Payments Basic Settings • Define Accounts for Overpayments/Underpayments

Account Determination for HR Interface
Payroll • Payroll: (Country) • Posting to Accounting • Activities for AC System • Assigning Accounts

Period-End Closing

Customizing the Foreign Currency Valuation
Financial Accounting (New) • General Ledger Accounting (New) • Periodic Processing • Valuate • Foreign Currency Valuation

Assign Accounting Principle
Financial Accounting (New) • General Ledger Accounting (New) • Periodic Processing • Valuate • Assign Valuation Areas and Accounting Principles

Assign Accounting Principle to Ledger Group
Financial Accounting (New) • Financial Accounting Global Settings (New) • Ledgers • Parallel Accounting • Assign Accounting Principle to Ledger Groups

Transfer and Sort Receivables and Payables
Financial Accounting (New) • General Ledger Accounting (New) • Periodic Processing · Reclassify • Transfer and Sort Receivables and Payables

Maintain Flat-Rate Value Adjustment
Financial Accounting (New) • Accounts Receivable and Accounts Payable • Business Transactions • Closing • Valuate • Valuations

Determine Retained Earnings Account (OB53)
Financial Accounting (New) • General Ledger Accounting (New) • Master Data • G/L Accounts • Preparations • Define Retained Earnings Account

Define Field Usage for Distribution/Assessment (GCA6/GCA1)
Financial Accounting (New) • General Ledger Accounting (New) • Periodic Processing • Allocation • Define Field Usage for Distribution/Assessment

Maintain Intercompany Reconciliation
Financial Accounting (New) • General Ledger Accounting (New) •Periodic Processing • Check/Count • Cross-System Intercompany Reconciliation

Define Financial Statements / P/L Structures (OB58)
Financial Accounting (New) • General Ledger Accounting (New) • Master Data • G/L Accounts • Define Financial Statements Versions

Maintain Account Determination for Asset Accounting (AO90)
Financial Accounting (New) • Asset Accounting • Asset Accounting (Lean Implementation) • Organizational Structures • Assign G/L Accounts

Asset History Sheet Customizing
Financial Accounting (New) • Asset Accounting • Information System • Asset History Sheet

B.3 Materials Management

B.3.1 Application

Invoice Verification

Enter Incoming Invoice (MIRO)
Logistics • Materials Management • Logistics Invoice Verification • Document Entry • Enter Invoice

Activate Financial Accounting Document Number Display in Transaction MIRO (SU3)
System • User Profile • Own Data

Release blocked Invoices (MRBR)
Logistics • Materials Management • Logistics Invoice Verification • Further Processing • Release blocked Invoices

GR/IR Clearing

Maintain GR/IR Clearing Account (MR11)
Logistics • Materials Management • Logistics Invoice Verification • GR/IR Account Maintenance • Maintain GR/IR Clearing Account

SAP General Ledger: GR/IR Clearing (F.19)
Accounting • Financial Accounting • General Ledger • Periodic Processing • Closing • Reclassify • GR/IR Clearing

Business Transactions

Execute Physical Inventory Count
Logistics • Materials Management • Physical Inventory • Inventory Count

Close Periods for Material Master Records (MMPV)
Logistics • Materials Management • Material Master • Other • Close Period

B.3.2 Customizing

Order Process

Define Purchasing Document Types
Materials Management • Purchasing • Purchase Order • Define Document Types

Change Account Assignment Category (OME9)
Materials Management • Purchasing • Account Assignment • Maintain Account Assignment Category

MM Account Determination

Account Determination Wizard (OMWW)
Materials Management • Valuation and Account Assignment • Account Determination • Account Determination Wizard

Specify Valuation Level (OX14)
Enterprise Structure • Definition • Logistics - General • Define Valuation Level

Activate Valuation Grouping Code (OMWM)
Materials Management • Valuation and Account Assignment • Account Determination • Account Determination Without Wizard • Define Valuation Control

Group Valuation Areas (OMWD)
Materials Management • Valuation and Account Assignment • Account Determination • Account Determination Without Wizard • Group Together Valuation Areas

Define Valuation Classes (OMSK)
Materials Management • Valuation and Account Assignment • Account Determination • Account Determination Without Wizard • Define Valuation Classes

MM-IM Account Grouping for Moving Types (OMWN)
Materials Management • Valuation and Account Assignment • Account Determination • Account Determination Without Wizard • Define Account Grouping for Movement Types

Configure Automatic Postings (OMWB)
Materials Management • Valuation and Account Assignment • Account Determination • Account Determination Without Wizard • Configure Automatic Postings

Set Material Type
Logistics - General • Material Master • Basic Settings • Material Types • Define Attributes of Material Types

Requirements Classes (OVZG)
Sales and Distribution • Basic Functions • Availability Check and Trans-

fer of Requirements • Transfer of Requirements • Define Requirement Classes

Business Transactions

Maintain Transaction Types (OMJJ)
Materials Management • Inventory Management and Physical Inventory • Movement Types • Copy, Change Movement Types

Settings for Logistics Invoice Verification
Materials Management • Logistics Invoice Verification

Settings for Unplanned Delivery Costs
Materials Management • Logistics Invoice Verification • Incoming Invoice • Configure How Unplanned Delivery Costs Are Posted

Activate Direct Posting to G/L Account and Material Stock Account
Materials Management • Logistics Invoice Verification • Incoming Invoice • Enable Direct Posting to G/L Account and Material Accounts

Specify Tolerance Limits (OMR6)
Materials Management • Logistics Invoice Verification • Invoice Block • Set Tolerance Limits

Define Behavior of Period Closing (OMSY)
Logistics - General • Material Master • Basic Settings •Maintain Company Codes for Materials Management

B.4 Production

B.4.1 Application

Master Data

Create / Change / Display Material BOM (CS01/CS02/CS03)
Logistics • Production • Master Data • Bills of Material • Bill of Material • Material BOM • Create / Change / Display

Multi-Level Bill of Material Explosion for Single-Level BOM (CS11)
Logistics • Production • Master Data • Bills of Material • Reporting • BOM Explosion • Material BOM • BOM Level by Level

Create / Change / Display Work Center (CR01/CR02/CR03)
Logistics • Production • Master Data • Work Centers • Work Center • Create / Change / Display

Create / Change / Display Routings (CA01/CA02/CA03)
Logistics • Production • Master Data • Routings • Routings • Standard Routings • Create / Change / Display

Production Process

Create Production Order (CO01)
Logistics • Production • Shop Floor Control • Order • Create •With Material

Change / Display Production Order (CO02/CO03)
Logistics • Production • Shop Floor Control • Order • Change/Display

B.4.2 Customizing

Define Order Type Parameters (Prepare Production Orders for Product Cost Collector) (OPL8)
Production • Shop Floor Control • Master Data • Order • Define Order Type-Dependent Parameters

B.5 Sales and Distribution

B.5.1 Application

Business Transactions

Create / Change / Display Sales Order (VA01/VA02/VA03)
Logistics • Sales and Distribution • Sales • Order • Create / Change / Display

Create / Change / Display Invoice (VF01/ VF02/ VF03)
Logistics • Sales and Distribution • Billing • Billing Document • Create / Change / Display

Edit Blocked Invoices (VFX3)
Logistics • Sales and Distribution • Billing • Billing Document • Blocked Billing Docs

Period-End Closing

Actual Overhead Calculation: Sales Order (VA44)
Logistics • Sales and Distribution • Sales • Product Cost by Sales Order • Period-End Closing • Single Functions • Overhead

B.5.2 Customizing

Business Transactions

Requirements Classes (OVZG)
Sales and Distribution • Basic Functions • Availability Check and Transfer of Requirements • Transfer of Requirements • Define Requirements Classes

Define Item Categories
Sales and Distribution • Sales • Sales Documents • Sales Document Item • **Define Item Categories**

Profit Center Derivation of Characteristics in Sales Orders (0KEM)
Financial Accounting (new) • General Ledger Accounting (new) • Tools • Validation/Substitution • Substitution of Profit Centers in Customer Orders • Define Substitution Rules

Define Pricing Procedure (V/08)
Sales and Distribution • Basic Functions • Pricing • Pricing Control • Define And Assign Pricing Procedures • Maintain pricing procedures

Determine Pricing Procedure in Sales Documents (OVKK)
Sales and Distribution • Basic Functions • Pricing • Pricing Control • Define and Assign Pricing Procedures • Define Pricing Procedure Determination

Define Condition Types
Sales and Distribution • Basic Functions • Pricing • Pricing Control • Define Condition Types

Define Invoice Types (VOFA)
Sales and Distribution • Billing • Billing Documents • Define Billing Types

SD – Financial Accounting Interface

Define alternative Reconciliation Accounts
Sales and Distribution • Basic Functions • Account Assignment/Costing • Reconciliation Account Determination

Revenue Recognition Customizing
Sales and Distribution • Basic Functions • Account Assignment/Costing • Revenue Recognition

Maintain Material/Customer Account Assignment Group
Sales and Distribution • Basic Functions • Account Assignment/Costing • Revenue Account Determination • Check Master Data Relevant For Account Assignment

Define Revenue Recognition Dependencies
Sales and Distribution • Basic Functions • Account Assignment/Costing • Revenue Account Determination • Define Dependencies Of Revenue Account Determination

B.6 SAP NetWeaver BW – Customizing in SAP ERP

You can access the Implementation Guide for transferring data to SAP NetWeaver Business Warehouse (SAP NetWeaver BW) using Transaction SBIW.

Data Warehousing Workbench: Modeling (RSA1)
Business Information Warehouse • Modeling • Data Warehousing Workbench: Modeling

Create Transaction Data DataSource (KEB0)
Settings for Application-Specific DataSources (PI) • Profitability Analysis • Create Transaction Data DataSource

B.7 Miscellaneous

Change Message Control (OBA5)
Controlling • General Controlling • Change Message Control

Posting Variant for HR Interface
Payroll • Payroll (Country) • Posting to Accounting • Activities in the HR System • Create Posting Variants

C The Authors

Andrea Hölzlwimmer has more than ten years of professional experience in industry and consulting. Her career path has been somewhat unusual: after coursework in vocational training and a degree in business, she began her first employment with a well-known international consumer goods manufacturing company. The main focus of her work at that time was on international SAP rollouts, setting up shared services centers for finance, and supporting users throughout Europe in the area of external accounting.

When she changed to consulting, Andrea added Controlling to her range of specializations. Specifically, integrated value flows became a particular area of expertise during her work in several national and international projects for both multinational and mid-sized companies. She was attracted to this area by her desire to connect specialized, process-oriented consulting and technical solution know-how, all on a cross-module basis.

Currently, Andrea is a manager at J&M Management Consulting. Together with J&M, her job in projects is to contribute a pragmatic, value flow-oriented approach with the goal of using innovative ideas to open new avenues and possibilities.

The following people in the financials area at J&M Management Consulting also made significant contributions to this book.

Jörg Daniels is a Consultant in the financials area. After his vocational training in banking, Jörg completed a degree in Economics at the University of Bonn, and then went on to work in Accounting. For several years, he was head of the accounting department of a well-known German knowledge organization. In his consulting work, Jörg specializes in SAP ERP Financials.

Thorsten Fülling is a manager in the business strategy area. He specializes in organizational and process consulting as part of business transformation projects and corporate performance management. During his many years of consulting experience, he has gained deep insight into the requirements of integrating supply chains and value flows.

Since his days as a student of Information Management, **Volkhard Korth** has focused on combining business administration management and IT. In his role as senior consultant, his project specializations are rolling out SAP General Ledger and successfully completing SAP projects in the financials area.

Christoph Streuber holds a degree in industrial engineering. As such, he is keenly aware of the significance of value flows in enterprises and specializes in combining production-related aspects with wider aspects of financials. As a consultant, his areas of expertise include product cost estimates as well as SAP General Ledger.

Antonia Wilms is a corporate controller at a large German company. With a degree in business administration, Antonia first worked in consulting, where her interest had already begun to focus on controlling. She is particularly involved with mapping production processes in controlling and with structuring reporting concepts to create optimal support for management.

After studying information management in Karlsruhe, Germany, **Stephan Wund** completed many successful projects over the years in the business intelligence area. His specializations today are financials and controlling. In his capacity as senior consultant, he regards SAP ERP and SAP NetWeaver Business Warehouse as two closely interlinked platforms for representing and controlling enterprise processes.

Index

A

B

C

D

E

F

G

H

I

L

M

Q

R

S

T

U

V

W

Y

Provides a detailed overview for transitioning SAP ERP Fi-nancials to IFRS

Features practical coverage of the complete conversion pro-ject, including a case study

Includes the US GAAP/IFRS deltas and their mapping to SAP ERP components

Paul Theobald

Transitioning to IFRS in SAP ERP Financials

This book will provide conversion project teams with a roadmap for preparing their SAP ERP Financials systems for conversion to IFRS. It will include detailed coverage of the transition process, an overview of the US GAAP/IFRS deltas and how they are mapped in ERP Financials, and real-world advice from an IFRS conversion project at a large petrochemical company. Its primary purpose is to gives finance professionals, executives, technical staff, project managers, and consultants a concise guide to jump-starting their IFRS projects in upgrade or non-upgrade scenarios.

approx. 320 pp., 79,95 Euro / US$ 79.95
ISBN 978-1-59229-319-3, Dec 2009

>> www.sap-press.com